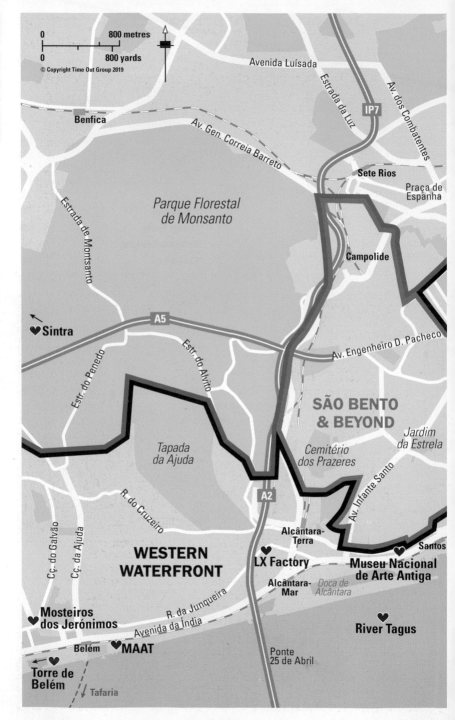

0   800 metres
0   800 yards
© Copyright Time Out Group 2019

Avenida Luísada

Estrada da Luz

Av. dos Combatentes

IP7

Benfica

Av. Gen. Correia Barreto

Sete Rios

Praça de España

Estrada de Montsanto

Parque Florestal de Monsanto

Campolide

♥ Sintra

A5

Estr. do Penedo

Estr. do Alvito

Av. Engenheiro D. Pacheco

SÃO BENTO & BEYOND

Jardim da Estrela

Tapada da Ajuda

Cemitério dos Prazeres

A2

R. do Cruzeiro

Av. Infante Santo

Cc. do Galvão

Cc. da Ajuda

WESTERN WATERFRONT

Alcântara-Terra

♥ LX Factory

Alcântara-Mar

Doca de Alcântara

♥ Museu Nacional de Arte Antiga

♥ Santos

♥ Mosteiros dos Jerónimos

R. da Junqueira

Avenida da Índia

♥ River Tagus

Belém ♥ MAAT

Ponte 25 de Abril

← ♥ Torre de Belém

↙ Tafaria

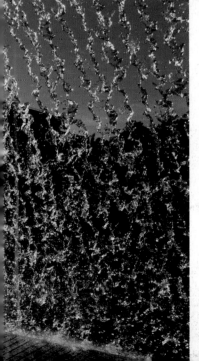

54

Contents

Introduction

Lisbon's geography is what most defines it: the city drapes itself across hills on a bend in the Tagus, at the point where that river widens into a vast estuary. Its waters reflect the southern light onto the gleaming surfaces of the city's buildings, to be admired from hilltop viewpoints by tourists and locals alike.

To enjoy Lisbon to the full, fall into its rhythm. Don't be fooled by the frenzy of construction and rush-hour traffic. The bleary-eyed commuters pouring off ferries and trains will nip out for mid-morning coffee in one of Lisbon's countless cafés and, later, eat a hearty lunch in a traditional *tasca*. Many Lisbon bars don't fill up until after midnight, and the city's laidback nightlife – much of it outdoors in summer – is one of its most engaging attractions (the region's beaches are another).

Locals are proud of the role Portugal played centuries ago in the first wave of what we now call globalisation. This has now rebounded, bringing the likes of McDonald's, Zara and even Starbucks to the city. But change has not undone the past: attendance at Catholic services may have slumped, but downtown churches still bustle with people dropping in to light a candle or say a prayer. Lisboans of all ages listen to fado music, and the whole city turns out for June's *Festas* – and you're more than welcome to join in.

ABOUT THE GUIDE

This is one of a series of Time Out guidebooks to cities across the globe. Written by local experts, our guides are thoroughly researched and meticulously updated. They aim to be inspiring, irrevcrent, well-informed and trustworthy.

Time Out Lisbon is divided into five sections: Discover, Explore, Experience, Understand and Plan.

Discover introduces the city and provides inspiration for your visit.

Explore is the main sightseeing section of the guide and includes detailed listings and reviews for sights and museums, restaurants ⑩, cafés & bars ⑩, and shops & services ⑩, all organised by area with a corresponding street map. To help navigation, each area of Lisbon has been assigned its own colour.

Experience covers the cultural life of the city in depth, including festivals, film, LGBT, music, nightlife, theatre and more.

Understand provides in-depth background information that places Lisbon in its historical and cultural context.

Plan offers practical visitor information, including accommodation options and details of public transport.

Hearts

We use hearts ❤ to pick out venues, sights and experiences in the city that we particularly recommend. The very best of these are featured in the Top 20 (see p10) and receive extended coverage in the guide.

Maps

A detachable fold-out map can be found on the inside back cover. There's also an overview map (see p8) and individual streets maps for each area of the city. The venues featured in the guide have been given a grid reference so that you can find them easily on the maps and on the ground.

Prices

All our **restaurant listings** are marked with a euro symbol category from budget to blow-out (€-€€€€), indicating the price you should expect to pay for an average main course: € = under €8; €€ = €8-€15; €€€ = €15-€25; €€€€ = over €25.

A similar system is used in our **Accommodation** chapter based on the hotel's standard prices for one night in a double room: **Budget** = under €100; **Moderate** = €100-€200; **Expensive** = €200-€300; **Luxury** = over €300.

Discover

Telecabine Lisboa

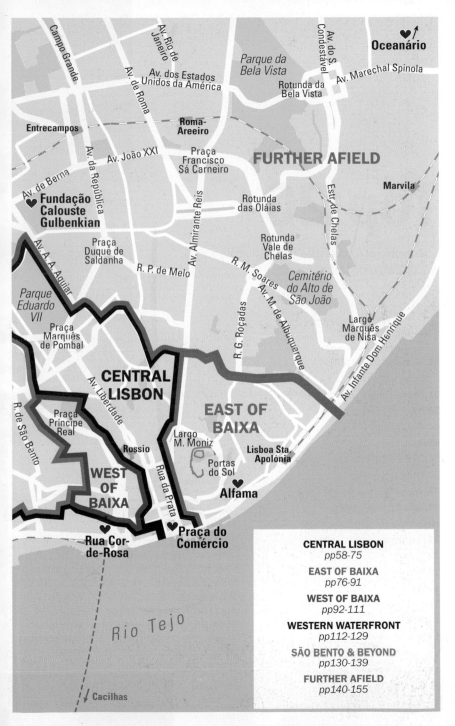

Oceanário

Av. do S. Condestável

Av. Marechal Spinola

Av. Rio de Janeiro

Campo Grande

Av. dos Estados Unidos da América

Av. de Roma

Parque da Bela Vista

Rotunda da Bela Vista

Entrecampos

Roma-Areeiro

FURTHER AFIELD

Av. João XXI

Praça Francisco Sá Carneiro

Marvila

Av. de Berna

Av. da República

Av. Almirante Reis

Rotunda das Oláias

Estr. de Chelas

❤ **Fundação Calouste Gulbenkian**

Av. A. A. Aguiar

Praça Duque de Saldanha

R. P. de Melo

R. M. Soares

Rotunda Vale de Chelas

Cemitério do Alto de São João

Av. M. de Albuquerque

Parque Eduardo VII

Praça Marquês de Pombal

R. G. Roçadas

Largo Marquês de Nisa

Av. Infante Dom Henrique

R. de São Bento

Praça Príncipe Real

CENTRAL LISBON

Av. Liberdade

EAST OF BAIXA

Rossio

Largo M. Moniz

Lisboa Sta. Apolónia

WEST OF BAIXA

Rua da Prata

Portas do Sol

❤ **Alfama**

❤ **Rua Cor-de-Rosa**

❤ **Praça do Comércio**

Rio Tejo

↓ Cacilhas

Top 20

Museums, markets and miradouros; *we count down the city's finest*

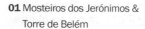

01

Mosteiros dos Jerónimos & Torre de Belém *p126*

They may not be the first sights you see, but these two monuments on the city's western edge hark back like no others to what locals still see as Portugal's glory days. Both the Jerónimos monastery and the Tower are prime examples of Manueline architecture – Portuguese late Gothic – the flamboyant expression of a confident regime in an era of maritime expansion.

02

Alfama *p84*

To lose yourself in ancient Lisbon, enter this hillside *bairro* (neighbourhood) whose maze of alleys has changed little since Moorish times. Traditions such as fado music are very much alive here – even part of daily life for many residents.

03

Praça do Comércio *p63*

This vast riverside square is one of several landmarks with more than one name; the older Terreiro do Paço (literally 'Palace Yard') tag reminds us that this was the seat of state power for centuries before the 1755 earthquake. Post-quake Lisbon was widely heralded as epitomising Enlightenment ideals of elegance and order, capped by this 'Commerce Square', with its colonnades and triumphal arch.

04

Miradouros *p83*

One of the disadvantages of Lisbon's hilly terrain is that sightseeing can be tiring; but one of the advantages is that walkers are regularly rewarded with fabulous views from *miradouros* (lookout points), each of which gives a different perspective on the city.

05

Azulejos *p234*

The most striking feature in architectural and interior decoration in Portugal, ceramic tiles have a history that stretches back to late medieval times. The peak was reached much later, in the 17th and 18th centuries, but today many artists are again favouring *azulejos* as a medium.

06

Coffee & pastries *p103*

The Portuguese know their coffee and are demanding enough that the quality of both the raw material and its handling is generally high. It's served in myriad ways: at the counter in scruffy *tascas* or on the terrace at sophisticated cafés – as often as not accompanied by a *pastél de nata* pastry.

07

Trams & funiculars *p67*

You're sure to catch sight of one of the city's antique trams as they clang through the streets, or perhaps an equally venerable funicular or elevator. Make sure to step on board for an eyeful of their wooden interior and carefully oiled antique machinery – though beware of pickpockets. Until the mid '90s, tram routes were being taken out of service; now there are two special tourist services, and one disused route has even been revived.

08

Museu Nacional de Arte Antiga *p117*

The only collection that gives a real sense of the course of Portuguese art through the centuries, Lisbon's premier national museum also harbours painting and statuary from across Europe as well as ceramics and furniture produced in China and India for the Portuguese market.

09

Gourmet food markets *p39*

Be it salted cod, a pork sandwich or a custard tart, you'll be able to find whatever your tastebuds are craving at one of the gourmet food markets that have sprung up in Lisbon. Many of Lisbon's best eateries have stalls at the wildly successful Time Out market at Cais do Sodré and there are similar, if smaller, markets in other, less touristy areas too.

10

Oceanário *p155*

The Oceanarium is one of the legacies of Expo '98 (World Fair), whose theme was the world's oceans. Its striking architecture conceals a range of habitats that teem with species, both above and below water. Information is copious and excellent. For families, this is a highlight of any visit to Lisbon.

11

Fundação Calouste Gulbenkian *p146*

Set in a delightful leafy park, the privately owned Gulbenkian Foundation runs the capital's premier museum of fine and applied art (both Western and oriental), a lively modern exhibition centre and a full season of classical music concerts in which performers include the Gulbenkian's own orchestra and choir.

12

Sintra *p164*

You'll need a full day to get the most out of this magical hill resort to the west of the capital, but Sintra should be included in any but the briefest visit to Lisbon. Classed by UNESCO as the world's first centre of Romantic architecture, it abounds in palaces and gardens and is one of Portugal's most-visited destinations.

13

MAAT *p124*

The ambitiously named Museum of Art, Architecture & Technology opened in 2016 on a prime riverside site in Belém: a gleaming, white-tiled swoosh of a building. Visitors can even stroll on the curved roof for great views, especially at sunset. Against all that, the art displays inside can feel like an after-thought, but it hosts some interesting installations.

14

Festa de Santo António *p175*

In June, the festivals of the 'people's saints' – António, João and Pedro – merge into one another, making for almost a month of solid partying. The most popular is Lisbon-born Santo António and the high point is 12 June, the eve of his saint's day, when revellers pack the old *bairros* for grilled sardines and sangria before dancing and singing along to local hits. Outsiders are welcomed with open arms, often literally.

15

LX Factory *p121*

In a former industrial complex in Alcântara, first ad agencies and design studios took up residence, then shops and restaurants with a difference, resulting in a 'creative city' that is one of the coolest places in town. From vintage clothing to cookery workshops, from a Sunday market to parties in cavernous warehouses, there's always something on.

16

Fado *p200*

Lisbon's fado music is perhaps the leading cultural expression of the city from which it emerged, but also of the nation. Its lyrics and sound express a very Portuguese *saudade* – an intense but vague yearning. Fado fell out of fashion after the 1974 Revolution, but the flame was kept burning in *casas de fado* in Alfama and elsewhere, and it is now enjoying a revival.

17

Beaches & watersports *p162*

They may be outside the city limits, but the region's beaches, both to the south and the west of the city, are an integral part of the rhythm of Lisbon life. And many offer a range of activities from gentle paddleboarding to exhilarating kitesurfing for both novices and the experienced. Easy access means that, even on a short break, you can combine sunbathing and surfing with sightseeing and bar hopping.

18

Traditional shops *p45*

Lisbon has long been known for its old-world charm, with long-established family businesses dotted around downtown. But a tourist boom sent rents soaring; recognising the danger, the council instituted a *Lojas com História* scheme to protect those of historical value. Meanwhile, strong demand for authentic local products has seen new stores open, selling prettily packaged vintage items and *azulejos*.

19

Rua Cor-de-Rosa *p196*

Once renowned for seediness, the 'Pink Street' – official name Rua Nova do Carvalho – has, at the time of writing, just had a fresh coat of paint, confirming its status as a place to socialise at night. Portugal's balmy climate and friendly locals make whiling away an hour or two drinking on the street feel relaxed and fun rather than the prelude to any alcohol-fuelled aggro. Opening hours are more limited than they were, but still later than in most of Europe – and there are sound-proofed clubs to go on to.

20

River Tagus *p57*

Although Lisbon's shore is bathed by the River Tagus rather than the Atlantic, the estuary is so broad visitors and locals alike often refer to it as 'the sea'. The vast reflective surface gives Lisbon a unique light. New riverside promenades are helping locals renew their acquaintance with the Tagus on foot or by bike, but it is only from the river itself that you get the best alternative panorama of the city.

Itineraries

Get the most out of your trip, whatever your timescale or your budget

ESSENTIAL WEEKEND

Budget €250 for two
Getting around Walking, trams, taxi

DAY 1

Morning

Chiado

After taking in the grand **Praça do Comércio** (*see p63*), head up into an older Lisbon aboard the antique 28 tram, or hop on a bus to ride all the way up to the **Castelo de São Jorge** (*see p84*), where the castle's battlements afford breathtaking views of the river and the city draped over a series of hills.

Wander down into the atmospheric **Alfama** neighbourhood (*see p85*). If you have a taste for applied arts, pop into the **Museu-Escola de Artes Decorativas** (*see p86*), or for ancient history step into the **Museu do Teatro Romano** (*see p79*) nearby. If *azulejo* tiles (*see p234*) take your fancy, the **Mosteiro de São Vicente** (*see p87*), further along the tram line, has magnificent panels – and more views.

▶ *Budgets include food, drink, transport and admission prices, but not accommodation or shopping.*

Praça do Comércio

Afternoon

In Alfama, lunch on grilled sardines or *bacalhau* (salt cod) at a local *tasca*, or go for a more exotic alternative such as Goan or Mozambican. Then catch the tram or a taxi across to Chiado for some window-shopping. Of the many local churches, the highlight is the **Igreja de São Roque** (*see p105*) just uphill, with its lavish Baroque decoration.

Art lovers may want to fit in a visit to the **Museu Nacional de Arte Antiga** (*see p117*) or **Museu Calouste Gulbenkian** (*see p147*), across town. The latter has a lovely garden, but keen botanists will find more to marvel at closer to hand in the **Jardim Botânico** (*see p108*) in Príncipe Real.

Evening

It is time for an aperitif, and the *miradouro* (lookout point) of the **Jardim de São Pedro de Alcântara** (*see p83*) is an excellent place for it. It's on the edge of the **Bairro Alto**, with its myriad restaurants (*see p106*) and late-opening bars (*see p191* Nightlife). But there is a cluster of top-notch restaurants in neighbouring Chiado too. For more bar and club crawling, head down to the **Rua Cor de Rosa** (Pink Street, *see p196*) and surrounding area. Or finish the night in style at **Lux** (*see p190*).

B.Leza *p195*

DAY 2

Morning

Set aside half a day to explore Belém, a district forever associated with the 'Discoveries' (*see p220*) – the golden age of Portuguese maritime exploration. As well as prime examples of late-Gothic Manueline architecture, the area has museums galore and a fine modern art collection at **Centro Cultural de Belém** (*see p125*). Take a break from culture to indulge in some of the famous custard tarts of the **Antiga Confeitaria de Belém** (*see p129*): it's almost considered a sin to walk past here without stepping inside to munch a few of its *pastéis de Belém*.

Padrão dos Descobrimentos

Time Out Market

Afternoon

Lunch in one of our recommended restaurants in Belém (*see p129*) or in Alcântara (*see p120*) or Santos (*see p118*), some of which offer views of the river from which the mariners set sail centuries ago, or pop into the **Time Out Market** at Cais do Sodré (*see p116*) for some gourmet fast food.

Then, continuing the maritime theme, cross town to the **Parque das Nações** (*see p153*), the former site of Expo '98. The park has attractions for all ages, with the **Oceanário** (*see p155*) the prime exhibit. To cover more ground, let the cable car take the strain, or hire a bike or electric scooter.

Mesa de Frades

Evening

Head back into town for a late-afternoon drink at yet another *miradouro* (*see p83*) and go on to dine at a *casa de fado* (*see p201*), where singers will pour their hearts out for you, accompanied by a lute-shaped Portuguese guitar. The origins of the *saudade* ('yearning') they are expressing (*see p32*) are intertwined with the seafarers' homesickness and the longing of the women they left behind.

BUDGET BREAK

Budget €50 for two
Getting around Walking, lifts, escalators

Morning

From downtown, take the free **Elevador do Castelo** on Rua dos Fanqueiros, then cross the street to the Mercado do Chão do Loureiro (a former market, now parking lot) where another lift will whisk you up to a roof terrace with a panoramic view of the city. From here, turn right on Costa do Castelo towards **Alfama** (*see p85*), peeking in at the **Museu do Teatro Romano** (*see p79*) on the way and the **Miradouro de Santa Luzia** for more views. In Alfama you can easily lose hours wandering the steep, narrow streets. If it's a Tuesday or Saturday, spend an hour or two browsing at the nearby **Feira da Ladra** flea market (*see p46*).

Museu do Teatro Romano

Feira da Ladra

Bairro Alto

Afternoon

For a tasty but well-priced lunch, head up to the workaday **Graça** neighbourhood (*see p86*), where most local restaurants still serve helpings that are more than enough for two people, as well as half and 'mini' sizes, and very drinkable house wine. Alternatively, head down through a fast-gentrifying Mouraria to Lisbon's most multicultural area along **Rua do Benformoso** for lots of cheap eats.

On Saturdays, art lovers may want to make the most of free admission at the **Museu Coleção Berardo** (*see p125*) in Belém; it is also free to admire the beautifully intricate exteriors of the area's historical monuments. On Sundays, the **Museu Calouste Gulbenkian** (*see p147*) is free from 2pm. Both museums are easily reached by public transport.

On other days, you might instead head for the Baixa-Chiado metro station and traverse it, emerging via a series of escalators up in the smart Chiado neighbourhood, for some very different people-watching. In summer there are often free open-air concerts here, while in winter they are hosted by local churches.

Evening

Head into the Bairro Alto and try to pick a bar that hands out free *tremoços* (lupin seeds) with your beer. For dinner, there are still a few traditional *tascas* that won't break the bank here, such as **1° de Maio** (*see p106*), or **Casa Liège** (*see p111*) in Bica. And bars here and down in the Cais do Sodré area often have DJs or live music for free.

FAMILY DAY OUT

Budget €180

Getting around Walking, tram, metro/taxi. If you can't face squeezing the family onto a regular yellow tram (free for under-5s, then full fare), note that a ticket on the city's Tramcar Tours (www.yellowbustours.com; €18, children €10) includes free access for the day to regular buses, trams and funiculars, as well as discounts to some monuments. (If you buy the Tramcar Tour ticket at the airport, you can take the Aerobus shuttle for free too.)

Lisboa Story Centre

Morning

For some educational fun to start, check out the multimedia displays at the **Lisbon Story Centre** (*see p64*). Or take the lift to the top of the **Arco da Rua Augusta** (*see p64*) – the giant figures up here and the 360-degree view are enough to make even the most jaded teenager's jaw drop.

Alternatively, head straight up to the **Castelo de São Jorge** (*see p84*) for a memorable experience, with cannons on the ramparts and a bird's-eye view of the city. Afterwards, just wandering on foot through the alleys of Alfama feels like a family adventure.

Tramcar Tours

Arco da Rua Augusta

Afternoon

Watching someone grill their lunch a few steps away from their table is sure to keep the kids entertained – try **Páteo 13** (*see p86*). After lunch, take the train (from Santa Apolónia, 7mins), metro or a taxi to the Parque das Nações, site of the **Oceanário** (*see p155*) – with its scary sharks and rays, but also cuddly penguins and otters – plus hands-on science exhibits at the **Pavilhão do Conhecimento** (*see p153*). Alternatively, a boat trip makes for some cheap family fun; various cruises are available, but we'd recommend just taking the ferry to **Cacilhas** (*see p57*) from Cais do Sodré.

Oceanário

Telecabine Lisboa

Evening

The wide open spaces of the **Parque das Nações** are great for burning off energy. If no one in the family has a problem with heights, the **Telecabine Lisboa** (*see p153*) cable car is a fun way to take in views of the estuary and Ponte Vasco da Gama bridge stretching into the distance. There's a good choice here of places to eat too, in the **Centro Vasco da Gama** mall or at **La Rúcula** (*see p154*), for example. If, instead, you did the ferry trip, Cacilhas is known for its lively seafood restaurants, where the kids will love watching locals smash crustaceans with plastic hammers. Back downtown, summer often sees free outdoor entertainment around Cais do Sodré or in Praça do Comércio.

When to Visit

Lisbon by season

These days Lisbon is popular with foreign visitors all year round, not least thanks to its mild climate, although winters can be rather wet. There are also now events, small and large, indoors and out, throughout the year, so you're never short of things to do and see. Still, some restaurants maintain the old tradition of closing down for a fortnight or two in August and/or in winter.

Spring

Portugal is a Catholic country, so Easter means Holy Week processions in many parishes. It also heralds the opening of the bullfighting season (*see p145*). March sees fashion show **Moda Lisboa** (*see p174*) and the first of a string of cinema-related events, with the **Monstra** festival of animation. For more, *see p182* Film. In April there's Lisbon's top gourmet event, **Peixe em Lisboa** (*see p174*) with fine wines, too.

Summer

June and July are the peak period for tourism, and the city organises free concerts and other events around town. June is the high point, with almost a full month of *arraiais* (neighbourhood grill-outs), often with live music, to mark the **Festas dos Santos Populares** (*see p176*) parties for the 'people's saints' – of whom **Santo António** (*see p175*) is the local favourite. Complementing this is an expanding roster of commercial music set-pieces (for which www.festivaisverao.com is a good source of information), such as **Super Bock Super Rock** (*see p177*), plus yet more film festivals (*see p182* Film). In August, many locals head for the Algarve, leaving the capital to a growing band of foreign tourists – and thereby making this a good month to explore the region's own beaches (*see p162*). The football season starts while many fans are still at the beach.

Rock in Rio Lisboa

Festa de Santo António

Estoril

Autumn

As locals return after their summer break, cultural life revives in what is known by Lisbon's francophile elite as the *rentrée*. As well as the start of the theatre and classical music seasons (*see p206* Performing Arts), this includes major film festivals such as **Queer Lisboa** (*see p178*) and **DocLisboa** (*see p179*) and, in mid October, another **Moda Lisboa** (*see p174*). Early autumn is also marked by the good-value **Festa do Avante** (*see p177*), the Portuguese Communist Party's massive annual shindig on a patch of land on the south bank. Later on there are more indoor concerts, with the most prominent series being **Música em São Roque**.

Winter

This is the season for more Catholic festivals, including **Natal** (Christmas) and a slew of classical concerts in Lisbon churches. The nights running up to **Ano Novo** (New Year) see outdoor concerts take place on Terreiro do Paço (Praça do Comércio), capped with fireworks on the 31st. Temperatures rarely drop low enough to put off either locals or tourists. **Carnaval**, by contrast, is no big deal in Lisbon, but you can find places in the region where it is (*see p179*).

Praça do Comércio

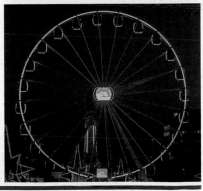

Lisbon Today

Tourism, tech and trams

There was a time when travellers visited Lisbon to sample a gentler way of life, in a place that time seemed to have all but forgotten and which was notably poorer than other western European capitals. Even today, there are remnants of that past – some of the city's traditional shops have secured protection from the council, although others have already been evicted by landlords keen to take advantage of a buoyant economy to raise rents. In the 1990s, Lisbon emerged as a nightlife hub – a status confirmed by the inauguration of Lux, one of Europe's coolest clubs. More recently, the city has become a mass-market destination, made fashionable by social media hype – famous for being famous, if you like. But that's underpinned by a more diverse range of accommodation, drinking and dining options than ever before – and, of course, by Lisbon's eternal charms: a fascinating history; a picture-perfect setting and 2,800 hours of sunshine a year.

Up and down, then up again

Mirroring Lisbon's undulating topography, the local economy has been on a rollercoaster in the past decade. The global financial crash and the long slump that followed even reshaped the city's population.

Portugal, traditionally a land of emigration despite the arrival since the 1970s of significant numbers of people from former colonies, only truly became a land of immigration in the 1990s. The economy was finally booming thanks to projects such as the Expo '98 World Fair and tumbling interest rates in anticipation of European and Monetary union (EMU), of which Portugal was a founder member. As well as an influx of Brazilians, there were at one point as many as 200,000 Ukrainian nationals in Portugal, most in the Lisbon region, and unprecedented numbers of migrants from Pakistan and other places.

But when the euro crisis hit, many packed up and went home; according to the National Statistics Institute, some 586,000 Portuguese also left the country from 2011 to 2015. In contrast to past outflows to France and other Continental countries, the top destination was the UK.

It's only since 2017 that Portugal has once more seen net positive immigration. Yet, it still faces demographic decline, with more than 21 per cent of its population over 65 and a low birth rate. The population is set to shrink by 40 per cent by 2060, a predicted fall that may just be kept at bay by the Socialist government's favourable attitude to increased immigration, announced in 2018.

Come back soon

Economic growth helps make the country a magnet for new immigrants or returning emigrants. In Lisbon, in particular, the recovery of recent years has also been driven by tourists. In 2017, their number jumped 12 per cent to a record 12.7 million. Tourism and travel now account for one-tenth of GDP, and an even bigger share of employment.

Economic growth helps make the country a magnet for new immigrants or returning emigrants

Lisbon, whose population is 500,000, now receives 4.5 million tourists a year

Lisbon, whose population is 500,000, now receives 4.5 million tourists a year. The quantity and quality of local hotels to receive them continues to rise, with 25 opening in the Lisbon region in 2018 alone. From funky hostels to luxurious mansions, many win awards. But they can't keep pace with the increase in visitor numbers; hence the explosion in short-term rentals, which now account for almost as many beds as the hotels and guesthouses. (Paddy Cosgrave, the founder of Web Summit, who in 2016 moved Europe's largest tech event here from Dublin, is among those who always stays in an Airbnb when in town.)

The influx delights city bosses but prompts many concerns for locals, who see the effects on infrastructure that has been starved of investment for years. From 2015, the city started levying a tourist tax: at first €1 per person per night; from 2019, twice that. But not all the proceeds go to mitigate the impact of tourism; indeed, some is used to attract more visitors.

The construction of luxury developments rarely helps locals struggling with increased rents

Housing schemes

Meanwhile, the national government has lured in €4 billion in foreign investment in seven years with the so called 'golden visa' scheme, which fast-tracks residence permits for non-EU citizens who spend €500,000 or more on property. Alternatively they can deposit €1 million in a local bank, create ten jobs or, now, spend 'just' €350,000 on rehabilitating property. But the vast bulk of funds pouring in (over half from Chinese nationals) goes into luxury property in and around Lisbon.

Then there's the Non-Habitual Residents programme, offering ten years' exemption for tax on some income, including pensions, to EU citizens not already living in Portugal. It's popular with wealthy French people convinced they're overtaxed at home and charmed by Lisbon.

Both schemes are widely resented for benefiting rich foreigners when ordinary

The vast bulk of foreign investment goes into luxury property

31

Portuguese are still paying the price of austerity in higher taxes and poorer services. 'Golden visas' are also seen as an invitation to launder money; the scheme has been hit by scandals, including one in which officials were accused of bribery and graft (which they deny). Privately, senior figures acknowledge the schemes must be rethought, despite the fact that the scale of urban renewal that has been undertaken since the crash might normally have taken 30 to 40 years, and so has made up for decades of underinvestment.

But the influx of foreign funds has contributed to other problems. It comes to something when even the association representing estate agents – who gain more than most from rising property prices – is warning of a crisis in which many locals can afford neither to buy nor rent.

Given all this, it is perhaps remarkable that locals are invariably friendly and helpful to the visitors that take over their housing and clog up their trams, and are happy to speak English too.

Transports of delight

Talking of trams, major investment in public transport seems finally on the way. In the first half of 2019, work started on a €210 million project to overhaul the metro by 2023: the yellow and green lines are to be extended – with new stations at Estrela and Santos – to meet in Alcântara, forming a circular line, with the red and blue lines as radials. The bus fleet is also expanding, with €55 million to be spent in 2019 alone on new electric- and gas-powered vehicles, and with more to come.

In the meantime, 80 kilometres (50 miles) of cycle paths are to more than double in length over two years, and 2018 saw the inauguration of a shared bike scheme. There are also privately run fleets of electric scooters – perhaps to keep things moving until the buses come into service. All of this helps make Lisbon a more liveable city, and more enjoyable for visitors too.

It is perhaps remarkable that locals are invariably friendly and helpful to the visitors that take over their housing and clog up their trams, and are happy to speak English too

In the know
Wish you were here, wish I were there

Central to the Portuguese sensibility is an evocative word with an elusive meaning. To feel *saudade* is to suffer an intense yearning for someone or something that is out of reach, maybe forever. Fado – the melancholy music that emerged from Lisbon's mean streets – is imbued with the *saudades* endured by this nation of seafarers and emigrants. For more on fado and where to hear it, *see p200*.

Modern Art is Rubbish

The city works with urban artists, and it's paid off

Economic upheaval has bequeathed the city a lot of derelict buildings, many ripe for transformation into giant canvasses. As a result of this but, crucially, also thanks to tolerance and encouragement on the part of the authorities, Lisbon has become a centre for urban art.

The most comprehensive overview of what's out there is afforded by **GAU** (Gabinete de Arte Urbana, http://gau.cm-lisboa.pt), the council department that helped turbo-charge the phenomenon back in 2008 by providing dedicated spaces – and paint – for local youngsters to explore their talents, starting with the panels at the top of Calçada da Glória. Its website has not only a gallery but a beautifully produced magazine and handy marked maps.

Over the years, municipal housing blocks have provided many of the large, smooth walls ideal for murals – for example in *bairros* such as Graça and Marvila. Beyond the city limits and GAU's purview, Quinta do Mocho in Sacavém has seen dozens of murals created in wildly different styles by Portuguese and foreign artists, many of them with community involvement. (For tours, see the GuiasdoMocho Facebook page.)

But urban art can be found on walls of all kinds, with themes of all kinds: works by Brazil's **Os Gémeos**, Italy's **Blu** and Spain's **Sam3** as part of a 2010 project with an anti-capitalist flavour are still visible on abandoned buildings on Avenida Fontes Pereira de Melo, in the business district, while in Mouraria there's a fado-themed mural by various artists on Escadinhas de São Cristóvão.

Urban art hotspots include **LX Factory** (see p121) and the **Muro Azul** ('Blue Wall', Rua das Murtas, Alvalade), the most ambitious GAU project, where some 60 artists worked on a one-kilometre stretch of wall round three sides of a psychiatric hospital; a handy cycle path runs along half of it.

As for individual artists, **Vhils** (real name Alexandre Farto, http://vhils.com) is best known around the world for his unique technique of sculpting (or dynamiting) faces on walls: his work is everywhere from the south-bank town of Barreiro where he grew up to Hong Kong. Having been backed by GAU from its inception, he has since helped found the Underdogs collective, which has its own gallery (see p153).

One of Vhils's most famous works, In Alcântara, disappeared in 2018 when the building was demolished. But others in town include one in his best-known style in Alfama, tucked away in Travessa das Merceeiras,

off the no.28 tram route, and another a ten-minute walk further uphill: a portrait in *calçada portuguesa*, traditional mosaic paving, of fado diva Amália Rodrigues, on Rua de São José.

Now another artist is attracting attention abroad, this time using rubbish (and rubbish bins) to create colourful large-scale works that criticise the throwaway society. **Bordalo II** – Artur Bordalo, grandson of painter Real Bordalo and himself a former fine-art student – is now a one-man upcycling industry. His 'Trash Animals', built up from old car parts, appliances and other detritus from wasteland or derelict factories, are dotted around Portugal and many other countries. Lisbon fauna includes a fox (Avenida 24 de Julho 28, Santos), a raccoon (Rua Bartolomeu Dias 43, Belém), a frog (Rua da Manutenção, Beato) and a monkey on the façade of his studio (Rua de Xabregas 49, Beato).

Exposure to sun, rain and curious visitors – not to mention the demolition men – takes its toll on this kind of art, but its creators profess not to be bothered. It's the flipside of having the privilege of being able to express themselves on a canvas that is the city itself.

Eating & Drinking

Local tradition, with more than a dash of global flavour

If there's anything the Portuguese think and talk about as much as football, it's food – invariably the traditional kind. Today, a new generation of chefs are reinventing the old standards, by applying modern techniques to the best fresh seafood and other local ingredients. You'll find the price-quality relationship here amazingly good, if you take care to avoid tourist traps and opt for places where locals themselves tuck into authentic *cozinha portuguesa*. In Lisbon, as in every town in Portugal, there are cafés and snack bars on every corner offering cheap, filling local fare, served up quickly at counter or table. But for a sit-down meal, there is now a wider choice than ever, from workaday *tascas* – small, usually family-run canteens – through bustling *cervejarias* serving up beer and seafood, to global cuisine and Michelin-starred hubs of creativity.

Portuguese cuisine

Local food tends to be simple, honest fare: globalised fast food is largely confined to shopping malls, while even in the ubiquitous *tascas*, with their paper tablecloths and chipped crockery, proper rituals are observed. That means any combination of appetisers are placed on the table first, with bread. (Note that you pay for what you eat, whether you ordered it or not; to avoid doubt, send back what you don't want.) Main courses are usually accompanied by potatoes or rice, greens or salad, though in more modest eateries, meat and two veg can become meat and two carbohydrates and your steak will come snuggled up to chips and rice.

This is one of the best places in Europe for seafood, at restaurants such as **Senhor Peixe** (*see p154*) or trendy **SEA ME** (*see p98*). Cod is invariably salted and dried – *bacalhau* – but fresh fish and shellfish abound. (To work out what's on offer *see p41* What's on the Menu?) Oilier fish such as sardines, a local favourite, are traditionally grilled outside.

Countless Portuguese dishes have as their base *refogado*, which, as with its Mediterranean equivalents, starts with frying onions in olive oil, invariably with garlic. Common seasonings include bay leaves and coriander, which the Portuguese use with gay abandon, particularly

❤ Seafood superstars

Aqui Há Peixe *p97*
Only the best fish here.

Páteo 13 *p86*
Keeping it simple.

Ramiro *p89*
Come early to beat the queues.

SEA ME *p98*
Restaurant and fish shop rolled into one.

Senhor Peixe *p154*
Choose from the day's catch.

SEA ME

In the know
Price categories

All our restaurant listings are marked with a euro symbol category, indicating the price you should expect to pay for a standard main course. The final bill will of course depend on the number of courses and drinks consumed.

€ = under €8

€€ = €8-€15

€€€ = €15-€25

€€€€ = over €25

in seafood dishes. But what really distinguishes the country from others in southern Europe is tastes picked up over centuries of seafaring, such as *piri piri*, a sauce made from crushed chilli peppers of which every *tasca* has its own version, kept in a tiny, power-packed bottle.

Lisbon has long been a good place to try Brazilian, Cape Verdean and Goan food, and the range of international cuisines on offer is expanding. The most notable recent

In the know
Water, water everywhere

Tap water is safe to drink in Lisbon, and in all but the snootiest restaurants staff won't bat an eyelid if you request it. But local bottled waters abound; aggressively fizzy Pedras Salgadas is an acquired taste but prized for its digestive qualities. Chilled is *fresca*, room temperature, *natural*.

EATING & DRINKING

Eleven

development is the emergence of chefs updating traditional Portuguese dishes. These include the empire-building José Avillez at **Belcanto** (*see p97*) or his many other outlets; the daring Alexandre Silva at **LOCO** (*see p136*); and the longer-established Vítor Sobral, who helped set up **Tasca da Esquina** (*see p139*). Foreign-born chefs such as Ljubomir Stanisic, at **100 Maneiras** (Rua do Teixeira 35, 91 091 8181, www. 100maneiras.com), and Joachim Koerper, at **Eleven** (*see p75*), make their own gastronomic contribution.

For diehard carnivores – or on Mondays, when locals spurn fish because the fleet stays home on Sundays – hearty dishes are popular, such as steak in Madeira sauce topped with

❤ **Best for gourmets**

Belcanto *p97*
Hub of José Avillez's empire.

Less Baixa *p65*
Fine food at affordable prices.

LOCO *p136*
Chef Silva explores wilder culinary shores.

a fried egg, and rich stews such as *feijoada* or *cozido* featuring beans, sausage and cheaper bits of pig. As in Spain, pork predominates; the free-range, acorn-fed *porco preto* (Iberian black pig) yields delicious meat.

You may see 'tapas' chalked up outside eateries, but both word and habit are imports. Still, trendy places that serve *petiscos* (snacks) are often good for vegetarians, whose options are still limited in traditional restaurants. One standby is thick vegetable soup, containing beans, cabbage, carrots or potato. But be on the alert for pieces of meat; *caldo verde* is mainly shredded kale but a slice of *chouriço* sausage is added on serving.

Grub's up

By 12.30pm the Portuguese are certainly thinking about lunch, if not already seated in their favourite *tasca*. Most restaurants serve lunch until at least 2.30pm – with some patrons enjoying food, chat and wine for over an hour, even on a work day.

Dinner starts any time from 8pm (although restaurants catering to tourists start serving at least an hour earlier); at weekends that can slide to 10pm. But if you are used to Spanish hours, beware: many kitchens don't stay open beyond 10pm during the week.

Except for very small or very fashionable places, you shouldn't need to book ahead except in high summer, and even then you may be able to do so on the day. Note that, away from touristy areas, Lisbon restaurants may close for part or all of August.

Menus at restaurants frequented by foreigners seek to cater to them, not always successfully (is 'sulking pig' really suckling pig or something more sinister?). But don't let that restrict you to a linguistically and gastronomically unchallenging diet of grilled chicken and omelettes. Many traditional places – particularly the *marisqueiras* specialising in

♥ **Tasty tascas**

1º de Maio *p106*
Unbeatable for price versus quality.

Casa Liège *p111*
A bustling student favourite.

Esquina da Fé *p72*
Cosy culinary den.

In the know
Imperial measures

If you want a draught beer, ask for *uma imperial*, which is the standard, small measure. Tourists may request *uma cerveja*, but that order means bottled beer. ('Imperial' was Lisbon's first beer served on tap, produced by Germânia – which in 1916 changed its inconvenient name to Portugália when the country entered World War I on Britain's side.) Two small draught beers is *duas imperiais*. For a large one, ask for *uma caneca*.

🖤 Gourmet food markets

Its slogan is 'The best of Lisbon under one roof' and that curatorial concept pays off at the **Time Out Market** (*see p116*), where some 40 rigorously selected traders offer everything from freshly squeezed juices and traditional Portuguese pastries to fine wines and 'signature cuisine' from some of Lisbon's top chefs.

Opened to fanfare in 2014, this food hall in Lisbon's main covered market, the Mercado da Ribeira, has been a roaring success. Every day, all day and well into the night, trendy locals and foreign visitors flock here, eager to sample delicacies dreamed up by local chefs. There are also cookery classes for adults and kids, and wine-tasting workshops.

It was in 2010 that the city council sought bids for the concession to manage the western nave of the dilapidated market hall and inject new life into it. The challenge was taken up by the local company (now part of the Time Out Group) responsible for our sister magazine, *Time Out Lisboa*, whose ambitious proposal to bring in top culinary talent and gourmet products won through.

Leading chefs whose creations can currently be sampled here include Alexandre Silva of **LOCO** (*see p136*) and Marlene Vieira of **Avenue**, as well as Dieter Koschina, of Michelin-starred Vila Joya in the Algarve, whose **Tartaria** stall serves amazing tartares, from goat's cheese to lobster.

You can order wine by the glass or choose from a great range of other tipples. For dessert there are the creamy *pastéis de nata* of **Manteigaria** (*see p100*), cakes or the elegant French-style creations of **L'Éclair** (*see p149*). If you just want a snack, there are various flavours of croquettes, veg and non-veg, at **Croqueteria**, and many other tasty tidbits.

It is a great option if you are a group (or couple) who can never agree what kind of food to go for. On the other hand, if your group is large you should try to come outside peak times. Time Out Market is a victim of its own success – at times it can be all but impossible to find a table to set your plate on, let alone a seat. Particularly in summer, we recommend braving it no later than noon (for lunch) or, in the afternoon, up until about 6pm.

Alternatively, catch the 28 tram to the middle-class neighbourhood of Campo de Ourique for a smaller version of the same gourmet food concept that actually predates the Time Out Market. At the **Mercado de Campo de Ourique** (*see p138*), the food court has real local atmosphere – it is right in the middle of the old fresh produce market – and a great range of stalls serving delicious fish, meat and vegetarian dishes, as well as fine wines.

Another local option, perhaps after visiting Belém, is the **Mercado de Algés** (*see p125*), just beyond the official city limits, which has extended hours and stalls serving everything from gourmet burgers and snacks to sushi, plus bars and regular live music programming. The current craze for gourmet markets started in Spain, but the Time Out Market's success in Lisbon probably helped prompt Spanish-owned department store **El Corte Inglés** (*see p149*) to open its own posh food court: **Gourmet Experience Lisboa**. Michelin-starred chefs here include seafood expert Pepe Soll, from Galicia, at **Atlántico**, and Roberto Ruíz, Mexican-born boss of Madrid's famous Punto Mx, with **Barra Cascabel**, in collaboration with Portugal's own José Avillez (*see p97*), who has two ventures here: **Tasca Chic** (www.tascachic.pt), serving traditional Portuguese food, and **Jacaré** (www.jacare.pt), which serves fine meats and vegetarian dishes with a Brazilian touch. There's also **Balcão**, a smart *taberna* run by Lisbon's other double-starred Michelin chef, Henrique Sá Pessoa.

seafood – display fresh produce in glass cases, so diners can see what's available and select before ordering. (It may be worth keeping an eye on the weighing process.) Restaurants that lack such a display are either very cheap – in which case they are best avoided unless we recommend them – or untypically modern or posh. Even in the latter, you can ask to see a particular fish or cut of meat before ordering.

To wash all this down, locals still prefer wine. Portugal produces a lot, most of it cheap and drinkable. If you are a stickler for etiquette, note that *bacalhau* matches with red. House wine comes in the bottle, unless bought in bulk, in which case it's served in jugs (*jarros*). Beer (*cerveja*) is popular with seafood – and on this note, Lisbon's *cervejarias* are bustling beer halls that specialise in surf and turf; usually open until late, they're good for a snack.

All restaurants have had to offer *menú turístico* by law for many years– a full set menu that nobody ever ordered, not least because it wasn't advertised. But many places clearly post up lunch deals, usually including soup and one of several *pratos do dia* (dishes of the day), plus a drink (which can be a glass of wine or beer) and coffee. Posher eateries often offer something similar (although of course called *menú executivo*) and this can be a great way of sampling gourmet creations. Even top chefs' restaurants may offer a proper *menu de degustação* (tasting menu) for less at lunchtime.

When the bill comes, the total will include IVA (VAT, with a higher rate for alcohol) but not, as a rule, a service charge – though at fancier establishments it's worth checking. There is little tradition of tipping here, perhaps because *tascas* have usually been staffed by family. Nowadays rounding up is normal, for a tip of around five per cent. But since tourists tend to be richer and from countries where tipping is more generous, your waiter may expect more. It's up to you.

♥ Best for drink connoisseurs

Chafariz do Vinho *p194*
Quiet haven for wine lovers.

Cinco *p194*
First and still best for cocktails.

Dois Corvos *p199*
For craft beer devotees.

Taberna Moderna *p80*
Its Lisbonita gin bar has 40 varieties.

What's on the Menu?

A primer of local cuisine

Basics

alho garlic; **almoço** lunch; **azeite** olive oil; **azeitona** olive; **coentro** coriander; **conta** bill; **dose** portion; **ementa** menu; **entrada** starter; **jantar** dinner; **lanche** snack; **lista da vinhos** wine list; **manteiga** butter; **meia** half; **ovo** egg; **pão** bread; **petisco** nibble; **piri-piri** chilli; **sal** salt; **salsa** parsley; **sandes** sandwich.

Cooking styles & techniques

açorda bread that has been soaked with olive oil, garlic, herbs and egg; **assado** roasted; **bem passado** well done; **caril** curry; **cebolada** cooked with onions; **caseiro** home-made; **churrasco** barbecue; **cozido** boiled; **espetada** skewer; **estufado** braised; **forno** oven; **frito** fried; **gratinado** baked with cheese on top; **grelhado** grilled; **guarnecido** garnished; **guisado** braised; **mal passado** rare; **massa** pastry/pasta; **médio** medium rare; **molho** sauce; **na brasa** charcoal-grilled; **no forno** oven-baked; **picante** spicy; **quente** hot/warm; **recheado** stuffed; **salteado** sautéed.

Sopas/ensopados (soups/stews)

Caldo verde shredded kale in potato broth; **canja** chicken broth; **cozido à portuguesa** stew of meats, sausages and cabbage; **feijoada** bean stew made with meat, seafood or snails.

Marisco (shellfish)

amêijoa clam; **camarão** shrimp; **gamba** prawn; **lagosta/lavagante** spiny/Norway lobster; **mexilhão** mussel; **ostra** oyster; **perceve** goose-necked barnacle; **sapateira** crab; **vieira** scallop.

Peixe (fish)

atum tuna; **bacalhau** salted cod (**...a brás** shredded, fried with potato and scrambled egg; **...a Gomes Sá** shredded, fried with onion, with boiled potato, egg and black olives; **... com natas** shredded, baked with cream and potato; **...cozido com grão** boiled, with chickpeas, potato and greens; **besugo** sea bream; **cação** dogfish; **caldeirada** fish stew; **cantaril** redfish; **carapau** mackerel; **cavala** horse mackerel; **cherne** large grouper; **choco** cuttlefish; **corvina** croaker; **dourada** gilthead bream; **enguia** eel; **espadarte** swordfish; **garoupa** grouper; **imperador** cardinal fish; **joaquinzinho** whitebait; **linguado** sole; **lula** squid; **pargo** sea bream; **pastel de bacalhau** deep-fried cod croquettes; **peixe espada** scabbard fish; **peixe galo** John Dory; **pescada** hake; **polvo** octopus; **pregado** turbot; **raia** skate/ray; **robalo** sea bass; **salmão** salmon; **salmonete** red mullet; **sardinha** sardine; **sargo** white bream; **solha** plaice; **truta** trout.

Carne (meat)

bifana slice of braised pork; **bife** steak (though not necessarily beef); **bitoque** slice of fried beef, served with chips and a fried egg; **borrego** lamb; **cabrito** kid; **caracois** snails; **chouriço** smoked sausage; **costoleta** chop; **dobrada** tripe; **entrecosto** pork rib; **entremeada** pork belly; **febras** boned slices of pork; **fiambre** uncured ham; **figado** liver; **ganso de vitela** topside of veal; **iscas** sliced liver; **leitão** suckling pig; **língua** tongue; **linguiça** spiced sausage; **lombinhos** tender pieces of meat; **lombo** loin; **medalhões** medallions; **mãozinha** trotter/hock; **morcela** blood sausage; **paio** cured sausage; **peito** breast; **perna** leg; **porco** pork; **porco preto** black pig; **prego** slice of beef, grilled; **presunto** cured ham; **posta** thick slice of meat (or fish); **rins** kidneys; **salpicão** spiced sausage; **salsicha** sausage; **toucinho** lard; **tripas** tripe; **vaca** cow/beef; **vazia** prime cut of beef; **veado** venison; **vitela** veal.

Aves e caça (poultry & game)

cabidela chicken with giblets; **codorniz** quail; **coelho** rabbit; **faisão** pheasant; **frango** chicken; **ganso** goose; **javalí** wild boar; **pato** duck; **perdiz** partridge; **perú** turkey.

Arroz, massa e feijao (rice, pasta & beans)

arroz rice; **esparguetes** spaghetti; **favas** broad beans; **feijão(ões)** bean(s); **lentilhas** lentils.

Legumes (vegetables)

alface lettuce; **batata (doce)** (sweet) potato; **cebola** onion; **cenoura** carrot; **cogumelo** mushroom; **couve** cabbage; **ervilhas** peas; **espargos** asparagus; **espinafres** spinach; **grelos** tender greens; **hortaliça** mixed vegetables; **pepino** cucumber; **pimenta** pepper.

Fruta (fruit)

ananás pineapple; **laranja** orange; **limão** lemon; **maçã** apple; **maracujá** passion fruit; **melancia** watermelon; **melão** cantaloupe; **meloa** melon; **morango** strawberry; **pêssego** peach; **uva** grape.

Sobremesa (dessert)

arroz doce rice pudding; **baba de camelo** dessert of yolks and sugar; **barriga de freira** dessert of breadcrumbs, sugar, egg and nuts; **bolo** cake; **gelado** ice-cream; **leite creme** custard; **pudim** caramel pudding; **toucinho do céu** dessert of almonds, eggs and sugar.

Drinks

vinho wine; **cerveja** beer; **àgua (com/sem gás)** (sparkling/still) water; **àgua da torneira** tap water; **café** coffee (espresso); **chá** tea.

Shopping

Traditional traders versus malls and mass tourism

Lisbon impresses many visitors with its era-spanning retail mix: long-established, often family-run stores in the Baixa contrasting with the luxury brands that emblazon façades on either side of the Avenida da Liberdade, and the bustling shopping centres further out. Traditional commerce is today under unprecedented pressure, yet many old-time traders cling on – some now with special protection from the city council. At the same time a more modern yet still quirky experience awaits in niches such as the Bairro Alto, while those looking for a more authentic local shop can head for one of the city's bustling residential neighbourhoods.

A Arte da Terra

43

Shopping in Portugal has in recent decades been a tale of two cities. Cast-iron leases enabled shopkeepers to go on paying tiny rents, so pursuing the same trade for decades – some stocking items that looked as though they had been around for decades too. They survived in a market where competition from the other city – the one with huge shopping centres – is fierce.

Beginning with **Amoreiras** (*see p139*) in 1987, malls were built near the heart of Lisbon, meaning that it's not just suburbanites who flock to them. When the burnt-out ruins of two department stores in Chiado, Lisbon's poshest shopping district, were turned into a mini-mall, many saw it as a Trojan horse, threatening local businesses by bringing foreign chains to their doorstep. Proponents argued that the intention was the opposite: to revitalise the old core by introducing greater variety. And a stroll around Chiado and Baixa, Lisbon's retail area since the late 18th century, doesn't suggest decline overall, despite some scars left by the economic crisis.

But this seemingly timeless scenario has, in fact, undergone rapid change since the current tourist boom began in the mid 2010s and the government – under pressure from the 'troika' of institutions that oversaw Portugal's eurozone bailout – loosened laws on rental contracts. That unleashed a wave of evictions, as property owners saw an opportunity to boost their financial returns and tourism-oriented businesses moved in. The resulting disappearance of several iconic establishments triggered an outcry, finally prodding the council into setting up a scheme to protect survivors (*see p45* Traditional shops).

What and where

In most Lisbon neighbourhoods there's still a *mercearia* (grocer's) on every other corner and any number of *padarias* (bakeries) and *talhos* (butchers), so you don't have to walk far to buy life's essentials. At the other

♥ **Best local food**

Antiga Confeitaria de Belém *p129*
Be prepared to queue for these traditional pastries.

Loja das Conservas *p66*
Compendium of tinned delicacies.

Manuel Tavares *p71*
Hams to honey, plus plenty of port.

Loja das Conservas

♥ **Best souvenirs**

A Arte da Terra *p80*
Crafts and other local products.

Lisbonlovers *p74*
Mementos with design flair.

A Vida Portuguesa *p104*
Vintage Portuguese brands.

💙 Traditional shops

Mercearias (grocers), *tabacarias* (tobacconists) and other specialists are still to be found squeezed into cramped spaces behind open doorways throughout the city. In particular, for those with time to browse, a wander through the traditional commercial area of the Baixa will reveal some amazing old shops.

Rua da Conceição still has colourful haberdashers with elaborate storefronts, offering a kaleidoscope of buttons, ribbons, tassels, lace, sequins and feather boas, as well as button-, belt- and buckle-covering services. Trades persist in streets long ago named after them, such as the Rua dos Sapateiros (cobblers), Rua dos Douradores (goldsmiths), Rua dos Fanqueiros (cloth merchants) and Rua da Prata (silversmiths). In some cases these are down to the final elegant survivors, such as **Victorino de Sousa** on Rua dos Correeiros, the last tanner's on Tanners' Street, just as **Azevedo Rua** is the last hatter's on Rossio.

Across town, every residential neighbourhood has any number of industrious cobblers hidden away in tiny rooms amid piles of shoes, and herbalists selling miracle teas for every ailment. You can also still get a haircut, shave, shoeshine, manicure and pedicure at an old-style barber's or hairdresser's.

But in the parts of Lisbon most impacted by the current tourism boom, commercial landmarks have been closing down at an alarming rate. After several years of debate, the council's *Lojas com História* programme (official English name 'Historic Shops') took effect in 2017, offering protection and support to 83 establishments — from wood-panelled pharmacies and tobacconists to jewellers and engravers, plus several cafés and restaurants. These establishments have the option to put up a plaque indicating their status, but for visitors looking for a classic Lisbon shopping experience, the website www.lojascomhistoria.pt is a good place to start.

For now, though, the initiative has almost as many advisors as it does protected shops, and the grim reaping continues. In the first few months of 2018 alone, Rua do Alecrim in Chiado saw the closure of several local stalwarts – including two booksellers and the showroom for *azulejo* specialist **Sant'ana** (*see p102*) – the latter to make way for yet more hotel rooms. All had, as newly exiled antiquarian António Trindade noted, helped make the street what it was. 'I don't feel like a victim,' he told *Público* newspaper. 'What I learned from my parents, grandparents and uncles no one can take away from me: I'll go somewhere else and rebuild. What pains me is what's happening to the city.'

Short of more radical action by the authorities, the main history lesson for residents and visitors alike is: use it or lose it.

extreme are hypermarkets Continente, Pão de Açucar/Jumbo or Carrefour, usually housed in shopping centres and broadly similar in terms of prices and selection. Stand-alone supermarket Pingo Doce has branches around town, while **El Corte Inglés** (*see p149*) has vast gourmet and wine sections. (For more on shopping for wine, *see p49* A Lot of Bottle.) There are, of course, products that even the biggest hypermarkets don't sell; for a concentration of African, Indian and Chinese wares, try **Centro Comercial Mouraria** on Largo Martim Moniz.

For Portuguese snacks, look out for *pastelarias* (cake shops) bearing the words *fábrico próprio* (own production). Biscuits are often sold by the kilo and staff will box up purchases *para levar* (to take away). **Antiga Confeitaria de Belém** (*see p129*) has what many maintain are Lisbon's best *pastéis de nata*, although **Manteigaria** (*see p100*) is a downtown contender.

After one too many cakes, drop into one of the surviving *ervanárias* (herbalists), where indigestion is among the many ailments, from alcoholism to ankle sprains, for which cures are stocked in 100-gram (3.5-ounce) bags, to be made into a tea. Regulars discuss their needs with staff in hushed tones; here, as elsewhere, shopping remains as much a social occasion as a functional one.

This social scene is evident even in the Bairro Alto, where bars sell clothes, hairdressers serve beer and some of the tiniest shops have DJs. Boutiques here open mid-afternoon and stay open into the night. It's a good place for club- and streetwear, but beware poor-quality imports with a hefty mark-up.

In general, Portuguese fashion is more conservative, and it is only since the '90s that a strong fashion industry has emerged, with regular catwalk events featuring up-and-coming talent as well as top names such as Anabela

In the know
To market

The **Feira da Ladra** (Campo Santa Clara; 21 817 0800; bus 712, 734, tram 28E; 9am-6pm Tues & Sat) is Lisbon's best-known flea market, but craft or produce stalls are set up weekly in areas from Graça to Príncipe Real. Official website www.visitlisboa. com has a list under Markets & Fairs. For a more authentic local experience, head for the multicultural open-air Sunday **Feira do Relógio** (Avenida Santo Condestável) or to a neighbourhood market hall such as **Mercado 31 de Janeiro** (Rua Engenheiro Vieira da Silva, closed Sun & Mon), or **Mercado de Arroios** (Rua Ângela Pinto, 21 351 1617, closed Mon). In all cases, hours are 7am to 2pm.

Feira da Ladra

Baldaque, Luís Buchinho, Paulo Cravo and Nuno Baltazar, Nuno Gama, Maria Gambina and Miguel Vieira. Only the most established can afford their own shops (clustered in Chiado) but El Corte Inglés stocks local designers' wares.

Footwear is one of Portugal's traditional industries and Lisbon has an abundance of shoe shops. Prices are competitive, but check the quality if they seem too cheap to be true. Larger chains are well represented in the malls; for a funkier approach, try **Gardénia** (*see p101*) and the boutiques in the Bairro Alto.

For souvenirs, the *azulejo* (tile) is a prime contender, showcased in the city's churches and palaces. Much tat is on offer but some fine hand-painted contemporary and antique tiles. can be browsed or bought at **Solar** (*see p107*). There are also distinctive regional ceramics and pottery, cork in ever more forms, a variety of textiles from linen tablecloths to woollen blankets, and *bordado* (embroidery) – the most expensive hails from Madeira and bears a seal guaranteeing authenticity.

Antique and bric-a-brac shops congregate in Rua de São Bento and Rua Dom Pedro V, and around the Sé. There's a cluster of junk shops in the area where the **Feira da Ladra** (*see p46*) market is held.

For a bit of local variety, hop off tram 28 at well-to-do Campo de Ourique and you'll find the streets lined not only with trees, but also with upmarket boutiques, children's clothes shops and stores selling household goods. These are interspersed with cafés and traditional shops and services, from *garrafeiras* (wine shops) to florists, and there's fresh produce at the local covered market.

Opening hours and tax

Along with Lisbon's quaint, traditional shops come quaint traditions, not least closing up for lunch from 1pm to 3pm or at some other random time when the owner pops out to see

❤ Best local fashion

Eureka *p101*
Striking modern footwear.

Lidija Kolovrat *p110*
Art meets fashion in Lisbon.

Luvaria Ulísses *p102*
Tiny jewel of a glove shop.

Lidija Kolovrat

**In the know
Out-of-town outlet**

Freeport (21 234 3500/1, www.freeport.pt) in Alcochete, across the Ponte Vasca da Gama bridge, has some 200 shops offering discounts of 50 per cent on big brands. They're open 10am to 10pm Sunday to Thursday and 10am to 11pm Friday and Saturday. Restaurants stay open an hour longer. As well as TST buses 431, 432 or 437 from Gare do Oriente (33mins), there is a dedicated shuttle that departs Marquês de Pombal at 10am and 1pm daily; the €10 return ticket gets you an extra 10 per cent off in some stores. Parking is free, except in the underground car park from October to May.

Solar

a man about a dog. A '*volto já*' (back soon) sign may or may not mean what it says, and it's not unusual for some family businesses to shut up shop for as much as a month in the summer. By contrast, in malls and chain stores such quirks have been ironed out.

Most shopkeepers are admirably patient when dealing with foreigners who don't speak the lingo, and almost anywhere volunteering the correct change (*troco*) will win you friends.

Value-added tax (IVA) is a stonking 23 per cent on most goods, but 13 per cent on some foodstuffs and six per cent on others; the lower rate also applies to books and pharmaceutical products. Non-EU residents may claim back IVA on purchases over €50 before tax if they take them home unused. At the store, have your passport ready and let the sales assistant know that you want to claim the refund; you will receive a code to punch into the 'e-Taxfree Portugal' terminal at the airport after checking in. There are private schemes that streamline the process. (See http://info.portaldasfinancas. gov.pt or www.ana.pt for more.)

♥ Best ceramics & azulejos

Sant'Anna *p102*
Handcrafted since 1741.

Solar *p107*
Antique dealer with top tiles.

Vista Alegre Atlantis *p104*
Classy ceramics and glass.

Viúva Lamego *p90*
Tiles to take you back in time.

A Lot of Bottle

How to shop for great port and wine

Portugal's burgeoning output of excellent wine is the obvious reason to head for a *garrafeira* (drink shop) such as **GN Cellar** (see *p66*) or **El Corte Inglés** (see *p149*), or indeed any large supermarket.

Portugal's largest producers are Sogrape, José Maria da Fonseca, Caves Aliança and Companhia das Quintas, any of whose names should be a guarantee of quality for anything from full-bodied reds to light, fizzy *vinho verde*. (A note on vintages: for most regions, you are usually safest buying the youngest wine that you can find, since many places store bottles in less than ideal conditions.) Don't expect to be bowled over by the lower-priced wines of big producers. Smaller producers often yield more interesting results, as they are more likely to be run by wine lovers. Here is a selection of producers by region.

Alentejo: Cortes de Cima; D'Avillez; Esporão; Fundação Eugénio de Almeida; Herdade do Porto da Bouga; João Portugal Ramos; Mouchão; Tapada de Coelheiros.

Bairrada: Luís Pato; Quinta das Bágeiras; Quinta de Baixo; Sidónio de Sousa.

Dão: Dão Sul (Quinta de Cabriz and others); Quinta da Pellada; Quinta dos Roques.

Douro: Calheiros Cruz; Domingos Alves de Sousa; Kolheita de Ideias; Lavradores de Feitoria; Niepoort; Quinta da Casa Amarela; Quinta de la Rosa; Quinta do Côtto; Quinta do Crasto; Vallado; Vale da Corça (Encostas do Tua, Brunheda).

Lisboa: Casa Santos Lima (Palha Canas and others); DFJ Vinhos; Quinta da Cortezia; Quinta de Pancas; Quinta do Monte d'Oiro.

Palmela/Setúbal: Cooperativa Agrícola de Santo Isidro de Pegões; Ermelinda Freitas; Hero do Castanheiro; JP Vinhos; Venâncio Costa Lima.

Tejo: Falua; Fiuza; Quinta da Alorna; Quinta da Lagoalva; Quinta do Alqueve; Quinta do Casal Branco (Falcoaria, Capucho); Quinta do Falcão.

As for port wine, a cornerstone of national identity, it is made only in the Douro valley and fortified with local brandy – but plenty of good stuff is available to buy in the capital. Port is traditionally divided into two broad categories: wood-aged and bottle-aged.

Bottle-aged port starts out deep and dark, with herbal and fruit aromas, gradually developing other flavours such as pepper, raisins and truffles. Vintage port is the king of bottle-aged ports: wine from a single harvest, which is bottled after two or three years. It is then supposedly left to mature for at least a decade; in reality much vintage port hits an eager market soon after bottling. Late-bottled vintage (LBV) refers to a process where wine from a single year has been kept in wood for between four and six years. If then bottled without filtration, it is known as a 'traditional' LBV and may compare well with a vintage. Filtered LBV can also be good.

Wood-aged port is a feast of aromas: dried fruit, walnut shell, toast or burnt wood – you name it, you'll sniff it. It has long been termed tawny, but is only of interest if it has had at least ten years in wood, so look for labels that say it is ten, 20, 30, 40 or over 40 years old. These labels are legally binding (being the minimum age in the blend), unlike terms such as 'fine old', 'aged' and 'reserve'. If you baulk at the prices, you may be better off with a ruby, which is an honestly young port.

Finally, two styles combine wood and bottle: *colheita* ('harvest') and *garrafeira*. Port labelled '*Colheita 1976*', for example, is wine from grapes harvested in 1976 and then aged in wood for at least seven years.

Madeira, from the sub-tropical island of that name, is another fortified wine that comes in a variety of styles: dry to be drunk on its own as an aperitif, or sweet to accompany dessert. There are also excellent sweet Muscat wines, particularly Moscatel de Setúbal; local liqueurs Licor Beirão (with herbs), Amêndoa Amarga (bitter almond) and *ginjinha* (morello cherries, see *p69* Sticky Situation); and *aguardente* (brandy) and *bagaçeira* (distilled from the skins and stems of grapes).

If you want to taste as many wines as possible before buying (and who doesn't?) look out for fairs where you may pay just a few euros to sample hundreds – and get the chance to chat to producers: **Vinho ao Vivo** (http://vinhoaovivo.pt) in July, **Mercado de Vinhos de Campo Pequeno** (www.campopequeno.pt) and **Grandes Escolhas –Vinhos e Sabores** (www.vinhosesabores.com) in October, **Encontro com Vinhos** (www.encontrovinhosesabores.com) in November, and **Adegga** (https://pt.adegga.com) in December.

Explore

Ponte 25 de Abril

Getting Started

From grand river vistas and Manueline monuments to labyrinths of alleyways and funny old funiculars – there's something round every corner on the slopes of Lisbon's seven hills. The city grew up along the River Tagus and you are likely to spend most of your time within a few hundred metres of it. But if you have more than a day or two, don't limit yourself to the older neighbourhoods huddled near the waterfront: some of the most interesting museums are in the modern business and residential districts inland. And the wider region has some fine sights, plus great beaches.

❤ Best museums

Belém *p122*
Museum-piece neighbourhood full of excellent museums.

Museu Calouste Gulbenkian *p147*
Art ancient and modern, western and eastern.

Museu do Aljube *p79*
Dictatorship and Revolution.

Museu Nacional de Arte Antiga *p117*
Portuguese art through the centuries, plus Old Masters.

Museu Nacional do Azulejo *p150*
An overview of locals' favourite decorative element.

Alfama p85

Cable ferry

♥ Best places to escape the crowd

Jardim do Torel *p83*
An oasis in the middle of the city.

Mouraria *p89*
Ancient bairro less touristy than Alfama.

Jardim Botânico de Lisboa *p108*
Shaded paths amid thousands of plants.

Fundação Arpad Szenes – Vieira da Silva *p138*
Excellent small art museum on a quiet square.

Campo de Ourique *p137*
Shop and snack among locals.

An overview of the city

As with most European capitals, foreign visitors these days tend to arrive in Lisbon by air, and flight paths usually sweep over the city centre. The view from the right side of the plane takes in the great curve of the River Tagus and its broad estuary, with the tangle of city-centre streets below. This is the 'peaceful harbour' – in Phoenician, 'Alis-Ubbo' – from which Lisbon probably earned its name, the mouth of the Iberian peninsula's longest river.

You should be able to spy the Ponte 25 de Abril, comparable in size and design to San Francisco's Golden Gate, spanning the river and presided over by the statue of Cristo Rei ('Christ the King') at its southern foot. Far to the east, the new Ponte Vasco da Gama also traverses the estuary, its white suspension cables looking, at this remove, like delicate white threads.

The city is fronted by the Praça do Comércio, a grand 18th-century square that opens out on to the water. From here, the city scrambles up on to seven hills. Rising above the clutter of terracotta rooftops, the skyline is dominated by the Castelo de São Jorge, with white-domed churches to east and west – the Panteão Nacional de Santa Engrácia just below the castle, and the Basílica da Estrela way over west.

For centuries, visitors would arrive by water – whether by ship or, later, on a seaplane landing in front of Praça do Comércio. Until the turn of the century, trains from the south terminated at Barreiro, on the south bank of the Tagus, and travellers entered the city by ferry. Express trains from the south now terminate at Oriente, at the former Expo '98 site, where services from Porto also stop before terminating at Santa Apolónia, further downtown. The overnight train from Madrid comes into the city along the same route.

The city may have turned its back on the river for decades, but many of the main sights are within a relatively narrow strip parallel to the bank. So by starting your exploration of the city down by the waterfront you will be able to better understand its history and layout.

We begin the Explore section with the Baixa, the flat 18th-century heart of the city and for centuries its business district, as part of **Central Lisbon** (*see pp58-75*). This chapter also takes in the city's main axis, the Avenida da Liberdade, which literally led the way to its later development – the first Metro line mirrored this, running up from Praça dos Restauradores to Praça Marquês de Pombal and beyond. In this area restaurants, cafés and shops abound.

East of Baixa (*see pp76-91*) are the hills where the oldest extant monuments are

Top Tours

Explore the city by land or water

Lisbon is not short of transport options, both public and private – from buses to boats and something very much in between. So when the seven hills of Lisbon prove too much, go easy on yourself and try one of the following.

Yellow Bus Tours

21 850 3225, www.carris.pt. **Tagus Tour** *Oct-May every 20mins 9am-5.30pm daily. June-Sept every 20mins 9am-7pm, then 7.30pm & 8pm, daily.* **Olisipo Tour** *Oct-May every 30mins 9.15am-5.45pm daily. June-Sept every 30mins 9.15am-7.15pm daily.* **Belém** *Oct-May every hr 10.40am-5.40pm daily. June-Sept every hr 10.40am-5.40pm daily.* **Tickets** *Tagus/Olisipo €16; €8 4-10s; free under-4s. Belém €10; €5 4-10s; free under-4s.*

Open-top hop-on/hop-off double-decker buses, with English commentary, set off from Praça da Figueira on two different circuits. The 1hr 40min Tagus Tour takes in the centre, the shopping hubs of El Corte Inglés and Amoreiras, Estrela, Belém, the docks, and the Museu de Oriente and Museu Nacional de Arte Antiga; the 1hr 45min Olisipo Tour trundles past Alfama, on to the Museu do Azulejo and out to Parque das Nações, before looping back via the Museu da Cidade, the bullring and the parliament building. In Belém, the service starts from the Mosteiro dos Jerónimos (see p126) and takes in the Torre de Belém, Padrão do Descobrimentos and Museu Nacional dos Coches.

This arm of Lisbon's public bus and tram operator Carris caters to the tourist trade. In addition to the tours, it offers single and combination tickets that all come with free public transport for the period of validity – including funiculars and the Elevador de Santa Justa – plus discounts on sights such as the Oceanário and zoo, and at some restaurants and stores. The €30 Bus & Tram and Bus & Boat tickets (€27 online) throw in the **Hills Tramcar Tour** or the **Yellow Boat Tour** respectively; the latter has a stop at Cacilhas, giving you the chance to visit the Cristo Rei statue (see p57 Appreciating the Tagus). There is also the All Bus ticket, which gives you 48 hours to do all three open-top bus circuits. It's good value for families at €25 per adult (€22.50 online) plus up to two under-12s. Note that all the company's tickets are cheaper online.

▶ *Several other highly visible private companies run hop-on, hop-off bus tours, including Cityrama (www.cityrama.pt), which,* *like its public rival, also does combined bus and boat tours.*

Yellow Boat Tour

21 850 3225, www.carris.pt. **Departures** *Terreiro do Paço Nov-Feb 10am, 1pm, 3pm daily. Mar, Apr 10am, 1pm, 3pm, 5pm daily. May-Oct 10am, 11.30am, 2pm, 3.30pm, 5pm daily. Belém 1hr later.* **Tickets** *€20; €10 4-10s; free under-4s.*

This hop-on, hop-off boat trip with English commentary is run by the Transtejo ferry company (http://ttsl.pt) and marketed by Yellow Bus. The 1hr 30min circuit starts at Terreiro do Paço, focusing on the city centre and Belém, where it stops at the ferry station. A cheaper alternative to this circuit is to take a ferry from Cais do Sodré to Cacilhas (15mins).

HIPPOtrip

21 192 2030, www.hippotrip.com. **Departures** *Oct-Mar 10am, noon, 2pm, 4pm daily. Apr-Sept 10am, noon, 2pm, 4pm, 6pm daily.* **Tickets** *€25; €15 reductions.*

This chunky yellow amphibious vehicle tours the city centre and Belém, where it plunges into the river to give you a different perspective of Lisbon and its history. It's the splashy transition that kids love, of course (but note that children under two are not allowed). In all, it's a 1hr 30min trip, starting from the Associação Naval de Lisboa at the Doca de Santo Amaro in Alcântara. In busy periods they lay on more trips than scheduled; conversely, conditions on the Tagus may prompt delays of 15 to 30 minutes to your departure. Whatever the weather, waterproofs are handy.

Tramcar Tours

21 850 3225, www.carris.pt. **Hills Tramcar Tour** *Oct-May every 30mins 9.30am-5.30pm daily. June-Sept every 2 mins 9.30am-7pm daily.* **Castle Tramcar Tour** *May-Oct every 30mins 10.30am-6pm daily.* **Tickets** *Hills Tramcar Tour €20; €10 4-10s; free under-4s. Castle Tramcar Tour €10; €5 4-10s; free under-4s*

The distinctive red tram sets off from Praça do Comércio for a 1hr 25min tour around Lisbon's hilly centre. Half the year the green tram does a cheaper 40min run past the castle and up to Graça. It's fun, but definitely on the expensive side for a large family, although it may be worth it to avoid the queuing and crowding of the city's standard yellow trams.

perched: castle, 12th-century cathedral and a church marking the birthplace of the city's favourite saint, Santo António (*see p79*), plus a bevy of small museums and the fascinating warren that is Alfama. Public transport in this area is limited to a minibus serving the castle and vintage trams – one of which clangs on up to the *miradouros* (lookout points) of Graça.

West of Baixa (*see pp92-111*) is another hill, on whose slopes are the Chiado's cafés and smart shops. Further uphill is the Bairro Alto, long a nightlife haven and now dotted with offbeat shops. Beyond that is Príncipio Real, still a focus of the LGBT community and now targeted by upmarket property developers. This area is a fine place to eat, shop and play.

Heading inland you reach a set of quieter, mainly residential districts that we review together as **São Bento & Beyond** (*see pp130-139*). They include Estrela, with its domed church and charming garden; the bustling middle-class neighbourhood of Campo de Ourique; and Amoreiras, old and new. Beyond that, from Campolide, Lisbon's 18th-century aqueduct stalks out across a valley.

But the Tagus calls: our priority now is to explore the **Western Waterfront** (*see pp112-129*), starting (as do trains, trams and buses) from Cais do Sodré, named for the local quay. From this once decadent, now trendy old port district we head west through Santos, where the city's prime museum for Portuguese art over the centuries stands, and Madragoa, whose residents' livelihoods once depended on the river. Next comes Alcântara, with another fine museum and a cluster of hip shops and restaurants, and finally Belém, with its iconic monuments.

The modern city is covered in our **Further Afield** chapter (*see pp140-155*). First we

look at Northern Lisbon, with several major museums amid the office buildings. Then there's Eastern Lisbon, where a landscape of once-derelict warehouses and contaminated land has been transformed – long-neglected Marvila, in particular, is buzzing – thanks in part to the craft breweries that have set up there. Much of this regeneration followed in the wake of the Expo '98 World Fair which was staged a little further north on a former industrial wasteland that is now the activity-filled Parque das Nações.

Finally, there are opportunities to get out of the city, whether by public transport or with your own wheels. Try not to miss Sintra or, in summer, the region's many miles of beaches. We've included some easily accessible highlights in **Day Trips** (*see pp156-169*).

Getting around

Lisbon's historic core is compact but everywhere except the Baixa is hilly. Keen walkers will be happy to cover most of it on foot, but others may want the tram to take the strain. For East of Baixa, tuk-tuks are another option, but they can't enter the ancient Alfama and Castelo *bairros* (neighbourhoods). Away from the centre, the Metro – comfortable and fairly regular – becomes an option, though not for Belém. For that there is the 15 tram and buses, or trains from Cais do Sodré, most of which stop there. In eastern Lisbon, trains run from Apolónia to Oriente station, at the Parque das Nações (some stopping at Braço de Prata in Marvila). Services are infrequent but take just seven minutes, compared to up to 40 minutes by Metro from downtown. For more on public transport, *see p246*.

Discount schemes

The **Lisboa Card** (www.visitlisboa.com, €19-€40) combines one to three days of unlimited public transport – including the iconic lifts, funiculars and trams, plus trains to day-trip destinations Cascais and Sintra – with free admission to 29 of the region's museums and other sights, and discounts at others. It also gives discounts of up to ten per cent on many tours, and at shops and restaurants. It's sold at tourist offices at the airport and in town, and online.

For dedicated consumers, the €6 Lisboa **Eat & Shop** card brings discounts of up to 20 per cent in 100 restaurants and shops for 72 hours.

▶ *The city's main tourist office is on the western side of Praça do Comércio, but the office in Palácio Foz on Praça dos Restauradores also dispenses help and leaflets on the city as well as on Portugal. For more information on tourist offices and booths, see p255.*

❤ River Tagus

The ferries that criss-cross the River Tagus are the equivalent of commuter trains in other cities and are packed at rush hours. In quieter periods, they give you a magnificent alternative perspective on Lisbon's cityscape. For a more leisurely trip, ferry company Transtejo does a 90-minute cruise (*see p55* Top Tours); several rival offers are listed on www.visitlisboa.com.

The busiest terminal on the south bank is at **Cacilhas**, ten minutes by boat from Cais do Sodré. There's a cluster of seafood restaurants that are full of families at weekends wielding plastic hammers over lobsters and crabs. Cacilhas is the gateway to **Almada**, a burgeoning metropolis whose cultural life includes Portugal's biggest annual theatre event, the **Festival Internacional de Teatro** (*see p177*); in summer, Lisbon residents pack on to buses at Cacilhas, headed for the **Costa da Caparica beaches** (*see p168*).

Further west along the river at Cais do Ginjal is a dirty river beach and the terrace of brilliant seafood restaurant **Atira-te ao rio** (Cais do Ginjal 69/70, 21 275 1380, www.atirateaorio.pt, €€€). Next door, **Ponto Final** (Cais do Ginjal 72, 21 276 0743, €€€) also has a waterfront patio and traditional cuisine. On the cliff above at the end is Almada's cute old town: a lift a little further on, the **Elevador Panorâmico da Boca do Vento** (Largo da Boca do Vento, €1) whisks you up to the *miradouro* behind the Câmara Municipal (City Hall) for great views – and a cocktail and tapas bar, and restaurant, named after the elevator (closed Wed). There are often free art exhibitions at the nearby **Casa da Cerca** (Rua da Cerca 2, 21 272 4950, closed Mon), a Baroque palace in lovely gardens, which also has a café with a view.

West again is the **Santuário do Cristo Rei** (Praceta do Cristo Rei 27A, 21 275 1000/1270, www.cristorei.pt), topped by a Christ the King statue that is a stiffer echo of Rio's statue of Christ the Redeemer, inaugurated in 1959. It's worth the trip (from the Cacilhas ferry terminal, by TST bus 101) to take the lift up 75 metres (246 feet) to the observation deck at the 28-metre (92-foot) high statue's feet, from which you are overlooking the suspension bridge. The ground-floor chapel, remodelled in 2006, is a site of pilgrimage.

Another way to enjoy the river is to take a ferry from the boat station at Belém across to Porto Brandão and **Trafaria**, where you can lunch cheaply on fresh fish. From here, a cycle path runs to the beaches of Caparica, so if you hire a bike in Lisbon first you are guaranteed a great day out.

Central Lisbon

The devastating 1755 earthquake paved the way for a despotic but enlightened first minister to stamp his rationalist mark on the heart of the city. The Baixa – literally 'low' – is a grid of streets leading down to the river at the majestic Praça do Comércio. Long the city's welcome mat, this grand square remains the entry point for thousands of commuters who cross over the Tagus from the south bank every day. At the northern end of the Baixa is the less formal square known as Rossio, from where it's just a short walk to Avenida da Liberdade, the city's main axis, forging up hill to the green expanse of Lisbon's central park, Parque Eduardo VII.

❤ **Don't miss**

1 Praça do Comércio *p63*
The vast riverside square that locals still call Terreiro do Paço.

2 Tram 28 *p67*
The number one route for Lisbon's top sights.

3 Elevador de Santa Justa *p64 and p67*
This century-old iron tower is just one of Lisbon's eccentric transport options.

4 Rossio *p68*
The city's crossroads for two millennia.

5 Avenida da Liberdade *p71*
Lisbon's central axis, lined with trees and luxury stores.

6 Igreja de São Domingos *p70*
Fire-ravaged but still imposing.

Praça dos Restauradores *p71*

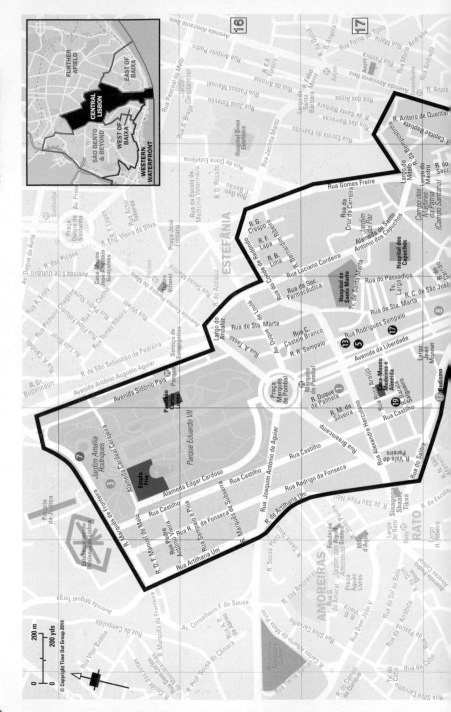

© Copyright Time Out Group 2019

200 m
200 yds

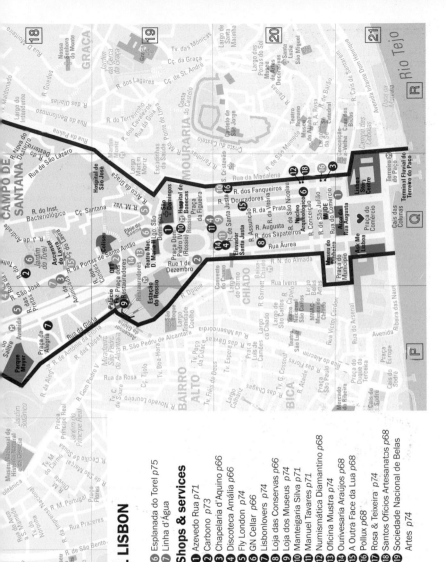

CENTRAL LISBON

Restaurants

1. Associação Caboverdeana *p75*
2. Bonjardim *p70*
3. Eleven *p75*
4. Esquina da Fé *p72*
5. Everest Montanha *p70*
6. Gambrinus *p70*
7. Jesus é Goês *p72*
8. JNcQUOI *p73*
9. João do Grão *p65*
10. Less Baixa *p65*
11. A Licorista *p65*
12. Maharaja *p73*
13. O Marques *p71*
14. Pinóquio *p73*
15. Solar dos Presuntos *p73*
16. Tasca Kome *p65*
17. Os Tibetanos *p73*

Cafés & bars

1. Café Martinho da Arcada *p66*
2. Café Nicola *p71*
3. Champanheria do Largo *p73*
4. Confeitaria Nacional *p71*
5. Delta Q *p73*
6. Esplanada do Torel *p75*
7. Linha d'Água

Shops & services

1. Azevedo Rua *p71*
2. Carbono *p73*
3. Chapelaria d'Aquino *p66*
4. Discoteca Amália *p66*
5. Fly London *p73*
6. GN Cellar *p66*
7. Lisbonlovers *p74*
8. Loja das Conservas *p66*
9. Loja dos Museus *p74*
10. Manteigaria Silva *p71*
11. Manuel Tavares *p71*
12. Numismática Diamantino *p68*
13. Oficina Mustra *p74*
14. Ourivesaria Araújos *p68*
15. A Outra Face da Lua *p68*
16. Pollux *p68*
17. Rosa & Teixeira *p74*
18. Santos Ofícios Artesanatos *p68*
19. Sociedade Nacional de Belas
Artes *p74*

THE BAIXA

A walk around the Baixa, Lisbon's traditional downtown, gives a flavour of how things were done in the days before shopping malls. You can wander down streets where trades have clustered for centuries: jewellers linger on **Rua do Ouro** (also marked on some maps by its old name, Rua Aurea); **Rua dos Sapateiros** is still a 'street of shoemakers'; and **Rua dos Fanqueiros** is home to textile merchants and fabric shops, as it has always been (*see also p45* Traditional shops).

Or, at least, as it's been since the mid 18th century. Before then, the heart of medieval Lisbon was a labyrinthine tangle of narrow streets. Then, as now, the poles were two squares: the **Terreiro do Paço** on the waterfront, later remade as the **Praça do Comércio** but more often known locally by its old name; and the **Rossio** (now officially Praça Dom Pedro IV) at its upper end. The largest of Lisbon's Jewish quarters, the Judiaria Grande, occupied a big chunk of the Baixa, centred round the synagogue that stood between Rua da Conceição and Rua de São Nicolau, at their eastern end.

The 1755 earthquake put paid to all that. Charged with the job of reconstruction, the Marquês de Pombal (*see also p223* Making of the Marquês) based his plan on a military encampment, with each street having a specific function. The overall project took until the next century to finish with the completion in 1873 of the **Arco Triunfal** (Triumphal Arch) and the waterfront Praça do Comércio (*see p63*) is as grand as any square in Europe.

The **Paços do Concelho**, housing Lisbon's Câmara Municipal (city council), sits on the west side of the Baixa on Praça do Município. Built in 1867, it was renovated after a 1996 fire that mysteriously broke out in the department of financial records. The Câmara's grand balcony was where the Republic was proclaimed on 5 October 1910, and the square is the setting for annual Republic Day celebrations. **Rua do Arsenal**, running west from here to Cais do Sodré, was long famous for the smell of *bacalhau* emanating from its storefronts but is now littered with souvenir shops.

Many of the Baixa's streets are now pedestrianised, notably the main drag, **Rua Augusta**, which has pavement cafés, shops (now mainly foreign chains) and buskers along its length. The workaday lunch crowd head for cheap restaurants on Rua dos Correeiros or to obscure eateries through unmarked doorways. Many businesses hereabouts still have appealing old fronts, such as the dilapidated button shops and haberdashers on **Rua da Conceição**.

Between the tram tracks near the street's junction with Rua da Prata, a manhole cover marks the way to some Roman tanks, probably the foundations of a temple or other large building. Normally flooded, they open to the public only once a year, in the autumn. For more information, head to the **Núcleo Arqueológico da Rua dos Correeiros**. If the medieval period is more your thing, in the basement of the free **Museu do Dinheiro** you can see a chunk of the 13th-century city wall.

Baixa's tallest landmark is the **Elevador de Santa Justa**, the 19th-century solution to the problem of getting up to the Chiado without breaking into a sweat. Today the series of escalators in Baixa-Chiado Metro station do part of the job, but underground. On the eastern side of the Baixa, the

---

♥ Time to eat & drink

From distant shores
Associação Caboverdeana *p75*, Tasca Kome *p65*

Mediterranean foodie heaven
Eleven *p75*

Rooftop dining
Less Baixa *p65*

Shrine to sugar
Confeitaria Nacional *p71*

Vegetarian and spiritual nourishment
Os Tibetanos *p73*

♥ Time to shop

Browse for music
Carbono *p73*, Discoteca Amália *p66*

Classy souvenirs
Lisbonlovers *p74*, Loja dos Museus *p74*

Hats and shoes
Azevedo Rua *p71*, Chapelaria D'Aquino *p66*, Fly London *p74*

Tinned fish galore
Loja das Conservas *p66*

Winning wine
GN Cellar *p66*

In the know
Getting around

The Baixa is pancake flat and several of its streets pedestrian-only. It is served by Metro station Baixa-Chiado and, at its northern end, stations Rossio and Praça dos Restauradores; above ground, buses stop at both squares before heading up Avenida da Liberdade. The 12 tram, which circles the castle hill, starts on Praça da Figueira, as does the 15 and buses running down to Praça do Comércio, whose Metro station takes the square's old name, Terreiro do Paço.

💙 Praça do Comércio

*Avenida da Ribeira das Naus. Metro Terreiro do Paco. **Open** 24hrs daily. **Admission** Free. **Map** p60 Q21.*

In the waterfront Praça do Comércio, 18th-century autocrat the Marquês de Pombal wanted a majestic square to rival anything found in Europe, and architects Carlos Mardel and Eugênio dos Santos more or less gave him what he wanted. It was designed with one side open to the river and the other three for government ministries, with a centrepiece 14-metre-high (46-foot-high) equestrian statue of Dom José I, monarch at the time of the Great Earthquake of 1755, by Joaquim Machado de Castro.

One thing that wasn't cleared away with the earthquake rubble was the area's name, Terreiro do Paço (Palace Yard, after the royal residence that stood here from the 16th century); it still trips off locals' tongues more easily than the official designation.

After several lost decades as a car park until the 1990s, the square has since been pedestrianised and cafés and restaurants with outdoor terraces now line its western and eastern flanks. Its central location make it a good place to start exploring, and the **Lisboa Story Centre** (*see p64*), on its eastern side, offers a fun introduction to the city's history.

Along the bottom edge of the square traffic still severs it from the river, but this is gradually being reduced. The **Cais das Colunas** – a monumental stone jetty that formed part of the original plan for the square – still draws canoodling couples and tourists in search of a scenic selfie.

A few steps east, rush-hour crowds pour on and off ferries linking the capital with the south-bank town of Barreiro. Along the bank in the other direction is the revamped **Ribeira dos Naus** riverfront, where for centuries ocean-going carracks were built and now tourists soak up the sun.

Under the arcades along the top of the square, handicrafts stalls set up on weekends and holidays. At the north-east corner, the **Café Martinho da Arcada** has been open since 1782; Lisbon's iconic poet Fernando Pessoa was a regular during the 1920s and '30s.

At the north-west corner is the main **Ask Me Lisboa** tourist office (9am-8pm daily), which also stocks a large range of souvenirs. A stone plaque on the wall nearby recalls the assassination, on 1 February 1908, of the then king, Dom Carlos I, and the crown prince, Luís Filipe. The gunmen represented the violent fringe of a movement that was to triumph two years later, with the proclamation of the Portuguese Republic round the corner at the City Hall.

The square's triumphal arch – usually known simply as the **Arco da Rua Augusta** (*see p64*) – was inaugurated in 1873, capping almost a century of post-quake rebuilding. That's Glory on top of the arch, holding wreaths above the heads of Genius and Bravery. Below are Viriatus, Nun'Álvares Pereira, Vasco da Gama and the Marquês de Pombal. The Tagus is the River God on the left, the Douro is on the right. Since 2013, the structure has been open to the public, for a unique perspective on the Baixa and its surroundings.

misleadingly named **Ascensor do Castelo** (Rua dos Fanqueiros 170) is a modern lift inside a building, and a first step up to the castle hill.

Sights & museums

Arco da Rua Augusta

Rua Augusta 2 (21 099 8599). Metro Terreiro do Paço. **Open** *9am-7pm daily.* **Admission** *€3; free under-6s. Joint ticket with Lisbon Story Centre €8; €4.50-€6.50 reductions; free under-6s.* **Map** *p60 Q21.*

There's nothing much to see in this grand structure, but its roof affords a unique view of the Baixa – and of the statues atop the arch – despite it being a comparatively low vantage point.

❤ Elevador de Santa Justa

Rua do Ouro (no phone, www.carris. pt). Metro Baixa-Chiado. **Lift** *Nov-Apr 7.30am-9pm daily. Easter weekend & May-Oct 7.30am-11pm daily.* **Miradouro** *Nov-Apr 9am-9pm daily, Easter weekend & May-Oct 9am-11pm daily.* **Admission** *Lift €5.15 return. Miradouro €1.50. No cards.* **Map** *p60 Q20.*

The industrial-age iron tracery of the Santa Justa lift – sometimes called the Elevador do Carmo – became a national monument in 2002. It was built by Portuguese-born Eiffel disciple Raul Mesnier de Ponsard, and officially opened in August 1901. It links downtown Rua do Ouro with the square next to the Carmo church up above, via a 15-m (49-ft) viaduct. On the top floor, up a spiral staircase, a viewing platform offers 360-degree views. The *elevador* is part of the public transport system, so if you have a pre-paid card (*see p246*) a one-way trip is equivalent to a bus journey; on-board, only pricey return tickets are on sale.

Lisbon Story Centre

Praça do Comércio 78-81 (21 194 1099, http://. lisboastorycentre.pt). Metro Terreiro do Paço. **Open** *10am-8pm daily (last entry 7pm).* **Admission** *€7; €3-€5 reductions;*

free under-6s. Joint ticket with Arco da Rua Augusta €8; €4.50-€6.50 reductions; free under-6s. **Map** *p60 Q21.*

This privately run space aims to take visitors on a journey through time, using sets with costumed figures, scale models, and multimedia and sensory experiences to recreate key events in Lisbon's history. These include the city's mythical and documented beginnings, its growth and status at the centre of a global empire, and the 1755 earthquake and its aftermath.

MUDE – Museu de Design e da Moda

Rua Augusta 24 (21 817 1892, www.mude.pt). Metro Baixa-Chiado or tram 12, 28. **Open** *check the website for details.* **Map** *p60 Q20.*

Elevador de Santa Justa

Lisbon's Museum of Design and Fashion was created to highlight the links between the two disciplines: the permanent collections of iconic and experimental clothing, footwear and accessories, along with household design and furniture were donated to the city by a businessman with an interest in both fields. It's housed in a cavernous former bank headquarters, which at the time of writing was closed to the public for refurbishment. In the meantime, keep an eye out for MUDE Fora de Portas shows around town.

Museu do Dinheiro
Largo de São Julião 9 (21 321 3240). Metro Baixa-Chiado or tram 28. **Open** *10am-6pm Wed-Sat.* **Admission** *free.* **Map** *p60 Q20.*

In a former church that long served as a garage for Portugal's central bank, the Money Museum opened in 2016 and is a great free attraction. In the crypt are the only extant remains of Lisbon's 13th-century city wall, with multimedia displays to help you understand the area's development. The museum's collections include coins and other treasures, but also interactive displays on the origins of money, barter systems and banking. For many visitors, though, the highlight is the chance to grasp a gold ingot – or try to.

Núcleo Arqueológico da Rua dos Correeiros
Rua dos Correeiros 9 (21 113 4496). Metro Baixa-Chiado or tram 12, 28. **Guided tours** *(English or Portuguese) hourly 10am-noon, 2-5pm Mon-Sat.* **Admission** *free.* **Map** *p60 Q20.*

Under the Millennium BCP bank headquarters in Rua Augusta (enter round the back), the Archaeological Centre offers a glimpse of what's lurking below the Baixa. In Roman times, this was a river beach, where locals made sauces by mixing fish and shellfish bits with salt, spices and herbs, leaving it all in tanks to rot over time. When the bank wanted to redo its head office in 1991, the construction teams unearthed the ancient complex. On display are artefacts found during the dig, as well as ancient walls, a holding tank and an intact section of mosaic floor.

Restaurants

João do Grão €€
Rua dos Correeiros 220-226 (21 342 4757). Metro Rossio or Baixa-Chiado, or tram 12, 15. **Open** *noon-3pm, 6-10pm daily.* **Map** *p60 Q20* ⑨ *Portuguese*

In a street packed with touristy eateries, this renowned restaurant has remained popular with locals and visitors by keeping standards up and prices down (relatively speaking). The *grão* (chickpeas) of the name turn up in one of the *bacalhau* staples and in *mão de vaca* (cow's hoof) *com grão*. There are grilled fish and meat dishes, plus game.

❤ Less Baixa €€
Rua dos Fanqueiros 276, 8th floor (91 320 4373, http://lessrestaurantes.pt). Metro Rossio or Baixa-Chiado. **Open** *noon-11.45pm Tue-Sat.* **Map** *p60 Q20* ⑩ *Portuguese/ Mediterranean*

Lisbon fans of the updated Portuguese cuisine of veteran chef Miguel Castro e Silva can sample the menu he devised for this rooftop restaurant (with amazing views) while he is busy in his native Porto. It's good for a relaxed lunch away from the hustle of Baixa; the executive menu is just €14.50. À la carte there are tartares, grilled seafood and steak, and a delicious veal liver. Enter through Pollux (*see p68*), taking the lift to the eighth floor.

A Licorista €€
Rua dos Sapateiros 220 (21 343 1415). Metro Rossio or Baixa-Chiado. **Open** *noon-3pm, 7-10pm Mon-Sat.* **Map** *p60 Q20* ⑪ *Portuguese*

Two restaurants run together – the other is O Bacalhoeiro – in a side street opposite a vintage peep show. In this unpromising setting, tasty traditional fare is served up to regulars and a sprinkling of tourists with bustling efficiency. Grilled meat and fish abound, but there are several dishes of the day –like *chanfana* (goat stew), *massada de peixe* (pasta with fish) or creamy *bacalhau com natas*.

❤ Tasca Kome €€
Rua da Madalena 57 (21 134 0117, www.kome-lisboa.com). Metro Baixa-Chiado or Terreiro do Paço. **Open** *noon-2.30pm, 7-10pm Tue-Thur; noon-3pm, 7-10pm Fri; 12.30-3pm, 7-10pm Sat.* **Map** *p60 Q20* ⑯ *Japanese*

Yuko Yamamoto grabbed the attention of local foodies soon after landing from her native Japan a decade or so ago, with a supper club where she served authentic dishes rarely seen in the city. Demand soon dictated that she open a restaurant. Among top sellers here are the *takoyaki* (fried octopus balls) and marinated salmon *zukedon*, but there are plenty of hot meaty and vegetable dishes as well as sushi, plus unusual desserts. The lunch menus (soup, salad and a main with rice) are stonking value at €11.50. The monthly Kaiseki dinners (€80) comprise a series of tiny, elegant dishes.

Tasca Kome

Cafés & bars

Café Martinho da Arcada

*Praça do Comércio 3 (21 887 9259, www. martinhodaarcada.com). Metro Terreiro do Paço or tram 15, 18, 28. **Café** 7am-11pm Mon-Sat. **Restaurant** noon-4pm, 7-11pm Mon-Sat. **Map** p60 Q21* ❶

This establishment began life in 1782 as a shop selling drinks and ice. The café and adjacent restaurant it was to become were two of poet Fernando Pessoa's favourite haunts. There is a restaurant serving full meals but you can just step into the café for the renowned *pastéis de nata*.

Shops & services

♥ Chapelaria d'Aquino

*Rua do Comércio 16A (91 227 7783). Metro Terreiro do Paço or Baixa-Chiado, or tram 12, 28. **Open** 10am-7pm Mon-Sat. **Map** p60 Q20* ❸ *Accessories*

A scion of one of Lisbon's long-established hatters has teamed up with another local retailer in this clean, modern space. It stocks a vast range of headgear, from top hats and panamas to flat caps and turbans. Most are products of Portugal's still thriving felt-hat industry, although some are imported.

♥ Discoteca Amália

*Rua Áurea (Rua do Ouro) 272 (21 342 0939). Metro Baixa-Chiado. **Open** 9.30am-1pm, 3-7pm Mon-Fri; 9.30am-1pm, 3-5pm Sat. **Map** p60 Q20* ❹ *Music*

A specialist in fado and other traditional music, with plenty of classics from Amália Rodrigues and her ilk, as well as contemporary artists. **Other location** Van on Rua do Carmo, Chiado (21 347 0276).

♥ GN Cellar

*Rua da Conceição 20-26 (21 885 2395). Metro Baixa-Chiado or Terreiro do Paço, or tram 12, 28. **Open** 10am-9pm daily. **Map** p60 Q20* ❻ *Food & drink*

A spin-off of leading wine and spirit merchant **Garrafeira Nacional** (Rua de Santa Justa 18-24, 21 887 9080, www.garrafeiranacional. com), this bright store with inventive window displays is aimed squarely at foreign wine-lovers. Stock is displayed clearly and staff are knowledgeable, with good English.

♥ Loja das Conservas

*Rua da Assunção 83 (91 355 2984, www. facebook.com/lojadasconservas). Metro Baixa-Chiado. **Open** noon-10.30pm Tue-Sun. **Map** p60 Q20* ❽ *Tinned goods*

Several fish-canning companies have opened lavish outlets in the Baixa *'para inglês ver'* – literally 'for Englishmen to see', meaning all fur coat and no knickers. This shop is different: run by the national industry association, it stocks products from 18 firms, in attractive displays that outline the history of each. It also has a great restaurant where specially trained chefs transform tinned sardines, mussels, eels and squid into delicious titbits. **Other location** Rua do Arsenal 130 (91 118 1210).

💙 Trams & funiculars

One of Lisbon's most enduring images is that of the yellow tram, clanking its way through narrow streets. Inside this *elétrico*, a uniformed driver pulls on his levers, exchanging gruff pleasantries with the pensioners who still brave the hordes of preoccupied tourists to clamber aboard. Visitors peer out, fascinated and delighted to have found such an authentic experience. Join them, but take note of the authentic local etiquette, too.

First rule: never jump the queue. Even if, by some miracle, there are seats free and it is just you and one old timer at the tram stop, an attempt to board out of turn will trigger a finger-wagging lecture about civilised society. And remember to get on at the front, off at the back.

Second: hold tight. Lisbon's trams have a knack of producing sudden jerks just as you are adjusting your balance. All too often, those caught unawares will fly across the boards, to be either fielded or scraped off the floor by tut-tutting fellow passengers.

Third: don't try to imitate local free riders. You may notice a couple of imps hanging off the back of the tram: these are ignored by the driver. Try it yourself and he will be less tolerant – and you will certainly leave your kneecap on a jutting street corner.

Fourth: watch your things. Small bands of pickpockets make light work of fat foreign wallets here.

Fifth: treat the driver well. Paid to navigate beloved streets in this engineering classic, surely his lot is a happy one? Look closer and you might notice the clenched jaw and wild stare as he mutters ironic gibes at the cars cutting across his path. All too often the protruding wing of a poorly parked vehicle brings everything to a grinding halt, prompting a cacophony of hooting from behind and complaints from within. Down the line impatient passengers are working themselves up into a lather, preparing a tirade for our tardy driver's ears. Meanwhile, tour groups will fray his nerves with linguistic challenges and a complete lack of small change.

Swarms of tuk-tuks around major sights have made Lisbon's streets even harder to negotiate of late. A better option for the city might have been to lay on more of the much-loved trams, but as these were made in long-closed factories in far-off places such as Glasgow, there literally are no more where they came from. Still, by April 2018 enough disused vehicles had been repaired for one more route to be revived after a 23-year break, resulting in a total of six routes served wholly or partly by antique trams.

The mood is more laid-back on board Lisbon's three funiculars or *ascensores*, which creak up steeper slopes with no traffic at all to contend with, and in the wood-panelled cab of the Elevador da Santa Justa (*see p64*) – all of which form part of the public transport system.

▶ *For more on routes and tickets, see p247.*

Numismática Diamantino

Rua da Madalena 89 (21 887 5113, www. nnd.com.pt). Metro Baixa-Chiado or tram 28. **Open** *9.30am-1pm, 2-7pm Mon-Fri; 9.30am-1pm Sat.* **Map** *p60 Q20* **⑫** *Coins*

A numismatist's delight, Diamantino sells notes and coins, mainly from Portugal and the former colonies, including currency dating back to monarchical times. On Saturdays, visitors are advised to call ahead. **Other location** Avenida Miguel Bombarda 1, Saldanha (21 887 5113).

Ourivesaria Araújos

Rua Áurea (Rua do Ouro) 261 (21 346 7810). Metro Rossio. **Open** *10am-7pm Mon-Fri.* **Map** *p60 Q20* **⑭** *Jewellery*

Established in 1878 and now run by the fourth generation of the same family – pretty much with the same decor as when it first opened – this jeweller has unusual gold and silver pieces, some of them copies of old designs. This is one of the best places to hunt for fine traditional Portuguese filigree.

A Outra Face da Lua

Rua da Assunção 22 (21 886 3430, www. aoutrafacedalua.com). Metro Baixa-Chiado or Rossio, or tram 12, 28. **Open** *10am-7.30pm Mon-Sat; noon-7pm Sun.* **Map** *p60 Q20* **⑮** *Fashion*

Recycled and second-hand clothes, plus retro gear such as flower-power minis. The shop also stocks vintage wallpaper and other decorative objects, smoking paraphernalia, kitsch tin toys and gadgets, and lots of different teas. **Other location** Avenida Almirante Reis 94A (21 826 9578).

Pollux

Rua dos Fanqueiros 276 (21 881 1200, www. pollux.pt). Metro Rossio or tram 12, 15. **Open** *10am-8pm Mon-Sat.* **Map** *p60 Q20* **⑯** *Department store*

This nine-storey department store is jammed with everything from fine glassware and ceramics to suitcases and stationery. Its top floor now hosts a gourmet restaurant, **Less Baixa** (*see p65*).

Santos Ofícios Artesanatos

Rua da Madalena 87 (21 887 2031, www. santosoficios-artesanato.pt). Metro Baixa-Chiado or Terreiro do Paço, or tram 12, 28. **Open** *10am-7.30pm Mon-Sat.* **Map** *p60 Q20* **⑱** *Handicrafts*

A cut above the usual souvenir shops, stocking a fine selection of handmade blankets, rugs, toys, pottery, clothes and baskets. There are also more modern offerings, such as tiles with unusual designs and bags made of coffee packets.

ROSSIO

Most people moving around the city will pass through Rossio at least once a day. It's also a meeting point and was once a market – florists still operate at the southern end. It was here that a flower seller is supposed to have given a carnation to a soldier on 25 April 1974, thus earning the Revolution the nickname Revolução dos Cravos (Carnation Revolution, *see p227*). But most of the cafés that the nervous dictator Salazar had 15 years earlier ordered to ban *tertúlias* – informal discussion groups – have disappeared. Of those that remain, **Café Nicola**, here since the late 18th century, has the most historical resonance. Around the square, commuters queue for buses and tourists hunt for foreign-language newspapers at kiosks or in the splendid vintage **Tabacaria Monaco** at no.21 (closed Sun).

Meanwhile, Africans gather around the steps of the **Teatro Nacional Dona Maria II** (*see p211*), catching up with news from Guinea-Bissau or other home countries; the area first became a magnet for them because the nearby **Igreja de São Domingos** traditionally had a black priest. In the square in front of the church, businessmen get a shoeshine and shopworkers fortify themselves with a nip of *ginjinha*, the cough syrup-like brandy made from morello cherries (*see p69* Sticky Situation).

Now believed to mark the site of the Roman hippodrome, by medieval times Rossio had become the open marketplace at the top of town. Pombal intended his more rectangular version to be secondary to the Praça do Comércio. Instead, Rossio increased in importance as the city expanded north. Its official name, Praça Dom Pedro IV, is something you'll only see on maps or the odd business card. King Pedro is remembered with a statue on top of the square's 23-metre (75-foot) high central

> ### In the know
> ### Cast-off bronze?
>
> Dom Pedro IV is the monarch whom the bronze figure atop the column in Rossio nominally represents. But a stubbornly persistent local rumour insists that it is actually a likeness of Emperor Maximilian of Mexico. In 1870, a ship bearing his statue is said to have docked at Lisbon, en route from Marseille, when word came of the emperor's assassination. By chance, Portugal had ordered a statue of Pedro IV from the same sculptor, Elias David, and a deal to take over the now unwanted Maximilian was supposedly struck.

Sticky Situation

A local drink for local people

Clustered around Rossio are tiny bars that survive almost entirely by selling a sour-cherry liqueur called *ginjinha* (sometimes written *ginginha* or just *ginja*) that is bottled with or without whole cherries. Opening early and closing at midnight, these bars never lack custom.

The biggest-selling brand is Ginja Sem Rival but Ginja Espinheira, showcased in **A Ginjinha** at Largo de São Domingos 8, provides competition. A fixture since 1840, this bar also serves home-made lemonade and Eduardino, a herbal liqueur. A few yards away, at Rua das Portas de Santo Antão 7, another minuscule place with an ancient frontage serves Ginja Sem Rival (open 8am-midnight daily) and Eduardino. At No.61, **Ginginha Popular** (open 7am-midnight Mon-Fri, 9am-midnight Sat, Sun) also sells a range of tasty snacks.

Round the corner at Rua Barros Queirós 27, **Ginjinha Rubi** is the only establishment with its own production in the city (in Anjos). On the southern side of Rossio, prettily tiled **Tendinha** (closed Sun) has been pouring drinks since 1840.

Across town, **Ginja d'Alfama** (Rua de São Pedro 12, open 10am-midnight Mon, Wed-Sun) and **Ginjinha da Sé** (Rua São João da Praça 3, closed Tue) sell the sticky stuff to a modish young crowd.

Local shops sell some attractive bottles of *ginjinha*. The best presented is Ginja Sem Rival with cherries, but the finest is Ginja de Alcobaça, a lighter tipple. After a few *ginjinhas* you might start thinking one of these would make a lovely souvenir. But face facts: it's best sipped in Lisbon, where it belongs.

column, while figures around the base represent Justice, Wisdom, Courage and Restraint. *See below* In the Know.

Restraint was not always the area's hallmark. A monument in **Largo de São Domingos** remembers the hundreds of alleged heretics massacred in April 1506, nine years after all Jews were forced to convert to Catholicism. The **Teatro Nacional** stands on the site of a royal palace that was taken over by the Inquisition three decades later, and many an auto-da-fé (public judging) ended with the condemned being burned at the stake in Rossio.

Next to Rossio lies the less gracious **Praça da Figueira**. The statue of Dom João I here was erected in 1971 at the square's centre but later moved during the construction of an underground car park, to align with the vista down Rua da Prata. Praça da Figueira is ringed with nondescript shops, the exception being the **Hospital das Bonecas**, a sweet doll's hospital and shop.

On the north side of Largo de São Domingos stands blood-red **Palácio de Independência** (21 324 1470), one of the few large structures in the area that survived the 1755 earthquake virtually intact. Its name comes from the fact that it was here, in 1640, that 40 aristocratic conspirators – known as the Conjurados – plotted to end decades of Spanish rule. Guided visits to the palace and its *azulejo* lined garden patio may be arranged during the week or you can just stop at the café-restaurant (91 660 3454, www.chaminesdopalacio.pt), which also has a patio.

The pedestrian-only **Rua das Portas de Santo Antão** leads north from here. It's lined with restaurants, many tourist traps. You could grab a tender *bifana* (braised pork) roll and draught beer at snack-bar **Ginginha Popular** (no.65, 21 342 7419) though, or venture through the discreet doorway at no.58, **Casa do Alentejo**, a home from home for *Alentejanos* with amazing neo-Moorish decor and a restaurant (21 340 5140) that serves so-so regional dishes. A few paces north, up Beco de São Luís da Pena, is the **Igreja de São Luís dos Franceses** (91 919 4614, www.saint-louis-des-francais. org)-the church of the French community since 1572. Normally open only for Sunday mass (11am), it's worth a look for its stucco work and a painting attributed to Amaro do Vale that depicts Lisbon before the 1755 earthquake.

Portas de Santo Antão is also the address of the cavernous **Coliseu dos Recreios** (*see p207*), the Lisbon Coliseum, opened in 1890. A smaller entrance in the same building, at no.100, leads into the Sociedade de Geografia (21 342 5401, www. socgeografialisboa.pt) and its colonial-style **Museu Etnográfico** (closed Sat-Sun). Opposite, the **Teatro Politeama** (*see p211*) stages corny musicals, usually with English subtitles. Further up is the **Ascensor da Lavra** (open 7.50am-7.55pm Mon-Fri; 9am-7-55pm Sat, Sun), a funicular that bears weary locals and wearier tourists up to **Campo de Santana**.

Praça Dom Pedro IV (Rossio) p68

Sights & museums

Hospital de Bonecas

Praça da Figueira 7 (21 342 8574, www. hospital debonecas.com). Metro Rossio. **Museum** *10am-1pm, 3-5pm Mon-Sat.* **Shop** *10am-7pm Mon-Fri; 10am-6pm Sat.* **Admission** *Museum €2. No cards.* **Map** *p60 Q19.*

Generations of Lisbon children have brought battered toys to this 'dolls' hospital' for surgery, which takes place upstairs. The little museum built up over the years here is a treasure trove of antique dolls and other toys and knick-knacks. In the ground-floor shop you can update your doll's wardrobe, pick up a Portuguese rag doll or porcelain doll, or choose from a selection of Barbies.

♥ Igreja de São Domingos

Largo de São Domingos (21 342 8275). Metro Rossio or tram 12, 15. **Open** *7.30am-7pm daily.* **Map** *p60 Q19.*

A succession of natural catastrophes has laid waste to this Dominican church since it was founded by Dom Sancho II in 1242: earthquakes in 1531 and 1755 but also a fire in 1959. After nearly 40 years of renovation it reopened in 1997, but the still-flame-ravaged interior makes for a cave-like look. The high altar was completed in 1748 to the designs of Ludovice, architect of the monastery of Mafra (*see p167*).

Restaurants

Bonjardim €€

Travessa de Santo Antão 7 & 10 (21 342 7424). Metro Rossio or Restauradores. **Open** *noon-11pm daily.* **Map** *p60 Q19* ❷ *Portuguese*

At the self-styled 'King of Chicken', comprising restaurants on either side of the street, chicken grilled over charcoal comes with chips, salad and (thankfully optional) piri-piri sauce. There are other dishes, but the place aims for quick turnover, so service can be brusque. Note that prices on the terrace are 20% higher.

Everest Montanha €€

Calçada do Garcia 15 (21 887 6428). Metro Rossio. **Open** *noon-3.30pm, 7-11pm daily.* **No cards.** **Map** *p60 Q19* ❺ *Indian*

Up an alley off Largo de São Domingos, this friendly Nepali-owned place offers tasty food at what are reasonable prices given its central location. The menu has a wide range of Indian standards, among them several vegetarian and vegan dishes.

Gambrinus €€€€

Rua das Portas de Santo Antão 23 (21 342 1466, www.gambrinuslisboa.com). Metro Rossio or Restauradores. **Open** *noon-1.30am daily.* **Map** *p60 Q19* ❻ *Portuguese*

In this discreet gourmet haven, amid stained glass and wood panelling, liveried waiters glide to and fro, bearing plates of seafood.

Eating here can cost a packet if you order any of these, or the fancier traditional dishes on offer, but the place also built its reputation with *pregos* (steak sandwiches) and delicious meat croquettes. Many locals just snack at the long bar.

O Marques €
Travesso do Ferro 11 (21 346 8070). Metro Restauradores or Rossio. **Open** *9am-10pm Mon-Sat.* **Map** *p60 Q19* ⑬ *Portuguese*

The last in a row of cheap *tascas*, O Marques offers the best value of any. Locals crowd in here for a reason, in the shape of tasty grilled fish and meats, and filling traditional fare such as *feijoada* (bean, meat and vegetable stew) or *alheira de caça* (game sausage). Order a *meia dose* (half serving) or split a full one.

Cafés & bars
Café Nicola
Praça Dom Pedro IV (Rossio) 24 (21 346 0579). Metro Rossio or tram 12, 15. **Open** *8am-midnight daily.* **Map** *p60 Q19* ❷

Nicola and its grand façade have been here since 1929 but they occupy the site of a famous 18th-century café where poet Manuel Maria Barbosa du Bocage held court (his statue is still toasted nightly). In the 20th century, Nicola was a centre for political intrigue, with the dictatorship's secret police keeping tabs on would-be agitators. Its marble, steel and glass interior results from a 1990s renovation, but the paintings are 1935 originals by Fernando Santos.

❤ Confeitaria Nacional
Praça da Figueira 18B (21 342 4470, www.confeitarianacional.pt). Metro Rossio or tram 12, 15. **Open** *8am-8pm Mon-Sat; 9am-8pm Sun.* **Map** *p60 Q19* ❹

The plaque outside boasting 'over 100 years of existence' is an antique; Nacional was founded in 1829 and retains its glass cases and painted panels. Fast service means it's a good place to buy biscuits or cakes to take away – locals queue up for the famous *bolo rei* fruitcake, and not only at Christmas – but there is also a sit-down café. It even has its own brand of coffee.

Shops & services
❤ Azevedo Rua
Praça Dom Pedro IV (Rossio) 69 & 72-73 (21 342 7511, 93 343 5294, www.azevedorua.com). Metro Rossio. **Open** *9.30am-7pm Mon-Fri; 10am-7pm Sat.* **Map** *p60 Q19* ❶ *Accessories*

Rossio used to be home to a community of hatters; only this one, founded in 1886,

remains. Black, rabbit-skin felt hats, worn by Portuguese horsemen, and the smaller-brimmed style favoured by Fernando Pessoa are stacked up to the ceiling. There's also a large range of berets, panama hats and bowlers.

Manteigaria Silva
Rua Dom Antão de Almada 1C-D (21 342 4905). Metro Rossio. **Open** *9am-7.30pm Mon-Sat.* **Map** *p60 Q19* ❿ *Food & drink*

The Portuguese have been eating *bacalhau* (salt cod) for centuries. It's sold dried and salted. In traditional places such as this one, the smelly, kite-shaped cod carcasses are stacked up whole, ready to be chopped up to order. Alternatively, you can buy *caras* (cod faces) and *línguas* (cod tongues). The shop also stocks canned fish and has a cheese and *presunto* (cured ham) counter. It now has a spin-off stall in the Time Out Market (*see p116*), open daily until 2am.

Manuel Tavares
Rua da Betesga 1A-B (21 342 4209, www.manueltavares.com). Metro Rossio. **Open** *9.30am-7.30pm Mon-Sat.* **Map** *p60 Q19* ⑪ *Food & drink*

Founded in 1860, this traditional delicatessen stocks a vast range of *presunto* (cured ham) and sausages, including *morçela* (black pudding) and *chouriço doce* (with honey and almonds). There are also smoked pig's tongues, Portuguese cheeses, dried fruit, *bacalhau* and a good range of ports.

RESTAURADORES & AVENIDA DA LIBERDADE

Avenida da Liberdade began as an extension of the Passeio Público, a late 18th-century garden promenade. The busy boulevard, built on the Champs-Elysées model, was completed in 1886. Where Lisbon had previously clustered along the river, now it expanded inland.

At the southern end, just north-west of Rossio, is the neo-Manueline façade of **Rossio station**, completed in 1892 and now the terminus of the Sintra line. The obelisk in **Praça dos Restauradores** commemorates the 1 December 1640 restoration of independence from Spain, inscribed with dates of decisive battles in the 28 years of war. The Eden cinema here was once an outstanding art deco landmark by Cassiano Branco; now an aparthotel, it retains only the façade and a monumental staircase.

Next door, the **Palácio Foz** housed a notorious nightclub in the 1920s, and later the Ministry of Propaganda. Its ground floor has a tourist office, the tourist police and the **Loja dos Museus**, a shop with replicas from Portugal's museums that make good souvenirs. Another entrance leads to the free **Museu Nacional do Desporto** (21 395 8629). There are also concerts some weekdays and Saturdays, upstairs in the gilded Sala de Espelhos – access is via the door on the far right of the façade, which is also the entrance to the Cinemateca Júnior, an offshoot of **Cinemateca Portuguesa** (see p184) with displays and Saturday film screenings aimed at kids.

Round the corner is the **Ascensor da Glória** (open 7.15am-11.55pm Mon-Thur, 7.15am-12.25am Fri, 8.45am-12.25am Sat, 9.15am-11.55pm Sun), a funicular that takes the strain if you're heading up to the Bairro Alto. Just beyond it, **Sunrise Press** (Avenida da Liberdade 9, 21 347 0204) has the city's best selection of foreign newspapers and specialist magazines. Across the square is the central post office and also the **ABEP kiosk** (see p206), which sells tickets for films, plays, bullfights and other sports and cultural events.

The tree-lined *avenida* was long a tolerated prostitution zone, spilling out from the red-light district around leafy **Praça da Alegria**, home to venerable jazz venue **Hot Clube** (see p189). Nowadays the boulevard is home to office blocks, expensive hotels and upmarket fashion shops. Ateliers **Rosa & Teixeira** and **Oficina Mustra** are here. Kiosks dotted either side of the avenue boast different specialities –from gourmet hot dogs to fruit cocktails. At night, groups of youngsters chat over DJ-driven soundtracks.

A few blocks north of Praça Restauradores on the west side, two art deco pillars mark the entrance to **Parque Mayer**, a decaying 1920s complex where Portuguese *revista* – revue theatre – once flourished, but all but one stage, at the **Teatro Maria Vitória** (see p211), have now gone dark. Architectural landmark **Capitólio** (see p236) has been restored but is little used.

Across the street, the curved lines of the modernist building at **no.170** stand out. Another work by Cassiano Branco, from 1936, as the Hotel Vitória it was frequented by German spies during World War II but is now owned by the Communist Party. A little further up is the **Teatro Tivoli** (see p211), a neoclassical former cinema built in 1924 by Raul Lino, now a venue for slick comedies. The striking red kiosk in front was installed in 1925 by the owners of **Diário de Notícias**, whose modernist former editorial offices (1936) stand further north.

Back on the west side of the avenue, the **Cinema São Jorge** (see p182), completed in 1950 to a design by Fernando Silva, is the last of Lisbon's old picture palaces, now used by the council for festivals. By contrast, the **Cinemateca Portuguesa** (see p184) round the corner in Rua Barata Salgueiro has a packed programme of Portuguese and international classics and art movies. Opposite, the **Sociedade Nacional de Belas Artes** is one of several art spaces in the area; on the next road north, the **Casa-Museu Medeiros e Almeida** boasts one of Portugal's finest collections of decorative arts.

If you want to get up, up and away from the city streets in summer, take the lift to the Tivoli hotel's **Sky Bar** (21 319 8900, www.tivolihotels.com) where you can loll on a pouffe as staff serve tasty cocktails and finger food, with DJs on duty from Thursday to Saturday.

Sights & museums

Casa-Museu Medeiros e Almeida
Rua Rosa Araújo 41 (21 354 7892, www.casa-museumedeirosealmeida.pt). Metro Marquês de Pombal. **Open** *10am-5pm Mon-Sat (last entry 4.30pm). Free guided tours noon 1st & 3rd Sat of mth (arrive 10mins before) or paid pre-booked tours (min 6) 1-5.30pm Mon-Sat.* **Admission** *€5, €3 over 64s, free under 18s & all Sat to 1pm.* **Map** *p60 P17.*

The foundation that late businessman António Medeiros e Almeida created in 1973 has 26 rooms across two floors showing 2,000 pieces (out of total holdings of 9,000), the legacy of years of hoarding. They include Chinese porcelain, clocks, paintings, furniture, gold and jewellery, sacred art, sculpture and textiles. The 19th-century building was previously the Vatican's embassy.

Restaurants

Esquina da Fé €
Rua da Fé 60 (21 342 0051, Metro Restauradores. **Open** *noon-3.30pm, 7-11.30pm Mon-Sat.* **Map** *p60 P18* ❹ *Portuguese*

Local workers hurry to this *tasca* in a side street in the São José neighbourhood, east of the Avenida, to tuck into traditional meat and fish dishes and eggy desserts such as *arroz doce* (rice pudding) and *pudim de ovos* (flan). Most mains come in full and half servings, the latter easily enough for one person. The Cantinho de São José, on the main drag (Rua de São José 94, 21 342 7866), is a smaller alternative.

Jesus é Goês €€
Rua São José 23 (21 154 5812). Metro Avenida. **Open** *noon-3pm, 7-11pm Tue-Sat.* **Map** *p60 Q18* ❼ *Indian*

Owner Jesus is indeed Goan, and this place offers an inventive take on that former Portuguese colony's cuisine. Coriander is much used, seafood includes shrimp curry with okra, and for afters there's classic *bebinca* cake. But there's also both a goat and a vegetarian *xacuti*, a spiced-up burger and unusual sweets such as date samosa with ginger and cardamom ice-cream.

JNcQUOI €€€€
Avenida da Liberdade 182-184 (21 936 9900, www.jncquoi.com). Metro Avenida. **Restaurant** *noon-midnight daily.* **Delibar** *noon-midnight Mon, Wed, Sun; noon-2am Fri, Sat.* **Map** *p60 P18* ❽ *French/Portuguese*

As the name suggests, this self-described 'lifestyle brand' aims at a Parisian *je ne sais quoi*, with a marble-and-glass decor and conspicuously fancy food. The restaurant serves chateaubriand and sole meunière, fresh cod as well as salted, and other seafood, plus fine French desserts. In the downstairs 'delibar' you can guzzle champagne and oysters or sample *burrata*, ceviche or *steak au poivre* at the counter – or buy fancy ingredients to take home. In the attached menswear store (www.fashionclinic.com, open 10am-8pm Mon-Sat, noon-8pm Sun) you can browse Valentino, Gucci and Tom Ford.

Maharaja €€
Rua do Cardal de São José 21-23 (21 346 9300, 96 256 1787). Metro Avenida. **Open** *noon-3pm, 6.30-11pm Tue-Sun.* **Map** *p60 P18* ⓬ *Indian*

This plush den specialising in Mughlai food is hidden away in a back street – make the effort, though, as it's great value. The kitchen turns out delicious tandoori kebabs, coconut shrimp curry and the like, and there are more than a dozen vegetarian mains.

Pinóquio €€
Praça dos Restauradores 79 (21 346 5106, www.restaurantepinoquio.pt). Metro Restauradores. **Open** *noon-11pm daily.* **Map** *p60 Q19* ⓮ *Portuguese*

Pinóquio stands out from its neighbours for its juicy clams and succulent prawns, plus delicious nibbles such as *pica pau* (marinated meat) and steak served with the famous house sauce.

Solar dos Presuntos €€€
Rua das Portas de Santo Antão 150 (21 342 4253, www.solardospresuntos.com). Metro Restauradores. **Open** *noon-3.30pm, 7-11pm Mon-Sat.* **Map** *p60 Q18* ⓯ *Portuguese*

Fans of Portuguese country cooking – particularly from the northern Minho

region – make a beeline for this upscale restaurant, with a wood-panelled interior lined with photos of celeb regulars. If you like *bacalhau* you should try it *assado* (roasted). The octopus is excellent too. In season, it also offers unusual dishes such as fried *sável* (shad).

❤ Os Tibetanos €€
Rua do Salitre 117 (21 314 2038, http://tibetanos.com). Metro Avenida. **Open** *12.15-2.45pm, 7.30-10.30pm Mon-Fri; 12.45-3.30pm, 7.45 10.45pm Sat, Sun.* **No cards.** **Map** *p60 P18* ⓱ *Vegetarian*

Lisbon's longest-running vegetarian dining option is as good as ever. It offers dishes including Tibetan *momo*, *seitan* steak and tofu sausages. The lunchtime set menus are excellent value, and there's French cider if you don't fancy one of the many herbal teas. Seating in the dining room is rather cramped; there is more space out back. A small shop at the entrance sells Tibetan items, and there's a Buddhist centre upstairs.

Cafés & bars

Champanheria do Largo
Largo da Anunciada 20 (21 347 0392). Metro Restauradores. **Open** *9am-midnight Mon-Sat.* **Map** *p60 Q18* ❸

Enjoy a champagne cocktail or two in this airy wine bar opposite the Lavra funicular accompanied by tasty snacks such as veal carpaccio or *queijo da ilha* (tangy cheese from the Azores). You can breakfast here all morning; and you can dine until 11.30pm on dishes such as suckling pig.

Delta Q
Avenida da Liberdade 144 (no phone). Metro Avenida. **Open** *9am-9pm Mon-Thur; 9am-11pm Fri, Sat; 9.30am-6.30pm Sun.* **Map** *p60 P18* ❺

This flagship store for Portugal's leading coffee company, Delta, is a pleasant place for a break from shopping or sightseeing, with a café and lounge, gourmet store and boutique.

Shops & services

❤ Carbono
Rua do Telhal 6B (21 342 3757, www.carbono.com.pt). Metro Avenida. **Open** *11am-7pm Tue-Sat.* **Map** *p60 Q18* ❷ *Music*

This alternative music store sells (and buys) local and international releases on CD, both new and second-hand, as well as lots of vinyl. It's a good source of information about new Portuguese artists and musical projects.

♥ Fly London

Avenida da Liberdade 230 (91 059 4564, www.flylondon.com). Metro Avenida. **Open** *10am-7pm Mon-Sat.* **Map** *p60 P17* ❺ *Fashion*

Despite the name, this well-known brand of distinctive footwear is Portuguese. This flagship store stocks the latest women's lines – plus the odd men's range – along with some clothes and accessories. ■

♥ Lisbonlovers

Avenida da Liberdade 83 (21 392 8799, http://shop.lisbonlovers.com). **Open** *10am-8pm daily.* **Map** *p60 P18* ❼ *Gifts & souvenirs*

This company produces and sells an amazing array of items bearing stylised local emblems such as sardines, historical monuments, trams, *guitarras* (Portuguese guitars used in fado music) and, of course, the city's favourite saint, António. You can also order online. **Other location** Praça do Príncipe Real 22 (21 347 1195). ■

♥ Loja dos Museus

Palácio Foz, Praça dos Restauradores (21 343 3008, www.patrimoniocultural.gov.pt). Metro Restauradores. **Open** *10am-1pm, 2-6pm Mon-Sat.* **Map** *p60 P19* ❾ *Gifts & souvenirs*

Porcelain, textiles, tiles, glassware and silverware are among the top-quality items stocked at this downtown outlet of the institution that runs Portugal's national monuments. **Other locations** national museums. ■

Oficina Mustra

Rua Rodrigues Sampaio 112 C/V (21 314 7009). Metro Avenida. **Open** *10am-7.30pm Mon-Sat.* **Map** *p60 P17* ⓭ *Fashion*

Off-the-peg and made-to-measure suits designed by a former creative director for an Italian clothing company. After your visit to the showroom, the resulting designs are sent to Naples, where a team of tailors stitch them together. Shirts, shoes and ties can also be made to order. ■

Rosa & Teixeira

Avenida da Liberdade 204 (21 311 0350, www.rosaeteixeira.pt). Metro Avenida. **Open** *10am-7.30pm Mon-Sat.* **Map** *p60 P17* ⓱ *Fashion*

Portugal's business elite have long had suits made to measure at this, the Avenida's longest-established menswear specialist. Techniques perfected over generations are applied by tailors upstairs, at prices that run to thousands of euros. Downstairs, off-the-peg suits from leading foreign brands line the racks. ■

Sociedade Nacional de Belas Artes

Rua Barata Salgueiro 36 (21 313 8510, www.snba.pt). Metro Marquês de Pombal. **Open** *Exhibitions noon-7pm Mon-Fri; 2-8pm Sat.* **Map** *p60 P17* ⓳ *Gallery*

Three airy exhibition spaces run by artists for artists, where many leading figures of the Portuguese scene began their careers. It also runs competitions. ■

MARQUÊS DE POMBAL & PARQUE EDUARDO VII

At the top of the Avenida stands an enormous column from which the statue of the Marquês de Pombal lords it over the eponymous Praça – really a roundabout that's a seething mass of cars. Atop his column, he serenely overlooks the distant urban plan he imposed on the old city.

Behind him is the **Parque Eduardo VII**, laid out in the late 19th century as the natural extension of the Avenida da Liberdade axis, and later named after the British king Edward VII during his 1903 visit to Portugal. Its layout is rather formal, but the **Estufa Fria** greenhouses on its west side provide welcome shade. Nearby, at posh sports club **Clube VII** (21 384 8300, www.clubevii.com), a day pass (€36.40) gets you access to a chlorine-free indoor pool and gym, plus two hours on covered tennis

Parque Eduardo VII

courts. Two fascist pillars at the park's upper end now bracket an eclectic grouping of stones – a sculpture by João Cutileiro –to commemorate the 1974 Revolution. A pond garden in the upper eastern corner has a café with a pleasant terrace. Beyond Alameda Cardeal Cerejeira is a garden named after fado singer Amália Rodrigues. Nearby is one of Lisbon's most serene esplanades, the **Linha d'Água**.

Sights & museums

Estufa Fria
Parque Eduardo VII (21 817 0996, http:// estufafria.cm-lisboa.pt). Metro Marquês de Pombal or Parque. **Open** *Summer (from last Sun in Mar) 10am-7pm daily. Winter (from last Sun in Oct) 9am-5pm daily.* **Admission** *€3.10; €1.55-€2.33 reductions; free under-6s & all Sun to 2pm. No cards.* **Map** *p60 O15.*

This greenhouse garden on the north-west side of Parque Eduardo VII was completed in 1930. The promenade around the pond leads into three areas containing a total of some 300 species: the Estufa Quente, or hothouse; the Estufa Fria itself, a cool greenhouse covered by a porous wooden roof; and the Estufa Doce, the 'sweet' greenhouse with drier conditions. The leafy groves, statues and cascades are ideal for a romantic stroll.

Restaurants

♥ Associação Caboverdeana €
Rua Duque de Palmela 2, 8th floor (21 353 1932). Metro Marquês de Pombal. **Open** *noon-3pm Mon-Fri.* **No cards.** **Map** *p60 P17* ❶ *African*

Take the lift to the eighth-floor canteen of this Cape Verdean social club, where inexpensive, tasty African dishes such as *cachupa*, fish *mukeca* or chicken with peanut sauce are served to an appreciative clientele that includes local office workers. On Tuesdays and Thursdays there's live music (1-2.30pm) and their lunch break is spent dancing cheek-to-cheek to *mornas*.

♥ Eleven €€€€
Rua Marquês de Fronteira, Parque Eduardo VII (21 386 2211, www.restauranteleven.com). Metro Parque. **Open** *12.30-3pm, 7.30-11pm Mon-Sat.* **Map** *p60 O15* ❸ *Mediterranean*

The first restaurant to bring a Michelin star to the city centre, in 2006, with the elegant Mediterranean cuisine of Joachim Koerper, Eleven briefly lost, then won back, that honour but now seems to have a firm grip. In a large, minimalist box – all wood, iron and stone – whose floor-to-ceiling windows afford panoramic views, Lisbon's elite coo over

dishes crafted using the freshest seafood, vegetables and herbs, and prime meats. Desserts, such as pear soufflé with saffron ice-cream, are divine. There are various tasting menus, including a vegetarian one (€75), plus a €35 set lunch.

Cafés & bars

Linha d'Água
Rua Marquês de Fronteira, Jardim Amália Rodrigues (21 381 4327, www.linhadeagua. pt). Metro São Sebastião. **Open** *Summer 10am-10pm daily. Winter 10am-8pm daily.* **No cards.** **Map** *p60 O15* ❼

At the very top of Parque Eduardo VII, this modern café by a circular pool is a haven of tranquillity. Fine salads, cakes and light meals are served inside to a cool musical soundtrack, while outside water laps beneath a boardwalk.

CAMPO DE SANTANA

Rising in the fork between the two *Avenidas*, Almirante Reis and da Liberdade, is a mixed bag of a neighbourhood with an uncommon number of hospitals. This makes it the perfect location for the statue of Sousa Martins, which stands on the well-greened square of **Campo dos Mártires de Pátria** (invariably known by its original name of Campo de Santana) outside the Faculdade de Medicina. José Thomaz de Sousa Martins died in 1897, having gained favour among the poor for treating them for little or no payment. Grateful locals keep candles burning in his memory and leave stone plaques round the statue's base in thanks.

The **Jardim do Torel**, a small park off Rua de Júlio de Andrade, has fine views and the **Esplanada do Torel**.

Cafés & bars

Esplanada do Torel
Jardim do Torel (21 302 6160, 96 957 3152). Metro Avenida then 10min walk, or Ascensor do Lavra. **Open** *Winter 11am-10pm daily. Summer 11am-midnight daily.* **Map** *p60 Q18* ❻

This large terrace – currently run by the Bananacafé crowd, who have kiosks serving snacks and drinks around town – is one of the city's best-kept secrets. The view makes it a great place for a sundowner, especially in summer when it often hosts live music, DJs or film screenings. A safe kids' playground is within eyeshot. In August, the area is transformed into an urban beach, with a large fountain serving as a pool (open 10am-8pm).

East of Baixa

From the orderly streets of Baixa, Lisbon loses all decorum as it scrambles on to its alleged seven hills, all of them with white churches dotted about. On its eastern side, above the clutter of terracotta rooftops, the skyline is topped by the brooding Castelo de São Jorge, with the higgledy-piggledy Alfama below it. Densely populated, Alfama is still a community. Poor pensioners linger in tiny rent-controlled apartments, though rooftop flats are much sought after by wealthier newcomers. It looks cheerful and postcard-perfect in summer, and the city, aware of the area's attractiveness to visitors, has long subsidised the maintenance of façades, but many houses remain in dire need of renovation. In this area, you'll also find the 12th-century Sé Catedral and many of the city's finest *miradouros*, lookout points that reward the efforts of footsore visitors.

❤ Don't miss

1 Castelo de São Jorge *p83 and p84*
A panoramic perspective on downtown.

2 Alfama *p84 and p85*
Get an overview of this medieval warren from a *miradouro* then lose yourself in its alleys.

3 Sé Catedral *p79*
Set the seal on the Christian Reconquest.

4 Museu-Escola de Artes Decorativas *p86*
A treasure house of applied arts.

5 Museu do Aljube *p79*
Tells a tale of dictatorship and Revolution.

6 Igreja e Mosteiro de São Vicente de Fora *p87*
Fabulous *azulejo* panels and panoramic views.

Panteão Nacional de Santa Engrácia *p87*

SÉ

Lisbon's most picturesque tram ride – the 28 east from Baixa up to Graça – heads past **Igreja de Santo António**, built at the birthplace of the city's favourite saint, the neighbouring **Museu de Santo António**, and the 12th-century **Sé Catedral**. As it skirts the hill below the Castelo, the street changes name so many times that locals often refer to it as Rua do Eléctrico da Sé – 'Street of the Tram of the Cathedral'. Today it is lined with souvenir, crafts and antique shops; the latter have some beautiful, but pricey, items on show.

Unlike nearby Alfama, this area was greatly modified after the 1755 earthquake, with the building of wider streets and elegant houses. It's also home to the **Museu do Aljube**, long a prison – most notoriously run by Salazar's secret police – and now an excellent museum on the dictatorship and 1974 Revolution.

The Teatro Romano, Portugal's only known Roman amphitheatre, was begun during the reign of Augustus and rebuilt under Nero in AD 57. A fenced-off section can be seen on Rua de São Mamede, but it isn't very revealing; a multimedia reconstruction can be seen at the **Museu de Lisboa – Teatro Romano**, across the street.

Follow any of the narrow alleys that run downhill to the right of the Sé and you'll pop out on to the Campo das Cebolas (Field of the Onions), formerly a market place that later moved to the site of the Mercado da Ribeira (*see p116*). A big, open square lined with souvenir shops and cheap restaurants, its main attraction is the spiky façade of the **Casa dos Bicos**, a 16th-century merchant's house. Turning west on Rua da Alfândega brings into view the medieval stone façade of the **Igreja da Conceição-a-Velha**.

Sights & museums

Casa dos Bicos
Rua dos Bacalhoeiros 10 (Museu de Lisboa 21 099 3811, www.museudelisboa.pt). Metro Terreiro do Paço. **Open** *10am-6pm Mon-Sat (last entry 5.30pm).* **Admission** *free.* **Map** *p80 R21.*

This striking building was erected between 1521 and 1523, on the orders of Brás de Albuquerque, the son of the first Viceroy of India. Its unusual façade, covered by a grid of point-cut diamond shapes commonly known in Portuguese as *bicos*, was inspired by Italian Renaissance models, namely the Palazzo dei Diamanti in Ferrara. Inside, a ground-floor exhibit run by the Museu de Lisboa lays bare (literally) the plot's history from Roman through medieval times. There are also ceramics and glassware from later centuries. The upper floors house the Fundação José Saramago (21 880 2040, www.josesaramago. org), which promotes the work of the late Nobel Prize-winning writer, hosts regular debates on literary and social topics and has a good bookshop.

Igreja da Conceição-a-Velha
Rua da Alfândega (parish 21 887 0202). Metro Terreiro do Paço, tram 15, 25. **Open** *9am-2pm, 3-6pm Mon-Fri; 10am-2pm, 3-8pm Sat, Sun. Mass 1pm Tue-Fri; 11am (in English), 12.30pm Sun.* **Map** *p80 Q21.*

On this site once stood a church built in 1534 dedicated to Nossa Senhora da Misericórdia (Our Lady of Mercy), who can be seen above the portal sheltering various notables under her mantle. The 1755 earthquake demolished the main structure, leaving only the wonderful Manueline-style façade, which has recently been restored. In 1770, the church reopened to house the congregation of Nossa Senhora da Conceição-a-Velha, whose

❤ Time to eat & drink

European flavours
Le Bar à Crêpes *p88*, Pois, Café *p86*

Fabulous fish
Páteo 13 *p86*, Ramiro *p89*

Portuguese twist
Bica do Sapato *p91*, Santa Clara dos Cogumelos *p88*

A taste of Africa
Cantinho do Aziz *p89*, Zambeze *p84*

❤ Time to shop

Bookish Lisbon
Fabula Urbis *p82*

Eye-popping crafts
A Arte da Terra *p80*

Party time
Flur *p91*

Tinned delicacies
Conserveira de Lisboa *p80*

Treasure and tat
Feira da Ladra *p46*

Vintage Portuguese
A Vida Portuguesa *p90*

In the know
Getting around

The 12 and 28 trams trundle past many churches and museums; for the castle, the 737 bus (from Praça da Figueira) gets you closer. But walking is the best way – and in the heart of Alfama the only way – to explore. If exhaustion sets in, yield to the blandishments of a tuk-tuk, but only if it is electric.

original home, a converted synagogue in the Baixa, had been flattened. The simple post-quake interior has one nave and contains an image of Our Lady of Restelo, donated to the earlier Conceição church by Prince Henry the Navigator.

Igreja de Santo António

Largo de Santo António da Sé (21 886 9145). Tram 12, 28 or bus 737. **Open** *8am-7pm Mon-Fri; 8am-8pm Sat, Sun.* **Map** *p80 R20.*

This small Baroque church opened in 1787, 20 years after construction began. It replaced a structure destroyed in the 1755 earthquake, on the spot where Fernando Bulhões, later known as St Anthony of Padua, was born around 1190. A tiny crypt below the church may or may not have been his bedroom, but as it was visited by Pope John Paul II in 1982, Catholics from all over the world now follow his example. St Anthony became famous as a travelling preacher and miracle worker, and is now the patron saint of things lost. Next door is a small museum (part of Museu de Lisboa) dedicated to him (21 886 0447, www.museudelisboa.pt). Mass marriages for those too poor to afford individual ceremonies, known as 'St Anthony's weddings', are held here in June (*see p176*).

Museu de Lisboa – Teatro Romano

Rua de São Mamede, 3A (21 581 8530, www.museudelisboa.pt). Tram 12, 28 or bus 737. **Open** *10am-6pm Tue-Sun.* **Admission** *€3; €1.50 reductions; free under-13s, students & all to 2pm Sun.* **Map** *p80 R20.*

This little museum, located just up from the Sé in a renovated 19th-century factory and recently revamped as part of the multipolar Museu de Lisboa (*see p147*), provides some context for the Roman theatre that's visible to passers-by on Rua de São Mamede. This Roman amphitheatre, which seated perhaps 5,000, is proof that Olisipo, as Lisbon was then known, was a major outpost. It also houses columns and other decorative elements from the site, including an inscription dedicating the theatre to Nero and a copy of a sculpture of Silenus.

♥ Museu do Aljube

Rua de Augusto Rosa 42 (21 581 8535, www.museudoaljube.pt). Tram 12, 28 or bus 737. **Open** *10am-6pm Tue-Sun.* **Admission** *€3; €2.60 over-64s; €1.50 13-25s; free under-13s.* **Map** *p80 R20.*

This engaging and informative municipal museum, inaugurated in 2015, ended the anomalous situation in which Portugal had no institution presenting to the public a history of the Salazar dictatorship, the resistance to it, and the 1974 Revolution (*see also p228* Talkin' About the Revolution).

There's no shortage of archive material on the subject, and the museum has fascinating and accessible displays. To understand modern Portugal, make a point of stopping by.

♥ Sé Catedral

Largo da Sé (21 886 6752). Tram 12, 28 or bus 737. **Church** *9am-6.30pm daily (mass 6.30pm Sat; 11.30pm, 7pm Sun).* **Treasury** *10am-6.30pm Mon-Sat (last entry 6.15pm).* **Admission** *Church free. Treasury €2.50; €1.25 reductions; free under-7s. No cards.* **Map** *p80 R20.*

Lisbon's cathedral is a symbol of the Christian Reconquest, having been built in the 12th century on the site of the main mosque. It was enlarged in subsequent centuries and facelifts were made necessary by earthquake damage, particularly after the 1755 quake: the south tower collapsed and the interior chancel, chapels and high altar were damaged. The Sé's current appearance is the result of restoration work completed in 1930 that removed many Baroque trappings and reconstructed the rose window from fragments of the original. In the original Romanesque scheme, the Sé was laid out in the form of a Latin cross with three naves. The treasury contains valuable artefacts and vestments. In the Gothic cloisters, added under Dom Dinis (early 14th century), parts of the mosque wall have been uncovered, as well as a section of Roman road and remains of the Visigothic occupation. The revamped cloisters were due to reopen in 2020.

Restaurants

Esperança da Sé €€

Rua São João da Praça 103 (21 887 0189). Tram 12, 28. **Open** *12.30-3.30pm, 6.30-10.30pm Mon-Thur; 12.30-3.30pm, 6.30pm-midnight Fri; 1-4pm, 6.30pm-midnight Sat; 1-4pm, 6.30-11.30pm.* **Map** *p80 R21* ❻ *Pizza*

A good range of thin-crust pizzas, risottos and burgers are served at this little place just

In the know
Pack it all in

Besides the Lisboa Card (see p56), a 90-day joint ticket exists for municipal monuments in this part of town – the Castelo de São Jorge, Museu do Fado, Museu do Aljube and offshoots of the Museu de Lisboa (Teatro Romano, Santo António and Casa dos Bicos) – that may be more useful for a longer stay. It costs €22.50 and is available from www.blueticket.pt: 'Pack 1 – Castelo de S. Jorge and Historical Lisbon - Museums and Monuments of Lisbon'.

EAST OF BAIXA

Restaurants

1. Arco do Castelo *p84*
2. Le Bar à Crêpes *p88*
3. Bica do Sapato *p91*
4. Cantinho da Fátima *p88*
5. Cantinho do Aziz *p89*
6. Esperança da Sé *p79*
7. Páteo 13 *p86*
8. Ramiro *p89*
9. Santa Clara dos Cogumelos *p88*
10. Santo António de Alfama *p86*
11. Taberna Moderna *p80*
12. Via Graça *p88*
13. Zambeze *p84*
14. Zé dos Cornos *p89*

Cafés & bars

1. Clara Clara *p88*
2. O das Joanas *p90*
3. Pois, Café *p86*

Shops & services

1. A Arte da Terra *p80*
2. Conserveira de Lisboa *p80*
3. Cortiço & Netos *p90*
4. Deli Delux *p91*
5. Fabula Urbis *p82*
6. Flur *p91*
7. A Vida Portuguesa *p90*
8. Viúva Lamego *p90*

below the cathedral – an offshoot of a popular restaurant in the Bairro Alto with a similar name. In summer, staff set up a pleasant little terrace across the street next to the cathedral wall. **Other location** Rua do Norte 95, Bairro Alto (21 343 2027).

Taberna Moderna €€

Rua dos Bacalhoeiros 18 (21 886 5039, http://tabernamoderna.com). Metro Terreiro do Paço or tram 12, 28. **Open** *7pm-midnight Mon, noon-midnight Tue-Sat.* **Map** *p80 R21* 11 *Portuguese*

With bright, modern decoration, a convivial terrace and a long list of cocktails, Taberna Moderna draws fashionable locals happy to mix and match the delicious tapas on offer. These include scrambled eggs with spring greens and garlicky *farinheira* sausage; seared tuna served with a mango purée; and creamy rice with leeks, thyme and chestnuts. The brownies are great too. While the kitchen closes at midnight, the Lisbonita Gin Bar stays open for another couple of hours.

Shops & services

❤ A Arte da Terra

Rua Augusto Rosa 40 (21 274 5975, www. aartedaterra.pt). Tram 12, 28 or bus 737. **Open** *11am-8pm daily.* **Map** *p80 R20* 1 *Souvenirs*

Displayed in stone mangers in the 12th-century former stables of the Sé cathedral is an immense variety of handicrafts and other *típico* products. Linen, embroidery, rustic clothing, fado and folk CDs, toys and pottery can all be found at this wonderful showcase of Portuguese culture, as well as dozens of figurines of the city's favourite son, Santo António.

❤ Conserveira de Lisboa

Rua dos Bacalhoeiros 34 (21 886 4009, www. conserveiradelisboa.pt). Metro Terreiro do Paço or tram 12, 28. **Open** *9am-7pm Mon-Sat.* **Map** *p80 Q20* 2 *Food & drink*

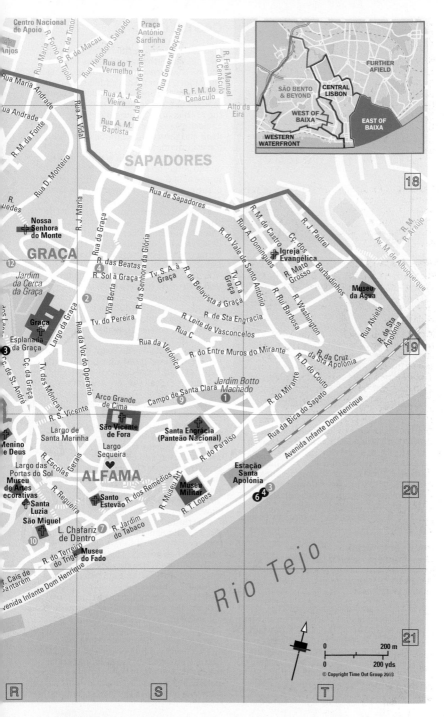

Centro Nacional
de Apoio

Anjos

Praça
António
Sardinha

R. Maria do Tijolo

R. de Timor

R. de Macau

Rua Heliodoro Salgado

Rua do T.
Vermelho

Rua da Penha de França

R. General Roçadas

R. Frei Manuel
do Cenáculo

Rua Maria Andrade

Rua A. J.
Vieira

R. F. M. do
Cenáculo

Alto da
Eira

ua Andrade

R. M. da Fonte

R. A. Vidal

Rua A. M.
Baptista

R. da Penha de França

FURTHER
AFIELD

SÃO BENTO
& BEYOND

CENTRAL
LISBON

WEST OF
BAIXA

EAST OF
BAIXA

WESTERN
WATERFRONT

SAPADORES

Rua D. Monteiro

Rua de Sapadores

R. M. de Castro

R. J. Padrel

Cç. dos Barbadinhos

R. M. Araújo

Av. M. de Albuquerque

R. uedes

Nossa
Senhora
do Monte

Rua da Graça

R. 'r.' Maria

R. do Vale de Santo António

Rua A. Domingues

R. Mato
Grosso

Igreja
Evangélica

Museu
da Água

GRAÇA

R. das Beatas

R. Sol à Graça

R. da Senhora da Glória

Tv. S. A. à
Graça

R. da Belavista à Graça

Tv. O. a
Graça

R. Rui Barbosa

R. Washington

Rua Alviela

R. de Sta
Apolónia

Jardim
da Cerca
da Graça

Vila Berta

R. de Sta Engracia

Largo da Graça

Tv. do Pereira

R. Leite de Vasconcelos

Rua C

R. da Cruz
da Sta Apolónia

Graça

Rua da Voz do Operário

Rua da Verónica

R. do Entre Muros do Mirante

R. D. do Couto

Esplanada
da Graça

Cç. de St. André

Jardim Botto
Machado

R. do Mirante

Cç. da Graça

Tv. das Mónicas

Arco Grande
de Cima

Campo de Santa Clara

R. S. Vicente

Largo de
Santa Marinha

São Vicente
de Fora

Santa Engrácia
(Panteão Nacional)

Rua da Bica do Sapato

Avenida Infante Dom Henrique

Menino
e Deus

R. Escolas Gerais

Largo
Sequeira

R. do Paraíso

Estação
Santa
Apolónia

Largo das
Portas do Sol

Museu
de Artes
ecorativas

ALFAMA

R. dos Remédios

R. Museu Art.

Museu
Militar

Santa
Luzia

R. Requeira

Santo
Estevão

R. T. Lopes

São Miguel

L. Chafariz
de Dentro

R. Jardim
do Tabaco

R. do Terreiro
do Trigo

Museu
do Fado

Cais de
Santarém

venida Infante Dom Henrique

Rio Tejo

0   200 m
0   200 yds

© Copyright Time Out Group 2010

18

19

20

21

R

S

T

Museu do Aljube

CASTELO

Lisbon began on the hill of Castelo, with an Iron Age settlement that was later occupied successively by Romans, Visigoths and Moors, all of whom added their own fortifications. Some of the oldest segments, thought to be of Roman origin, are near the 737 bus stop. These are the outer walls, enclosing both the **Castelo de São Jorge** itself and the small neighbourhood within the walls named after it.

From here, the way in is through the Arco de São Jorge; on the left a niche houses an image of St George, dragon-killing patron of the castle – and of Portugal. The ticket office for the castle proper is beyond it, in the Casa do Governador at the top of the rise. Off to the right, narrow streets lead into a neighbourhood where the older residents living in rent-controlled flats are gradually being replaced by incomers who will pay fortunes for renovated pads. At the end of Rua da Santa Cruz do Castelo, the **Igreja da Santa Cruz do Castelo** is on the shady *largo* of the same name and contains a statue of St George. The original church was built on top of a mosque right after the 1147 Reconquest; the present post-earthquake one dates from 1776.

In the Castelo de São Jorge itself, the open square just past the entrance has unrivalled views over the city. Cannons projecting over the parapet recall the fortification's original purpose, but today overlook orange and lemon trees in the gardens below. Further in are a moat and keep, whose courtyards and ramparted walkways make up the heart of the medieval castle.

Just outside the walls of the Castelo area, at the far end of Chão da Feira from the Arco de São Jorge, is a curious, much-photographed urinal. The **Palácio Belmonte**, through the nearby archway, was renovated with city council funds and is now a top-notch hotel.

The tunnel here through to the Pátio de Dom Fradique is a public right of way; take it to pass through a square surrounded by tumbledown houses. Through the arch at the bottom is Rua dos Cegos – Street of the Blind – where the 16th-century house at no.20 is one of the city's oldest. The octagonal shape of the large church to your left, the Baroque **Igreja do Menino de Deus** (96 967 2419, open 10am-12:30pm Wed) is unique in Portugal. From here, streets lead down into Alfama and Mouraria.

The street circling below and round the castle from just beyond here, and in the other direction from the Arco de São Jorge, is called Costa do Castelo. It rewards walkers with views out over the city, including those

This small, wood-panelled space opened in 1930 and is lined with a dazzling array of colourfully packaged tins – sardines, tuna, anchovies, fish paste and the like. The store now also stocks a range of gourmet jams and liqueurs for tourists. Rival **Comur** at no.12 (91 649 0709, www.comur.pt) also calls its shop 'A Conserveira' but is a newcomer here, with packaging aimed squarely at tourists, despite its antique look.

❤ Fabula Urbis

Rua de Augusto Rosa 27 (21 888 5032, www. fabula-urbis.pt). Tram 12, 28 or bus 737. **Open** *11am-1.30pm, 3-8pm Thur-Sat.* **Map** *p80 R20* ❺ *Books*

Most Lisbon bookshops have English-language sections but stock few books about the city itself. This little place fills that gap. As well as a fine selection of Portuguese non-fiction and fiction, translated into English, French, German and several other languages, there are plenty of glossy coffee-table tomes about Portuguese country gardens and the like.

💙 Miradouros

Outdoor seating at bars and restaurants was not so common in Lisbon until fairly recently – perhaps a legacy of the dictatorship, when people were supposed to know their place and get back to work, not fritter away hours at pavement cafés. But Lisbon's many hills guaranteed the existence of plenty of *miradouros*, or lookout points, where people could pause and take in the view. Kiosks are now ensconced on many of them, serving drinks and snacks.

Castelo de São Jorge
See p84.

You have to pay to enter the castle grounds, but its ramparts, on top one of Lisbon's highest hills, are the place to head first for an overview of the city's topography.

Esplanada da Graça
Largo da Graça, Graça. Tram 28. **Open** *24hrs daily.* **Admission** *Free.* **Map** *p80 R20.*

This large paved area next to the church in Graça is patronised by both tourists and locals, enjoying a range of snacks and drinks, including fresh lemonade. The view is at its best in the late afternoon, but this place often buzzes at night, too.

Estacionamento Chão do Loureiro
Calçada do Marquês de Tancos 18, Edifício EMEL, Mercado Chao do Loureiro, Castelo. Tram 28. **Open** *10am-midnight daily.* **Admission** *Free.* **Map** *p80 R19.*

It doesn't sound promising – the roof of a multi-storey car park – but it boasts a magnificent panoramic view of the Baixa. The Zambeze restaurant (*see p84*) that occupies most of the rooftop serves traditional Portuguese and Mozambican food, but you can also sip a cocktail or beer on its terrace.

Jardim de São Pedro de Alcântara
Rua de São Pedro de Alcântara, Bairro Alto. Ascensor da Gloria. **Open** *24hrs daily.* **Admission** *Free.* **Map** *p95 P19.*

On the western side of Baixa, at the edge of the Bairro Alto, this is one of Lisbon's best vantage points, taking in castle, cathedral, river and even part of Parque Eduardo VII. After lengthy restoration, it now boasts two kiosks (one on the lower level, down a flight of steps) and benches from which to enjoy the view.

Jardim do Torel
Rua Júlio de Andrade, Elevador do Lavra. **Open** *7am-10pm daily.* **Admission** *Free.* **Map** *p60 Q18.*

To reach this pretty garden and *miradouro* with a view over the Avenida da Liberdade, Baixa and river, climb the stairs off Rua do Telhal – only advisable if you have a strong pair of legs – or, from downtown, take the vintage funicular, the Elevador do Lavra. A kiosk just down from the garden serves salads, toasties and wine.

Nossa Senhora do Monte
Largo Monte, Graça. Tram 28. **Open** *24hrs daily.* **Admission** *Free.* **Map** *p80 R18.*

From this, the highest point in the city, just uphill from Graça, you can see right across to Monsanto Forest Park. There is no kiosk, but watching the sunset from here is magical.

Santa Luzia
Largo de Santa Luzia, Alfama. Tram 28. **Open** *24hrs daily.* **Admission** *Free.* **Map** *p80 R20.*

Just down from the Largo das Portas do Sol (which has its own panoramic view of Alfama) is this most romantic of Lisbon *miradouros*, in a garden framed by *azulejos*. From here you can see not only the river's full expanse, but also the Igreja de São Vicente de Fora and Panteão Nacional.

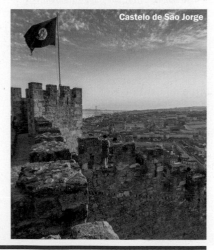

Castelo de São Jorge

from the terraces of the **Chapitô** (*see p212*) restaurant-bar and theatre, and the café of the restored 19th-century **Teatro Taborda** (*see p213*). A staircase, the Escadinhas de São Crispim, follows the course of the old Moorish walls down towards the Sé from near Chapitô.

Sights & museums
❤ Castelo de São Jorge
*Rua de Santa Cruz do Castelo (21 880 0620, www.castelodesaojorge.pt). Tram 12, 28 or bus 737. **Open** Nov-Feb 9am-6pm daily. Mar-Oct 9am-9pm daily. **Admission** €10; €5-€8.50 reductions; free under-13s. **Map** p80 R20.*

The hilltop was fortified even before the arrival of the Roman legions; in later centuries the castle walls were strengthened by Visigoths and Moors, before falling to Portugal's first king, Afonso Henriques, in 1147. His statue stands in the square just past the main gate. From the 14th to the 16th centuries, Portugal's kings resided in the Palácio de Alcáçovas, the remains of which now house a snack bar and a display of finds from the ongoing archaeological digs. The castle itself has undergone numerous transformations. Back in the 1930s, several government offices and a firehouse were removed from the grounds, exposing the walls, which were duly topped with supposedly authentic-looking battlements. There have been several makeovers since then. The battlements of the Castelejo (keep) have ten towers, which may be climbed; in one is a Cámara Obscura from which you can see key city monuments and spy on people downtown, as well as learning how the contraption works. Beyond the keep is an area where labelled displays trace out dwellings from prehistoric times and the late Islamic period, as well as the ruins of the last palatial residence on this hill, which was destroyed by the 1755 earthquake.

Restaurants
Arco do Castelo €€
*Rua Chão da Feira 25 (21 887 6598, 96 625 7902). Tram 12, 28 or bus 737. **Open** noon-11pm Mon-Thur; noon-midnight Fri, Sat. **Map** p80 R20 ❶ Indian*

This tiny place with basic furniture, plain tablecloths and bottle-lined walls is one of Lisbon's few genuinely Goan restaurants. The menu only runs to two pages, but includes *xacuti* (chicken with coconut and aromatic spices), *balchão de porco* (pork in a rich sauce containing dried shrimp) and *sarapatel* (pork in a rich ginger gravy). Booking is essential for dinner; note that the kitchen closes at 10pm even on weekends.

❤ Zambeze €€€
*Calçada Marquês dos Tancos, Mercado Chão do Loureiro (21 887 7056, 92 520 0631, http://zambezerestaurante.pt). Tram 28. **Open** 10am-11pm daily. **Map** p80 Q20 ⓭ African/Portuguese*

Dishes from Mozambique, beautifully prepared and presented in an airy space, plus a huge terrace with stunning views of Lisbon: what's not to like? The place also has dishes from the Beiras region of central Portugal. There's a Portuguese touch to the decoration, too, in the form of Bordallo Pinheiro ceramics. Zambeze is on the roof of a multi-storey car park, so if you're on foot in the Baixa take the Elevador do Castelo (Rua dos Fanqueiros 170) then cross the road to the car park, where another lift (by the Pingo Doce supermarket) whisks you up to the roof.

ALFAMA

A *miradouro* with a beautiful view introduces visitors to Alfama. On the 12 and 28 tram lines, the **Miradouro de Santa Luzia**, just below Largo das Portas do Sol, has a rose garden, decorative pool and grapevine trellises that combine to provide one of Lisbon's most serene views. On the outside wall of the nearby **Igreja de Santa Luzia** (the Order of Malta's headquarters in Portugal), are two tile panels: one maps downtown Lisbon before the 1755 quake, the other shows Christians storming the castle in 1147. Another twist of the road up the hill leads to Largo das Portas do Sol (Sun Gate Square), graced by a statue of Lisbon's official patron, São Vicente (St Vincent), bearing the city's symbol (a boat with two ravens).

On the southern side of the square, the former city palace of the Visconde de Azurara is now occupied by the **Museu-Escola de Artes Decorativas**, next to an old stone tower that was once part of the Moorish siege walls. Across the road a terrace overlooks an expanse of red Alfama roofs. Over the next hill, the white marble churches of São Vicente and Santa Engrácia mark the eastern boundary of Alfama. The ugly slab in the foreground is the neighbourhood car park, where vehicles are stored and fetched completely automatically. From here you can plunge down into Alfama proper (*see p85* Alfama), losing yourself until you pop out downhill onto Largo de Chafariz do Dentro or at **Santa Apolónia** train station (*see p90*).

💙 Alfama

Running down the south-eastern slope of the hill topped by the Castelo de São Jorge, Alfama is Lisbon's oldest *bairro* (quarter) after Castelo – the castle quarter. It's an appealing warren of narrow streets and blind alleys, stooping archways and twisting staircases. Some buildings stand on foundations dating back to the Visigoths, but the street pattern is Moorish. Washing flutters everywhere. Children chase through alleys as grown-ups chatter outside shops and cafés.

The name Alfama probably comes from the Arabic word *al-hama*, meaning springs or fountains. Most of this well-watered area stood outside the Moorish siege walls, which stretched from the Largo das Portas do Sol along Rua Norberto Araújo and Rua da Adiça down to the river. The fountain in Largo do Chafariz de Dentro, after which the square is named, has been in use since medieval times, while the Chafariz d'el Rei on Rua dos Cais de Santarém has also been dishing out water for more than 700 years. In the 17th and 18th centuries, the taps were segregated: Moors used the tap on one side, Europeans the other.

At the western end of narrow Rua de São Pedro, Largo de São Rafael opens on to a remaining portion of the Moorish siege walls, complete with a private lemon-tree garden on top. Below this, Rua da Judiaria is a small side street that was home to Alfama's Jewish community in medieval times. A museum dedicated to its history is planned on nearby Largo de São Miguel, but construction is stalled as a legal battle rumbles on over its architecture. The white-fronted Igreja de São Miguel here is, like so many churches, a post-earthquake reconstruction of an earlier one. East from here, narrow Rua de São Miguel is a main street of sorts, although nowadays only a handful of traditional businesses survive in the neighbourhood. The tiny alleys off Rua de São Miguel lead into wondrous networks of staircases, terraces and gardens.

What's missing in Alfama is the sound of motor vehicles. They can't get in here – a factor that long acted as a brake on gentrification. Still, the current tourist boom has wrought major change in Alfama: while morning rush hour is still accompanied by the sound of birds singing and footsteps scurrying to work, this is often drowned out by the trundle of wheelie suitcases.

On summer evenings, crowds head into Alfama looking for an outside table, a plate of grilled sardines and plenty of red wine. Across from Largo do Chafariz de Dentro, where tour buses decant their camera-toting passengers, stands the **Museu do Fado** (*see p86*). A number of fado houses crowd this bottom end of the neighbourhood: the **Parreirinha de Alfama** see is one of the city's most renowned.

A good way to get a more intimate look at Alfama is to make your way up (via Rua dos Remédios) to the Igreja de Santo Estevão, whose veranda-cum-*miradouro* provides yet another fine view. From here you can see grapevines growing in the back lots of some houses. Leading off here are streets up to the Igreja de São Vicente de Fora and the neighbourhood named after it, and to the more bustling Graça district. But the ideal way to get to know this most atmospheric of Lisbon *bairros* is to wander and get a little lost – something visitors will find almost impossible to avoid. Be aware, though: pickpockets do operate in this area.

Sights & museums

♥ Museu-Escola de Artes Decorativas

Largo das Portas do Sol 2 (21 888 1991, www.fress.pt). Tram 12, 28, or bus 737. **Open** *10am-1pm, 1.30-5pm Mon, Wed-Sun.* **Admission** *€4; €2 reductions; free under-15s.* **Map** *p80 R20.*

Banker Ricardo do Espírito Santo Silva – admirer of Salazar, intimate with *fadista* Amália, builder of Lisbon's Ritz Hotel – was also a leading collector of Portuguese applied arts. In 1947, he bought a 17th-century palace and created the Museum of Applied Arts and attached school. The collection of 16th- to 19th-century Portuguese, French and English furniture is the most important in the country, and is displayed in reconstructions of the original rooms. Tapestries, silverware, porcelain, antique books and tiles make up the rest of the exhibits. The shop sells items produced by the school and workshops' staff, who are skilled in 21 different crafts; the shop and café have the same hours as the museum.

Museu do Fado

Largo do Chafariz de Dentro 1 (21 882 3470, www.museudofado.pt). Metro Santa Apolónia. **Open** *10am-6pm Tue-Sun (last entry 5.30pm).* **Admission** *€5; €2.50-€4.30 reductions; free under-13s.* **Map** *p80 R20.*

Permanent displays at this city museum tell the history of this ever-popular musical form; you can book a guided visit that includes a live fado performance. On summer weekends there are also excellent free fado tours of Alfama during which local singers perform – check the website for details. There is a museum café, and the attached restaurant, **A Travessa do Fado** (21 887 0144) serves up delicious snacks and has a good selection of wines. Fado singers often perform here too; on such evenings, be sure to book ahead.

Restaurants

♥ Páteo 13 €

Calçadinha de Santo Estêvão 13 (21 888 2325). Metro Terreiro do Paço or Santa Apolónia. **Open** *(summer/early autumn only) 11am-11pm Tue-Sun.* **Map** *p80 S20* ❼ *Portuguese*

Shaded by vines, Páteo 13 is one of the most atmospheric places to eat fish or cuts of meat straight off the charcoal grill. The big seller is sardines, traditionally served with boiled potatoes, salad and grilled peppers, all washed down with sangria. What you see on arrival – the terrace – is what you get: there's no indoor dining room, so Páteo 13 only functions in the warmer/drier months. It's best to arrive early to avoid a wait.

Santo António de Alfama €€

Beco de São Miguel 7 (21 888 1328, www.siteantonio.com). Metro Terreiro do Paço or Santa Apolónia, or tram 12, 28. **Open** *12.30-5pm, 7.30pm-2am daily.* **Map** *p80 R20* ❿ *Portuguese*

This restaurant became an Alfama fixture by being a tad more sophisticated than its local rivals (slogan: 'no fado or sardines') and is sticking to the formula after two decades. It has a wide variety of starters and desserts, and some decent main courses, though grilled fish and steak dominate. It's all served to a jazz soundtrack.

Cafés & bars

♥ Pois, Café

Rua São João da Praça 93 (21 886 2497, www.pois cafe.com). Tram 12, 28 or bus 737. **Open** *10am-6pm Mon-Fri, Sun; 10am-10pm Sat.* **Map** *p80 R21* ❸

This Austrian-run café is a great place in which to lounge, reading the foreign newspapers and magazines provided. The rustic decoration, mismatched furniture, and games and toys scattered about add to the informal atmosphere. Sandwiches, salads, fine cakes and fragrant Austrian lemonade are all on offer, plus brunch at weekends.

SÃO VICENTE & GRAÇA

Between the **Igreja e Mosteiro de São Vicente de Fora** and the white dome of the **Panteão Nacional de Santa Engrácia** – both of whose roofs offer fabulous views of Lisbon – lies the hillside space known as the Campo de Santa Clara. Here, from dawn until early afternoon on Tuesdays and Saturdays, the **Feira da Ladra** flea market is held.

Whereas Alfama feels like a busy village, Graça, on the hill above São Vicente, is more like a small town. Indeed, it has several *vilas operários*, built by the more enlightened late 19th-century industrialists to house their workers in decent conditions, with patios and verandas. The 28 tram stops at Largo da Graça, site of one of the largest, Vila Sousa. This isn't much of an area for nightlife, but **Damas** (*see p190*) is fun. To the west is the **Esplanada da Graça**, an open-air café with great sunset views serving excellent toasties and fresh lemonade. The **Igreja da Graça** is one of Lisbon's oldest churches, built in 1271 but enlarged in the mid 16th century. The attached monastery became a military barracks after religious orders were dissolved in 1834.

The small promontory above Graça (turn left on Rua Damasceno Monteiro, then bear right up the Calçada do Monte) is the highest of Lisbon's hills, topped by the chapel of **Nossa Senhora do Monte**. In front of the chapel is a glass-encased image of the Virgin, while a sit-down inside on the stone chair of St Gens – a bishop martyred during Roman times, after whom the chapel was originally named – is supposed to ease the pangs of childbirth; the chair was popular with Portuguese queens over the centuries. The *miradouro* is a favourite with lovers and a fine place to catch the sunset. Down the hill is the **Jardim da Cerca da Graça**, Lisbon's newest park and the largest in the old *bairros*. A kiosk here serves soups, toasties and home-made ice teas.

Sights & museums

Igreja da Graça

Largo da Graça (21 887 3943). Tram 28 or bus 734. **Open** *9.30am-12.30pm, 2-5pm Mon-Sat; 9.30am-12.30pm, 5-7pm Sun.* **Admission** *free.* **Map** *p80 R19.*

The original monastery of Graça was built in 1271 and completed with an image of Nossa Senhora da Graça (Our Lady of Grace), salvaged from the sea off Cascais that same year. Renovated in the mid 16th century, most of the church fell in the 1755 earthquake. The later renovation reduced three naves to one, and removed much austere marble in favour of rococo decoration. During Lent, the church organises the Senhor dos Passos procession.

♥ Igreja e Mosteiro de São Vicente de Fora

Largo de São Vicente (21 882 4400 church, 21 888 5652 cloisters). Tram 28 or bus 734. **Church** *8am-1pm, 2.30-5pm Tue-Sat; 8am-noon Sun.* **Cloisters** *10am-6pm Tue-Sun (last entry 5pm).* **Admission** *Church free. Cloisters €5; €2.50 reductions; free under-13s. No cards.* **Map** *p80 S20.*

Portugal's first king, Afonso Henriques, laid the foundation stone for the first church of St Vincent 'Outside' – that is, beyond the then city walls – hardly a month after taking Lisbon from the Moors in 1147. He was fulfilling a vow to construct Christian houses of worship on the sites where Portuguese soldiers and northern European crusaders lay buried. In 1580, Portugal's then ruler, King Philip II of Spain, decided to start from scratch and brought in his own architect, Juan Herrera (builder of the Escorial). With Italian architect Filippo Terzi, Herrera designed a new church in Italian mannerist style. It was inaugurated in 1629, but was severely damaged in the 1755 earthquake, when the main dome and roof collapsed on a crowd of worshippers. The big draw are the cloisters, richly decorated with early 18th-century tile panels, some illustrating La Fontaine fables. Inside there's the royal pantheon of the Braganza family, the last dynasty to rule Portugal. The figure of a weeping woman kneels before the twin tombs of Dom Carlos I and Crown Prince Luís Filipe, shot by assassins in 1908. The imposing church is the seat of Portugal's top cleric. The church's fine organ is used for concerts at 5pm on the second Saturday of most months.

Panteão Nacional de Santa Engrácia

Campo de Santa Clara (21 885 4820). Tram 28 or bus 734. **Open** *10am-5pm Tue-Sun.* **Admission** *€4; €2 reductions; free under-13s & all 1st Sun of mth. No cards.* **Map** *p80 S20.*

The dome of this church was completed in 1966, a mere 285 years after the building was begun; hence the Lisbon expression 'a job like Santa Engrácia' – one that takes forever. The church is on the site of an earlier one, which was torn down after being desecrated by a robbery in 1630. A Jew was blamed and executed, but later exonerated. Before dying he is said to have prophesied that the new church would never be completed because an innocent man had been convicted. The first attempt at a new Santa Engrácia duly collapsed in 1681 (construction error, compounded by a storm, may have been to blame) and work restarted the following year. The new plan, by master stonemason João Antunes, bears many similarities to Peruzzi's plans for St Peter's in Rome, and marble in various colours dominates the interior. In 1916, the Republican government decided the then still roofless Santa Engrácia would become the national Pantheon, a temple to honour dead Portuguese heroes. Among those since laid to rest here is General Humberto Delgado, an opposition leader assassinated by the secret police in 1962, and fado diva Amália Rodrigues. Amália's tomb in the Pantheon is always heaped with flowers. Guides say you can tell which are from people who knew her personally – look for the meadow blooms she loved.

In the know
Riverfront bargains

A €7 joint ticket is avalable for the **Panteão Nacional** (see above) and the **Museu Nactional do Azulejo** (see *p150*), which is located a little further east along the river. There is also a €15 'Frente Ribeirinha' ticket that takes in both these state-run monuments and one other that overlooks the Tagus, the **Museu Nacional de Arte Antiga** (see *p117*).

EAST OF BAIXA

87

Mosteiro de São Vicente de Fora

Restaurants

❤ Le Bar à Crêpes €€
Largo da Graça 18 (91 150 0259). Tram 28, bus 734. **Open** *noon-3pm, 7-10pm Tue-Fri; noon-10pm Sat.* **No cards.** **Map** *p80 S19* ❷ *Pancakes*

Graça has emerged as a magnet for French expats, and the friendly young couple who run this cosy crêperie are among those who have been given the warmest welcome. It's a good place for anyone avoiding gluten as all their delicious and filling savoury galettes (whimsically named after French stars of stage and screen) are made with buckwheat. There's Normandy cider to wash them down, to a suitably Gallic soundtrack. They also do tasty salads and, for dessert, a range of sweet pancakes (from wheat flour).

Cantinho da Fátima €
Rua da Graça 11 (21 887 8772). Tram 28, bus 734. **Open** *7am-5pm Mon-Sat.* **Map** *p80 S19* ❹ *Portuguese*

Graça's high street is dotted with *tascas* serving rigorously traditional fare. This one, open only for breakfast and lunch, is among the best value and is patronised by regulars. Several dishes on the menu come in half servings that are more than enough for one person. Not the spot for a quiet, intimate meal but great for local atmos.

❤ Santa Clara dos Cogumelos €€
Mercado de Santa Clara, Campo de Santa Clara 7 (21 887 0661, 91 304 3302, www. santaclaradoscogumelos.com). Tram 28 or bus 734. **Open** *7.30-11pm Tue-Fri, Sun; 1-3pm, 7.30-11pm Sat.* **Map** *p80 S19* ❾ *Portuguese/International*

As the name suggests, the focus is on mushrooms (*cogumelos*) in this snug place above the old Santa Clara market hall,

from pâtés and risottos to vegan takes on Portuguese standards, such as shitake *à bulhão pato* (cooked with garlic and coriander, in a dish normally made with clams). There is also tender steak from the Azores and several fish dishes, including *bacalhau*. Signature desserts include porcini ice cream (with glacé chestnuts) and crème brûlée with truffle.

Via Graça €€€
Rua Damasceno Monteiro 9B (21 887 0830, www.restauranteviagraca.com). Tram 28 or bus 734. **Open** *12.30-3pm, 7.30-11pm Mon-Fri; 7.30-11pm Sat, Sun.* **Map** *p80 R19* ❷ *Portuguese*

Via Graça serves up one of Lisbon's best views, attentive service and excellent traditional dishes. Choose from one of the *bacalhau* dishes on offer, or perhaps shellfish rice or game pie, and wash it down with a full-bodied Alentejo red, as you gaze at the illuminated castle ramparts.

Cafés & bars

Clara Clara
Jardim Botto Machado, Campo de Santa Clara (21 885 0172, http://clara-clara-cafe. business.site). Metro Santa Apolónia, tram 12 or bus 712, 734. **Open** *Nov-Feb 10am-7pm daily. Mar-Oct 10am-midnight daily.* **Map** *p80 S19* ❶

On days when there's no **Feira da Ladra** (*see p46*), the little park in Campo de Santa Clara is a peaceful oasis with a view over the river. It has shaded lawns, a children's playground, tables where old locals play cards, and now this little kiosk and terrace, with coffee, herbal tea, home-made snacks and lemonade, and free Wi-Fi. Note that on chilly or rainy days, it may close slightly early.

MOURARIA & INTENDENTE

Mouraria is the district wedged on the hillside between the Castelo and Graça. The defeated Moors were allowed to settle here, and in the 12th and 13th centuries two mosques were still functioning. A 1471 Muslim petition to the king mentions that Mouraria was enclosed by walls and that residents locked the gates at night. Twenty-five years later, non-Christians were either converted or expelled from the country.

In the 19th century, Mouraria was known for its prostitutes, seedy *tascas* and fado houses – the area is still scruffy, but no less authentically Lisboeta than Alfama, and considerably less touristy. The most famous fado house of the 19th century, run by singer A Severa, was in Rua do Capelão; Casa da Severa, was renovated by the city in 2013 and is now fado house **Maria da Mouraria** (*see p202*), run by *fadista* Hélder Moutinho, brother of the more famous Camané.

Mouraria's main street is Rua dos Cavaleiros/Calçada do Santo André, which the 12 tram climbs up. The lower part of it has been taken over by Indian-run discount stores, and the Centro Comercial Mouraria, down on Largo do Martim Moniz, bustles with Asian and African shops.

This multi-ethnic area is, appropriately, where the Society of Jesus began training missionaries, including St Francis Xavier, to send out across the world. On Rua Marquês de Ponte de Lima is the former Convento de Santo Antão-o-Velho (now the Socorro parish church); a plaque indicates that the world's first Jesuit foundation was set up here in 1542.

Mouraria meets the Baixa in **Largo do Martim Moniz**. Once the heart of Mouraria, in the 1950s and '60s old byways, patios and churches were bulldozed in the name of urban renewal. Successive city administrations inflicted architectural atrocities on the area. Another overhaul is planned, but its ultimate shape is unclear.

For now, Martim Moniz serves as a meeting place for the immigrants who have adopted it; on Sundays, you might even catch a cricket game at the southern end of the square. The Hotel Mundial here has a rooftop bar with one of Lisbon's best views.

Running north from Martim Moniz, the Rua da Palma/Avenida Almirante Reis axis is a workaday contrast to the glitzier Avenida da Liberdade. The municipal **Arquivo Fotográfico** at Rua da Palma 246 (218 844 060), has regular exhibitions and a pleasant bar-café.

The narrow street behind this block, Rua do Benformoso, is believed to date back to Roman times. The medieval house at no.101 may be Lisbon's oldest. Lined with Chinese shops, Pakistani butchers and Portuguese *tascas*, and with residents hailing from dozens of other nations, this street finally opens up into a large open space, Largo do Intendente. Intendente has undergone a miraculous makeover in the past couple of years to become one of the city's trendiest areas – though still with a bit of an edge. For now, as well as the flagship **A Vida Portuguesa** store and hustling **Largo Café Estúdio** (no. 16, 21 888 5420, http://largoresidencias.com), the square is also home to the popular bar **Casa Independente** (*see p190*), among others.

EAST OF BAIXA

Restaurants

❤ Cantinho do Aziz €
Rua São Lourenço 3 (21 887 6472). Metro Martim Moniz or Rossio, or tram 12, 28. Open noon-11pm daily. Map p80 Q19 ❺
African/Indian

For a real taste of Africa in Europe, you could do far worse than this long-established canteen, now with a little terrace. The cuisine is Mozambican, with Goan recipes thrown in for good measure, and all of it is halal. As well as the *chamussas* (samosas), we recommend the *frango à Zambeziana* (grilled chicken marinated in coconut milk). It delivers too.

❤ Ramiro €€€
Avenida Almirante Reis 1H (21 885 1024, www.cervejariaramiro.pt). Metro Intendente or tram 28. Open noon-1am Tue-Sun. Closed Aug. Map p80 R18 ❽ *Seafood*

Senhor Ramiro, a native of Galícia in Spain, is what Lisboetas call a *cromo*, 'a card'. After helping his father run a snack bar in what was then a dodgy part of town, he transformed it into this celebrated *marisqueira* (seafood restaurant). As the fame of his sublime Spanish-style *gambas a ajillo* (garlic prawns) and other fresh shellfish spread, Ramiro bought the shop next door, then the next and the next. Service and turnover are rapid, but if you can't face the queue, Marisqueira do Lis at no.27B (21 885 0739) is pretty good too.

Zé dos Cornos €
Beco dos Surradores 5 (21 886 9641). Metro Rossio/Martim Moniz or tram 12, 28. Open 11.40am-4pm Mon-Wed; 11.40am-4pm, 7-10pm Thur-Sat. No cards. Map p80 Q19 ⓮ *Portuguese*

This tiny *tasca* at the bottom of Mouraria is a favourite with students for its rock-bottom prices and informal atmosphere. Grilled meats and fish are the speciality; there are more elaborate dishes, mainly from northern Portugal, but nothing fancy, and do the usual

A Vida Portuguesa

eggy desserts such as cinnamon-strewn *arroz doce* (rice pudding). Come early to bag a table – although you may end up sharing one anyway.

Cafés & bars

O das Joanas

*Largo do Intendente 28 (21 887 9401). Metro Intendente. **Open** Dec-Mar 9am-midnight Mon, Fri; 9am-10pm Wed, Thur; 10am-midnight Sat; 10am-10pm Sun. Apr-Nov 9am-midnight Mon-Thur; 9am-2am Fri; 10am-2am Sat; 10am-midnight Sun. **No cards**. Map p80 R21* ❸

This capacious café sells breakfast, brunch and a great variety of soups, salads, quiches and cakes. Drinks made in-house include lemonade, herbal tea and mulled wine. There's plenty of space inside the *azulejo*-fronted building, but on warm days the large terrace is the big attraction. There are often late-afternoon happy hours when drinks are cut-price or snacks free with an aperitif. Closed on Tuesdays in winter.

Shops & services

Cortiço & Netos

*Calçada de Santo André 66 (21 136 2376, 91 970 3705, www.corticoenetos.com). Metro Martim Moniz or tram 12. **Open** 10am-1pm, 2-7pm Mon-Sat. Map p80 R19* ❸ *Tiles*

Unlike other *azulejo* shops listed in this guide, this place stocks mostly mass-produced tiles. But with hundreds of discontinued lines, it's a veritable museum of style through the decades and a great place to pick up one-off decorative bargains. For years, the owner snapped up stock from factories as they closed; now his grandchildren are busy selling it. Buy now while you can.

❤ A Vida Portuguesa

*Largo do Intendente 23 (21 197 4512, www. avidaportuguesa.com). Metro Intendente. **Open** 10.30am-7.30pm daily. Map p80 R18* ❼ *Vintage*

This wasn't the first of Catarina Portas's wildly successful vintage shops to open, but it's the largest and most painstakingly restored. Everything from the shelving and cabinets to the packaging of the products is calculated to delight. Stock includes many of the best and most unusual Portuguese gourmet products, as well as traditional soaps and creams. There are also large items for the home. **Other locations** Rua Anchieta 11, Chiado (21 346 5073); Time Out Market (*see p116*).

❤ Viúva Lamego

*Largo do Intendente 25 (21 231 4274, www. viuvalamego.com). Metro Intendente. **Open** 10am-1pm, 2-6.30pm Mon-Fri. Map p80 R18* ❽ *Azulejos*

The façade of this former factory (founded in 1849) is a magnificent showcase for the *azulejos* of one of Portugal's most famous tile manufacturers. Production moved out of town in the 1940s, but the shop remained, selling ceramics as well as tiles. The company also undertakes major projects (including in Lisbon's Metro, *see p246*) from its base in Sintra.

SANTA APOLÓNIA

Santa Apolónia railway station at the foot of Alfama is the terminus for lines going to Oporto, Madrid, Paris and beyond, and now finally on the Metro network. Santa Apolónia was built in the 1860s on the Cais dos Soldados – 'Quay of the Soldiers' – from where troops departed on their way to colonial campaigns in Africa and India, Timor and Macao. Fittingly, the **Museu Militar** is opposite the station. In the 19th century, there was no road to the right of the station; ships would tie up next to the tracks. Nowadays the warehouses that sprang up on landfill across the way have been cleared and a new cruise ship terminal has been installed – and is being expanded – along with a string of trendy shops, restaurants and clubs, including **Lux** (see p190). Behind Santa Apolónia station, the **Clube Ferroviário** (see p190) has a rooftop terrace bar that's great for summer nights.

▶ For details of sights east of Santa Apolónia, see p140.

Sights & museums

Museu da Água – Estação Elevatória a Vapor dos Barbadinhos
Rua do Alviela 12 (21 810 0215, www.epal. pt). Metro Santa Apolónia or bus 794. **Open** 10am-5.30pm Tue-Sat. **Admission** €4; €2 reductions; free under-13s. No cards. **Map** p80 T19.

As with Belém's Central Tejo (see p124 MAAT), the Water Museum and its contents are important parts of Portugal's industrial archaeology and still run by a utility firm – in this case, state water company EPAL, which is headquartered at the Barbadinhos Steam Pumping Station, the first to serve Lisbon. The station is dominated by four huge steam engines from the 1880s, one of which is set in motion every month or so. The museum's well-designed displays trace the history of Lisbon's water supply from Roman times to the present. A joint ticket (€10) for all four of the musuem's branches – including the Aqueduto das Águas Livres (see p137), Mãe d'Água (see p138) and Reservatório da Patriarcal (see p108).

Museu Militar
Largo do Museu do Artilharia (21 884 2453, www.exercito.pt). Metro Santa Apolónia. **Open** 10am-5pm Tue-Sun (last entry 4.15pm). **Admission** €3; €1 reductions; free under-12s. No cards. **Map** p80 S20.

A former 17th-century weapons factory provides an appropriate setting for the Military Museum. The tour begins upstairs, with two rooms devoted to the Napoleonic invasions, and a display on World War I (the Portuguese suffered heavy losses in the 1918 Battle of Le Lys, known to the British as Estaires). A series of rooms with elaborately carved and gilded decoration leads to a comprehensive display of Portuguese arms up to the 20th century. Downstairs you'll

find a plethora of cannons and a mind-boggling variety of weaponry captured from adversaries during the colonial wars of the 1960s and '70s.

Restaurants

❤ Bica do Sapato €€€
Avenida Infante D Henrique, Armazém B (21 881 0320, 91 761 5065, www.bicadosapato. com). Metro Santa Apolónia or bus 728. **Restaurant** noon-3.30pm, 7pm-midnight Tue-Sat. **Sushi bar** 7.30pm-midnight Mon-Fri; 12.30pm-midnight Sat. **Map** p80 T20 ❸ Portuguese/International

This large modern dockside space, dotted with designer furniture, features a main restaurant, a large terrace on the river, and an excellent sushi bar upstairs. Its kitchen is now run by Henrique Mouro, one of Portugal's most admired chefs, carrying forward Bica do Sapato's record of combining tradition and modernity. The changing menu might offer the likes of roast or grilled squid or octopus, bacalhau with white beans and sames (the cod's swim bladder), confit of rabbit, or pork from the Iberian black pig served with snail rice – all served with tasty sides. Salads, interesting vegan mains and lovely light desserts are standard.

Shops & services

Deli Delux
Avenida Infante D Henrique, Armazém B, Loja 8 (21 886 2070, www.delidelux.pt). Metro Santa Apolónia. **Open** Winter 10am-10pm Mon-Thur, Sun; 10am-11pm Fri, Sat. Summer 10am-11pm Mon-Thur; 10am-midnight Fri, Sat. **Map** p80 T20 ❹ Food & drink

'O Deli', as devotees call it, caters largely to diplomats and the local bourgeoisie, who come here to snuffle for truffles and similarly pricey fare, from fine wines, hams and cheeses to dried mushrooms and cranberry sauce. The café has a healthy gourmet menu and a riverside terrace. **Other location** Rua Alexandre Herculano 15A, Avenida da Liberdade (21 314 1474).

❤ Flur
Avenida Infante D Henrique, Armazém B, Loja 4 (21 882 1101, www.flur.pt). Metro Santa Apolónia. **Open** 1-8pm Mon-Sat. **Map** p80 T20 ❻ Music

A magnet for DJs and fans of independent music, vinyl specialist Flur is also one of the best places in town to pick up flyers and tickets for parties and shows. It also sells CDs and vinyls via the website.

West of Baixa

During the 19th and early 20th centuries, the Chiado, with Rua Garrett as its main axis, was the very centre of Lisbon's intellectual life. The dictatorship, not keen on the life of the mind, suppressed this inheritance. Then, in August 1988, much of what remained went up in smoke when fire destroyed Lisbon's only two department stores. Reconstruction work was overseen by renowned Porto architect Alvaro Siza Vieira, who ensured that some of the former grandeur endured in this neighbourhood of cafés and booksellers, theatres and boutiques. The neighbouring areas of Bica and Bairro Alto are a contradiction in terms: they're old-fashioned residential areas that are dotted with bars and restaurants and, increasingly, funky shops. Further uphill, Príncipe Real is known as the city's thriving gay hub, and is undergoing major development, but it still has bookshops and antiques traders, and a garden favoured by card-playing oldies.

❤ Don't miss

1 Café A Brasileira *p99 and p103*
Coffee and pastries in Chiado.

2 Igreja de São Roque *p105*
Home to the city's most lavish chapel.

3 Igreja do Carmo *p96*
Ruined church still seen by many as Lisbon's loveliest.

4 Bar bonanza *p191*
A taste of Bairro Alto nightlife.

5 Praça do Príncipe Real *p108*
Leafy garden that's great for people watching.

6 Museu Nacional de Arte Contemporânea *p96*
For a crash course in modern Portuguese art.

Ascensor da Bica

WEST OF BAIXA

Restaurants

Cafés & bars

Shops & services

♥ Time to eat & drink

A better class of tasca
Antigo 1º de Maio *p106*, Fidalgo *p106*

Inventive chefs
Alma *p97*, Belcanto *p97*

Seafood and sweets
Aqui Há Peixe *p97*

Sweet treats
Alcôa *p99*, Manteigaria *p100*, Santini *p100*

Traditional food on a budget
Casa Liège *p111*, Das Flores *p98*

Vegetarian heaven
Terra *p109*

♥ Time to shop

Portuguese showcase
Embaixada *p110*

Traditional tiles galore
Sant'Anna *p102*, Solar *p107*

Fine crafts and manufactures
Luvaria Ulisses *p102*, Leitão & Irmão *p102*, Vista Alegre Atlantis *p104*

Fashion favourites
Eureka *p101*, Lanidor Outlet *p101*, Salsa *p102*, Storytailors *p104*

Unusual gifts
Burel *p100*, A Vida Portuguesa *p104*

Books and music
Fnac *p101*

In the know
Getting around

Chiado is on a hillside but best experienced in leisurely fashion, on foot. From the Baixa you could take the **Elevador da Santa Justa** (see *p64*) up to Largo do Carmo, then wander down. The escalators inside Baixa-Chiado Metro station take you as far as Largo do Chiado, where the 28 tram also stops; its route skirts the bottom of the Bairro Alto and the top of Bica. For the upper half of the Bairro Alto, there's the **Ascensor da Glória** (see *p72*) from Praça dos Restauradores; bus 758 also runs past, from Cais do Sodré and Chiado, then on to Príncipe Real, Largo do Rato and beyond. The 24 tram accompanies it part of the way, from Praça Luís de Camões. For Príncipe Real itself, the Metro at Rato is just a 10-minute walk.

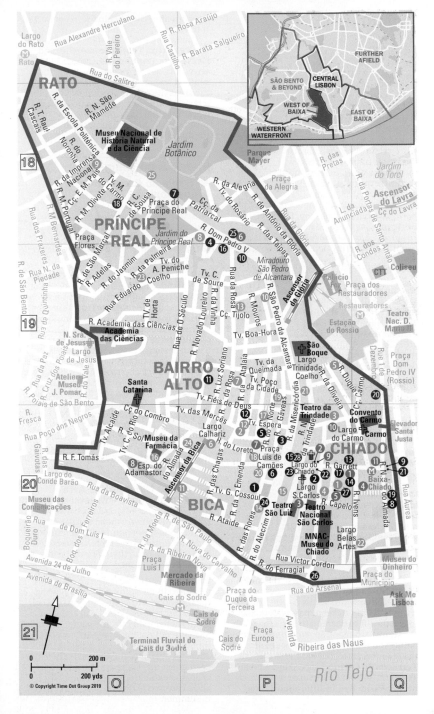

CHIADO

The gentle ascent from Rossio up Rua do Carmo and then along Rua Garrett leads into the heart of the Chiado, known for its upmarket shops and fashion ateliers. On the way, modern boutiques rub shoulders with ancient establishments selling first editions or fine gloves. At the bottom of Rua Garrett is the **Armazéns do Chiado**, a compact mall anchored by Fnac, whose top-floor food court has some good local eateries, plus loos with a view. To enjoy a similar panorama, but comfortably seated and with a well-mixed drink in your hand, head next door to the **Entretanto** bar of the Hotel do Chiado on Rua Nova de Almada.

As you climb Rua Garrett, you pass Portugal's oldest bookshop, **Livraria Bertrand**, inaugurated here in 1773. On Largo do Chiado, **Café A Brasileira** is a traditional meeting point and was once a haunt of writer Fernando Pessoa, whose bronze likeness has a seat on the terrace. Down towards the river, the **Museu Nacional de Arte Contemporânea** houses a collection of Portuguese art from the 19th and 20th centuries. The nearby **Teatro Nacional de São Carlos** (*see p208*), inaugurated in 1793, was modelled on the great Italian opera houses of the time. On the street above stands the Teatro Municipal de São Luiz (*see p210*), whose programme ranges from stand-up to jazz. Further downhill, on Rua do Alecrim, is a cluster of antique and antiquarian bookshops, as well as the over-the-top **Palácio Chiado** – worth exploring even if you don't eat there.

Uphill on the other side of Rua Garrett, Largo do Carmo is one of Lisbon's prettiest squares, fronted by the ruined **Igreja do Carmo**. The former convent of the same name next door is the headquarters of the GNR – the paramilitary National Republican Guard. This was the scene of one of the most memorable moments of the 1974 Revolution: part of the building is now the **Museu da GNR** (21 321 7222, www.arquivomuseugnr.pt), including the room where the then prime minister, Marcello Caetano, took refuge from besieging soldiers (*see p227*).

The walkway from the top of the towering **Elevador da Santa Justa** (*see p64*) runs beside the convent; access is unrestricted. A bus and tram ticket or pass allows you to use the lift to descend to Baixa; to climb the stairs to the rooftop *miradouro* (viewing point) you must have the on-board lift ticket or pay extra. Behind the church, the **Terraços do Carmo** – served by café-bar **TOPO** (21 342 0626) – are part of a project by Siza Vieira that in 2016, almost three decades after the Chiado fire, reconnected it to Carmo.

On nearby Rua Nova da Trindade stands the **Teatro da Trindade** (*see p210*) and **Cervejaria Trindade** (no.20C, 21 342 3506, www.cervejariatrindade.pt), where the seafood and steak is unremarkable but the fabulous tile panels warrant stopping for a beer. Nearby is the **Bairro do Avillez**, a gourmet 'neighbourhood' created by prolific chef, José Avillez (*see p97* Cheffing in Chiado).

Sights & museums

♥ Igreja do Carmo/Museu Arqueológico

Largo do Carmo (21 347 8629, www.museuarqueologicodocarmo.pt). Metro Baixa-Chiado or tram 24, 28. **Open** *10am-6pm Mon-Sat (to 7pm June-Sept).* **Admission** *€4; €3 reductions; free under-15s. No cards.* **Map** *p95 Q20.*

The Gothic lines of the Church of Our Lady of Mount Carmel went up on the orders of Nun'Álvares Pereira, who helped Dom João I consolidate the rule of Portugal's second dynasty, the House of Avis. Pereira, known as the Condestável, or Constable, founded the church and attached convent to fulfil a pledge made before a battle, and was adamant in his choice of location – despite the nearby precipice and various false starts after foundations caved in. During the 1755 earthquake the roof fell in on a crowd of All Saints' Day worshippers, leaving only the walls and some vault ribbing still standing. Said by many to be the most beautiful church in Lisbon, it remains roofless. The Archaeological Museum, a ragbag of European finds, is at the far end of the church.

♥ Museu Nacional de Arte Contemporânea – Museu do Chiado

Rua Serpa Pinto 4 (21 343 2148, www.museuartecontemporanea.gov.pt). Metro Baixa-Chiado or tram 28. **Open** *10am-6pm Tue-Sun (last entry 5.30pm).* **Admission** *€4.50; €2.25 reductions; free under-13s. No cards.* **Map** *p95 P20.*

Founded in 1911, this state-run museum reopened in 1994 after a hiatus following the Chiado fire. Notwithstanding the cool, modernist redesign by French architect Jean-Michel Wilmotte, the name – National Museum of Contemporary Art – overstates things somewhat given its small size. Still, it offers an overview of 19th- and 20th-century Portuguese art. There are also ambitious changing exhibitions of contemporary art, and a café and patio that host jazz concerts in summer.

Cheffing in Chiado

One local chef's empire just keeps growing

José Avillez may no longer be the only Portuguese chef to oversee a restaurant with two Michelin stars – his **Belcanto** (*see below*) is in 2019 joined by Henrique Sá Pessoa's **Alma** (*see p97*). But his achievement in hanging on to them – thanks also to his head chef, David Jesus – is all the more impressive given his growing culinary empire.

Avillez is the leading figure in a new generation (he was born in 1979) of chefs who value Portuguese traditions while using modern techniques – in his case after working with Ferran Adrià and Alain Ducasse. The recognition won by such talents as Alexandre Silva of **LOCO** (*see p136*) is in part thanks to Avillez's promotion of this new cuisine. It was back in 2009 that he became the first Portuguese chef to bring a Michelin star to Lisbon, at Tavares (*see p105*), a restaurant dating back to 1784 previously known for unchallenging gourmet cuisine. Avillez flew the coop two years later and Tavares lost its star. Within a year the Michelin judges had starred his new place, Belcanto – another long-established haven from whose old menu he salvaged *ovos à professor* – an egg dish devised by a customer in the 1960s –in a '21st-century' version served at **Cantinho do Avillez** (Rua dos Duques de Bragança 7, 21 199 2369, http://cantinhodoavillez.pt, €€€), his informal eaterie nearby.

There are further riffs on tradition at his **Café Lisboa** (21 191 4498, www.cafelisboa. pt, €€€) in the Teatro Nacional de São Carlos: the coffee sauce on the house steak is a Chiado classic, while the *pastel Lisboa*, a meat pasty, has 12th-century origins.

Round the corner in the Teatro São Luiz are gourmet snacks, modish house drinks and a DJ-driven ambience at **Mini Bar** (21 130 5393, www.minibar.pt, €€€), which has an offshoot in Porto. Down from the Cantinho on Rua Duques de Bragança is his **Pizzaria Lisboa** (no.5H, 21 155 4945, www.pizzarialisboa.pt, €€) and there's street food uphill at **Pitaria** (Rua Nova da Trindade 11, www.pitaria.pt, €), which peddles posh stuffed pitta. But nearby Avillez has a whole 'neighbourhood', **Bairro do Avillez** (Rua Nova da Trindade 18, 21 099 8320, www.bairrodoavillez. pt): **Mercearia** for light snacks; **Taberna** (€€€) for more elaborate dishes; **Páteo** (€€€€) for seafood and **Beco** (€€€€) for haute cuisine and a show.

His company, Grupo José Avillez (www. joseavillez.pt), now has other ventures around the city, several in partnership with foreign chefs. All these ventures offer great food and good value, but for a real sense of Avillez's culinary wizardry you must eat at Belcanto, where signature dishes include 'Dip in the Sea' (sea bass with seaweed and bivalves) and 'Suckling Pig Revisited'. From *amuse-bouches* to petits fours, a meal here is a dining experience involving all the senses.

WEST OF BAIXA

Restaurants

💙 Alma €€€€
*Rua de Anchieta 15 (21 347 0650, www. almalisboa.pt). Metro Baixa-Chiado. **Open** 12.30-3.30pm, 7-11pm Tue-Sun. **Map** p95 P20* ❶ *Portuguese*

Chef Henrique Sá Pessoa was Lisbon's big winner at the launch of the 2019 *Michelin Guide*, securing a second star for this restaurant. Dishes here are based on a deep knowledge of traditional Portuguese cuisine, but also Sá Pessoa's experience working in top kitchens abroad, which shows through above all in Asian influences. There's a five-course seafood menu and a tasting menu with five signature dishes; you can also order à la carte, though there's little for vegetarians.

💙 Aqui Há Peixe €€€
*Rua da Trindade 18A (21 343 2154, www. aquihapeixe.pt). Metro Baixa-Chiado. **Open** noon-4pm, 7-11pm Tue-Fri; 7-11pm Sat, Sun. **Map** p95 P20* ❸ *Seafood*

This prettily decorated restaurant brings a breath of sea air to the city: its regulars include local artists and politicians but it retains an informal ambience. The seafood is wonderful – from the more affordable grilled fish of the day, or squid in *beurre blanc* sauce, to the blowout *cataplana* stew or shellfish sold by the kilo. The homemade desserts are a big draw too. For unreconstructed meat-eaters there's Brazilian *picanha* beef, served with black beans.

💙 Belcanto €€€€
*Largo de São Carlos 10 (21 342 0607, www. belcanto.pt). Metro Baixa-Chiado. **Open** 12.30-3pm, 7.30-11pm Tue-Sat. **Map** p95 P20* ❹ *Portuguese*

José Avillez (*see also p97* Cheffing in Chiado) had already made his name when he took over this space opposite the opera house in 2010. Within a year, it had won a Michelin star and, for many, established itself as Lisbon's top restaurant. In 2014, it won a second star; this has been reconfirmed for 2019. His

Igreja do Carmo p96

'revisited' Portuguese cuisine is exemplified in dishes such as *cozido à portuguesa* – a traditional stew, but here with each flavour clearly distinguishable. There are two different tasting menus but you can order à la carte.

Café Buenos Aires €€€
Calçada do Duque 31 (21 342 0739, www. cafebuenosaires.pt). Metro Rossio or Baixa-Chiado. **Open** *noon-1am daily.* **No cards.** **Map** *p95 P19* ⑤ *Argentinian/ International*

It's all about the cross-cultural vibe at this evocatively decorated little bistro run by an Argentinian and a Portuguese who met in Paris. The steak is good, as are the Margaritas, though there isn't much else beyond *tartines* and salads, and it's not cheap. But the wine list is decent and the terrace buzzes in summer. There's now a larger and equally charmingly decorated offshoot round the corner, **Café Buenos Aires na Fábrica** (Rua do Duque 22).

❤ Das Flores €
Rua das Flores 76 (21 342 8828). Metro Baixa-Chiado or tram 28. **Open** *noon-3.30pm Mon-Sat.* **Map** *p95 p20* ⑭ *Portuguese*

Beware: there are several places on and around Rua das Flores with similar names; this one, which only opens for lunch, undoubtedly offers the best value. So book ahead or arrive early. The meat croquettes are famous, but there's plenty of other delicious simple fare such as *alheira* (garlic sausage)

and grilled or steamed fish, as well as soups and salads.

Palácio Chiado €€€
Rua do Alecrim 70 (21 010 1184, www. palaciochiado.pt). **Open** *noon-midnight Mon-Thur, Sun (kitchen closes 11pm); noon-2am Fri, Sat (kitchen closes midnight).* **Map** *p95 P20* ⑮ *International*

Various bars and restaurants in this luxurious 18th-century former mansion are overseen by one chef, Manuel Boía, but their concepts vary dramatically: from gourmet Portuguese snacks through Italian risottos and 'healthy and veggie' options to roast octopus and aged entrecôte. One bar is named after Junot, the French general who lived here after invading Portugal in 1807.

SEA ME €€
Rua do Loreto 21 (21 346 1564, www. peixariamoderna.com). Metro Baixa-Chiado or tram 28. **Open** *12.30-3.30pm, 7pm-midnight Mon-Thur; 12.30-3.30pm, 7pm-1am Fri; 12.30pm-1am Sat; 12.30pm-midnight Sun.* **Map** *p95 P20* ⑱ *Seafood/Japanese*

'*Peixaria Moderna*' – a modern fishmonger – is how SEA ME styles itself: it seeks to combine the excellence of the fresh seafood found in gourmet restaurants with the informality of traditional Lisbon *marisqueiras*. It's not the place for a leisurely or intimate meal – the tables are packed in tight and noise levels can be alarming – but it is good for a fast feast of molluscs, grilled fish or sushi, and there's an excellent wine list to boot. Like any *marisqueira*, it also does *prego* (steak sandwich), served here in a sweet *bolo do caco* from Madeira – it's so popular that there's now a spinoff chain, **O Prego da Peixaria** (www.opregodapeixaria.com). **Other location** Time Out Mercado da Ribeira (*see p116*).

Taberna da Rua das Flores €€
*Rua das Flores 103 (21 347 9418). Metro Baixa-Chiado or tram 28. **Open** noon-4pm, 5-11.30pm Mon-Sat. **No cards**. Map p95 P20* 20 *Portuguese*

Founded by three veterans of the Lisbon scene, this tiny place (come early or queue) specialises in traditional lunch fare such as *iscas com elas* (liver in pig's spleen sauce), *meiadesfeita de bacalhau* (codfish fins) and *miomba* (a sandwich made with sliced pork shoulder). For dinner, there might be *mexilhões à bulhão pato* (mussels in garlic and coriander sauce), *lingueirão na chapa* (seared razor clams) or *pâté de ovas de pescada* (haddock roe pâté with toast). Only Lisbon wines are served, drunk from a traditional tiny *copo de três*. You can also buy gourmet products to take away.

Tacho à Mesa by Faz Gostos €€€
*Rua Nova da Trindade 11 (92 528 6086, www.fazgostoslx.com). Metro Baixa-Chiado. **Open** noon-3pm, 7-11.30pm Mon-Fri; 7-11.30pm Sat. Map p95 P19* 21 *Portuguese*

A transplant from the Algarve that thankfully brought with it some of the region's best food. That means rice dishes with *ameijoas* (clams) or *lingueirão* (razor clams), as well as a range of meats and sausages. The decor blends modernity with tradition in the form of a lovely sweep of *azulejos*, and informality: your food arrives still in the cooking pot – ideal for splitting between diners to keep prices down. The all-in menus are good value.

Tágide €€€€
*Largo da Academia Nacional de Belas Artes 18 (21 340 4010, www.restaurantetagide.com). Tram 28 or metro Baixa-Chiado. **Open** 12.30-3pm, 7.30pm-midnight Mon-Sat. Map p95 Q20* 22 *Portuguese*

Away from the hustle of Chiado's main drag, this refined yet friendly place has one of the most amazing views you'll find in any Lisbon restaurant. The food is fairly conservative Portuguese fare, expertly prepared and served. Reservations are essential but downstairs is walk-in bar **Tágide Wine & Tapas**, with a similarly stunning view and excellent Portuguese wines and snacks. Tágide also manages the tram-themed café in the square (noon-9pm Mon-Thur, noon-10pm Fri, Sat).

Cafés & bars
❤ Alcôa
*Rua Garrett 37 (21 136 7183, www.pastelaria-alcoa.com). Metro Baixa-Chiado or tram 28. **Open** 9am-11pm daily. Map p95 P20* 1

Alcôa, a famous pastry maker based in Alcobaça, opened this branch in 2017, and it is a sight for sore eyes. Not only is it in a listed premises lined with modern *azulejos* by Querubim Lapa, but it has a dazzling array of *doces conventuais* – sweets originally devised by nuns with time and a lot of egg yolks on their hands. **Other location** Gourmet Experience Lisboa, El Corte Inglés (*p149*).

❤ Café A Brasileira
*Rua Garrett 120 (21 346 9541). Metro Baixa-Chiado or tram 28. **Open** 8am-2am daily. Map p95 P20* 2

When this café opened in 1905, customers not only got a free *bica* (espresso) when they bought a bag of beans, but the waiters were courteous too. These days prices are steep (especially outside) and the service is offhand. Inside is a little cheaper and you can gawp at the carved wood interior and modern art. At its 1920s peak, A Brasileira underpinned the idea that while Coimbra studied and Porto worked, Lisbon talked and made revolution. Now it's mainly tourists taking snaps by the Pessoa statue or listening to buskers playing in the square. The atmosphere is best after midnight, when flotsam from the Bairro Alto – including the odd tipsy local intellectual – washes in.

Café no Chiado
*Largo do Picadeiro 10 (21 346 0501, www.cafenochiado.com). Metro Baixa-Chiado or tram 28. **Open** 10am-midnight daily. Map p95 P20* 3

Civilised yet informal, this café is great for settling down to an afternoon with the papers. The terrace has better and cheaper coffee than Café A Brasileira and is more peaceful; even the trams rattling past provide a photo opportunity. The place is a lunch favourite with media types, who tuck into Caesar salad and English roast beef, as well as Portuguese fare. It's owned by the Centro Nacional de Cultura, which was a much-needed cultural catalyst under the Salazar dictatorship; its library and internet space are upstairs (open 10am-1pm, 2-6pm Mon-Fri).

Fábulas
*Calçada Nova de São Francisco 14 (21 601 8472, www.fabulas.pt). Metro Baixa-Chiado. **Open** Nov-Feb 11am-11pm Mon, Wed, Thur, Sun; 11am-midnight Fri, Sat. Mar-Oct 11am-11pm Mon-Thur, Sun; 11am-midnight Fri, Sat. Map p95 Q20* 4

The jumble of old furniture dotted about this cave-like former storage space makes for a pleasantly informal drinking experience. As well as substantial salads and unusual toasted sandwiches, which go down nicely with the well-priced house red, there are several mains, tasty cakes and tarts, and a range of herbal teas. A roomy annexe has more seating and art exhibitions.

Kaffeehaus
Rua Anchieta 3 (21 095 6828, www. kaffeehaus-lisboa.com). Metro Baixa-Chiado or tram 28. **Open** *9.30am-4pm Mon; 9.30am-midnight Tue- Sat; 9.30am-8pm Sun.* **Map** *p95 P20* ❺

This Austrian-owned café brings a touch of Viennese class to Lisbon. The filling fare on offer includes Wiener schnitzel, *spätzle*, *apfelstrudel* and Sachertorte, and there's delicious hot chocolate too. There are also vegetarian options and a brunch menu every day until noon. A range of foreign newspapers hangs by the door.

❤ Manteigaria
Rua do Loreto 2 (21 347 1492). **Open** *8am-midnight daily.* **Map** *p95 P20* ❼

The chiselled name on the façade – Manteigaria União – is of the dairy that once occupied this space. This 'butter shop' opened only in 2014 but rapidly established its reputation with crisp and creamy *pastéis de nata* (custard tarts) that some locals maintain are better even than those of the famous pastry shop in Belém (*see p129*). Test them yourself – ideally just after the bell rings, heralding a batch warm from the oven. **Other location** Time Out Market, Mercado da Ribeira (*see p116*).

Pastelaria Bénard
Rua Garrett 104 (21 347 3133). Metro Baixa-Chiado or tram 28. **Open** *8am-11pm Mon-Sat.* **Map** *p95 P20* ❾

Top-notch coffee and cakes are served here, in a tearoom that's one of Lisbon's oldest (and whose waiting staff certainly act as though they've seen it all before). You can also lunch here, but, as at nearby Café A Brasileira (*see p99*), prices all but triple if you sit outside.

Royale Café
Largo Rafael Bordalo Pinheiro 29 R/C E (21 346 9125, 93 861 1370, www.royalecafe.com). Metro Baixa-Chiado. **Open** *noon-midnight Mon-Fri, 11am-midnight Sat; 11am-11pm Sun.* **Map** *p95 P20* ❿

A Scandinavian café serving Mediterranean food – that sums up this stylish place with a patio where everything except the rye bread is made on site. Ingredients feature organic

or regional specialities such as *chouriço de cebola* (onion sausage) and *queijo da serra* cheese; herbal teas are made from loose leaves, and there are old-fashioned tipples such as *quinado* (a fortified wine flavoured with quinine) and *licor de pinho* (pine liqueur) served with orange, mint and cinnamon.

❤ Santini
Rua do Carmo 9 (21 346 8431, deliveries 91 500 1103, www.santini.pt). Metro Baixa-Chiado. **Open** *11am-midnight daily.* **Map** *p95 Q20* ⓫

The original ice-cream parlour in Cascais, opened in 1949 by Italian expat Attilio Santini, was patronised by local high society, including the Spanish royal family in exile. At this downtown outlet the firm's all-natural ice-creams and sorbets are just as popular. It delivers too. **Other locations** Time Out Market, Mercado da Ribeira (*see p116*); Museu Nacional dos Coches, Belém (*see p128*); Avenida Dom João II, Lote 1.16.01, Parque das Nações.

Shops & services

BdMania
Rua das Flores 67 (21 346 1208, 93 446 1207, www.bdmania.pt). Metro Baixa-Chiado or tram 28. **Open** *10.30am-7.30pm Mon-Sat.* **Map** *p95 P20* ❶ *Comics*

As well as importing comics from the US, France, Spain and Belgium, BdMania issues some of its own publications. Avid collectors will also find all the related merchandise (posters, models and T-shirts) they could possibly want.

❤ Burel
Rua Serpa Pinto 15B (21 245 6910, www. burelfactory.com). Metro Baixa-Chiado. **Open** *10am-8pm Mon-Sat, 11am-7pm Sun.* **Map** *p95 P20* ❷ *Fashion & handicrafts*

Burel is a material made from compacted wool, long used by shepherds in the Serra da Estrela, Portugal's highest mountain range, to protect them from cold, wet winters. The capes, jackets and bags sold here are made in one of the last remaining factories in the town of Manteigas, in both traditional and colourful new designs, so helping preserve the culture of a unique region.

A Carioca
Rua da Misericórdia 9 (21 346 9567, 21 342 0377). Metro Baixa-Chiado or tram 28. **Open** *9am-7pm Mon-Fri; 9am-1pm Sat.* **No cards.** **Map** *p95 P20* ❸ *Food & drink*

Established in 1936, and still retaining its original interior, this shop sells everything

Fernando Pessoa

gold-trimmed, handmade pieces with striking designs in stainless steel or silver, plus a selection of other high-quality homewares.

♥ Eureka
Rua Nova do Almada 26 (21 346 8173, www.eurekashoes.com). Metro Baixa-Chiado. **Open** *10am-7.30pm daily.* **Map** *p95 Q20* **8** *Fashion*

Striking modern footwear by local designers including Lidija Kolovrat (*see p110*) and Nuno Gama are on sale at this store owned by Alberto Sousa, one of Portugal's largest shoe manufacturers. There's a wide range of men's and women's styles, from restrained to bold. **Other locations** Rua Bernardino Costa 43, Cais do Sodré (21 137 9771); Dolce Vita Monumental, Avenida Fontes Pereira de Melo 51, Saldanha (21 315 0466).

♥ Fnac
Armazéns do Chiado, Rua do Carmo 2 (707 313 435, www.fnac.pt). Metro Baixa-Chiado or tram 28. **Open** *10am-10pm daily.* **Map** *p95 Q20* **9** *Books & music*

The anchor store for the Armazéns do Chiado mini-mall, Fnac is a pleasant place to while away an hour or two browsing the shelves. It has a good range of Portuguese literature in translation, as well as lots of originals in English, French and Spanish. The music department also has a great selection: Portuguese, Brazilian and African music, plus jazz, classical, world, pop and rock. There are decent computer, camera and audiovisual departments, a counter where you can buy tickets for most major shows, and a café with a programme of talks, films and concerts. **Other locations** Amoreiras Shopping Center (*see p139*); Atrium Saldanha, Praça Duque de Saldanha 1; Centro Colombo (*see p149*); Centro Vasco da Gama (*see p154*).

Gardénia
Rua Garrett 54 (93 451 3158, www.gardenia.com.pt). Metro Baixa-Chiado or tram 28. **Open** *10am-10pm daily.* **Map** *p95 P20* **13** *Fashion & acessories*

Tiny Gardénia is a compulsory stop for local footwear fetishists, thanks to an always interesting selection of funky Portuguese and foreign brands. Its other shop uphill stocks men's shoes only. **Other location** Largo Rafael Bordalo Pinheiro 2, Chiado (91 192 3287).

♥ Lanidor Outlet
Rua Ivens 70 (93 203 2520, www.lanidor.com). Metro Baixa-Chiado or tram 28. **Open** *11am-8pm Mon-Sat.* **Map** *p95 P20* **14** *Fashion*

Lanidor is one of the more upmarket Portuguese fashion chains, a safe bet in

from cheap coffee-chicory mixtures to specialist beans costing up to €20 per kilo. Staff make up blends on request and grind them to suit your coffee-maker; they're also happy to let you taste other products. The shop also stocks teas and tisanes. Round the corner at Rua Garrett 38, **Casa Pereira** operates a similar business, but also imports a handsome range of tea, biscuits and chocolates.

Cutipol
Rua do Alecrim 84 (21 322 5075, www.cutipol.pt). Metro Baixa-Chiado or tram 28. **Open** *10am-2pm, 3-7pm Tue-Sat.* **Map** *p95 P20* **6** *Homewares*

Portugal's leading Portuguese cutlery maker, Cutipol sells both machine-produced and

terms of both price and quality, offering stylish and restrained womenswear plus clothes for children and young teens. This small store (which also carries items from its trendier stablemate, Globe) is its only presence downtown. **Other locations** throughout the city.

♥ Leitão & Irmão

Largo do Chiado 16 (21 325 7870, www.leitao-irmao.com). Metro Baixa-Chiado or tram 28. **Open** *10am-7pm daily. Closed Jan-Mar .* **Map** *p95 P20* **⑮** *Jewellery/tableware*

The flagship store of Portugal's most famous gold- and silversmith, whose workshop is in the Bairro Alto, showcases its tableware and jewellery to stunning effect. Leitão & Irmão first opened a store here in 1877 and it was patronised by the court as it spearheaded a revival of Portuguese gold-working traditions. Some pieces, such as the 1942 crown of Our Lady of Fátima, are one-offs, but other historic lines, such as a 1917 silver cutlery set by René Lalique, are still in production. **Other locations** Travessa da Espera 8, Bairro Alto (21 342 4107); Hotel Ritz Four Seasons (*see p242*).

Livraria Bertrand

Rua Garrett 73-75 (21 347 6122, www.bertrand.pt). Metro Baixa-Chiado or tram 28. **Open** *9am-10pm daily.* **Map** *p95 P20* **⑰** *Books*

Bertrand was founded in 1732 (it moved to its current location some 50 years later), making it Portugal's oldest bookshop. Apart from local literature, it stocks a reasonable selection of English novels, as well as guidebooks and foreign magazines. **Other locations** throughout the city.

♥ Luvaria Ulisses

Rua do Carmo 87A (21 342 0295, www.luvariaulisses.com). Metro Baixa-Chiado or Rossio. **Open** *10am-7pm Mon-Sat.* **Map** *p95 Q19* **⑳** *Accessories*

In the know
Refreshing changes

The kiosk that does a roaring trade on Praça Luís de Camões is a relatively new arrival; it used to be in far-off Jardim das Amoreiras. Many of these structures – which for a century served as cafés, news stands or lottery agencies – had fallen into disuse. In recent years, licences have been issued for renovated kiosks (and several new ones) to sell traditional non-alcholic *refrescos* such as *capilé* (a lemon and chicory drink), home-made lemonade and redcurrant *groselha*.

In this tiny shop – in business since 1925 and now the only one of its kind in the country – rows of drawers contain exquisite gloves indexed by size, colour and material, available in quarter sizes. There are leather, lace, crocheted and sporting varieties, lined with fur, cashmere or silk. All come with a simple guarantee: a free, unlimited repair service.

Parfois

Armazéns do Chiado, Rua do Carmo 2 (93 226 4370, www.parfois.com). Metro Baixa-Chiado. **Open** *10am-10pm daily.* **Map** *p95 Q20* **㉑** *Accessories*

With scores of outlets in Portugal, this nimble chain has now spread to dozens of other countries where it's battling it out with British rival Accessorize. Its products feature cheap and cheerful styles, from earrings and keychains to travel bags and umbrellas. **Other locations** throughout the city.

Paris em Lisboa

Rua Garrett 77 (21 342 4329, www.parisemlisboa.pt). Metro Baixa-Chiado or tram 28. **Open** *10am-7pm Mon-Sat.* **Map** *p95 P20* **㉒** *Home furnishings*

The name and façade reflect a Portuguese fixation with French style that predates 1888, when the shop opened. Local *senhoras bem* (posh ladies) still flock here to stock up on towels, bedlinen and tablecloths, even if some of the best are now made in Portugal.

♥ Salsa

Largo do Chiado 13-15 (21 098 7295, www.salsa.pt). Metro Baixa-Chiado or tram 28. **Open** *10am-8pm Mon-Sat; 11am-7pm Sun.* **Map** *p95 P20* **㉓** *Jeans*

Don't be fooled by the name: this jeans manufacturer is Portuguese (here *salsa* means 'parsley'). It found favour with local youngsters with its fitted and push-up models and is now striving to take the brand upmarket and expand abroad. **Other locations** throughout the city.

♥ Sant'Anna

Rua do Alecrim 95 (21 342 2537, www.santanna.com.pt). Metro Baixa-Chiado or tram 28. **Open** *9.30am-7pm Mon-Fri; 10am-7pm Sat.* **Map** *p95 P20* **㉔** *Tiles*

Sant'Anna has been producing handmade tiles since 1741 and sells copies of designs dating from the 17th and 18th centuries. The firm is happy to manufacture to order and ship abroad. If you love beautiful old things, note the brace of antiquarian bookshops opposite.**Other location** Factory showroom, Calçada da Boa-Hora 94B, Ajuda (21 363 8292).

💜 Coffee & pastries

Cafés ready to fuel the local addiction to coffee and sugar are everywhere in Lisbon, ranging from workaday *pastelarias* (pastry shops) to smart *esplanadas* (outdoor seating) on the main avenues.

This is no recent phenomenon: Portugal, as one-time ruler of the world's largest coffee producer, Brazil, has long had access to the finest of beans. In Lisbon, the growth of empire and rise of the bourgeoisie saw an artistic and political café society emerge in Chiado. Later, the larger cafés on Rossio had popular appeal and a stream of customers from the new railway station. In the 1940s, with the rest of Europe at war, they all flourished; however, two decades later, most were gone. Recent years have seen a revival of the Chiado, and now Lisbon has more places to sip coffee than ever.

Beans here come in four levels of quality; gold (highest), platinum, diamond and bar (lowest). The finest coffee will be freshly ground gold; it is worth asking staff which grade they are using. As for what to order, you could just say '*um café, por favor*', but expect a tiny dose of a bitter brew. In any case, why not test the staff's patience by showing your appreciation of Portuguese culture?

For a milky coffee, served in a glass, ask for *um galão*, but tack on *da máquina* (from the machine) or else the coffee may come from a tankful that's been standing around (a budget option). The nearest thing to a cappuccino is *uma meia da leite* ('half milk'). To make sure it's strong and hot, end the phrase with *da máquina com leite quente* (with hot milk).

Most locals opt for a straight café (*uma bica*, in Lisbon waiters' slang) or, if desperate, *um duplo* (double), and then offset the bitterness with sugar. Dieters might instead cut it with a drop (*pingo*) of milk, ordering *um café pingado*. The other way round – a few drops of coffee in milk – is *um garoto* (literally, 'a young boy'); this can be qualified with *claro* or *escuro* (light/dark).

Coffee drinkers who like the strength just so can order *um café cheio/curto* (more/less diluted). Strongest of all is *uma italiana*, while *um carioca* (not to be confused with *carioca de limão*, which is lemon rind in hot water – great for a cold) is a tad weaker than a *cheio*. *Um abatanado* is still more diluted, and so comes in a larger cup. For a different kind of boost, try *um café com cheirinho* – 'with a whiff' of *aguardente* (grape mash distillate). A decaf is *um descafeinado*.

Some fans of piping hot coffee spurn cups from on top of the machine, where crockery is left to dry, for fear of burning their lips. They order *um café escaldado numa chávena fria* (scalded, in a cold cup). Perhaps no one goes so far as to request *um café descafeinado escaldado pingado numa chávena fria*, but all other orders cited above can be heard in Lisbon cafés.

Thankfully, ordering a cake or pastry to accompany your coffee is more straightforward: the offer is laid out before you, so you can just point at what you fancy. The best-known Portuguese pastry is the *pastel de nata*, or custard tart, which reaches its acme at **Antiga Confeitaria de Belém** (*see p129*), more commonly known as Pastéis de Belém, and, downtown, **Manteigaria** (*see p100*). The many others includes *pastéis de feijão*, with a filling made from beans; *bolos de arroz*, little rice-flour cakes; *sonhos* ('dreams'), jam-free doughnuts; and *broas de mel*, honey-flavoured cornbread.

Vista Alegre

♥ Storytailors

Calçada do Ferragial 8 (21 343 2306, www. storytailors.pt). Metro Baixa-Chiado or tram 28. **Open** *11am-7pm Tue-Sat.* **Map** *p95 P21* **㉖** *Fashion*

Plunge into a world of fantasy tales with Storytailors' funky yet sophisticated ready-to-wear and made-to-measure clothes. Everything from corsets to capes feature exquisite detail and opulent fabrics. The atelier-cum-store is an atmospheric place to indulge.

♥ A Vida Portuguesa

Rua Anchieta 11 (21 346 5073, www. avidaportuguesa.com). Metro Baixa-Chiado or tram 28. **Open** *10am-8pm Mon-Sat; 11am-8pm Sun.* **Map** *p95 P20* **㉗** *Gifts & souvenirs*

Though this shop stocks handicrafts, it's best known for giving a new lease of life to venerable Portuguese brands of soap and other toiletries, foodstuffs, stationery and toys. All are beautifully presented, many in old-style packaging that triggers bouts of nostalgia among older customers. **Other locations** Rua Ivens 2, Chiado (21 007 9536); Largo do Intendente Pina Manique 23 (21 197 4512); Time Out Market, Mercado da Ribeira (*see p116*)

♥ Vista Alegre

Largo do Chiado 20 (21 346 1401, www. vistaalegre.pt). Metro Baixa-Chiado or tram 28. **Open** *10am-8pm daily.* **Map** *p95 P20* **㉘** *Tableware*

Vista Alegre is the best-known Portuguese porcelain brand, with a wide range of plates, other crockery, vases and bowls in traditional designs, oriental styles and modern classics. It also has handmade Portuguese lead crystal, ranging from copies of 18th-century goblets to modern glassware. **Other locations** throughout the city.

BAIRRO ALTO

When Dom Manuel I moved his residence down from the castle to the waterfront in the early 1500s, the axis of Lisbon's development shifted west: harbour activity expanded along Cais do Sodré, while up the hill the level ground outside the 14th-century Muralha Fernandina city wall was divided into lots and sold to aristocrats and the emerging merchant class. The Jesuits set up in the **Igreja de São Roque** and the quarter – its more or less regular street plan predating the Baixa – became known as the Bairro Alto de São Roque (upper neighbourhood of St Roch). Wealthy merchants later gave way to small shopkeepers and, for a while, there were print shops and newspaper offices. Both Rua de O Século and Rua do Diário de Notícias are named after newspapers once based here.

During the day the Bairro Alto is relatively quiet, especially since almost all cars were banished years ago. A few shops are dotted about, plus arts hotspot **Galeria Zé dos Bois**, which for 25 years has promoted new artists working in less conventional fields.

But this is mainly a residential area and by day the streets rarely bustle.

At night it's another story. The area is full of restaurants, ranging from *tascas* to places serving smart cosmopolitan cuisine. As the night wears on, thousands of revellers cram into these narrow streets, hopping from bar to bar. For more on the area's nightlife, *see p191*.

The Bairro Alto has also long had Lisbon's largest collection of fado houses. **Café Luso** on Travessa da Queimada is Lisbon's oldest, with **Adega Machado** (for both, *see p201*) on Rua do Norte almost as venerable, whereas **Tasca do Chico** (*see p203*) is cheaper and less formal. All these places love tourists, but Portuguese frequent them too.

At the southern edge of the Bairro Alto is **Praça Luís de Camões**, adjoining Largo do Chiado to the east. A monumental statue designed by Vítor Bastos was unveiled in 1867 at its centre; it represents the 16th-century epic poet Luís de Camões, standing on a pedestal ringed by smaller statues of Portuguese authors – all now atop an underground car park.

From here, if you walk up Rua da Misericórdia you will pass **Tavares** (no.37, 21 342 1112, http://restaurantetavares. pt), a gilded restaurant that's been in business since 1784. Further uphill is the **Associação 25 de Abril** (no.95, 21 324 1420), which strives to keep memories of the 1974 Revolution alive. The square in front of the **Igreja de São Roque** is Largo de Trindade Coelho, although locals tend to call it Largo da Misericórdia, after the social welfare institution whose head offices are there. On the square's western side stands the Palácio de São Roque, which from 2019 is to house a new museum, the **Casa Ásia – Colecção Francisco Capelo**, showcasing some 1,200 artworks from across Asia collected by the eponymous businessman who also amassed the fashion and design collections of **MUDE** (*see p64*). Antiquarian and second-hand bookshops once clustered here but are gradually being edged out. A scenic staircase, the Calçada do Duque, leads from Largo da Misericórdia down to Rossio, passing **Café Buenos Aires** (*see p98*) and other restaurants, and more bookshops.

Further uphill is the **Jardim de São Pedro de Alcântara**, a garden *miradouro* on two levels laid out in the early 19th century that offers splendid views over the Avenida da Liberdade business district, the Baixa, Castelo and the river. There is live music here some nights in summer. The **Ascensor da Glória** funicular has been whisking passengers down and up the steep Calçada da Glória between the *miradouro* and Restauradores since 1885. The **Solar do Vinho do Porto** (www.ivdp.pt), a swish

bar dedicated to port wine where you can choose from some 300 varieties, is across from the funicular's upper terminal but is closed while the building is turned into a port-themed hotel.

The bit of street running past the *miradouro* is named after the Convento de São Pedro de Alcântara, at its upper end; it's worth a look at the blue-tiled depiction of St Peter of Alcantara's stigmata, by the entrance. The north of the Bairro Alto was barely affected by the 1755 earthquake. An alley halfway down Rua da Rosa leads to the Colégio dos Inglesinhos, founded in 1628, a time when English Catholics were forced to flee their country or be thrown in prison. The religious foundation was closed in 1973; the building is now a luxury residential complex.

On the Bairro Alto's western edge, Rua do Século is home to Portugal's constitutional court, a dance conservatory and galleries. At no.79 is the 16th-century palace built by Sebastião de Carvalho e Melo, grandfather of the future Marquês de Pombal, who was born here. Now municipally owned, it houses a lively arts space, **Carpe Diem** (21 197 7102). At no.123, the **Convento de Cardaes** (21 342 7525) is an active convent that also runs guided tours; its shop has lovely handicrafts. Round the corner in Rua da Academia das Ciências is a venerable scientific academy whose **Museu Geológico** (no.19, 21 346 3915) has historically important collections, including a vast range of fossils.

Sights & museums

♥ Igreja de São Roque/ Museu de São Roque

Largo de Trindade Coelho (21 323 5444, www.museudesaoroque.com). Metro Baixo-Chiado or Restauradores then Ascensor da Glória. **Church** *(with break for mass 12.30pm Tue-Sun) Oct-Mar 2-6pm Mon; 9am-6pm Tue-Sun. Apr-Sept 2-7pm Mon; 9am-7pm Tue, Wed, Fri-Sun; 9am-8pm Thur.* **Museum** *Opens one hour later Tue-Sun.* **Admission** *Church free. Museum €2.50; €1 reductions; free under-15s, over-64s & all Sun to 2pm. No cards.* **Map** *p95 P19.*

The Igreja de São Roque was built for the Jesuits with the assistance of Filippo Terzi on the site of an earlier chapel dedicated to St Roch. Most of the single-nave structure was built between 1565 and 1573, although it was roofless for another decade. The original architect had planned a vaulted roof, but in 1582 a decision was made to flatroof the space in wood, and sturdy timber from Prussia was richly painted. The paintings in the inner sacristy are worth seeing, but the main attraction is the side chapel dedicated to St John the Baptist: its lavish ivory, gold and lapis lazuli attests to Portugal's colonial wealth and extravagance. Built in Rome and shipped to Lisbon in 1749 after being blessed by the Pope, it took four years to reassemble. The museum's treasures include Italian goldsmiths' work and richly embroidered vestments.

Restaurants

♥ Antigo 1° de Maio €€

Rua da Atalaia 8 (21 342 6840). Metro Baixa-Chiado or tram 28. **Open** *noon-3pm, 7-11pm Mon-Fri; 7-11pm Sat.* **Map** *p95 P20* ❷
Portuguese

The queue outside the saloon-style swing doors every night testifies to the popularity of this budget classic. At lunchtime, too, canny regulars cram round snugly fitted tables, tucking into grilled fish or meat dishes, served fast and with a smile, at reasonable prices. For something a bit fancier, go for *osso buco* (stewed oxtail) or partridge. Traditional desserts include *bolo de bolacha* (a biscuit-and-cream layer cake) and eggy *sericaia*, flavoured with cinnamon and lemon.

Casanostra €€

Travessa Poço da Cidade 60 (21 342 5931, http://casanostra.pt). Metro Baixa-Chiado or tram 28. **Open** *12.30-2.30pm, 8-11pm Mon-Fri; 8-11pm Sat; 1-3pm, 8-11pm Sun.* **Map** *p95 P19* ❼ *Italian*

Portugal's first decent Italian when it opened in 1986, Casanostra is still a Bairro Alto staple. It keeps ahead of the pack with authentic ingredients flown over from Italy and designer pasta from owner Maria Paola. For pizza, look to its takeaway spin-off in Príncipe Real, **Pizza à Pezzi** (Rua Dom Pedro V 84, 93 456 3170, http://pizzapezzi.pt).

Decadente €€

Rua de São Pedro de Alcântara 81 (21 346 1381, www.thedecadente.pt). Metro Baixa-Chiado. **Restaurant** *noon-3pm, 7pm-midnight Mon-Fri; noon-4pm, 7pm-midnight Sat,Sun.* **Bar** *6pm-midnight Mon-Wed, Sun; 6pm-1am Thur; 6pm-2am Fri, Sat.* **Map** *p95 P19* ❿ *Portuguese*

This restaurant on the ground floor of a funky hostel offers interesting dishes made from Portuguese ingredients. It's popular, so it's worth booking ahead. The back patio is sheltered from sun and wind, and has a retractable roof for when it rains. Of snacks available all day, the tomato soup and *pica pau* (marinated beef) are good. This is a nice spot for weekend brunch, a mid-afternoon snack or a cocktail. On the hostel's roof, the

pricier **Insólito** has a breathtaking view across to the castle and a menu that ranges from oysters and carpaccio to sophisticated vegetarian fare.

♥ Fidalgo €€

Rua da Barroca 27 (21 342 2900). Metro Baixa-Chiado or tram 28. **Open** *noon-3pm, 7-11pm Mon-Sat.* **Map** *p95 P20* ⓬
Portuguese

Fidalgo has remained a *tasca* at heart for decades, despite today's contemporary decor and occasional flight of culinary fancy. You'll find well-prepared dishes such as octopus rice, medallions of wild boar and *bacalhau à Brás*. The desserts are delicious: try profiteroles or berry tart.

Flor da Laranja €€

Rua da Rosa 206 (21 342 2996). Metro Baixa-Chiado or bus 758, 790. **Open** *Lunch by reservation only. Dinner 7-11pm daily.* **Map** *p95 P19* ⓭ *Moroccan*

The most authentic of Lisbon's few Moroccan eateries, with traditional starters such as spinach with preserved lemon and marinated carrots, and then decent helpings of couscous royale or lamb tagine with prunes (or vegetarian alternatives). To finish, the passion fruit and orange egg pudding is a house standard.

Primavera do Jerónimo €€

Travessa da Espera 34 (21 342 0477). Metro Baixa-Chiado or tram 28. **Open** *7.30-11.30pm Mon-Sat.* **No cards**. **Map** *p95 P20* ⓱
Portuguese

Igreja de São Roque *p105*

Solar

At this long-established haven, known to locals simply as Primavera, the menu features hearty soups, clams in white wine, braised liver and other meaty concoctions, as well as grilled fresh fish and *bacalhau*. The kitchen is on full view from the tiny dining room, where talking points are provided by tiles bearing Portuguese proverbs, framed articles and a photograph of Josephine Baker above the table where she ate.

Sinal Vermelho €€

Rua das Gáveas 89 (21 346 1252). Metro Baixa-Chiado or tram 28. **Open** *6.30pm-midnight Mon, Sat; noon-midnight Tue-Fri.* **Map** *p95 P19* ⑲ *Portuguese*

Stop at the 'Red Light' for reliably good food from this bustling Bairro Alto standard, now with tables outside in summer. *Peixinhos da horta* (tempura green beans) and baked cod are among the house staples.

Shops & services

Cork & Co

Rua das Salgadeiras 10 (21 609 0231, www. corkandcompany.pt). Metro Baixa-Chiado or tram 28. **Open** *11am-8pm Mon-Sat; 5-7pm Sun.* **Map** *p95 P20* ⑤ *Accessories*

One of several companies that are finding amazing uses for one of Portugal's most important products. Here you'll find everything from handbags to lampshades and umbrellas made from cork. If you don't know how the raw material is harvested and processed, do ask – it's fascinating.

Galeria da Arcada

Rua Dom Pedro V 49, Porta A (91 474 9417, 91 978 7521, www.galeriadaarcada.com). Bus 758, 790. **Open** *10am-1pm, 3-7pm Mon-Fri; 3-7pm Sat.* **Map** *p95 P19* ⑩ *Antiques*

An impressive collection of religious carvings from the 15th to the 19th centuries, primarily from Portugal, ranging from tiny crucifixes right up to life-size depictions of Biblical scenes.

Galeria Graça Brandão

Rua dos Caetanos 26A (21 346 9183, 91 986 1469, www.galeriagracabrandao.com). Metro Baixa-Chiado. **Open** *11am-7pm Tue-Sat. Closed Aug.* **No cards.** **Map** *p95 P19* ⑪ *Gallery*

The spotlight at this commercial gallery is on high-quality art from Portuguese-speaking countries, especially Brazil. Albano Afonso and Victor Arruda are among artists represented in a modern space that retains traces of its industrial past.

Galeria Zé dos Bois

Rua da Barroca 59 (21 343 0205, www. zedosbois.org). Metro Baixa-Chiado or tram 28. **Open** *Exhibitions 6-10pm Wed-Sat.* **Admission** *Exhibitions €3.* **Map** *p95 P20* ⑫ *Gallery*

For 25 years now, this not-for-profit centre based in an 18th-century former palace has showcased and promoted contemporary creativity of various kinds: from visual and performing arts to film and music. It hosts frequently changing exhibitions, as well as artist residencies, workshops, theatre and dance performances, and concerts of experimental music (*see p192*). Its bars stay open well past midnight; its rooftop terrace is a great place to lounge on summer nights.

Louie Louie

Escadinhas do Santo Espírito da Pedreira 23 (21 347 2232, www.louielouie.biz). Metro Baixa-Chiado. **Open** *11am-7.30pm Mon-Sat; 3-7.30pm Sun.* **Map** *p95 Q20* ⑲ *Music*

Thousands of new and second-hand CDs (from €5) and vinyl records are on display in this airy store accessed via a quiet stairway that connects Rua Nova de Almada to Rua do Crucifixo. Genres range widely, from hip hop to dark and industrial, and there's plenty of Portuguese and Brazilian music to delve into.

❤ Solar

Rua Dom Pedro V 70 (21 346 5522, www.solar. com.pt). Metro Rato or Baixo-Chiado, or bus 58. **Open** *10am-7pm Mon-Fri; 10am-1pm Sat (closed Sat in July & Aug).* **Map** *p95 P18* ㉕ *Tiles*

An incredible collection of over half a million antique *azulejos* from the 15th to the 19th centuries, displayed chronologically. They come mainly from old palaces, churches and houses.

PRÍNCIPE REAL

Rua Dom Pedro V, the continuation of Rua de São Pedro de Alcântara, leads north to **Praça do Príncipe Real**. There are antique stores and bookshops here, as well as the **Pavilhão Chinês** (*see p194*), the bar with the best interior decor in Lisbon. Príncipe Real is to an extent a continuation of the Bairro Alto, especially for the gay and lesbian community, which still has plenty of bars and clubs to choose from here (*see p193*), but the area is changing as foreign money floods in – the **Memmo Príncipe Real** (*see p242*) is one of several hip hotels to open here of late. There are still remnants of olden days, though, such as **Faz Frio** at no.96, where the wooden dining booths once common in Lisbon restaurants have been beautifully restored.

The **Jardim do Príncipe Real** at the neighbourhood's heart is one of the city's most romantic gardens, with two café terraces on which to linger until midnight or later. The park was laid out in 1860, with lots of exotic imported greenery. On sunny afternoons old men play cards at one end, while lovers curl up on benches under the 150-year-old cedar tree, grown out horizontally to provide more shade. Nearby, a memorial to victims of homophobia represents someone inside a closet, trying to get out, according to local rights group Opus Gay (its name a pun on that of ultra-conservative Opus Dei, which has clout in Catholic Portugal).

At the garden's centre, steps lead down into the **Reservatório da Patriarcal**, an underground reservoir inaugurated in 1856 that has been disused since the 1940s; it is now part of the **Museu da Água** (*see p91*). On Saturdays the garden also hosts the weekly **Mercado Biológico do Príncipe Real**, Lisbon's oldest organic market, where you can pick up herbs, olive oil and bread as well as fresh produce.

The square is ringed by pastel-painted buildings, the most notable being the Arabesque palace at no.26, built in the late 19th century as the Palácio Ribeiro da Cunha and now redeveloped as a trendy shopping gallery, **Embaixada**. The streets between Príncipe Real and Rua de São Bento are a grid of townhouses that are home to, among others, the British Council on Rua de São Marçal.

On Rua da Escola Politécnica is the **Museu Nacional de História Natural e da Ciência**; a path alongside it leads to the **Jardim Botânico de Lisboa**. On the way you'll pass the **Teatro da Politécnica** (*see p213*), home to one of Lisbon's most active theatre troupes, Artistas Unidos.

Sights & museums

Jardim Botânico de Lisboa

Rua da Escola Politécnica (21 392 1800, www.museus.ulisboa.pt/en) . Metro Rato. **Open** *Oct-Mar 9am-5pm daily. Apr-Sept 9am-8pm daily. Last entry 30mins before closing.* **Admission** *€3; €1.50 reductions; free under-6s. Joint ticket with Museu Nacional de História Natural e da Ciência €6; €3.50 reductions. No cards.* **Map** *p95 P18.*

The shaded walkways of the university's Botanical Garden, laid out between 1858 and 1878, are surrounded by some 10,000 plants. It's a lovely place to wander on hot days – though do remember that what goes down must come up, and the garden is on the slope of a hill. The Borboletário (butterfly house), home to an unrivalled range of Iberian species, is open from mid March to mid November.

Museu Nacional de História Natural e da Ciência

Rua da Escola Politécnica 56 (21 392 1808, www.museus.ulisboa.pt/en). Metro Rato. **Open** *10am-5pm Tue-Fri; 11am-6pm Sat, Sun. Last entry 30mins before closing.* **Admission** *€5; €3 reductions; free under-6s & all Sun to 2pm. Joint ticket with Jardim Botânico €6; €3.50 reductions. No cards.* **Map** *p95 O18.*

The National Museum of Natural History and Science brings together several university-run museums under one roof. Phenomena such as momentum, centripetal force, the properties of a vacuum and the speed of sound are demonstrated in entertaining and practical ways. The museum has a collection of antique instruments and organises temporary exhibitions, lectures and courses for non-specialists, some taking place next door in the 19th-century planetarium. There are also historically important anthropological and zoological collections, from seashells to stuffed animals, and a mineralogical department with astonishing glittery rocks.

Restaurants

A Cevicheria €€€

Rua Dom Pedro V 129 (21 803 8815, www. chefkiko.com). Metro Rato or bus 758, 773. **Open** *12.30pm-midnight daily.* **Map** *p95 P18* ❽ *Ceviche*

Five years after it opened, queues still form daily (you can't book) outside this bright little place for the chance to savour the excellent ceviche and pisco sours served inside. Don't worry: staff serve bites and drinks through the window as you wait. The chef behind it, Kiko Martins – born in Brazil to Portuguese parents, studied cuisine in Paris and trotted the globe – is nothing if not eclectic. His temple to meat near the Gulbenkian, **O Talho** (Rua Carlos Testa 1B, 21 315 4105), predates Cevicheria, while **O Asiático** in the Bairro Alto (Rua da Rosa 317, 21 131 9369) tours Asia's cuisines.

Comida de Santo €€€

Calçada Engenheiro Miguel Pais 39 (21 396 3339, www.comidadesanto.pt). Metro Rato. **Open** *12.30-3.30pm, 7.30pm-midnight Mon, Wed-Sun. Closed lunch Aug.* **Map** *p95 O18* ❾ *Brazilian*

This deservedly enduring restaurant serves hearty Brazilian food in hearty Brazilian surroundings: greenery, papier-mâché toucans and other tropical tat. Its *feijoada* and other classic dishes are as good as any in town, but the real secret is the cosy atmosphere. There's a surprisingly good selection of vegetarian dishes on offer, plus lots of sticky Brazilian desserts.

❤ Terra €€

Rua da Palmeira 15 (21 342 1407, www. restaurante terra.pt). Metro Rato. **Open** *12.30-3pm, 7.30pm-midnight Tue-Sun (kitchen closes 10.30pm).* **Map** *p95 O19* ㉓ *Vegetarian*

Buffet dining only (€15.90, weekday lunch €12.50), with a plethora of organic vegetarian delights: sushi, kebabs, an adaptation of *cozido* (Portuguese stew), plus homemade vegan ice-cream and crumble. You pay extra for drinks, which include juices made on the premises (try the ginger), beer and wines. In an 18th-century building, two dining areas are filled with Portuguese furniture and decorative items from around the world. Out back are more tables in a garden.

ZeroZero €€

Rua da Escola Politécnica 32 (21 342 0091, www.pizzeriazerozero.pt). Metro Rato. **Open** *noon-midnight Mon-Thur, Sun; noon-1am Fri, Sat.* **Map** *p95 O18* ㉕ *Pizza*

Praça do Príncipe Real

Here pizzas are made with slow-fermented dough and topped with authentic Italian ingredients, then cooked in a wood-fired oven. There are also great cocktails, best sipped in the back garden. At busy times you may have to queue – giving you time to browse the Italian salamis and cheeses for sale. For a takeaway, rival **Pizza a Pezzi** down the street (Rua Dom Pedro V 84) is also good. **Other locations** Alameda dos Oceanos, Lote 2.11.01H, Parque das Nações (21 895 7016).

Cafés & bars

Lost In

Rua Dom Pedro V 56D (91 775 9282, www. lostinesplanada.com) Metro Baixa-Chiado, or metro Avenida then Ascensor da Glória. **Open** *4pm-midnight Mon; 12.30pm-midnight Tue-Sat.* **No cards.** **Map** *p95 P18* ❻

Duck through a tunnel past the store selling funky Indian clothing and trinkets to a terrace with a breathtaking view over central Lisbon. Here you can nestle in a wicker chair and sip a drink or snack on a salad or wrap (full meals are available 7.30-10.30pm). You can order tea and scones at any time too. On the same block, the **Memmo Príncipe Real** (*see p242*) hotel affords a similar panorama and has a swish cocktail bar.

Shops & services

Charcutaria Moy

Rua Dom Pedro V 111 (21 346 7011). Metro Rato or bus 758, 790. **Open** *10am-8pm daily (closed 1-2pm Sat, Sun).* **Map** *p95 P18* ❹ *Food & drink*

This rather pricey delicatessen carries a decent range of French and Italian luxury foods, as well as good-quality local products, including fine wines.

❤ Embaixada

Praça do Príncipe Real 26 (96 530 9154, www.embaixadalx.pt). Metro Rato. **Shops** *11am-7pm daily.* **Café-bar** *noon-midnight Mon-Thur, Sun; noon-2am Fri, Sat.* **Map** *p95 O18* ❼ *Mall*

This self-appointed 'conceptual shopping gallery' in an iconic 19th-century neo-Moorish building, revamped by Pritzker Prize winner Eduardo Souto Moura, hosts the grooviest of Portuguese retailers. There's everything from exclusive footwear to jewellery, organic cosmetics and babywear, and you can eat and drink here with a view of the botanical garden.

Lidija Kolovrat

Rua Dom Pedro V 79 (21 387 4536, www. lidijakolovrat.org). Metro Rato. **Open** *11am-8pm Mon-Sat.* **Map** *p95 P19* ❶❻ *Fashion & accessories*

Art meets fashion in this magnificently revamped former bakery run by Bosnian-born, long-time Lisbon resident Kolovrat. The price tags on her creations are reasonable; whether you'd walk down the street in them is another matter. The space also showcases other designers' work, accessories and perfumes, as well as staging art shows and events.

Livraria Britânica

Rua de São Marçal 83 (21 342 8472, http:// livrariabritanica.pt). Metro Rato. **Open** *9.30am-8pm Mon-Fri; 9.30am-1pm Sat.* **Map** *p95 O18* ❶❽ *Books & music*

Although a specialist in study books, this English-language bookshop hard by the British Council also has an excellent range of novels, classics, children's books, bestsellers and recent releases.

BICA & SANTA CATARINA

The **Ascensor da Bica** funicular (7am-8.55pm Mon-Sat, 9am-8.55pm Sun) snails its way up a steep street from Cais do Sodré to the lower end of the Bairro Alto, beginning its journey in a building down on Rua de São Paulo. It climbs through one of Lisbon's quirkiest old *bairros*, an area where fashionable restaurants and bars coexist with tatty grocers and taverns.

A landslide swept away much of an earlier Bica during an earthquake in 1598. Topping out the neighbourhood now is the **Esplanada do Adamastor** (aka Santa Catarina *miradouro*), where the kiosk often serves drinks deep into a summer night. Crowds admire the wonderful view over the Tagus or lie on the lawn under the statue of the Adamastor – the mythical monster who guarded the Cape of Good Hope in Camões's *Lusiads*. The pink mansion overlooking the square above the *miradouro* is the HQ of the Pharmacists' Association, housing the surprisingly good **Museu da Farmácia** and restaurant **Pharmácia**. Nearby stands the **Verride Palácio Santa Catarina** (*see p242*), a hip luxury hotel.

If you like to wash away your sins in gilt, head down Calçada do Combro to the **Igreja de Santa Catarina**, which boasts one of the city's most sumptuous interiors. Behind the church (under the arch and down the alley beside it) is a quiet esplanade mainly patronised by locals. For somewhere more fashionable – and great views – walk back up to the multi-storey car park and take the lift to fashionable rooftop bar **Park** (*see p192*).

Sights & museums

Igreja de Santa Catarina
Calçada do Combro (21 346 4443). Tram 28. **Open** *8.30am-12.30pm, 2-5pm daily.* **Admission** *free.* **Map** *p95 O19.*

The original religious foundation here dates from 1647, but it was remodelled after the 1755 earthquake. The adjoining monastery is now a National Guard barracks, but the church is still in use and contains gilt dating to the late 17th century, as well as a ceiling that's a masterpiece of 18th-century stucco in rococo style. Paintings on the side walls include works by Vieira Lusitano and André Gonçalves, two of Portugal's leading 18th-century artists.

Museu da Farmácia
Rua Marechal Saldanha 1 (21 340 0680, www.museudafarmacia.pt). Metro Baixa-Chiado or tram 28. **Open** *10am-7pm daily (last entry 6.30p)m.* **Admission** *€5; €3.50 reductions. No cards.* **Map** *p95 O20.*

The Pharmaceutical Museum is packed with fascinating items: European medical implements and model infirmaries from medieval times onwards; ancient Roman and Greek artefacts; Tibetan medical charts and Arab medicine chests. The full-scale mock-ups of pharmacies through the centuries are painstakingly done. The building also houses a fine restaurant, **Pharmácia** (*see p111*).

Restaurants

❤ Casa Liège €
Rua da Bica de Duarte Belo 72 (21 342 2794, 91 898 3036). Metro Baixa-Chiado or tram 28. **Open** *noon-3pm, 7-10pm Mon-Sat.* **No cards.** **Map** *p95 P20* ❻ *Portuguese*

A friendly *tasca* at the top of the Ascensor da Bica, Casa Liège makes a great pit stop if you're on a budget, like the groups of students that often pile in. For three decades, the cook has turned out local favourites such as *pernil de porco* (leg of pork), *pataniscas de bacalhau* (cod fritters), *bitoque* (cheap steak, served with egg and chips) and, in summer, grilled meats.

Estrela da Bica €€
Travessa do Cabral 33 (21 347 3310). Metro Baixa-Chiado or Cais do Sodré, or tram 28. **Open** *7.30pm-midnight daily Mon-Sat; 6.30pm-midnight Sun (dinner from 7.30pm).* **Map** *p95 P20* ⓫ *Portuguese/International*

This trendy café-bar-restaurant at the lower end of Bica, with battered wooden furniture, draws an arty crowd. The food is very different from your average Lisbon tavern: beetroot burgers, say, or salmon with a chia crust. Staff make their own bread, too.

Pharmácia €€
Rua Marechal Saldanha 1 (21 346 2146). Metro Baixa-Chiado or tram 28. **Open** *noon-1am daily.* **Map** *p95 O20* ⓰ *Portuguese*

The garden of the **Museu da Farmácia** (*see p111*) is its big draw, but the kitchen that serves it is overseen by Susana Felicidade, a leading light of Lisbon's *taberna* revival. Tasty snacks abound, from salads and *tibornas* (open sandwiches) to duck croquettes, aubergine rolls with goat's cheese, dates and fresh mint, and fried cuttlefish. More substantial dishes include rice with razor clams and coriander. As well as excellent Portuguese wines, there are cocktails with alarming pharmaceutical names. Chef Susana also has a stall, **Cozinha da Felicidade**, in the Time Out Market, Mercado da Ribeira (*see p116*).

Toma Lá Dá Cá €€
Travessa do Sequeiro 38 (21 347 9243). Metro Baixa-Chiado or tram 28. **Open** *noon-3pm, 7.30-11pm Mon-Sat.* **Map** *p95 P20* ㉔ *Portuguese/International*

This unpretentious little restaurant with a *calçada à portuguesa* mosaic floor serves food that's fancy for the price. Dishes range from *nacos de vitela Maronesa* (succulent veal chunks) or pork steak *gratiné*, to fondue and *emincé* with rösti, as well as a dozen types of fish, including grilled tuna and salmon. You can't book, so turn up early or be prepared to wait on the street.

Cafés & bars

Noobai
Miradouro do Adamastor (21 346 5014, www.noobaicafe.com). Metro Baixa-Chiado or tram 28. **Open** *10.30am-midnight daily.* **No cards.** **Map** *p95 O20* ❽

Right next to the Esplanada do Adamastor and boasting the same river views, Noobai is set apart from the noisy scene that takes over the area as the night wears on. On sunny days staff set out tables on the rooftop terrace, but there's more space downstairs. A modish menu offers Mediterranean snacks such as stuffed vegetables, risottos and couscous. There are also tarts, cakes and scones, plus great caipirinhas. It's good for families, as there's a well-stocked play area.

Western Waterfront

The banks of the River Tagus once provided the berths for fishing boats and the shipyards that fitted out the caravels and *naus* (sailing ships) of the Discoveries. With the reclamation of land and laying of a rail line and roads, Lisbon turned its back on the river. It finally woke up to the wonders of the waterfront in the 1990s, and the area has drawn restaurants, bars and joggers ever since. Tourists troop daily through Belém's raft of museums ranging from the awe-inspiring Mosteiro dos Jerónimos to the city's leading arts hub, the Centro Cultural de Belém (CCB), with anything and everything from naval history to carriages to planets in between. Once you've gorged yourself on culture, take time to indulge in another of the area's unmissable treats – the famous custard tarts of the Antiga Confeitaria de Belém in its beautifully tiled restaurant.

❤ **Don't miss**

1 Belém's monuments *p126*
Redolent of past maritime exploits.

2 Museu Nacional de Arte Antiga *p117*
Portuguese art in full.

3 Time Out Market - Mercado da Ribeira *p116* *and p39*
Gourmet food hall pioneered by *Time Out Lisboa*.

4 MAAT *p124*
Gleaming Museum of Art, Architecture and Technology.

5 LX Factory *p121*
Fashion and food for those in the know.

6 CCB/Museu Coleção Berardo *p125*
Culture galore, especially modern art.

7 Museu do Oriente *p119*
An abundance of Asian artefacts.

Padrão dos Descobrimentos *p128*

CAIS DO SODRÉ

Immediately west of Praça do Comércio is a walkway along the river to the Cais do Sodré train, Metro and boat stations. This area – the **Ribeira das Naus** – has been transformed in recent years, with a new promenade, steps down to the river and lawns laid out next to the remains (now open to view) of the docks where ocean-exploring ships were built during the 15th and 16th centuries.

At rush hour at Cais do Sodré, commuters head every which way (beachgoers too in summer) as this is the end of the line for many buses and trains, as well as the terminal for ferries to Cacilhas. From here, a cycle path runs along the river to **Belém** (*see p122*), with Pessoa's *Ode to the Tagus* spooling out on the tarmac.

As is the tradition in port areas, there has long been a red-light area just in from the river, and a few prostitutes still loll around Praça de São Paulo. Otherwise, the area has been all but taken over by a stream of trendy bars and offers some of the city's buzziest nightlife (*see p195*).

The **Mercado da Ribeira**, built in 1882, is a grand old market hall on Avenida 24 de Julho; with cafés that open early, it's a popular spot for late-night revellers to sip hot chocolate in winter while waiting for the first train home. A little later, stallholders start unpacking fruit and veg, and in the afternoon the place is a blaze of colour as the flower sellers take over. In recent years the western nave of the market has been transformed into a foodie heaven (*see p39* Gourmet Food Markets).

▶ *For boat trips on the River Tagus, see p57 River Tagus.*

Restaurants

Confraria Lx €€€

Rua do Alecrim 12A (21 342 6292, www. lxboutiquehotel.com/en/restaurant). Metro Cais do Sodré or tram 15, 18. **Open** *noon-3pm, 7.30pm-midnight Mon-Thur, Sun; noon-3pm, 7.30pm-2am Fri; noon-4pm, 7.30pm-2am Sat.* **Map** *p114 P21* ❷ *Japanese*

It can be hard to get a table at this prettily decorated offshoot of Cascais favourite Confraria (Rua Luis Xavier Palmeirim 14, 21 483 4614), housed in a boutique hotel, so book ahead. All the sushi is good, but the *gyoza* and *niguiri* are really special. There's occasional live music too.

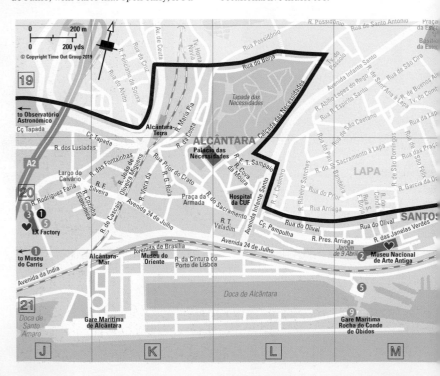

♥ Time to eat & drink

All-day decadence
Pensão Amor *p116*

Culinary travels
Feitoria *p129*

Gourmet food on the go
Time Out Market *p116*

Portuguese perfection
Antiga Confeitaria de Belém
p129, Guarda-Mor *p118*

Too much to choose from
LX Factory *p121*

♥ Time to shop

Museum treasure
Centro Cultural de
Belém *p125*, Museu Nacional
de Arte Antiga *p117*

Best for books
Ler Devagar *p120*

In the know
Getting around

Cais do Sodré is a terminal
for the Metro green line;
from here mainline trains
run west via Santos,
Alcântara and Belém to
Algés and beyond. Trams
15 and 18 stop nearby,
as do a plethora of buses,
running mostly parallel
to the river. Bus 728 is
the fastest bus to Belém
from downtown, starting
at Parque das Nações and
passing Santa Apolónia
and Cais do Sodré. The 714
starts at Praça da Figueira
and runs via Santos, where
it's joined by the 727
from Marquês de Pombal;
both run past the Museu
Nacional de Arte Antiga and
LX Factory in Alcântara,
then to Belém.

WESTERN WATERFRONT

Restaurants
1. Cantina LX *p120*
2. Confraria Lx *p114*
3. Guarda-Mor *p118*
4. Ibo *p116*
5. Malaca Too *p120*
6. Pap'Açôrda *p116*
7. Taberna Tosca *p116*
8. A Travessa *p118*
9. Último Porto *p118*

Cafés & bars
1. Buzz Lisboeta *p120*
2. Le Chat *p118*
3. Landeau Chocolate *p120*
4. Pensão Amor *p116*
5. Zazah Good View *p119*

Shops & services
1. Ler Devagar *p120*
2. Time Out Market/Mercado da Ribeira *p116*

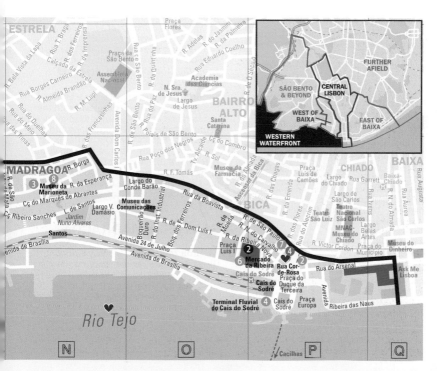

Ibo €€€

*Cais do Sodré (21 342 3611, www.ibo-
restaurante.pt). Metro Cais do Sodré.* **Open**
*12.30-3pm, 7.30-11pm Tue-Fri; 12.30-3pm,
7.30pm-1am Sat; 12.30-3.30pm Sun.* **Map**
p114 P21 ❹ *African/Portuguese*

Best known for serving food with a
Mozambican influence, Ibo is also notable
for its pleasing design and fantastic riverside
location. The menu ranges from chicken and
goat curries (with a strong Goan influence)
through a panoply of top-notch seafood to
tenderloin steak served with various sauces.
For dessert, try the stuffed papaya.

Pap'Açôrda €€€

*Mercado da Ribeira (1st floor), Avenida 24 de
Julho 50 (21 346 4811).* **Open** *noon-midnight Tue, Wed, Sun; noon-
2am Fri, Sat.* **Map** *p114 O21* ❻ *Portuguese*

This Lisbon institution's (formerly of the
Bairro Alto) key elements are the *pastéis de
massa tenra* (fried meat pasties), the rich
açordas (seafood bread soups) from which the
restaurant takes its name, its famed chocolate
mousse, and even the huge chandelier that
greets guests as they enter. A lunchtime
three-course Market Menu, made with
seasonal ingredients, is now available for €20
including a glass of wine and a coffee.

Taberna Tosca €€

*Praça de São Paulo 21 (21 803 4563, http://
tabernatosca.com). Metro Cais do Sodré.*
Open *12.30pm-midnight Mon-Thur, Sun;
12.30pm-2am Fri, Sat.* **Map** *p114 P20* ❼
Portuguese

Tosca is one of the new breed of gourmet
tabernas situated in Lisbon's hottest nightlife
zone. It serves traditional snacks, such as
fried cuttlefish, *pataniscas de bacalhau* (cod
fritters) or eggs with *farinheira* sausage, in
decent portions – three or four choices make
a light supper for two. There's a wide range
of wines served by the glass. You can eat in
the tastefully renovated interior, complete
with stone arches, or out on the square. The
place keeps relatively late hours, but note
that the kitchen closes an hour before staff
shut up shop.

Cafés & bars

❤ Pensão Amor

*Rua do Alecrim 19, (21 314 3399/www.
artbuilding.eu). Metro Cais do Sodré.* **Open**
*2pm-3am Mon-Wed, Sun; 2pm-4am Thur-
Sat.* **Map** *p114 P21* ❹

The name means 'Love Boarding House'
– a nod at the building's past as a place of
business for sex workers and their clients.

Time Out Market

Trendy locals now flock here to see and be
seen in the over-the-top lounge bar – a sort
of decadent tearoom, open all afternoon
and into the night – and attached rooms,
including a shop selling erotic books. The
background music, though invariably fairly
unintrusive, is eclectic. Later on there is live
music or an old-style disco. There is another
entrance down on Rua Nova do Carvalho
('Pink Street').

Shops & services

❤ Time Out Market/Mercado da Ribeira

*Avenida 24 de Julho 50 (21 346 2966). Metro
Cais do Sodré.* **Fresh produce** *6am-2pm
daily.* **Flowers** *6am-8pm daily.* **Time Out
Market** *10am-midnight Mon-Wed, Sun;
10am-2am Thur-Sat.* **Map** *p114 P21* ❷
Market

Lisbon's main market hall is a tale of two
halves: the old fresh produce market in the
eastern nave, and the gourmet food court
in the western one. Every afternoon and
evening the latter's Time Out Market pulls in
hundreds of trendy locals and foreign visitors
eager to sample snacks and drinks dreamed
up by top local chefs (*see p39* Gourmet food
markets). Upstairs is the new home of classic
Lisbon restaurant **Pap'Açôrda** (*see left*).

SANTOS & MADRAGOA

Avenida 24 de Julho is pretty empty during
the day, but at night bar-hopping youngsters
are often out until dawn. Fast-food outlets
in Santos stay open late, serving *caldo verde*
(cabbage soup with a slice of sausage) and
pão com chouriço (sausage bread), warm
from brick ovens.

Santos was named after three saintly
Christian siblings – Verissimus, Julia and
Maxima – who according to tradition were

💙 Museu Nacional de Arte Antiga

Rua das Janelas Verdes (21 391 2800, www. museudearteantiga.pt). Tram 15, 18, 25. **Open** *10am-6pm Tue-Sun. (Last entry 5.30pm.)* **Admission** *€6; €3 reductions; free under-13s. Joint ticket with Museu Nacional do Azulejo & Panteão Nacional €15.* **Map** *p114 M20.*

Housed in a 17th-century former palace, the National Museum of Ancient Art offers the only truly comprehensive panorama of Portuguese art from the 12th to the early 19th centuries.

Its most prized painting is Nuno Gonçalves's enigmatic late 15th-century masterpiece, usually known as the Panels of St Vincent, although its subject is hotly disputed: some say the central figure is Dom Fernando, the Infante Santo (holy prince) who died in captivity in Fez in 1443.

Another priceless treasure is the Custódia de Belém (Belém Monstrance), the most famous work by a Portuguese goldsmith, attributed to Gil Vicente (who is best known as a playwright). Commissioned by the king Dom Manuel I for Monsteiro dos Jerónimos, it was made from metal paid as a tribute by the king of Kilwa (in present-day Tanzania) and brought back by Vasco da Gama from his second voyage to India, in 1503. Its tiny spires exemplify the late Gothic taste for 'micro-architecture'.

Also on display here are important Renaissance paintings from northern Europe, including works by Hieronymous Bosch, Albrecht Dürer and Lucas Cranach, as well as top-notch Chinese porcelain, Indian furniture and African carvings.

Some of the most fascinating exhibits are products of the stylistic mix fostered by the 15th- and 16th-century Discoveries and empire, such as Indo-Portuguese cabinets with legs in the form of snarling tigers or topless women, and chinaware made with designs to order for customers in Portugal from the 16th century onwards. Among the loot from Asia are two Japanese lacquer screens which depict the landing in the 1540s of the 'long noses' from Portugal – a snapshot of what was a key moment for both cultures.

Private sponsorship recently helped fund a new top-floor gallery to showcase the Portuguese furniture collection, which includes two thrones. Since its completion, though, it has spent more time closed than open for lack of security: an ongoing budget squeeze at the Ministry of Culture stopped the museum from taking on the staff it needs. And, for now, plans to expand beyond the current premises have been shelved. Still, this traditionally staid institution has been partnering recently with a promoter better known for staging one of Lisbon's biggest music festivals to put together major exhibitions involving swaps with Madrid's Prado or other foreign museums. (Admission to such shows is separate from the main ticket.)

Here you will also find one of Lisbon's best museum shops, with plenty of books in English, along with a lovely range of tiles, pottery and other arty wares. And the shaded rear garden, with a view out over the river, serves as a terrace for the museum café and is an oasis for the foot-weary.

WESTERN WATERFRONT

martyred by the Romans on the beach here in the early fourth century. It remains home to crumbling monasteries and nunneries, and there are tales of secret tunnels used by enterprising monks in search of lonely nuns. One old royal palace on Rua de Santos-o-Velho is now the French Embassy; legend has it that Christopher Columbus was introduced to his (Portuguese) wife here.

The road running west from the Igreja de Santos-o-Velho – the church believed to stand on the site of the fourth-century shrine – is Rua das Janelas Verdes or 'Street of the Green Windows', after the nickname of the old Alvor Palace that now houses the **Museu Nacional de Arte Antiga** (*see p117*). The museum's shaded rear garden, with a view out over the river, serves as a terrace for the museum café. The area has long been a favourite of visiting artists and writers. Graham Greene and John le Carré are among past guests of nearby posh *pensão* (guesthouse) **York House**, while charming hotel **As Janelas Verdes** was for a time the home of Portuguese novelist Eça de Queiroz and is said to have inspired two of his novels. Another nearby mansion with links to Eça, the Palácio Ramalhete, is now the Lisbon home of Madonna.

Just above the eastern end of Santos is one of Lisbon's most traditional neighbourhoods, **Madragoa**. A feast of fado and fishwives, it once housed a colony of African fishermen, their waterfront irreverence contrasting with the holy orders dwelling in the many nearby houses of religion. Since those days, the railway line and Avenida 24 de Julho have cut the neighbourhood off from the river, and the religious orders were abolished in Portugal back in 1834. The former Convento das Berardas on Rua da Esperança now hosts the **Museu da Marioneta** and a fine restaurant, Luso-Belgian **Travessa**.

Sights & museums

Museu da Marioneta

Convento das Bernardas, Rua da Esperança (21 394 2810, www.museudamarioneta.pt). Tram 15, 18, 25. **Open** *10am-6pm Tue-Sun (last entry 5.30pm).* **Admission** *Museum €5; €4.30 over 65s; €2.50 13-25s; free under-13s & all Sun before 2pm. Shows €7.50; €5 reductions. No cards.* **Map** *p114 N20.*

Housed in a grand 18th-century former convent, the Puppet Museum contains more than 800 marionettes from Portugal and around the world, some created for operas staged by its founders, puppet-maker Helena Vaz and the late composer João Alberto Gil. The convent's former chapel serves as a theatre for puppet shows.

Restaurants

💙 Guarda-Mor €€

Rua do Guarda-Mor 8 (21 397 8663, 96 275 2752, 91 839 3817, www.guarda-mor.com). Tram 25. **Open** *12.30-3pm, 8pm-midnight Tue Fri; 8pm-midnight Sat, Sun.* **Map** *p114 N20* ❸ *Portuguese*

This smart, friendly place serves affordable traditional dishes. As well as some great fried snacks, there's a legendary fish soup. There are fado sessions on Wednesday nights.

A Travessa €€€€

Travessa do Convento das Bernardas 12 (21 390 2034, 21 394 0800, www.atravessa. com). Tram 25, 28. **Open** *7.30pm-midnight Mon-Sat.* **Map** *p114 N20* ❽ *Portuguese/ International*

This Luso-Belgian restaurant is in the Convento das Bernardas – a former nunnery that also houses the Museu da Marioneta (*see p118*). Owners Viviane Durieu and António Moita are usually on hand to guide you through a seasonal menu with five dishes each of fish and meat, plus steak cooked several ways. Look out for *tamboril flamejado* (seared monkfish), *raie au beurre noir* (steamed ray with a burned butter sauce), and their very own partridge pie, featuring wild mushrooms and foie gras. The wine list is exhaustive and there's Belgian beer too.

Último Porto €€

Estação Marítima da Rocha do Conde de Óbidos (21 397 9498). Tram 15, 18. **Open** *12.30-3.30pm Mon-Sat.* **Map** *p114 M21* ❾ *Seafood*

This dockside restaurant (lunch only) in an old boat station is known as one of the best places in Lisbon to tuck into fresh fish, grilled over charcoal, at affordable prices. There are grilled meats too. If the weather's fine, come early to snag an outside table.

Cafés & bars

Le Chat

Jardim 9 de Abril, Rua das Janelas Verdes (21 396 3668, www.facebook.com/ Le.Chat.Lisboa). Tram 25 or bus 713, 714, 727, 760. **Open** *12.30pm-2am Mon-Sat; 12.30pm-midnight Sun. Winter 12.30pm-2am Mon-Sat; 12.30-8pm Sun.* **Map** *p114 M21* ❷

Perched on a cliff next to the Museu Nacional de Arte Antiga (*see p117*), the glass-walled Le Chat is a great place for a coffee or early-evening cocktail. There are DJ sets most evenings from 5pm and 11pm. At weekends, brunch is served until 5.30pm.

Zazah Good View
*Edifício LACS, Cais da Rocha Conde de Óbidos (91 411 3272, http://zazahgoodview. pt). Tram 15, 18. **Open** 4pm-midnight daily.
Map p114 M21* ⑤

The second part of the name says it all: this lounge bar in reconditioned shipping containers sits atop a co-working building in the docks. To your left is a shipyard, to your right a container terminal; beyond lies the River Tagus. An offshoot of an eaterie in Príncipe Real, the bar buzzes at the end of the day when workers pile out of their offices. The attached Okah restaurant (which serves lunch from noon) offers eclectic dishes inspired by Asian cuisines, many with seafood.

ALCÂNTARA & DOCAS

The westernmost end of Avenida 24 de Julho meets the **Alcântara** district in the shadow of the **Ponte 25 de Abril**. It was the longest suspension bridge in Europe when it was built in 1966 as the Ponte Salazar. Its four lanes were then more than enough to handle Lisbon's traffic, but within a few decades it was renowned for rush-hour jams that lasted hours. The opening in 1998 of the Ponte Vasco da Gama in eastern Lisbon to relieve the pressure hasn't solved beach-related jams. In 1999, a railway track that was part of the original design was finally suspended underneath. Since 2017, the **Pilar 7** (Avenida da Índia, 21 111 7880) visitor centre has offered a unique perspective on the structure.

High on the eastern side of the Alcântara valley are the pink walls of the 18th-century Palácio das Necessidades, now the Foreign Ministry. Its leafy park, a former royal hunting ground known as the **Tapada das Necessidades** (closes 6pm in winter, 7pm in summer), contains a notable collection of exotic plants, including one of Europe's oldest cactus gardens. Concerts and DJ sets are staged on the lawn on summer weekends; at other times women are advised not to wander here alone.

Up on the western slopes of the valley is the **Tapada de Ajuda** (entrance on Rua Jau, open 7am-midnight daily), another former hunting ground now attached to an agricultural institute and which contains an important 100-hectare botanical garden that is also the setting for the **Observatório Astronómico de Lisboa** (21 361 6730, http://oal.ul.pt), an elegant institution completed in 1867. To book a guided visit to the still-working astronomical observatory email geral@museus.ul.pt or call 21 392 1808/24/25, if possible two weeks in advance. A little further west is the

hilltop **Capela de Santo Amaro**, a pretty, round hermitage built in 1549. It opens once a month for mass (10am, 1st Sun), but early 17th-century polychrome tile panels recounting the life of St Amaro can be seen in the porch.

The lower part of Alcântara, around the busy public transport hub of Largo do Calvário, was transformed in the 1990s, with nightclubs and restaurants carved out of old warehouses. Along Rua Rodrigues Faria are a couple of African nightclubs popular with kids from the suburbs. At its far end, a new 'creative city' has taken shape in the form of **LX Factory** (*see p121*). Across thousands of square metres, former workshops and storerooms house design studios and art spaces, shops, cafés, restaurants and clubs. The neighbouring tram terminal houses the **Museu do Carris**.

Across the railway tracks and under a flyover is the **Doca de Santo Amaro**, a yachting marina with outdoor terraces, indoor bars and most of the restaurants offering conveyor-belt cuisine. If you live on a boat, the **Doca de Alcântara**, to the east, is a better place to tie up and is home to a fascinating museum, the **Museu do Oriente**.

Sights & museums
Museu do Carris
*Rua 1º de Maio 101 (21 361 3087, http://museu. carris.pt). Tram 15, 18. **Open** 10am-6pm Mon-Fri; 10am-1pm, 2-6pm Sat. (Last entry 30 mins before closing.) **Admission** €4; €2 reductions; free under 6s. **Map** p114 J21.*

At the city transport company's Alcântara hub, kids will delight in decommissioned horse-drawn and electric trams and double-decker buses, while adult buffs can pore over plans and scale models – such as an 1892 model of a funicular.

❤ Museu do Oriente
*Avenida de Brasília (21 358 5200, www. museudooriente.pt). Alcântara Mar rail from Cais do Sodré, bus 712, or tram 15, 18, bus 728, 732, 760 then 10min walk. **Open** 10am-6pm Tue-Thur, Sat, Sun; 10am-10pm Fri. **Admission** €6; €2-€3.50 reductions; free under-6s; free 6-10pm Fri. **Map** p114 K21.*

The Portuguese were the first Europeans to have an enduring presence in Asia, and the Museum of the Orient, opened in 2008, tells the story. The core exhibition includes unique maps and charts, priceless 17th- and 18th-century Chinese and Japanese painted screens and other Namban (Western-influenced) art, and an important collection of artefacts from Timor. The separate 'Shadows of Asia' display has shadow puppets from a swathe of countries from Turkey to South-East Asia, drawn from the vast Kwok On collection. The museum runs courses on everything from languages to cuisine and *ikebana*, as well as hosting music and dance events. The top-floor restaurant has fine views and is popular for weekend brunch.

Restaurants

♥ Cantina LX €€

LX Factory (Edifício C), Rua Rodrigues Faria 21 (21 362 8239, www.cantinalx.com). Tram 15, 18 or bus 714, 727, 732, 751, 756. **Open** *noon-11pm daily.* **Map** *p114 J20* ❶ *Portuguese*

In this former industrial space – the restaurant makes use of the wood-fired oven and battered tables and chairs from its previous long life as a workers' canteen – you can eat well and cheaply. There are several fresh fish and *bacalhau* dishes, while meat options might include pork cheek with asparagus *migas* or duck leg.

♥ Malaca Too €€

LX Factory (Edifício G), Rua Rodrigues Faria 103 (213 477 082, 96 710 4142). Train to Alcântara Mar from Cais do Sodré or tram 15, 18. **Open** *12.30-3pm, 8-11.30pm daily.* **Map** *p114 J20* ❺ *Asian*

This restaurant takes its inspiration from the voyages through Asia of 15th- and 16th-century Portuguese mariners. You might find tempura and *yakitori*, satay, Thai salad, red and green curries, Korean beef (stir-fried with peppers and mushrooms) or spicy steamed fish, plus at least one vegetarian option. Desserts invariably include black sticky rice pudding and green tea ice-cream.

Cafés & bars

Buzz Lisboeta

Village Underground, Mueu da Carris, Estação de Santo Amaro, Rua 1º de Maio 103 (91 111 5533, http://vulisboa.com). Alcântara Mar rail from Cais do Sodré or tram 15, 18. **Open** *11am-7pm daily.* **Map** *p114 J20* ❶

An old double-decker bus perched amid old shipping containers is home for this buzzy snack bar in the Village Underground co-working initiative, modelled on a similarly named one in London. It serves toasties, salads and other light meals, plus waffles and homemade cakes. The €18 weekend brunches are lavish. At the weekend, when Village Underground hosts parties, the café may stay open longer.

♥ Landeau Chocolate

LX Factory, Rua Rodrigues Faria 103 (91 727 8939, www.landeau.pt). Alcântara Mar rail from Cais do Sodré or tram 15, 18. **Open** *7pm Mon-Thur, Sun; noon-11pm Fri, Sat.* **Map** *p114 J20* ❸

When a place makes a good living by selling only one thing, you know there has to be something special about it. In this case, it's a rich chocolate cake deemed by many to be the city's best. **Other location** Rua das Flores 70, Chiado (91 181 0801); Gourmet Experience Lisboa (*see p150*).

Shops & services

♥ Ler Devagar

LX Factory (Edifício G), Rua Rodrigues Faria 103 (21 325 9992, www.lerdevagar. com). Alcântara Mar rail from Cais do Sodré or tram 15, 18. **Open** *11am-9pm Mon, Sun; 11am-11pm Tue-Thur; 11am-1am Fri, Sat.* **Map** *p114 J20* ❶ *Books*

Housed in an old printing works, this ambitious venture – dubbed 'Read Slowly' – is an important cultural centre with a busy programme of debates and exhibitions. As for the books, the English section has political and social science tomes, as well as literature and the arts, but the shop is stronger on French- and Portuguese-language titles.

Ler Devagar

❤ LX Factory

Rua Rodrigues Faria 103 (21 314 3399, www. lxfactory.com). Tram 15, 18 or bus 714, 720, 727, 732, 738, 742, 751, 756, 760. Map p114 J20.

For decades this area was abandoned, but since 2008 it has come back to life as LX Factory, a 'creative city' within a city with late-opening shops, cafés, restaurants and creative ateliers, and other micro-enterprises, all thriving within the old (and often still crumbling) walls. Its mix of bustle and leisure makes it Lisbon's hippest district.

The old industrial ambience has been maintained here; from 1846 it was home to textile manufacturer Companhia de Fiação e Tecidos Lisbonense and later to a string of other industrial companies, some of which have left behind massive machines.

For shopping, the best day is Sunday, when the popular **LX Market** (www. lxmarket.com.pt) runs from 11am to 6pm: a jumble of stalls with fashion accessories, secondhand clothing (in good condition), crafts, jams, wine and much more. But there is plenty to buy on other days, and the space can be explored *edifício* (building) by *edifício*. Near the entrance is **India That Wears You** (Ed. E, 91 611 2762), which specialises in silk saris and other Indian-style clothing. For something more western, try the **Trend Hunter's Closet** (Ed. G, 21 590 1297), a multi-brand store for womenswear and accessories. Neighbour **KARE Design** (Ed. I, www.kare-design.com/pt/en) is a treasure house of original items, from alarm clocks and posters to sofas and lamps. For vintage pieces, drop into **Retroshop** (Ed. G, 93 355 9798). Then there's **Bairro Arte** (Ed. I, 91 443 9543, www.bairroarte.com), a local standard for original and humorous souvenirs. Fans of organic cosmetics will love Portuguese chain **Organii** (Ed. H, 21 099 9763, http://organii.com), while bibliophiles will lose themselves amid the soaring shelves at **Ler Devagar** *(see p120)*, which has its own café with WiFi.

Speaking of food and drink, you can also head for **Café na Fábrica** (Ed. E, 21 401 1807), opposite the main entrance. It's great for breakfast, with a range of fresh juices, homemade cakes and pastries; at weekends it serves brunch. In front, in the former printing works canteen, is restaurant **Cantina LX** *(see p120)*. At **1300 Taberna** (Ed. H, 21 364 9170, www.1300taberna. com) the food is fancier: chef Nuno Barros

is a wizard at being creative with the best Portuguese ingredients, such as Barrosã veal or pork cheek. His shop next door, **Mercado 1143** (Loja A, 21 590 0963), sells and serves top-quality Portuguese products and more elaborate nibbles.

But it isn't all traditional fare here. For cheaper but still tasty snacks, head for the fourth-floor **Quarto com Vista** (Ed. I, 21 606 6960), the cafeteria at CoWork, which offers flexible workspaces from €10/day in, as the name puts it, a 'Room with a View'. For Asian flavours, head for **Malaca Too** *(see p120)* or **Sushi Factory** (Ed. I, 21 363 0131). For pizza, there's **A Mesa** (Ed. I, 21 362 4351, 91 888 5154), whose single long table gives it its name. For dessert there's chocolate cake at **Landeau Chocolate** *(see p120)* or ices and crêpes at **Chef Nino** (Ed. H, 91 017 9279).

Want more interaction? **Kiss the Cook** (Ed. H, 96 811 9652, www.kissthecook.pt), runs workshops where participants make their own delicious lunch. You can pick up tips on fashion at ateliers run by **Madame Evasê** (Ed. I, 3rd floor; 927654101) or on interior decoration and renovation at **Atelier Maria Moinhos** (Ed. H, 93 628 7550).

At night, spaces dotted around LX Factory often host parties and concerts, with sounds veering from hip hop to Brazilian funk. Most events are flagged in advance on the main website. But on any night (except Monday), for a bit of Brazilian atmosphere – and fabulous views – head up to fourth-floor **Rio Maravilha** *(see p198)* in Edifício I.

BELÉM, AJUDA & ALGÉS

Belém

Belém was originally separate from the city of Lisbon, and bore the name Restelo (now limited to the residential region uphill). The lower part was dubbed Belém (Bethlehem) in the 16th century by Dom Manuel I. Once a prime anchorage spot, its history is intertwined with the Discoveries. In 1415, the first overseas expedition left Restelo beach on the way to conquer Ceuta in Morocco. In March 1493, Christopher Colombus stopped in on his way back from the Americas; and in 1497, Vasco da Gama departed with his fleet for India – a scene recorded in Luís de Camões's 16th-century epic poem *The Lusiads*. In 1588, during Spanish rule, Belém was the assembly point for the Spanish Armada sent forth against England.

For a trip through history, start at the **Torre de Belém** (*see p126*), one of Lisbon's most recognisable symbols. Nearby is a V-shaped monument to Portugal's dead in the African colonial wars that raged through the 1960s, ending only with the 1974 Revolution.

In 1940, the Salazar regime put on a show called the Exhibition of the Portuguese World, celebrating various anniversaries, including 300 years since the restoration of Portugal's independence from Spain. The waterfront at Belém was dolled up and the Praça do Império levelled out in front of the Mosteiro dos Jerónimos. Remnants of the show are the reflecting pools, a building that houses a branch of the Portugália chain of beer halls, and the monolithic **Padrão dos Descobrimentos**, beside the marina.

Inland, the **Mosteiro dos Jerónimos** (*see p126*) is one of Portugal's most famous landmarks, containing the tombs of Vasco da Gama and Luís de Camões. The longer wing, facing the Praça do Império, was built in the 19th century and houses the **Museu Nacional de Arqueológia**. (Tickets for both – and, until 3pm, for the Torre de Belém – are usually available at the tourism booth across the road from the monastery, which is a good way to avoid the queues.) Beyond it are the **Museu da Marinha** and **Planetário Calouste Gulbenkian**. Uphill from Jerónimos are Belenenses, the Lisbon football club with the best view, and the **Museu Nacional de Etnologia**.

The modern complex facing Praça do Império is the **Centro Cultural de Belém**, or CCB (*see p125*), erected as a showpiece for Portugal's 1992 presidency of the European Union. Originally controversial for its cost, this striking building soon settled into its role as host of cultural events and, since 2007, home to the priceless modern art collection of the **Museu Colecção Berardo**.

Opposite the one remiaining block of Belém's old residential district on Rua de Belém is the **Antiga Confeitaria de Belém**. It has been serving its lovely speciality *pastéis de Belém*, a creamy custard tart topped with cinnamon and sugar, since 1837; the place is invariably packed.

An alley leading off the main street, next to no.118, leads into a tiny square with a column. The five bands on this *pelourinho* (pillory) stand for the five members of the aristocratic Távora family who were executed here in 1759 for their alleged complicity in an assassination attempt against Dom José I. Salt was spread on their property so nothing would grow there; today weeds peek up among the cobbles around the *pelourinho*. Round the corner and up the Calçada do Galvão, the elegant neoclassical **Igreja da Memória** (Calçada do Galvão, 21 363 5295) marks the spot of the assassination attempt.

On the way up there you'll pass the entrance to one of two botanical gardens in the area. Created in 1906 as the Jardim do Ultramar, the **Jardim Botânico Tropical** (Largo dos Jerónimos, 21 392 1808, www.museus.ulisboa.pt) features ponds and exotic lush foliage. One building houses the Xiloteca, a scholarly collection of woods from some 15,000 species of tree (visits by appointment only).

Between the eastern end of Rua de Belém and the river is shady Praça Afonso de Albuquerque, named after the fiery Indian Ocean governor who established Portugal's pepper empire in the early 16th century. The salmon-coloured building opposite is the official residence of the president of Portugal, watched over by the National Republican Guard (GNR); a changing of the guard ceremony takes place on the third Sunday of the month (11am). The **Museu da Presidência** (21 361 4660, www.museu.presidencia.pt) has curiosity value, but the palace itself is more interesting and the gardens pretty. Several guided tours take place every Saturday unless the president's schedule intervenes. Next door to the palace is the former Picadeiro Real (Royal Riding School) that was long home to the **Museu Nacional dos Coches**. The longstanding tourist favourite has now been moved lock, stock and carriage into the hulking concrete structure on the eastern side of the square – designed by Paulo Mendes da Rocha, a Pritzker Prize-winning Brazilian architect.

On the river side of the railway tracks is the Belém boat station for ferries to Trafaria (beyond which stretches the Costa da Caparica, weekend beach destination of many locals). Beside it stands the old Central Tejo power station, which was Portugal's first. It is now part of the **Museu de Arte, Arquitetura e Tecnologia (MAAT)** (*see p124*).

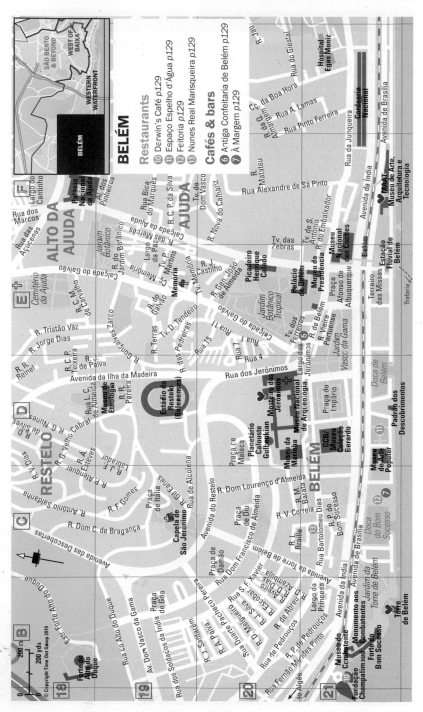

BELÉM

Restaurants

10 Derwin's Café p129
11 Espaço Espelho d'Água p129
12 Feitoria p129
13 Nunes Real Marisqueira p129

Cafés & bars

6 Antiga Confeitaria de Belém p129
7 À Margem p129

❤ MAAT – Museu de Arte, Arquitetura e Tecnologia

*Avenida Brasília, Belém (21 002 8130, www. maat.pt). Cais do Sodré rail to Belém or tram 15, 18, bus 728. **Open** 11am-7pm Mon, Wed-Sun. **Admission** MAAT €5; Central Tejo €5, €2.50 reductions. MAAT & Central Tejo €9; €4.50 reductions. Free under 18s & all on 1st Sun of mth. **Map** p123 F21.*

The Museum of Art, Architecture and Technology is Belém's latest architectural landmark, a gleaming white swoosh of a building designed by British architect Amanda Levete. From the side, it resembles a great wave breaking; from the river, a wide, half-closed eye.

The chief executive of EDP, the energy company whose non-profit foundation had the new museum built, predicted at the time of its inauguration in 2016 that it would become 'the hotspot of hotspots', and it certainly draws many visitors to gaze at the curving white-tiled exterior and clamber on its roof, which affords an amazing view over the River Tagus.

It all fits well with the city's strategy of encouraging more use of the riverfront, with the cycle path from Cais do Sodré to Belém now much used by locals and tourists alike, and plenty of new cafés and restaurants establishing themselves along its route.

Fewer visitors actually enter the new museum building, although its cavernous central space has housed some interesting site-specific installations by artists, and several smaller spaces have hosted video and sound shows. Much thought went into allowing natural lighting into the building and the technology available is, as you would expect, up to date.

The imposing red-brick Central Tejo power station next door – now part of MAAT – draws many visitors too, and is worth a visit in its own right for a glimpse of the antique machinery still in situ, around which new art spaces have been squeezed.

MAAT has a busy programme of events, a restaurant and spaces for artistic residences. With the Fundação EDP generously endowed (and the company keen to curry favour with the public, many of whom are convinced that energy prices are too high and that EDP is largely to blame), money seems to be no object, so there is always something interesting happening at Lisbon's newest museum.

Ajuda

Back inland, the Calçada de Ajuda runs up the side of the Coach Museum and past the **Picadeiro Henrique Calado** (next to no.23), a riding ring that hosts dressage shows most mornings with elegant Lusitano horses and riders dressed in full 18th-century costume, staged by the Escola Portuguesa de Arte Equestre (21 923 7300, http://arteequestre. pt). Further uphill is the 18th-century **Jardim Botânico da Ajuda** (21 362 2503, www.isa.ulisboa.pt/jba), Portugal's first botanical garden; it was created by order of Dom José I to grow plants from around the world. Further uphill is the **Palácio da Ajuda**, begun in 1802 but left unfinished.

Beyond Ajuda is **Monsanto Forest Park** (*see p147*).

Algés

West of Belém lies Algés, a transport hub. The covered market, **Mercado de Algés** (www.mercadodealges.pt), has been given a makeover similar to that of the Mercado da Ribeira, albeit on a smaller scale, with gourmet food stalls and regular live concerts (*see p39* Gourmet Food Markets). On the riverbank between Belém and Algés looms the **Champalimaud Centre for the Unknown**, a privately funded scientific research and clinical centre designed by Indian architect Charles Correa that is one of Portugal's most impressive modern buildings. It houses a lovely restaurant, **Darwin's Café**, and a cheaper cafeteria (open 8am-8pm Mon-Fri) with a terrace offering views right across the mouth of the Tagus.

Sights & museums

♥ Centro Cultural de Belém/Museu Colecção Berardo

Praça do Império (box office 21 361 2627, www.ccb.pt; museum 21 361 2878, www. museuberardo.pt). Belém rail from Cais do Sodré, tram 15, or bus 28, 714, 727, 751. **Museum** *10am-7pm daily (last entry 6.30pm).* **Admission** *Museum €5; reductions €2.50; free under 7s and all Sat.* **Map** *p123 D21.*

The culturally vital Centro Cultural de Belém (CCB) opened in 1993. Most of its main exhibition art space has, since 2007, been taken up by a museum showcasing the collection of Madeiran-born mining-to-media magnate José 'Joe' Berardo, which runs to hundreds of pieces, from Picasso and Duchamp to Warhol, Bacon and local girl Paula Rego (*see p161*). In fact, there's only room for some 900 of the more than 4,000 works Berardo owns (by some 550 different artists), representing dozens of modern movements. The CCB's other indoor and outdoor spaces are used for concerts, dance and other arts-related activities, while an underground car park, the Garagem Sul, hosts architecture exhibitions. The centre also houses several shops that are good for art, souvenirs and books. Several cafés and canteens are dotted around the building, with gourmet snack and wine bar Topo Belém having the best view.

Museu da Marinha

Praça do Império (21 097 7388 , http:// ccm.marinha.pt). Belém rail from Cais do Sodré, tram 15, or bus 714, 727, 728, 729, 751. **Open** *Oct-Apr 10am-5pm daily. May-Sept 10am-6pm daily.* **Admission** *€6.50; €3.25 reductions; free under-4s & all 1st Sun of mth. No cards.* **Map** *p123 D20.*

The Naval Museum has an enormous collection, all owned by the Ministry of Defence. The display starts with scale models of every type of Portuguese boat, and ends with a hangar full of gilded royal barges. Along the way are maps, navigational instruments, and crypto-fascist statues from the Salazar years.

Museu Nacional de Arqueologia

Praça do Império (21 362 0000, www. museunacionalarqueologia.gov.pt). Belém rail from Cais do Sodré, tram 15, or bus 714, 727, 728, 729, 751. **Open** *10am-6pm Tue-Sun.* **Admission** *€5 (€12 with Mosteiro dos Jerónimos); €2.50 reductions; free under-13s. No cards.* **Map** *p123 D20.*

The Archaeological Museum, housed in a wing of the Mosteiro dos Jerónimos, has too little space to display more than a small proportion of the permanent collection at any one time, but on show are usually an impressive collection of Egyptian artefacts and (often excellent) temporary exhibitions. Note that you can beat the queues for Jerónimos itself by buying your ticket here.

> **In the know**
> **Regal Rego**
>
> The Museu da Presidência (see p122) isn't a big draw for foreign visitors, but art lovers joining the Saturday guided tours will get to see Paula Rego's specially commissioned series on the life of the Virgin Mary inside the presidential palace itself. The theme is unusual for the artist, but recalls the area's name, which means Bethlehem. For more works by Rego, visit the Casa das Histórias (see p160) in Cascais, a museum dedicated to her work.

💙 Mosteiro dos Jerónimos & Torre de Belém

WESTERN WATERFRONT

Mosteiro dos Jerónimos *Praça do Império (21 362 0034, www.mosteirojeronimos.gov. pt). Belém rail from Cais do Sodré then 10min walk, tram 15, or bus 714, 727, 728, 729, 751.* **Open** *Oct-Apr 10am-5.30pm Tue-Sun. May-Sept 10am-6.30pm Tue-Sun. (Last entry 30mins before closing.)* **Admission** *Church free. Cloisters €10; €5 reductions; free under-13s. Combined ticket with Museu Nacional de Aqueologia €12.* **Map** *p123 D20.*

Torre de Belém *Praça da Torre de São Vicente (21 362 0034, www.torrebelem.gov.pt). Tram 15 or bus 729.* **Open** *Same hours as the Mosteiro.* **Admission** *€6; €3 reductions; free under-13s.* **Map** *p123 B21.*

The history of the Belém area is intertwined with Portugal's age of maritime Discoveries and its main monuments – the Mosteiro dos Jerónimos and the Torre de Belém, both UNESCO World Heritage sites – reflect that singular period in their architecture and decoration.

Much of the verdant stretch now overrun by tourists was once underwater: the beach at Restelo, as it was then known, ran in front of where the monastery and its church now stand. As a prime anchorage spot, it was witness to many key moments in Portugal's sea-faring history, including Vasco da Gama's departure for India. The phrase 'velho do Restelo' – a reference to an elderly character in Luís de Camões's 16th-century epic *The Lusiads* who dismisses da Gama's India expedition as dangerous folly – is still hurled at naysayers. Belém takes its name from the patron saint of the monastery's church, Santa Maria de Belém (St Mary of Bethlehem).

Mosteiro dos Jerónimos as a whole is a masterpiece of the Manueline style, a Portuguese twist (often literally) on late Gothic, built using *lioz*, a local limestone. Construction of this home for the Hieronymite religious order began in 1501 on the orders of Dom Manuel I, in thanks for the divine favour bestowed through the Discoveries. The west front of the church is obscured by a 19th-century extension that is now the Museu Nacional de Arqueologia (*see p125*), but the sculptural relief of the south

Mosteiro dos Jerónimos

lateral entrance still captivates, with its hierarchy of saints framing Santa Maria. As you enter the church, the tombs of Camões and Vasco da Gama are on either side; then the nave soars up into a space famed for the quality of light that sweeps in during the day. Camões's tomb is always the first stop for heads of state visiting Portugal, to lay a wreath. The exquisite cloisters, designed by master architect Diogo de Boytac and completed by João de Castilho, often host concerts and other events.

The Tower of Belém, a 15-minute stroll away, was built from 1514 to 1521 to guard the entrance to Lisbon harbour (it once stood on a small island but changes to the river's course beached it). Most of its stonework motifs recall the Discoveries, among them twisted rope and the Cross of Christ, as well as Lisbon's patron saint St Vincent and a rhinoceros (the first to be depicted in Europe), but there is Moorish influence in the sentry boxes. The tower is a symbol of Lisbon, despite its small size. It gets very crowded in summer, when you may be best off admiring its exterior from the bank.

Torre de Belém

Mosteiro dos Jerónimos

Museu Nacional de Etnologia

Avenida da Ilha da Madeira (21 304 1160). Bus 714, 728, 732. **Museum** *2-6pm Tue; 10am-6pm Wed-Sun.* **Library** *9.30am-12.30pm, 2-5.15pm Mon-Fri.* **Admission** *€3; €1.50 reductions; free under-13s. No cards.* **Map** *p123 D19.*

The National Museum of Ethnology has a vast collection of items from rural Portugal and the former colonies that are regularly rotated and displayed in well-researched temporary exhibitions. A permanent show on rural life comprising some 3,000 pieces may be visited with a guided tour (weekends only, must be booked in advance by phone or email visitasguiadas@mnetnologia.dgpc.pt).

Museu Nacional dos Coches

Avenida da Índia 136 (21 361 0850, http:// museudoscoches.gov.pt). Belém rail from Cais do Sodré, tram 15, or bus 714, 727, 728, 729, 751. **Museum** *10am-6pm Tue-Sun (last entry 5.30pm).* **Picadeiro** *10am-12.30pm, 2-6pm Tue-Sun (last entry 5.30pm).* **Admission** *Museum €8; €4 reductions. Picadeiro €4, €2 reductions. Museum & Picadeiro €10; €5 reductions. Museum, Picadeiro & Palácio Nacional de Ajuda €12; €6 reductions. Free under-13s.* **Map** *p123 E21.*

The National Coach Museum claims to have the world's largest and most valuable collection of horse-drawn vehicles – 45 in all. The oldest, used by Spanish incomer Philip II (Philip III of Spain) in the early 17th century, was outwardly austere so as not to stoke resentment among his new subjects, but plush inside. The art of coach-making reached its height in three Italian Baroque confections sent to Pope Clement XI by Dom João V; even their wheels are elaborately carved. The main collection is housed in a hangar-like building designed by Brazilian architect Paulo Mendes da Rocha that was inaugurated in 2015, where the carriages have room to breathe and are enhanced by informative multimedia labels. Across the road, the Picadeiro Real (Royal Riding School), which was commissioned by Dom João V in 1726, still keeps a number of 18th-century carriages that are also worth seeing.

Padrão dos Descobrimentos

Avenida de Brasília (21 303 1950, www. padrao dosdescobrimentos.pt). Train to Belém rail from Cais do Sodré, tram 15, or bus 714, 727, 728, 729, 751. **Open** *10am-6pm Tue-Sun. Mar-Sept 10am-7pm daily. Last entry 30mins before closing.* **Admission** *€6; €5 over-64s; €3 13-18s; free under-13s.* **Map** *p123 D21.*

. The original temporary Monument to the Discoveries was put up for the 1940

Feitoria

Exhibition, and the permanent stone Salazarist glorification of the Discoveries opened to the public only in 1960. From the side, it takes the form of a tall oblong; at the base, sculpted figures of discoverers – led by Prince Henry the Navigator – line a stylised prow jutting over the Tagus. Viewed head on, the monument appears as a giant sword-cum-cross, its point embedded in the riverbank, marking the entrance to the little exhibition space. Inside there's a lift to the top for fine views. As the sun follows its course, the shadow of the monument traces the progress of Portuguese explorers around a marble map of the world on the square below. Key dates, such as Vasco da Gama's rounding of the Cape of Good Hope in 1498 and Pedro Álvares Cabral's landing in Brazil in 1500, are marked.

Palácio Nacional da Ajuda

Largo da Ajuda (21 363 7095, www. palacioajuda.gov.pt). Tram 18 or bus 729, 732. **Open** *10am-6pm Mon, Tue, Thur-Sun (last entry 5.30pm).* **Admission** *€5; €2.50 reductions; free under-13s* **Map** *p123 F18.*

Construction began in 1802, but was interrupted in 1807 when the royal family high-tailed it to Brazil to escape Napoleon's armies. The palace was never finished. In the past couple of years the once gaping western wing has finally been filled with a new museum, with a striking contemporary façade, which will display the Tesouro Real (crown jewels); it is slated to open in 2020. The palace itself served as a royal residence in the late 19th century and is the only museum in Lisbon with original interiors from the period. Its collections include noteworthy gold- and silverware, jewellery, textiles, furniture, glass and ceramics, as well as paintings, prints and sculpture. One wing of the palace houses the Ministry of Culture.

Planetário Calouste Gulbenkian

Praça do Império, Belém (21 097 7350, http://ccm.marinha.pt/pt/planetario). Cais do Sodré rail to Belém or tram 15. **Open** *times vary; check website for details.* **Admission** *€5; €2.50 reductions; free to all 1st Sun of mth. No cards.* **Map** *p123 D20.*

The 330-seater planetarium is a real buzz for children. Many of the sessions are aimed at Portuguese school groups; the times and themes for the public sessions change periodically, so check the website for details. Family tickets are available.

Restaurants

Darwin's Café €€€

Champalimaud Centre for the Unknown, Avenida Brasília (21 048 0222, www.darwincafe.com). *Tram 15.* **Open** *12.30-4pm Mon; 12.30-3.30pm, 4.30-6.30pm, 7.30-11pm Tue-Sun.* **Map** *p123 B21* ❿ *International*

The location of this restaurant, in a private scientific foundation on a curve of the river just before it meets the ocean, is enough to take your breath away. Add to that the landmark building and the restaurant's dramatic interior, and dining here becomes a real occasion. The food is inevitably hard pressed to match the setting, but is good and pretty well priced, with a range of pasta and risotto dishes as well as more elaborate *bacalhau* and meat dishes, plus an excellent wine list. You can also enjoy tea or a drink on the café terrace.

Espaço Espelho d'Água €€€

Avenida Brasília, Belém (21 301 0510, http://espacoespelhodagua.negocio.site). Tram 15. **Open** *11am-midnight daily.* **Map** *p123 D21* ⓫ *Portuguese/African/Brazilian*

This low modernist building stands on an artificial island in the water feature after which it is named and which dates back to the 1940 Exhibition. Since 2014, it has housed a laidback café/bar and restaurant that is a great place to enjoy the river view. Smart waiters serve tasty Portuguese dishes such as roast octopus or duck rice, or more exotic fare such as *bacalhau* ceviche, *moqueca* (Brazilian fish stew) or tagine. The wine list is limited, but there are classic cocktails and three kinds of caipirinhas – best enjoyed out on the terrace.

♥ Feitoria €€€€

Altis Belém Hotel, Doca do Bom Sucesso (21 040 0200, www.restaurantefeitoria.com). Tram 15. **Open** *7-11pm Tue-Sat. Closed 1st half Jan.* **Map** *p123 C21* ⓬ *Portuguese/Asian*

This Michelin-starred restaurant and wine bar in the riverside Altis Belém hotel offers a chance to get back in touch with nature in the most sophisticated way possible. Its head chef, João Rodrigues, lays stress on the best and freshest ingredients, above all seafood, reinventing traditional dishes and drawing on international influences to offer a range of distinctive yet subtle flavours.

Nunes Real Marisqueira €€€

Rua Bartolomeu Dias 112, Belém (213 019 899, http://nunesmarisqueira.pt. Tram 15. **Open** *noon-midnight Tue-Sun.* **Map** *p123 C21* ⓭ *Seafood*

Despite the stray apostrophe that creeps into the name on occasions (as in Nune's), staff really know what they are doing at this sophisticated modern shrine to *marisco* (shellfish). The crustaceans are fresh, the service relatively swift and the price tag justifiably high. Don't hesitate here to brave more unusual fare such as *percebes* (goose barnacles), a real taste of the sea. There are also lots of steak options (including Kobe) and other traditional meat dishes such as *iscas* (liver).

Cafés & bars

♥ Antiga Confeitaria de Belém

Rua de Belém 84-92 (21 363 7423, www.pasteisdebelem.pt). Belém rail from Cais do Sodré or tram 15, bus 714, 727, 751. **Open** *July-Sept 8am-midnight daily. Oct-June 8am-11pm daily.* **Map** *p123 E21* ❻

Often known just as 'Pastéis de Belém' after its world-famous product – warm, creamy tarts with puff pastry made according to a secret recipe – which fairly fly out of the door here. Customers with time to spare scoff them two at a time in a warren of rooms lined with tiles depicting Belém in the early 17th century. Others take them away by the half-dozen in specially designed cardboard tubes. It opens every day of the year, only closing early (7pm) on Christmas Eve and Day, and on New Year's Eve and Day.

À Margem

Doca do Bom Sucesso (91 862 0032, www.amargem.com). Belém rail from Cais do Sodré or tram 15. **Open** *Apr-Oct 10am-1am Mon-Sat; 10am-10pm Sun. Nov-Mar 10am-10pm Mon-Thur, Sun; 10am-1am Fri, Sat.* **Map** *p123 C21* ❼

On sunny days, this riverside terrace is one of Lisbon's busiest. At weekends book ahead or be prepared to wait for a table. The secret of À Margem's success is its simplicity: it's a white steel-and-glass box, as pleasant inside as out, with ambient music to suit the hour. The food isn't outstanding, but the spot is ideal for a lunchtime salad, afternoon tea and scones, or a glass of wine at sunset.

São Bento & Beyond

Parliamentarians gather at the Assembly of the Republic in São Bento, an area that in historical terms could be labelled the African inner city, and which still retains something of an African feel. Up the hill towards Príncipe Real and Rato is the domain of antiques shops and twee cafés, as well as the former home of famed fado diva Amália Rodrigues. Further west are Estrela, with its white-domed basilica built on the orders of Dona Maria I to fulfil a promise over the birth of a male heir; middle-class Campo de Ourique; and the well-heeled Lapa district – home to many foreign diplomats. With several interesting museums and pleasant gardens, yet off the main tourist track, these areas are good for relaxed sightseeing, with or without the aid of the antique trams that cut through this part of the city.

❤ Don't miss

1 Basílica da Estrela *p136*
Serene church with stunning views.

2 Fundação Arpad Szenes – Vieira da Silva *p138*
Striking modern art on show.

3 Aqueduto das Águas Livres *p137*
This aqueduct withstood the quake.

4 Jardim da Estrela *p136*
Charming local park with shows on summer weekends.

5 LOCO *p136*
Foodies shouldn't miss this experimental gourmet haven.

Palácio da Assembleia da República *p134*

SÃO BENTO

Restaurants

1. Café de São Bento p135
2. Estórias na Casa da Comida p138
3. LOCO p136
4. Mercado do Campo de Ourique p138
5. Stop do Bairro p138
6. Tambarina p135
7. Tasca da Esquina p139

Cafés & bars

1. Casa de Chá de Santa Isabel p135
2. Gelateria Nannarella p135
3. Lomar p139
4. Panificação Mecânica p139
5. Pão de Canela p135
6. Pastelaria Aloma p139

Shops & services

1. Amoreiras Shopping Center p139
2. Companhia Portugueza do Chá p135
3. Cristina Guerra Contemporary Art p136
4. Depósito da Marinha Grande p135
5. Módulo – Centro Difusor de Arte p139

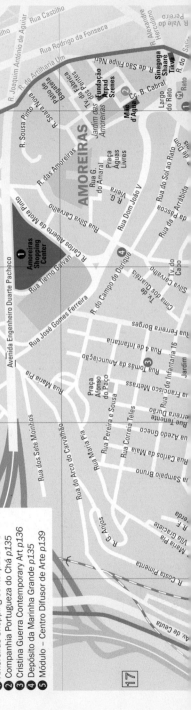

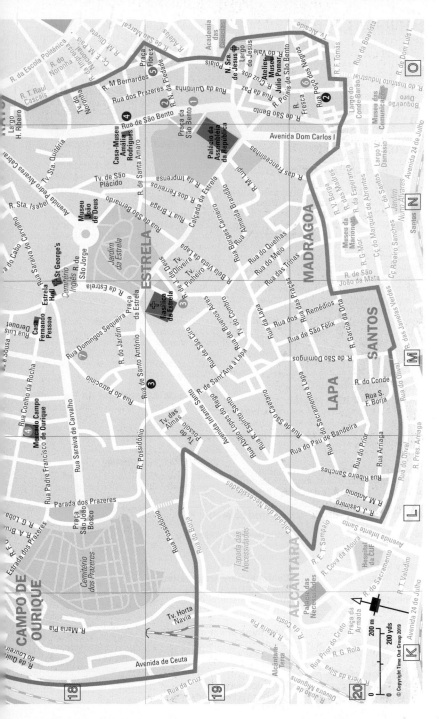

CAMPO DE OURIQUE

ESTRELA

MADRAGOA

SANTOS

LAPA

ALCÂNTARA

Avenida Dom Carlos I

Avenida de Ceuta

Avenida 24 de Julho

Palácio da Assembleia da República

Basílica da Estrela

Jardim da Estrela

Cemitério dos Prazeres

Tapada das Necessidades

Palácio das Necessidades

Museu João de Deus

Casa-Museu Amália Rodrigues

Casa Fernando Pessoa

Mercado Campo de Ourique

Museu das Comunicações

Museu das Marionetas

Estrela Hall

St George's

N. Sra. de Jesus

Atelier-Museu Julio Pomar

Largo do Vale de Jesus

Largo do Conde-Barão

Hospital da CUF

Alcântara-Terra

© Copyright Time Out Group 2019

200 m

200 yds

SÃO BENTO

The neighbourhood in front of the Palácio de São Bento, the massive Benedictine monastery now known as the **Palácio da Assembléia da República** as it that now houses the Portuguese parliament, takes its name from the building. Perhaps the best approach to the *palácio* is from the narrow Travessa da Arrochela, a typical old street with laundry draped from windows. Capping the view at the bottom of the street are the huge pediment and columns of the palace. Up Rua de São Bento, a street dotted with antiques shops, is the former home of Amália, the greatest 20th-century *fadista*; it's now the **Casa-Museu Amália Rodrigues**.

In the 16th century, the area around busy Rua do Poço dos Negros (Well of Negroes) to the east of Avenida Dom Carlos I reeked of rotting bodies – African slaves dumped in a depository at the bottom of the hill after serving their use. It's now a lively residential area served by cheap *tascas*.

Turn into Rua do Vale for a view up to the imposing former Convento de Jesus (now the parish church of Mercês) and a well-hidden museum, the **Atelier-Museu Júlio Pomar** modern art space. Further uphill, Praça das Flores is a delightfully leafy square with a cluster of fashionable cafés and restaurants.

Sights & museums

Atelier-Museu Júlio Pomar
Rua do Vale 7 (21 588 0793, www.ateliermuseu juliopomar.pt). Tram 28. **Open** *10am-1pm, 2-6pm Tue-Sun.* **Admission** *€2; €1-€1.70 reductions; free under-13s & all Sun.* **Map** *p132 O19.*

This workshop-cum-museum for Lisbon native Júlio Pomar, one of Portugal's leading artists was finally unveiled in 2013. The new art space – a former derelict 17th-century warehouse transformed by renowned Porto architect Álvaro Siza Vieira – comprises an airy central exhibition area and mezzanine, plus an auditorium. As well as showcasing several hundred paintings, sculptures, drawings, engravings, collages, ceramics and installations donated by Pomar (who passed away in 2018), it also hosts exhibitions of fellow artists' works.

Casa-Museu Amália Rodrigues
Rua de São Bento 193 (21 397 1896, http:// amaliarodrigues.pt). Metro Rato or bus 706, 727, 773. **Open** *10am-6pm daily.* **Admission** *Guided tours €6.50; reductions €4-€5.50; free under-13s.* **Map** *p132 N18.*

The house of fado diva Amália Rodrigues is a shrine to the memory of the greatest exponent of Lisbon's soulful music (for more on fado, *see p200*). Lined with 18th-century *azulejos*, it has been restored and adapted, displaying portraits of the star by leading Portuguese artists, her favourite glittery outfits, jewellery and decorations awarded by adoring politicians. Guided tours are conducted in Portuguese or English. Amália, as she is invariably known, died in October 1999 after a career that spanned decades, having won the hearts of her compatriots and found fame in Italy, France and Brazil. Since 2002, her remains have been in the National Pantheon (*see p87*).

Palácio da Assembléia da República
Largo das Cortes, Rua de São Bento (21 391 9000, www.parlamento.pt). Tram 25, 28 or bus 6, 713, 727, 773. **Open** *Sessions from 3pm Wed, Thur; from 10am Fri. Guided visits 3pm & 4pm last Sat of mth (except Aug & Dec).* **Admission** *free.* **Map** *p132 N19.*

The imposing façade of the Palácio de São Bento, home to Portugal's Assembly of the

---

💜 Time to eat & drink

Booking required
LOCO *p136*

Hearty fare
Stop do Bairro *p138*

Keeping African traditions alive
Tambarina *p135*

Prize-winning pastéis
Pastelaria Aloma *p139*

Sophisticated cuisine
Estórias na Casa da Comida *p138*

💜 Time to shop

Antiques and glassware
Depósito da Marinha Grande *p135*

Contemporary art galleries
Cristina Guerra Contemporary Art *p136*, Modulo – Centro Difusor de Arte *p139*

Everything under one roof
Amoreiras Shopping Center *p139*, Mercado do Campo de Ourique *p138*

For a proper brew
Companhia Portugueza do Chá *p135*

In the know
Getting around

Tram 28 runs up to Estrela and Campo de Ourique, crossing the Rua de São Bento, on which buses link Santos, down by the river, with the Metro station at Largo do Rato. Other buses run from the Praça Marquês de Pombal, downtown, via Rato to Estrela and via Amoreiras to Campolide; the latter two neighbourhoods are also on the route of the recently revived tram 24 from Chiado.

Republic, seems as if it ought to face more than just a huddle of red-roofed neighbourhoods kept at bay by the stone lions at its entrance. A former monastery, the Mosteiro de São Bento (St Benedict) was turned over to parliament in 1834 when religious orders were abolished. Major renovation work has left little evidence of the original late 16th-century structure, but the building contains notable artworks, especially the upstairs murals (1920-26) by Rafael Bordalo Pinheiro. When parliament is in session, you can enter the viewing galleries (entrance on Praça de São Bento, to the right of the palace; have ID handy), and guided tours are available once a month. Up the hill behind parliament is the prime minister's official residence.

Restaurants

Café de São Bento €€€

Rua de São Bento 212 (21 395 2911, 91 365 8343, www.cafesaobento.com). Metro Rato then 10min walk, tram 28 or bus 706, 727, 773. Open 12.30-2.30pm, 7pm-2am Mon-Fri; 7pm-2am Sat, Sun. Aug closed for lunch. Map p132 O19 ❶ *Steakhouse*

The Café de São Bento is small and rather formal, but the quality of the steak and accompanying sauces and chips, not to mention the well-pulled beer, are the main thing here – plus the fact that it stays open well after midnight. There are uncomplicated salads and starters involving smoked salmon or fine cheeses and hams, plus a range of desserts that include a delicious tarte Tatin.

♥ Tambarina €

Rua do Poço dos Negros 94 (21 012 7556). Tram 28. Open 9am-2am Mon-Sat; 5pm-2am Sun. Map p132 O20 ❻ *West African*

This little place on the 28 tram route serves up large helpings of simple but tasty food from the Cape Verde archipelago, a former colony of Portugal. Dishes include muamba fish curry, various types of *cachupa* stew, and manioc with beef. Try the *grogue* or *ponche* – traditional drinks from the islands – if you dare. They stay open late, often with live music. **Other location** Travessa dos Pescadores 32, São Bento (21 808 4324).

Cafés & bars

Casa de Chá de Santa Isabel

Rua de São Bento 700 (91 742 2749, www. casadecha.org). Metro Rato. Open Jun, Jul, Sept 3.30-7pm Mon; 11.30am-7pm Tue-Fri. Oct-May 11.30am-7pm Tue-Fri; 3.30-7pm Sat, Sun. Closed Aug. No cards. Map p132 O17 ❶

Still known to locals as 'As Vicentinhas', after the religious order that ran it for decades, this

now revamped tearoom hands all its profits to local charitable works. As well as sweet and savoury snacks, full meals are available between 12.45 and 3pm. After that, home-made scones and cakes are displayed in all their sticky glory for what is arguably Lisbon's best afternoon tea.

Gelateria Nannarella

Rua Nova da Piedade 68 (92 687 8553, www. nannarella.pt). Tram 28. Open noon-10pm daily. Map p132 O19 ❷

This little ice-cream parlour was opened by a couple from Rome in 2013 and quickly found success, with queues forming outside at peak hours. Ingredients in the sorbets and ices include locally sourced fresh fruit (such as the very Portuguese Rocha pear), pistachios and almonds imported from Italy, port wine and Óbidos *ginginha* (cherry liqueur).

Pão de Canela

Praça das Flores 27 (21 397 2220, www. canela.pt). Metro Rato or bus 706, 727, 773. Open 8am-midnight daily. Map p132 O19 ❺

This discreetly fashionable café serves tasty quiches and cakes. Its terrace is blissfully free of traffic fumes, and there's even a mini-café for kids with craft activities to complement the playground in the square. The attached restaurant stays open until 11pm, and at weekends lays on a great brunch.

Shops & services

♥ Companhia Portugueza do Chá

Rua dos Poços dos Negros 105 (21 395 1614). Tram 28. Open 10.30am-6.30pm Mon-Fri; 10.30am-7.30pm Sat. Map p132 O20 ❷ *Food & drink*

This wood-panelled shop, dating back to 1880, has since 2014 been home to Lisbon's foremost tea specialist, with lacquered jars containing leaves from China and India, of course, but also from Korea, Malawi and the Azores. The latter is used in the 'Lisbon Breakfast' blend, created by its very own 'tea sommelier'. The company logo is a cameo of Catherine of Braganza (known in her homeland as Catarina de Bragança): she was responsible for taking the tea-drinking habit to England, on marrying Charles II.

♥ Depósito da Marinha Grande

Rua de São Bento 418 (21 396 3096, www.dmg. com.pt). Tram 28 or bus 706, 727, 773. Open 9am-7pm Mon-Fri; 9am-1pm Sat. Map p132 O18 ❹ *Glassware*

Thousands of pieces of hand-blown glasswork in copies of old, unusual designs from the town of Marinha Grande, where the industry dates back to 1769, can be found here. Prices are reasonable, with large goblets selling for around €15. There's another, smaller, shop at no.234 (21 396 3234) .

LAPA & ESTRELA

West of São Bento, the neighbourhoods are more well-to-do. **Lapa**, on a hillside facing south over the river, is home to Lisbon's diplomats. A walk along Rua do Sacramento, Rua do Caetano or Rua de São Domingos shows what Lisbon has to offer in the way of discreet luxury. **Estrela** is based around the late 18th-century **Basílica da Estrela**. Tram 28 passes by here, on the west end of its run up and down old Lisbon. The **Jardim da Estrela** opposite the church is a popular stop for parents with children in tow and often has live events in summer

Beyond the roundabout at its eastern end is an art nouveau building housing the free **Museu João de Deus** (Avenida Álvares Cabral 69, 21 396 0854, www.joaodeus. com), dedicated to the poet-pedagogue of that name but most interesting for its 19th-century art. There are paintings by José Malhoa,Rodrigo Soares and the conference room are cartoons and a vase by the multi-talented Bordalo Pinheiro. On the other side of Rua de São Jorge is the **Cemitério Inglês** and, round the corner, **St George's Church**; these are just two of several local features with Anglo connections; the am-dram group the Lisbon Players are based (for now) at **Estrela Hall** (*see p212*).

Sights & museums

♥ Basílica da Estrela
Praça da Estrela (21 396 0915). Tram 25, 28. **Church** *9am-7pm daily (closed 1-2pm Tue, Thur).* **Roof terrace** *10-11.30am, 1-6.30pm daily.* **Admission** *Church free. Roof terrace €4; €2 under-13s.* **Map** *p132 M19.*

The ornate white dome of the Basílica da Estrela is one of Lisbon's best-loved landmarks. Construction took ten years (1779-89), with statues sculpted by artists from the Mafra School, all to fulfil a vow made by the queen, Dona Maria I, after she succeeded in producing a son and heir. The church is richly decorated inside with Portuguese marble, although many of the paintings are by Italian masters. Climb the 114 steps for fine views of the city.

Cemitério Inglês
Rua de São Jorge à Estrela (93 210 1805, http://lisbonanglicans.org). Tram 25, 28 or bus 709, 720, 738. **Open** *10.30am-1pm Mon-Fri.* **Map** *p132 N18.*

Across the street from the top end of the Jardim da Estrela, a tall wall encloses the English cemetery, which dates back to a 1654 agreement between Dom João IV and Oliver Cromwell over the need for a Protestant burial ground, given the many British merchants in Lisbon. Intentions were made good seven decades later, and the first body was officially laid to rest in 1729. Among them is 18th-century novelist Henry Fielding, who came to Lisbon to improve his health and promptly died. A small Jewish area – in use in the first half of the 19th century – is hidden behind a wall on the west side. If the gate isn't open, ring the bell (repeatedly if necessary) and somebody should come and let you in.

♥ Jardim da Estrela
Praça da Estrela (no phone). Tram 25, 28 or bus 709, 720, 738, 773. **Open** *7am-midnight daily.* **Map** *p132 N18.*

Also known as the Jardim Guerra Junqueiro, the Estrela Garden was laid out in 1842 across the street from the Basílica. The bandstand near the top end of the park once graced the public promenade that became Avenida da Liberdade. There's a lake with swans overlooked by a café, several other kiosks, and a large playground. On summer weekends the garden often hosts live music performances or DJ sets.

Restaurants

♥ LOCO €€€€
Rua dos Navegantes 53B, Lapa (21 395 1861, www.loco.pt). **Open** *7-11pm Tue-Sat. Closed 2 wks Nov, 1st wk Jan.* **Map** *p132 M19* ❸
Portuguese/International

Alexandre Silva is perhaps Portugal's most daring chef and at this compact restaurant, with its suitably contemporary decor, he tests his talents to the limit. It secured a Michelin star less than a year after its opening in 2015, with dishes inspired by Portuguese traditions but taken to another level, based on Silva's experiments with new techniques. It's tasting menus only here, some of which are sure to make you sit up. Booking is essential: there are just seven tables, all with an unimpeded view of the kitchen.

Shops & services

♥ Cristina Guerra Contemporary Art
Rua Santo António à Estrela 33 (21 395 9559, www. cristinaguerra.com). Tram 25, 28. **Open** *noon-8pm Tue-Fri; 3-8pm Sat.* **Map** *pp132 M19* ❸ *Gallery*

This gallery showcases works in a range of media by heavyweights such as Matt

Basílica da Estrela

Mullican, André Cepeda, Ângela Ferreira and João Onofre, who has been with Guerra almost from the start of his career. New shows appear every couple of months.

CAMPO DE OURIQUE, AMOREIRAS & CAMPOLIDE

Campo de Ourique is a middle-class district above Estrela that was laid out in the 19th century on a grid pattern, whose streets are lined with local shops and services. The house on Rua Coelho da Rocha where poet Fernando Pessoa spent the last 15 years of his life is now the **Casa Fernando Pessoa**, one of Lisbon's more active small cultural institutions. The **Mercado de Campo de Ourique**, one of the city's best markets, is now home to a host of gourmet food stalls too. To the west, at the end of the tram 28 route, is a vast city of the dead spread beneath lonely cypresses, the municipal **Cemitério dos Prazeres** (literally 'Pleasures', named after the local church dedicated to Our Lady of that ilk). The cemetery has a small museum (closed Mon).

The northern end of Campo de Ourique is marked by a pile of pastel postmodernism. Architect Tomás Taveira boasted in the mid 1980s that his goal with the **Amoreiras**

Shopping Center towers – which look a bit like giant Liquorice Allsorts studded with smoked glass – was to provide a skyline counterbalance to the Castelo de São Jorge. Most feel he missed the mark, but the towers are still there and the mall is one of the capital's most popular. Beyond it is the bustling residential neighbourhood of **Campolide**, from where the **Aqueduto das Águas Livres** stalks across the Alcântara valley to the **Parque Florestal de Monsanto** (*see p147*), Lisbon's green lung. Back down Rua das Amoreiras, above busy Largo do Rato, is the pretty **Jardim das Amoreiras** (whose mulberry trees gave the garden and neighbourhood the name); along one side run the arches at the end of the aqueduct before it terminates at the **Mãe d'Água** reservoir. A kiosk in the garden serves light lunches.

The **Fundação Arpad Szenes – Vieira da Silva** has a permanent collection of the work of Portuguese modernist painter Maria Helena Vieira da Silva and her Hungarian husband, along with works by associated artists. The museum is housed in a former textile workshop. The whole area was set up as an industrial park in the late 18th century, so many of the streets are named after factories, such as Travessa da Fábrica dos Pentes (Comb Factory Way).

Lisbon's central synagogue, the **Sinagoga Shaaré Tikvá** (Alexandre Herculano 59, 21 393 1130, www.cilisboa.org), is just off Largo do Rato, set well back from the street: when it was built, in 1904, non-Catholic places of worship weren't permitted to front on to a public thoroughfare.

Sights & museums

❤ Aqueduto das Águas Livres
*Access from Calçada da Quintinha (EPAL gate), Campolide (21 325 1652). Bus 702, or tram 24 then 10min walk. **Open** 10am-5.30pm Tue-Sat. Guided visits 11am 1st Sat of mth. **Admission** €3; €1.50 reductions; free under-13s. **Map** p132 M15.*

Lisbon's aqueduct spans the Alcântara valley. Construction began in 1731, and by 1748 the first water was flowing from a source 58km (36 miles) to the north-west. It bridges the valley on a series of 35 arches, the largest of which rises 64m (210 ft) from the ground; giddy heights indeed when you walk along the parapet. When built, these were the tallest stone arches in the world. They were sturdy too – they survived the 1755 earthquake unscathed. The aqueduct was taken out of service in 1967 and now forms part of the Museu de Água (*see p91*); joint tickets with the Mãe d'Água (*see p138*) and other offshoots of the museum are available.

Casa Fernando Pessoa

Rua Coelho da Rocha 16, Campo de Ourique (21 391 3270, www.casafernandopessoa. pt). Tram 25, 28. **Open** *10am-6pm Mon-Sat (library Mon-Fri). Last entry 5.30pm.* **Admission** *€3; €1.50-€2.60 reductions; free under-13s. Guided visits €4.* **Map** *p132 M18.*

Dedicated to poetry in general, and Portugal's most celebrated modernist poet in particular, the Casa Fernando Pessoa is where he lived during the last 15 years of his life. The Casa has daily guided visits in English (11.30am) in July and August, and on Mondays, Fridays and Saturdays the rest of the year. It also organises poetry readings and publishes monographs on Pessoa, as well as hosting art exhibitions and the odd jazz concert. There's a restaurant (21 395 0704) round the back.

♥ Fundação Arpad Szenes – Vieira da Silva

Praça das Amoreiras 56 (21 388 0044/0053, www.fasvs.pt). Metro Rato, tram 24, or bus 713, 774. **Open** *10am-6pm Tue-Sun.* **Admission** *€5; €2.50 reductions; free under 13s & all before 2pm Sun.* **Map** *p132 O17.*

A plain building that was once the Royal Silk and Textile Workshop now houses this foundation, dedicated to exhibiting and promoting research into the work of Portuguese modernist Maria Helena Vieira da Silva and her Hungarian husband and fellow painter Arpad Szenes. As well as housing and displaying its large permanent collection of their works, the foundation puts on regular exhibitions of artists with links to the couple, such as Fernand Léger and Marc Chagall. The museum's prettily tiled café (accessible without ticket) serves tasty light meals as well as scones and cakes.

Mãe d'Água

Praça das Amoreiras (Museum 21 810 0215). Metro Rato, tram 24, or bus 713, 774. **Open** *10am-12.30pm, 1.30-5.30pm Tue-Sat.* **Admission** *€3; €1.50 reductions; free under-13s.* **Map** *p132 O17.*

The Aqueduto das Águas Livres ends at the Mãe d'Água (Mother of Water), a large stone building that looms behind the Socialist Party headquarters on Largo do Rato. Construction began in 1745 and work carried on until 1834. Inside, the central tank has a capacity of 5,500 cubic metres, and the cool stone interior has the feel of an eerie grotto. Arriving water tumbles into the central pool over an ever-growing mound of limescale. The walkways round the tank and a floating platform are used for art exhibitions. Visitors can climb the stairs to peer down the aqueduct passage. The monument is part of the Museu de Água *(see p91)*; joint tickets with other offshoots of the museum are available.

Restaurants

♥ Estórias na Casa da Comida €€€€

Travessa das Amoreiras 1, Amoreiras (21 388 5376, www.casadacomida.pt). Metro Rato. **Open** *7pm-midnight Mon-Sat.* **Map** *p132 O17* **❷** *Portuguese*

A famous gourmet spot, the Casa da Comida is currently overseen by talented young chef João Pereira. His seasonal menus (€45 or €60 with wine pairing, €60 or €90 with wine pairing) include elaborate dishes based on traditional Portuguese cuisine, but with an international twist; the à la carte menu takes the same approach. You can just drink and snack in the wine bar, or head for the restaurant and its romantic *azulejo*-lined patio.

♥ Mercado do Campo de Ourique €€

Rua Coelho da Rocha, Campo de Ourique (21 132 3701, www.mercadodecampodeourique. pt). Tram 25, 28 or bus 709, 774. **Open** *May-Sept 10am-11pm Mon-Wed, Sun; 10am-midnight Thur; 10am-1am Fri, Sat. Oct-Apr 10am-11pm Mon-Thur, Sun; 10am-1am Fri, Sat.* **Map** *p132 M18* **❹** *Portuguese/International*

Not one restaurant but a whole gourmet food court in one of Lisbon's liveliest surviving market halls. Stalls include a gin bar and a seafood specialist with oysters and a great fish soup, as well as Portuguese favourites such as suckling pig and gourmet burgers. On weekend nights there's live music or DJs. Meanwhile the old business of selling fruit, vegetables, fish and meat goes on around you.

♥ Stop do Bairro €€

Rua Marquês de Fronteira 173-A, Campolide (21 585 2893). Tram 24 or bus 701, 702, 712, 713, 742, 758. **Open** *noon-4pm, 7-11pm Tue-Sun.* **Map** *p132 N15* **❺** *Portuguese*

This old favourite, formerly of Campo de Ourique for more than four decades, relocated to new (larger) premises in Campolide in 2017. It remains as resolutely unglamorous as ever, its walls decked with football scarves (and a Portugal shirt from the 1966 World Cup, signed by Eusébio); its extensive menu of Portuguese standards, and a few Angolan specialities, has moved with it. Among well-priced dishes are *caras de bacalhau* (codfish cheeks), Azorean *polvo guisado* (stewed octopus) and, on Fridays, *cabidela de galinha* (chicken cooked in blood). Helpings are generous – in some cases even a *meia dose* (half serving) is enough for two – and it's worth saving space for dessert. The wine list is outstanding for this price bracket. You can't reserve, so come early.

Tasca da Esquina €€

Rua Domingues Sequeira 41C, Campo de Ourique (21 099 3939, 91 983 7255, www. tascadaesquina.com). Tram 25, 28 or bus 709. **Open** *12.30-3.30pm, 7.30-11.30pm Tue-Fri, Sun; 1-3.30pm, 7.30-11.30pm Sat.* **Map** *p132 M18* ❼ *Portuguese*

A *tasca* in name only, this recession-busting gourmet restaurant founded in 2009 by leading Portuguese chef Vítor Sobral is now overseen on a day-to-day basis by the equally creative Hugo Nascimento. There are two ways to approach a meal here, both involving delicious starters: order à la carte from a menu that includes dishes of the day, or go for a combo with four to eight starters. Offal looms large here but there are other options, such as squid sautéed with mushrooms or flaked *bacalhau* with potato and egg.

Cafés & bars

Lomar

Rua Tomás de Anunciação 72, Campo de Ourique (21 385 8417). Tram 25, 28. **Open** *7.30am-7.30pm Mon-Fri; 7.30am-4pm Sat.* **No cards.** **Map** *p132 M17* ❸

This stylish neighbourhood *pastelaria* attracts a mixture of local *tias* (literally 'aunts' – ladies who lunch) and students, who come in to natter over coffee and sample the sweets and savouries that are made on the premises.

Panificação Mecânica

Rua Silva Carvalho 209, Campo de Ourique (21 381 2260, http://panificacaomecanica.pt/pt). Metro Rato or bus 758. **Open** *7am-8pm Mon-Fri; 7am-3pm Sat.* **No cards.** **Map** *p132 N17* ❹

Chandeliers, tiles depicting ears of wheat, coloured enamel pillars, painted moulded ceilings and wall mirrors make this one of Lisbon's most over-the-top *pastelarias*. It has been supplying the middle classes and local businesses with top-notch bread and cakes for more than a century. There's no seating area, but you can stand at the high table or counter for a drink and a snack. Note that on Saturdays, if business is slack, they close a little earlier.

❤ Pastelaria Aloma

Rua Francisco Metrass 67, Campo de Ourique (21 396 3797/www.aloma.pt). Tram 25, 28. **Open** *8am-7pm daily.* **No cards.** **Map** *p132 M17* ❻

Inaugurated in 1943 and named after a sarong-clad character played by film star Dorothy Lamour, this place won national fame in 2012 and 2013 when its *pastéis de nata* (custard tartlets) were declared Portugal's best in a blind tasting.

Shops & services

❤ Amoreiras Shopping Center

Avenida Engenheiro Duarte Pacheco (21 381 0240, www.amoreiras.com). Metro Rato or tram 24, or bus 711, 718, 723, 748, 753, 758. **Open** *10am-11pm daily.* **Map** *p132 N16* ❶ *Mall*

Architect Tomás Taveira based the postmodernist design for Portugal's first shopping centre on the Brazilian concept of many small entrances to make it easy to get in. Expect the usual selection of local and international chains, one of Lisbon's best supermarkets (jumbo), a multiplex with seven screens, dozens of eateries and a chapel. For an overview of the whole city, not just downtown, check out the Amoreiras 360˚ Panoramic View on the roof, tickets are available at the information desk or online (www.amoreiras360view.com).

❤ Módulo – Centro Difusor de Arte

Calçada dos Mestres 34A-B, Campolide (21 388 5570). Tram 24 or bus 701, 702, 712, 742. **Open** *3-7.30pm Mon-Sat.* **No cards.** **Map** *p132 M15* ❺ *Gallery*

This 'art diffusion centre' is home to one of Lisbon's most interesting exhibition spaces. Work by exciting new artists predominates, with photography a particular focus.

Aqueduto das Águas Livres p137

Further Afield

The wooded walkways that became the Avenida da Liberdade once marked the northern edge of the city. Now, the roundabout at its far end is just the starting point for avenues that spin off towards today's office districts. Still, many points of interest for visitors are dotted across northern Lisbon.

To the east, the low hills outside Lisbon were described by writer Almeida Garrett in the 1800s as full of gardens and orchards. By the 1860s, trains chugged alongside the river, heralding the arrival of factories and warehouses. After decades of decline and abandonment, changes set in motion by the Expo '98 World Fair – whose site is now the fun-filled Parque das Nações – are transforming this waterfront.

❤ **Don't miss**

1 Fundaçao & Museu Calouste Gulbenkian *p146 & p147*
Treasure house of art and culture.

2 Oceanário *p155*
Top aquarium in the wide open spaces of the former Expo '98 site.

3 Museu Nacional do Azulejo *p150*
The national showcase for tiles.

4 Marvila *p150*
Lisbon's most happening *bairro*.

5 Palácio dos Marqueses da Fronteira *p148*
Impressive tile panels and a bucolic setting.

NORTHERN LISBON

Restaurants
1 Grand'Elias *p149*
2 O Nobre *p149*
3 Portugália *p149*
4 Rabo d'Pêxe *p149*

Cafés & bars
1 L'Éclair *p149*
2 Pastelaria Mexicana *p149*
3 Pastelaria Versailles *p149*

Shops & services
1 Centro Colombo *p149*
2 El Corte Inglés *p149*
3 Galeria 111 *p150*
4 Miosótis *p150*

© Copyright Time Out Group 2019

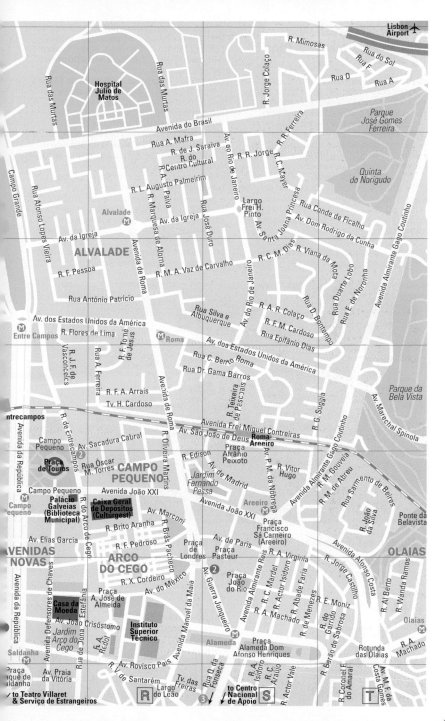

NORTHERN LISBON
Praça de Espanha, Sete Rios and Benfica

Praça de Espanha is infamous at rush hour; the grassy space in the middle sports an aqueduct arch that was once used to constrict traffic further downtown until it was uprooted to here. On one side is Palácio de Palhavã, the official residence of the Spanish ambassador.Uphill, towering department store El Corte Inglés, with its well-stocked supermarket, cinema and now a fashionable top-floor food court overseen by Michelin-starred chefs, also does sterling work for Spanish-Portuguese relations.

Opposite the embassy is the landscaped garden that is home to **Fundação Calouste Gulbenkian** (*see p146*), one of Lisbon's most important cultural institutions. Its Museu Calouste Gulbenkian has a rich collection of artefacts, plus a separate showcase for modern art and, in summer, open-air jazz. There are more shows on offer on the south-western corner of Praça de Espanha, at the **Teatro Aberto** (*see p212*) and **Teatro da Comuna** (*see p213*). To the north, at **Sete Rios**, is the city's zoo, the **Jardim Zoológico de Lisboa**.

Now a sprawl of bank headquarters and airport-style hotels, the area still has some old jewels, such as the **Palácio dos Marqueses da Fronteira**, famed for its gardens and tiles depicting exotic hunting scenes. The **Museu da Música** is nearby, inside the Alto dos Moinhos Metro station. From here it's a short walk to the 65,000-seater stadium of **Sport Lisboa e Benfica** (museum 707 200 100, www. slbenfica.pt), a powerhouse of European football in the 1960s and a perennial candidate, with FC Porto and Sporting, for the league title. The pre-match ritual, in which an eagle swoops above the crowd to land on its handler's glove, makes it worth arriving well before kick-off.

Centro Colombo

❤ Time to eat & drink

Fancy food with a view
Gourmet Experience *p150*

The freshest fish
Rabo d'Pêxe *p149*, Senhor Peixe *p154*

Lisbon beer district
Marvila's craft brewers *p199*

Pastries in style
Pastelaria Versailles *p149*

Traditional fare at its best
O Nobre *p149*

❤ Time to shop

Browse for art
Galeria 111 *p150*, Galeria Filomena Soares *p152*, Galeria Francisco Fino *p152*, Kunsthalle Lissabon *p152*, Underdogs Gallery *p153*

Major malls
Centro Colombo *p149*, Centro Vasca da Gama *p154*

Top brands, local and foreign
El Corte Inglés *p149*

Across Lisbon's ring road, the Segunda Circular, is the mega-mall **Centro Colombo** and, beyond it, **Benfica** itself, once a quiet town, now a concrete suburb.

Saldanha and Avenidas Novas

There are office blocks along the new avenues off Avenida da República and busy shopping centres around Praça Duque de Saldanha. Yet bits of an older, gentler city remain: the **Casa-Museu José Anastácio Gonçalves** is a monument to tasteful acquisitiveness; at the beginning of Avenida da República, **Pastelaria Versailles** retains its bourgeois appeal; and across the avenue at no.38 stands an art nouveau gem.

Further up Avenida da República, ringed by brick-red cupolas, is a neo-Moorish bullring, the 1892 **Praça de Touros do Campo Pequeno** (21 799 8450, www.campopequeno. com). In Portugal, it's illegal to kill the bull in the ring – and a major part of the spectacle is unarmed *forcados* wrestling it to a standstill – but the animal is still butchered afterwards.

The arena also hosts concerts and other shows, has an underground shopping centre with multiplex (*see p183*) and restaurants with terraces around the building. On the south side of the square is the **Palácio Galveias** (21 817 3090, closed Sun), an elegant former palace that houses Lisbon's central library, where José Saramago spent countless hours feeding his passion for literature, long before he won fame and a Nobel Prize. The palace's lovely walled garden has a kiosk café. Round the corner is Portugal's biggest building, the headquarters of state bank Caixa Geral de Depósitos, which is home to **Culturgest**, one of the city's leading arts venues.

Avenida da República continues north to the traffic snarl of Entrecampos roundabout, beyond which is Campo Grande, home of the **Biblioteca Nacional** (no.83, 21 798 2000, www.bnportugal.pt, closed Sun), Portugal's main copyright library. To consult any publication, bring ID.

Further up Campo Grande, as it widens out to form a proper park, are astounding ceramics in the **Museu Rafael Bordalo Pinheiro** and, at its northern end, historic exhibits in the **Museu de Lisboa**. On the other side of the Segunda Circular is the stadium of **Sporting Clube de Portugal** (21 751 6164, www.sporting.pt), designed by Tomás Taveira and dubbed 'the bathroom' by Benfica fans because of its external tiling. Both clubs' stadiums were built for the 2004 European championships.

A few blocks east from Campo Grande, Avenida da Roma cuts through Alvalade, a smart residential and shopping area. To the north, again beyond the ring road, is the airport.

Lumiar

North of Campo Grande, Avenida Padre Cruz skirts Telheiras – where the results of a decade-long building boom are much in evidence – towards Lumiar. Once a sleepy village, it's now a dreary suburb choked with traffic, despite now being served by the Metro. But the **Parque da Quinta das Conchas** on Alameda Linhas das Torres has ample lawns, a playground and six large slides embedded in a slope, plus two terrace cafés (open past 8pm). The **Museu Nacional do Traje** and **Museu Nacional do Teatro e da Dança** are housed in wings of an 18th-century former palace that overlooks the **Parque Botânico do Monteiro-Mor** (closed Mon; €3, €1.50 reductions), a reminder of more bucolic times. The park's glades are dotted with sculptures.

Sights & museums

Casa-Museu José Anastácio Gonçalves
Avenida 5 de Outubro 8 (21 354 0923, www.cmag.dgpc.pt). Metro Picoas. **Open** *10am-6pm Tue-Sun.* **Admission** *€3; €1.50 reductions; free under-13s & all 1st Sun of mth.* **Map** *p142 Q15.*

Originally commissioned by painter José Malhoa, who had his atelier upstairs, this house was bought by art enthusiast Dr Gonçalves. He favoured landscapes and portraits by Mário Augusto, Bordalo Pinheiro and his chum Silva Porto. Gonçalves also amassed a collection of Chinese porcelain from the Ming and Transition periods, as well as 18th- and 19th-century English, French and Portuguese furniture.

Culturgest
Edifício Caixa Geral de Depósitos, Rua Arco do Cego 1 (21 790 5155, www.culturgest. pt). Metro Campo Pequeno. **Open** *Gallery 11am-6pm Tue-Sun.* **Admission** *€4; €2 reductions; free under-13s & all Sun.* **Map** *p142 R13.*

The programming at this bank-owned foundation is the most avant-garde of Lisbon's major art institutions, regularly hosting interesting and challenging exhibitions. Its auditoria are used to stage everything from showcases of foreign film to jazz concerts.

Jardim Zoológico de Lisboa
Estrada de Benfica 158-60, Sete Rios (21 723 2910, www.zoolisboa.pt). Metro Jardim Zoológico. **Open** *21 Mar-20 Sept 10am-8pm daily (last entry 6.45pm). 21 Sept-20 Mar 10am-6pm daily (last entry 5.15pm).* **Admission** *€21.50; €14.50-€16 reductions; free under-3s. No cards.* **Map** *p142 M12.*

🖤 Fundação Calouste Gulbenkian

*Avenida de Berna 45A, Northern Lisbon
(21 782 3000, gulbenkian.pt). Metro São
Sebastião. **Museums** 10am-6pm, Mon,
Wed-Sun. **Garden** 10am-sunset daily.
Map p142 P13.*

Sixty years since its creation, the Gulbenkian
Foundation remains Lisbon's most important
cultural institution: unchallenged and,
perhaps, unchallengeable.

Its museum (*see p147*) boasts one of
Europe's leading collections of Islamic and
oriental art, but also an excellent range of
European fine and applied art – paintings,
tapestry, silverwork, jewellery – from
medieval to modern times. Exhibition
spaces in the foundation's main building
are also used for temporary shows: either
themed or retrospectives of leading artists.

At the other end of what is one of Lisbon's
loveliest gardens stands the building that
houses the Gulbenkian's Modern Collection
– the most representative grouping
anywhere of works by 20th-century
Portuguese artists, including Amadeo de
Souza-Cardoso, Maria Helena Vieira da
Silva and Paula Rego, but also boasting an
important selection of British works dating
from the 1950s onwards.

As if all this were not enough, the
Foundation has its own orchestra and
100-strong choir, and stages a full classical
season from October to May that features
renowned visiting orchestras and solo
musicians, performing in its acoustically
excellent main auditorium. For more
information, *see p207*.

So how did all this take shape, and
why does the foundation have such a
very un-Portuguese name?

Calouste Gulbenkian was born in Istanbul
in 1869, into a family of Armenian traders.
He made his money in oil, his deal-making
with the British authorities, above all in
what is now Iraq, ultimately earning him
the nickname 'Mr Five Per Cent'. Though a
British citizen, he ended up in Lisbon during
World War II after the British government
seized his assets as 'enemy property' and
neutral Portugal offered him asylum.

Gulbenkian is said to have begun his
collection in his teens, after picking up some
coins in a bazaar. By the time he died in 1955,
it comprised some 6,000 items and was one
of the most valuable in private hands, with a
clear emphasis on oriental (and Armenian)
art. His will stipulated that all this should
go to a new Lisbon-based foundation, to
be endowed with his fortune; the museum
to house the Founder's Collection was
finally inaugurated in 1969, coinciding
with the completion of the foundation's
iconic garden – a masterpiece of Portuguese
landscape architecture.

Over the decades the Gulbenkian filled a
gaping hole in Portugal left by feeble state
funding (prompting locals to joke that it was
the Ministry of Culture, back when there was
no such thing). Besides the arts programme at
its own venues, it provides grants to students,
publishes arts-related material, and runs
a specialist central library and nationwide
network that put the state's efforts to shame.

Its pockets are not bottomless, however, and
a few years ago it disbanded its much-admired
ballet company on the grounds that the funds
would go further if meted out to other dance
troupes – but in the field of music in particular
and the arts in general Fundação Calouste
Gulbenkian has done its founder proud.

Modern Collection

Lisbon's green lung, **Parque Florestal de Monsanto** or Monsanto Forest Park (www.cm-lisboa.pt/en/living-in/environment/monsanto-forest-park) was long dismissed by locals as the haunt of drug dealers and prostitutes, but it has gained huge popularity thanks to substantial municipal investment and regular open-air events. Its 306 kilometres (190 miles) of hiking and bike trails now link up with central Lisbon, and it has several playgrounds. The largest and busiest is the hilltop **Parque Recreativo do Alto da Serafina**, near where the Aqueduto das Águas Livres (see *p137*) enters Monsanto. It has a leafy picnic area, driving circuit for children, climbing wall, boating lake and restaurant – as well as marvellous views; you can reach it by taking bus 770 from Sete Rios metro station. For ecological exhibitions and information, visit the Centro de Interpretação Monsanto (bus 770).

Lisbon's zoo strikes an excellent balance between fun and conservation. Home to some 2,000 creatures of more than 300 different species, from every continent, it also has a botanical garden, pleasant cafés and an amusement park. A miniature train takes the strain on hot days. Check the website for feeding times and shows.

❤ Museu Calouste Gulbenkian

Avenida de Berna 45 (21 782 3000, guided group visits & activities 21 782 3800, http://gulbenkian.pt/museu). Metro Praça de Espanha (Founder's Collection), São Sebastião (Modern Collection). **Museum** *10am-6pm Mon, Wed-Sun (last entry 5.30pm).* **Library** *9.30am-7pm Mon-Fri.* **Admission** *€10 (€14 with all exhibitions); €5 reductions (€7 with exhibitions); free under-13s & all Sun from 2pm. Exhibitions prices vary. No cards.* **Map** *p142 P13.*

It's difficult to know where to start in this, one of Europe's leading fine arts museums, whose main **Founder's Collection** comprises exhibits dating from 2000 BC to the early 20th century. From the ancient world come Egyptian scarabs, Greco-Roman jewellery and a giant ninth-century BC Assyrian bas-relief in alabaster of a warrior. The Islamic and oriental art is outstanding: carpets, robes, tapestries, tiles and glassware, mainly from 16th- and 17th-century Persia, Turkey, Syria and India; and porcelain, jade, paintings and lacquered boxes from China and Japan.

The section on European art displays medieval manuscripts and ivory and wood diptychs. Further on are Italian Renaissance majolica ware and tapestries, and a selection of 18th-century French furniture and silverware. Among the painters represented are Domenico Ghirlandaio, Rubens, Hals and Rembrandt, Gainsborough, Manet and Corot. Save time for the final room's breathtaking art nouveau jewellery by René Lalique.

Audio-guides help you get the most from the experience; free guided tours in English are at 11am on Mondays and Sundays. There are also excellent temporary exhibitions, with pieces lent by foreign institutions. Downstairs is an art library, an excellent café and a small gift shop. Your ticket includes admission to the **Modern Collection** – the city's premier showcase for Portuguese art from the last century, as well as having a fine collection of modern British art – housed in a fine modernist building at the southern end of the park with its own bookshop and canteen.

Museu da Música

Alto dos Moinhos Metro station, Rua de Freitas Branco (21 771 0990, www.museunacionaldamusica.pt). **Open** *10am-6pm Mon-Sat.* **Admission** *€3; €1.50 reductions; free under-13s. No cards.* **Map** *p142 O10.*

Although it's off the beaten track, the Museum of Music has some real treasures from the 16th to the 20th centuries – from pocket fiddles and a plethora of *guitarras* (12-stringed Portuguese guitars) to Baroque harpsichords. There's also a specially strengthened piano that Franz Liszt brought to Lisbon for a much-fêted series of concerts, and which he left behind as a gift to the queen, Dona Maria II. The shop has a good range of books and classical CDs, plus miniature instruments.

Museu de Lisboa – Palácio Pimenta

Campo Grande 245 (21 751 3200, www.museudelisboa.pt). Metro Campo Grande. **Open** *10am-6pm Tue-Sun (last entry 5.30pm).* **Admission** *€3; €1.50 reductions; free under-13s, students & all Sun to 2pm. No cards.* **Map** *p142 P9.*

An 18th-century mansion houses this city-run museum charting Lisbon's history. Displays rush from the Stone Age through Roman times to the Visigoths and Moors and into the modern age. The highlights, though, are a scale model of Lisbon before the 1755 earthquake, the fabulous kitchens and the formal garden with its peacocks and display of giant ceramic wasps, lobsters and frogs by Bordalo Pinheiro (see *p148* Museu Rafael Bordalo Pinheiro). The modern Pavilhão Branco annexe is an important contemporary art space.

Palácio dos Marqueses da Fronteira

Museu Nacional do Teatro e da Dança

Estrada do Lumiar 10 (21 756 7418, www. museudoteatro.pt). Metro Lumiar. **Open** *10am-6pm Tue-Sun.* **Admission** *€4; €2 reductions; free under-13s. Combined ticket with Museu do Traje & park €6; €3 reductions.*

Opened in 1985, this theatre museum has more than 300,000 items, including costumes, stage designs, manuscripts and many photographs. The cafeteria has a shaded terrace overlooking the garden.

Museu Nacional do Traje

Largo Júlio Castilho (21 756 7620, www. museudotraje.gov.pt). Metro Lumiar. **Open** *10am-6pm Tue-Sun.* **Admission** *€4; €2 reductions; free under-13s & all 1st Sun of mth. Combined ticket with Museu do Teatro & park €6; €3 reductions. No cards.*

Despite the limited display, the Costume Museum is worth a visit just to see the prettier parts of the former Palácio de Angela-Palmela. Walls are decorated with garlands and musical instruments in pastel colours, and most of the original wall tiles remain. Round the back, in a neo-Gothic pavilion, a fancy restaurant serves lunch and afternoon tea until 6pm (92 445 0786, www. restaurantemonteiromor.com, closed Mon).

Museu Rafael Bordalo Pinheiro

Campo Grande 382 (21 581 8544, http:// museubordalopinheiro.cm-lisboa.pt). Metro Campo Grande. **Open** *10am-6pm Tue-Sun.* **Admission** *€3; €1.50-€2.70 reductions; free under 13s & all Sun to 2pm. No cards.* **Map** *p142 Q9.*

Portuguese architect and artist Rafael Bordalo Pinheiro (1846-1905) had his own ceramics factory in Caldas da Rainha, where he produced fantastic designs. Examples include a pig's head on a platter, lobsters in baskets and frogs sat on plates or climbing vases and poles. He was a prolific caricaturist, using his everyman character Zé Povinho to puncture the pomposity of public figures.

♥ Palácio dos Marqueses da Fronteira

Largo de São Domingos de Benfica 1 (21 778 2023, www.fronteira-alorna.pt). Metro Parque Zoológico then 15min walk, or bus 770. **Guided tours** *(palace and garden) June-Sept 10.30am, 11am, 11.30am, noon Mon-Sat. Oct-May 11am, noon Mon-Sat.* **Garden** *June-Sept 10.30am-1pm, 2-5pm Mon-Fri; 10.30am-1pm Sat. Oct-May 9.30am-1pm, 2-5pm Mon-Fri; 9.30am-1pm Sat.* **Admission** *Tours €9; free under-12s. Gardens €4; free under-12s. No cards.* **Map** *p142 M12.*

The idyllic setting of this palace, at the foot of Monsanto Forest Park (*see p147*), is in sharp contrast to the concrete jungle of Sete Rios, across the railway tracks. The palace was built for the Mascarenhas family, who still own it. Most of the palace was erected in the 1670s, then rebuilt after the 1755 earthquake. Its Sala das Batalhas is decorated with 17th-century *azulejos* depicting battles against Spain during the War of Restoration (1640-68), while the halls, courtyards and gardens are full of statuary. You may visit the garden independently but the palace is only accessible with a guided tour. Tours last about an hour; arrive a few minutes early.

Restaurants

Grand'Elias €€
Avenida Elias Garcia 109 (21 797 5359, www. restaurantegrandelias.pai.pt). Metro Campo Pequeno. **Open** *noon-4 pm, 6 pm-midnight daily.* **Map** *p142 P13* ❶ *Portuguese*

A specialist in rustic fare from the northern Minho region, Grande Elias has built up its reputation over decades with dishes such as roast bacalhau and octopus, grilled javali (wild boar), rojões com castanhas (pork loin with chestnuts) and tender rabo de boi (oxtail). The decor is quaint, to say the least, staff are friendly and the wine cellar is vast.

❤ O Nobre €€€
Avenida Sacadura Cabral 53B (21 797 0760, www.justanobre.pt). Metro Campo Pequeno. **Open** *noon-3pm, 7.30-11pm Tue-Fri, Sun; 7.30-11pm Sat.* **Map** *p142 Q13* ❷ *Portuguese*

This is a showcase for the rural cuisine of Justa Nobre, who learned her tricks growing up in rural Trás-os-Montes. Try one of her specialities such as shellfish soup, baked *robalo* (sea bass) or stewed partridge: you won't find better in Lisbon. Desserts runs from ultra-light egg *farófias* to a filling chestnut and hazelnut tart. On Sundays, locals make a special trip for the *cozido à portuguesa*. Nobre recently opened another restaurant near Belém, **À Justa** (Calçada da Ajuda 107, 21 363 0993).

Portugália €€
Avenida Almirante Reis 117 (21 314 0002, www.portugalia.pt). Metro Arroios. **Open** *noon-midnight Mon-Thur, Sun; noon-1am Fri, Sat.* **Map** *p142 S15* ❸ *Beer hall*

This old brewery, originally called Germania (a name hastily changed when Portugal entered World War I on the Allied side), has morphed into a chain. But there's nothing like going to the original. It's pretty much just shellfish, steaks and lots of beer, served up with brusque efficiency. Of the other branches, the best located is the one on the river near Cais do Sodré. **Other locations** throughout the city.

❤ Rabo d'Pêxe €€
Avenida Duque de Ávila 42B, Saldanha (21 314 1605, www.rabodpexe.pt). Metro Saldanha. **Open** *noon-3pm, 7-11.30pm Mon-Thur, Sun; noon-3pm, 7pm-midnight Fri, Sat.* **Map** *p142 Q14* ❹ *Seafood*

The 'Fish Tail', a swish modern restaurant, is among the best places in Lisbon to enjoy the sea's bounty, thanks to head chef Abel Cunha's experience working with sushi. Grilled fresh fish from the impressive display is also a good option, and there's even fish and chips (and steaks).

Cafés & bars

L'Éclair
Avenida Duque d'Ávila 44 (21 136 3877). Metro Saldanha. **Open** *9am-8pm Tue-Fri, 9am-7pm Sat, Sun.* **Map** *p142 Q14* ❶

This is the first of three shops opened in quick succession by a pastry maker from Paris whose fancy concoctions are like little jewels. éclairs range from lemon and strawberry-Matcha to black forest and tatin. Pricey, but you're worth it. **Other locations** Time Out Market; Rua dos Bacalhoeiros 113, Alfama.

Pastelaria Mexicana
Avenida Guerra Junqueiro 30C (21 848 6117, http://mexicana.pt). Metro Alameda. **Open** *7.30am-10pm daily.* **Map** *p142 S14* ❷

This large snack bar (with nothing Mexican about it) on a smart shopping street opened in 1946 – and is still owned by the same family – but the striking tiled decor dates from 1962. The cakes, pastries and scones are all made on the premises. Like **Pastelaria Versailles** (*see p149*), Mexicana is on the protected 'Lojas Com História' list (*see p45*).

❤ Pastelaria Versailles
Avenida da República 15A (21 354 6340). Metro Saldanha. **Open** *7.30am-11pm daily.* **Map** *p142 Q14* ❸

How many places are there where you can take afternoon tea or a late-night hot chocolate surrounded by chandeliers, carved wooden display cases and stained glass? This 1922 gem has a huge selection of cakes, meringues and pastries. You can lunch or dine here too: the desserts are fantastic.

Shops & services

❤ Centro Colombo
Avenida Lusíada, Benfica (21 711 3600, www. colombo.pt). Metro Colégio Militar-Luz. **Open** *10am-midnight daily.* **Map** *p142 O10* ❶ *Mall*

This giant mall boasts a wealth of international and Portuguese chains, lots of fast food (including some local stalls of reasonable quality), a cinema (*see p150*) and a bowling alley (www.bowling-city.pt).

❤ El Corte Inglés
Avenida António Augusto de Aguiar 31, Praça de Espanha (21 371 1700, www.elcorteingles. pt). Metro São Sebastião. **Open** *10am-10pm Mon-Thur; 10am-11.30pm Fri, Sat; 10am-8pm Sun.* **Map** *p142 O14* ❼ *Department store*

This flagship branch of the Spanish chain has 12 floors of departments from stationery and electronics through surfwear to home textiles.

Galeria 111

In the basement is one of Lisbon's best supermarkets and a separate gourmet deli, plus cinemas and a varied food court. On the top-floor you will find **Gourmet Experience Lisboa** (10am-midnight Mon-Thur, Sun; 10am-1 am Fri & Sat), a food court hosting outlets from Michelin-starred chefs that's a magnet for Lisbon's smart set.

♥ Galeria 111
*Campo Grande 113 (21 797 7418, https://111. pt). Metro Campo Grande. **Open** 10am-7pm Tue-Sat. **No cards**. **Map** p142 P10* ❸ *Gallery*

This high-profile gallery, founded before the 1974 Revolution, boasts a huge stock of work by the likes of Paula Rego, Alexandre Pomar and António Dacosta. It has a fine collection of prints and drawings, plus a bookshop. There's overspill round the corner at Rua Dr João Soares 5B (21 781 9907).

Miosótis
*Rua Latino Coelho 89 (21 136 9849, 21 314 7841). Metro São Sebastião. **Open** 9am-9pm Mon-Sat. **No cards**. **Map** p142 P15* ❹ *Food & drink*

This organic grocery has a wide range of local and imported fresh produce and prepared dishes, herbal teas and vitamins, plus hard-to-find ingredients such as pecans. There is a restaurant (lunch only) and cafeteria with yummy cakes.

EASTERN LISBON

Xabregas and Beato

The **Museu Nacional do Azulejo** took up residence in 1980 in one of the city's most important Manueline landmarks, the 16th-century **Convento da Madre de Deus**, in Xabregas. It once stood on the waterfront but is now separated from the river by a bewildering assortment of streets, overpasses, railways and cranes. Upriver, the **Convento do Beato** was built in the 16th century; in the mid 19th century it was annexed to the Nacional biscuit factory, but has now been restored and is used for special events. Several old warehouses and even former churches (such as **Teatro Ibérico**, *see p213*) in the area have become performance spaces, and galleries have moved in.

Marvila

Further upriver, the fever surrounding Expo '98 (*see p153*) saw warehouses in Marvila host parties. But more permanent nightlife only moved in a decade later, when **Fábrica Braço da Prata** (*see p199*) took over a disused munitions factory, joining **Teatro Meridional** (*see p213*) in the area. It was another decade again before other businesses multiplied, from bicycle repair shops to rock-climbing gyms, plus craft breweries Lince, **MUSA** and **Dois Corvos** (for the latter two's tap rooms, *see p199*). Today, this is one of Lisbon's trendiest *bairros*, yet still relatively untouristy.

Sights & museums
♥ Museu Nacional do Azulejo
*Rua da Madre de Deus 4, Xabregas (21 810 0340, www.museudoazulejo.pt). Bus 718, 742, 794. **Open** 10am-6pm Tue-Sun (last entry 5.30pm). **Admission** €5; €2.50 reductions; free under-13s. No cards. **Map** p151 U18.*

The Tile Museum, housed in a former convent, charts the development of the art of Portuguese *azulejos* since the 15th century, including a panel depicting Lisbon before the 1755 earthquake and some striking contemporary tiles. The building is a treat, with a tiny Manueline cloister and a barrel-vaulted church. The shop sells superior tiles, and there's a lovely café.

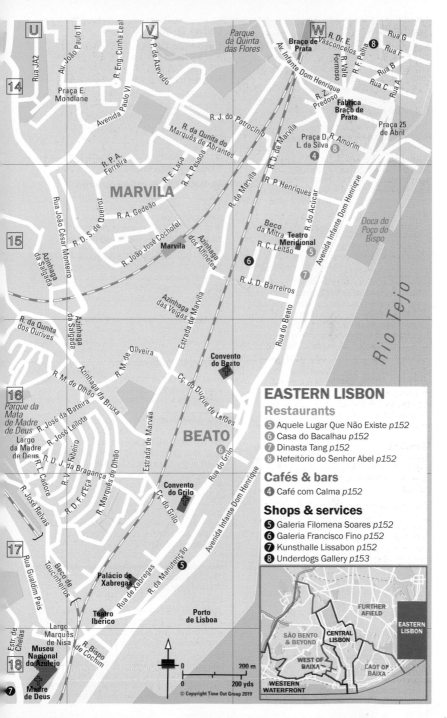

EASTERN LISBON

Restaurants

5 Aquele Lugar Que Não Existe *p152*
6 Casa do Bacalhau *p152*
7 Dinasta Tang *p152*
8 Refeitório do Senhor Abel *p152*

Cafés & bars

4 Café com Calma *p152*

Shops & services

5 Galeria Filomena Soares *p152*
6 Galeria Francisco Fino *p152*
7 Kunsthalle Lissabon *p152*
8 Underdogs Gallery *p153*

© Copyright Time Out Group 2019

Restaurants

Aquele Lugar Que Não Existe €€
Rua do Açúcar 89, Marvila (96 001 6208).
Braço de Prata rail from Santa Apolónia
or bus 718, 728, 755, 781, 782. **Open**
12.30pm-00.30am Mon-Thur; 12.30pm-2am
Fri; 11.30am-2am Sat; 11.30am-00.30am
Sun. Map p151 W15 **5** *International*

The name means 'That Place That Doesn't
Exist' – but it is hard to miss. Past a heap of
old doors is a space furnished in spectacularly
mismatched fashion: wine bottles are
displayed in an old piano, a suitcase serves
as a chandelier, and there are more doors
hanging from the walls. The food is an
inventive mixture of Italian and Indian, much
of it spicy.

Casa do Bacalhau €€
Rua do Grilo 54, Beato (21 862 0000, www.
acasado bacalhau.com). Bus 718, 728. **Open**
noon-3pm, 7.30-11pm Mon-Sat; noon-3pm
Sun. Map p151 V16 **6** *Portuguese*

Although there are other fish and meat dishes
at the 'House of Bacalhau' – and even some
vegetarian fare – the focus here is cod. The
range of *bacalhau* dishes is unrivalled: from
accessible standards to rarer treats such as
feijoada de sames (bean stew with the cod's
float bladder). There's a good wine cellar too.

Dinasta Tang €€
Rua do Açúcar 107, Marvila (21 868 0467).
Bus 718, 728, 755, 781, 782. **Open** *noon-3pm,*
7-11pm daily. Map p151 W15 **7** *Chinese*

Yet another old warehouse, this space has
since 2014 served as the roomy home for this
restaurant serving mainly Cantonese fare.
There's dim sum and starters that include
tofu with Century Egg and lotus roots with
sticky rice, plus a long list of standard mains.
Decorated niches are good for a romantic or
family dinner, some with a view of the docks.

Refeitório do Senhor Abel €€
Praça David Leandro da Silva 5, Marvila (21
868 8023, http://senhorabel.pt). Bus 718, 728,
755, 781, 782. **Open** *noon-3pm, 7.30-11pm*
Tue-Sat; noon-3pm Sun. Map p151 W14 **8**
Pizzas

Sicilian *pizzaiolo* Roberto Mezzapelle teamed
up with Chakall, Argentinian chef and long-
time Lisbon resident, to open this pizzeria
in the refectory of a magnificent old wine
warehouse. Doughs are slow-fermented, and
made with hemp, activated charcoal and the
like, with Italian-style toppings. There are tasty
carpaccios too. The kitchen also serves the
neighbouring Heterónimo BAAR (*see p199*). At
nearby no.9, Chakall lets rip, South American
style, in the cavernous El Bulo Social Club.

Cafés & bars

Café com Calma
Rua do Açúcar 10, Marvila (21 868 0398). Bus
718, 728, 755, 781, 782. **Open** *8am-7pm Mon-*
Fri; noon-6pm Sat. Map p151 W14 **4**

Best known for its unusual and scrumptious
cakes and tarts, this café with a vintage vibe
also serves healthy lunches. The Saturday
brunches (to 4pm) are popular, so come
early or queue.

Shops & services

♥ Galeria Filomena Soares
Rua da Manutenção 80, Xabregas (21 862
4122, www.gfilomenasoares.com). Metro
Santa Apolónia then 25min walk, or bus
718, 728, 742, 759. **Open** *10am-7pm Tue-Sat.*
Closed Aug. Map p151 V17 **5** *Gallery*

Soares is one of Europe's most influential
female art dealers, representing a roster of
local heavyweights such as Rui Chafes and
the late Helena Almeida, plus global stars
such as Shirin Neshat and Dan Graham.

♥ Galeria Francisco Fino
Rua Capitão Leitão 76, Marvila (21 584 2211,
www.franciscofino.com). Bus 718, 728, 755,
781, 782. **Open** *noon-7pm Tue-Fri; 2-7pm Sat.*
Map p151 W15 **6** *Gallery*

A more recent arrival, in 2017, this gallery
shares a street with two craft beer joints and
showcases less mainstream local and foreign
artists. As well as shows there are other
themed events.

♥ Kunsthalle Lissabon
Rua José Sobral Cid 9E, Xabregas (91 204
5650, www.kunsthalle-lissabon.org). Metro
Santa Apolónia. **Open** *3-7pm Thur-Sat.* **Map**
p151 U18 **7** *Gallery*

The name wryly contrasts this gallery's
modest size with Germany's grand 'art halls',
but is a statement of intent: the Portuguese
duo who run it aim to stoke debate about
contemporary art.

In the know
Take flight

Visitors crossing the Ponte Vasco da Gama
pass over a large area of old salt pans near
Alcochete. This is the start of the **Reserva
Natural do Estuário do Tejo** (21 234 8021,
http://www.natural.pt), a birdwatcher's
paradise. Local experts **Birds & Nature**
(www.birds.pt, 91 329 9990) offer half- and
full-day private tours (from €40/person) and
can arrange three-hour guided boat trips.

Underdogs Gallery

♥ Underdogs Gallery

*Rua Fernando Palha, Armazém 56, Marvila (21 868 0462, www.under-dogs.net). Braço de Prata rail from Santa Apolónia or bus 728, 781. **Open** 2-8pm Tue-Sat. **Map** p151 W14 ⑧ Gallery*

The Underdogs cultural platform, whose best-known collaborator is graffiti/street artist Vhils, promotes urban-inspired art with exhibitions at this large space near Braço de Prata train station. The gallery is also a meeting point for artists, with a loungey café. You can pick up artworks here or at their store in Cais do Sodré (Rua da Cintura do Porto de Lisboa, Armazém A, no.20, 21 099 1678, closed Mon).

PARQUE DAS NAÇÕES

In 1990, the area around Cabo Ruivo was a wasteland of near-derelict warehouses, the municipal abattoir, an oil refinery and dozens of oil tanks. It was a far cry from back when the Companhia dos Diamantes on Avenida Marechal Gomes da Costa (now home to public broadcaster RTP) oversaw Africa's diamond trade, and Pan-American Clipper seaplanes docked on the Olivais quay, where the ultra-modern **Oceanário** (*see p155*) now stands.

In the mid 1990s, a site measuring 330 hectares was levelled as armies of bulldozers and workers transformed the area for the opening of Expo '98 on 22 May 1998. The four-month World's Fair was timed to coincide with the 500th anniversary of the discovery of the sea route to India, with oceans as its theme. A new Metro line was built, with impressive artistic input (*see p234* Azulejos).

After Expo '98 ended, the area was recast as a new district dubbed Parque das Nações, where urban development has continued ever since. Above a riverside walkway, the cable cars of **Telecabine Lisboa** (www.telecabinelisboa.pt) dangle as they travel towards **Torre Vasco da Gama**, Lisbon's tallest structure, now the Myriad hotel. In late 2018, Spain's most decorated chef, Martin Berasategui, inaugurated a restaurant on its top floor.

Across the dock, the **Pavilhão de Portugal**, designed by Álvaro Siza Vieira, hosts occasional exhibitions. Next door, the futuristic beetle-shaped building is the Pavilhão Atlântico (now officially the **Altice Arena**, *see p207*), which hosts everything from rock concerts to ice spectaculars. South of the Oceanário, the **Pavilhão do Conhecimento** (*see p153*) delights children and their parents with hands-on science exhibits. By the river, the **Teatro Camões** (*see p209*) is home to the Companhia Nacional de Bailado.

The **Ponte Vasco da Gama**, completed in 1998, was briefly Europe's longest bridge. The project was dogged by controversy because of the disruption to wildlife. On the south bank, it triggered a building boom and the appearance of the **Freeport** shopping outlet (*see p17*).

Sights & museums

Pavilhão do Conhecimento

*Alameda dos Oceanos, Parque das Nações (21 891 7100, www.pavconhecimento.pt). Metro Oriente. **Open** 10am-6pm Tue-Fri; 11am-7pm Sat, Sun. (Last entry 30mins before closing.) **Admission** €9; €6-€7 reductions; free under-3s; €24 family ticket. **Map** p154 Z10.*

The Pavilion of Knowledge, an interactive science and technology centre, has changing interactive exhibitions that make for an excellent mix of fun and learning for visitors of all ages. The hands-on displays are sure to pique kids' curiosity, with experiences that help to explain the reasons behind natural phenomena. Examples include the chance to start your own tornado or blow a giant soap bubble.

Restaurants

D'Avis €€

*Avenida Dom João II, Lote 1.06.23 (21 868 1354, 96 884 8961). Metro Oriente or bus 728. **Open** noon-3.30pm, 7.30-11pm Mon-Sat. **Map** p154 Z8 ⑨ Portuguese*

This famed rustic tavern recently moved from Marvila, bringing with it authentic Alentejo regional specialities such as *ensopada de*

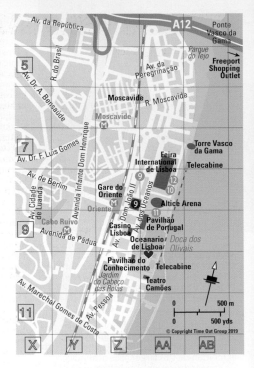

PARQUE DAS NAÇÕES

Restaurants

⑨ D'Avis *p153*
⑩ The Old House *p154*
⑪ La Rúcula *p154*
⑫ Senhor Peixe *p154*

Shops & services

⑨ Centro Vasco da Gama *p154*

---

borrego (lamb stew), *caldeta de cação com poejo* (dogfish soup) and *pezinhos de porco de coentrada* (pork trotters with coriander).

The Old House €€€
Rua Pimenta 9 (96 932 2771, www. theoldhouseportugal.pt). Metro Oriente. **Open** *noon-3pm, 7-11pm daily.* **Map** *p154 AA8* ⑩ *Chinese*

Arguably Lisbon's best Chinese food, and with impeccable decoration and service, this large restaurant near the waterfront is great for a blowout. The menu runs to dozens of pages, from *gyozas*, crêpes and a vast array of soups, to myriad vegetable dishes and Sichuan specialities. The wine list is extensive and you can sample Chinese spirits as well as teas.

La Rúcula €€
Rossio dos Olivais (21 892 2747, www. larucula.com.pt). Metro Oriente. **Open** *noon-3.30pm, 7.30-11pm Mon-Fri; noon-3.30pm, 7.30-11.30pm Sat, Sun (winter lunch only Sun).* **Map** *p154 AA8* ⑪ *Italian*

This airy space with a terrace and lovely river views is a pleasant choice for lunch. Offerings include tasty carpaccio and decent pizzas cooked in a wood-fired oven.

❤ Senhor Peixe €€€
Rua da Pimenta (21 895 5892, 91 467 1702, http://senhorpeixe.pt). Metro Oriente. **Open** *noon-3.30pm, 7-10.30pm Tue-Sat; noon-3.30pm Sun.* **Map** *p154 AA8* ⑫ *Seafood*

At 'Mr Fish', a sign in Portuguese boasts that this is 'Setúbal in Lisbon': their man is at the dockside market each morning to snap up the day's catch when it comes in. There are 15 or so kinds of fish on offer, most served charcoal-grilled, plus various pasta and rice dishes. The house speciality is a lavish *caldeirada* (fish stew) for two, good value at €35.

Shops & services

❤ Centro Vasco da Gama
Avenida Dom João II (21 893 0601, www. centrovascodagama.pt). Metro Oriente. **Open** *9am-midnight daily. Shops from 10am.* **Map** *p154 Z8* ⑨ *Mall*

Stores at this compact, three-floor mall are clustered by genre. There's also a hypermarket and a small multiplex. When you're done, go up to the beer deck and gaze out at the Tagus.

💙 Oceanário

*Esplanada Dom Carlos I (21 891 7002, www. oceanario.pt). Metro Oriente. **Open** Summer 10am-8pm daily (last entry 7pm). Winter 10am-7pm daily (last entry 6pm). **Admission** €15; €10 reductions; free under-4s; €39 family. **Map** p154 AA10.*

The Oceanarium, designed by US architect Peter Chermayeff to be the centrepiece for the ocean-themed Expo '98, was built on a pier in the former Doca das Olivias – where seaplanes coming in from the Atlantic once landed and, later, abandoned boats rotted before the area was transformed. This seawater aquarium is one of Europe's largest and best-run showcases for marine life, with 26,000 fish, birds, mammals and other organisms, from invertebrates to plants.

Observation decks on two levels make the huge (5 million litres) central tank – where sharks, rays and a large sunfish from the Algarve are the stars –ideal for other-worldly selfies. Four other tanks around it are sealed off by sheets of acrylic, generating the illusion that the water is continuous. These smaller tanks represent different habitats that visitors can also experience above water: North Atlantic rocky coast, Antarctic coastal line, Temperate Pacific kelp forests and Tropical Indian coral reefs. Here, children will particularly appreciate the penguins and sea otters – the adult otters are named Amália and Eusébio, after Portugal's two national heroes. But in the dozens of mini-aquariums elsewhere in the building there are plenty of octopi and jellyfish to keep them entranced, too, not to mention seahorses, starfish, corals, cuttlefish, sea snails and myriad beautiful and intriguing plants from both land and sea.

In addition to this permanent showcase of the world's marine life, the Oceanário also hosts interesting temporary exhibits relating to the oceans, sometimes with an artistic or musical bent.

It all makes for a terrific day out – or night if you book the popular 'Sleeping with sharks' package (€60/person) for your six- to 12-year-old. There are also concerts for under-fours at 9am on Saturdays (€35, with two adults, Oceanário visit included). Email reservas@ occanario.pt to book either activity.

The Oceanário also does a lot of educational outreach, engaging more than 160,000 children and adults a year in activities across the country, and funding conservation programmes. Since 2017 it has been working in this area in partnership with the Fundação Ocean Azul (Blue Ocean Foundation, www.oceanoazulfoundation. org) set up by supermarket group Jerónimo Martins. Its new Ocean Conservation Fund awards €150,000 to new scientific projects in Portugal or abroad that contribute to greater knowledge of endangered marine species. And there are plans for a new permanent exhibit on the seas around Portugal, though the inauguration date has not yet been announced.

All this investment is made easier by booming ticket revenues, of course: some 1.3 million people come through the Oceanário's doors each year. It also has a shop with an impressive array of ocean-related items for all ages, from stuffed animals to clothing and homeware (holders of family tickets get a 10% discount). In keeping with the conservation theme, management has pledged to ensure that within the next couple of years 95% of items on sale here are sustainable. And at restaurant **Tejo** (www.oceanario.pt/en/visit/ plan-your-visit/where-to-eat), which serves Mediterranean cuisine, chef Kiko Martins of Cevicheria (*see p108*) has drawn up a menu that aims for reduced environmental impact.

Day Trips

One of the best things about a visit to Lisbon is that you can enjoy a city break – complete with historic sights, fine food and drink, and great nightlife – with a beach holiday thrown in for good measure. Or, if you have an extra day, head for romantic Sintra, with its hilltop castle, palaces and gardens; the picture-postcard walled village of Óbidos; the palaces of Queluz and Mafra; or continental Europe's westernmost point at Cabo da Roca. Other options include the Estoril coast, sometimes known as the 'Portuguese Riviera', with a grand old resort and the country's biggest casino, as well as Cascais – an ancient fishing port that's also home to a fine museum dedicated to artist Paula Rego. All are within reach of the capital by public transport.

❤ **Don't miss**

1 Palácio Nacional da Pena, Sintra *p164*
A royal palace bursting with colour.

2 Praia de Carcavelos *p158 and p162*
Sunbathe or surf on the Estoril coast's biggest beach.

3 Praia do Rei to Praia da Sereia *p169*
Fun stretch of Caparica's endless strand.

4 Casa das Histórias, Cascais *p160*
Showcase for Paula Rego's intriguing art.

5 Praia do Guincho *p163 and p162*
Top windsurfing spot in a stunning setting.

Palácio Nacional da Pena

WEST OF LISBON
The Estoril coast

Catch a train from Cais do Sodré and you can be on your towel – or a rented sun lounger – in 45 minutes. The further you go, the more resort-like the surroundings. The return journey offers fine sunset views; the N6 Avenida Marginal coast road also makes for a stunning drive.

We wouldn't recommend any *praia* (beach) up to the São Julião da Barra headland, 20 kilometres (12 miles) west of Lisbon, for swimming. But just before it, a 20-minute walk from Santo Amaro or Oeiras rail stations, is a fun seawater pool, the **Piscina Oceânica** (http://piscinaoceanica. oeirasviva.pt, open May-Sept), with daily water quality updates on the website. Or carry on past the headland to **Carcavelos**, whose broad sands are unmatched along this coast. In summer it attracts hordes of local youngsters. There are volleyball nets and the beach is popular with surfers year-round. For eats, **A Pastorinha** (Avenida Marginal, 21 457 1892, www.apastorinha. com, €€€) serves good fish.

At **Parede**, the next major beach, the sheltered patch of sand is quieter and good for bathing. The high iodine content in the waters is supposedly good for treating rheumatism. West from Parede, shelves of rock reach into the sea, creating pools where waves break low.

An attractive beach, little used by tourists but crowded on summer weekends, **São Pedro do Estoril** is a narrow strip of sand that slips into clear waters, where rock slabs create shades of blue and green: a big draw for divers, but it makes for a dodgy dip at low tide. Below the cliff-top car park is **Praia da Bafureira**, where a restaurant (**Bafureira**, Avenida Marginal 2754, 21 452 5209, €€€) with the same name has sushi, hamburgers and giddy sea views.

Heading further west, to São João do Estoril, above the tidal **Praia da Forte**, funky cliff-top shack **Alcatruz** (Rua Vasco da Gama 2, 91 045 0447) serves snacks and drinks from noon until the wee hours. Beyond the area's two main beaches, linked by a promenade: first the pretty and peaceful **Praia da Azarujinha**, and then, after a headland, larger **Praia da Poça**, a 'locals' beach with a seawater pool, which offers respite from the crowds. A continuous promenade runs from São João do Estoril westwards; restaurants and bars with outdoor seating abound, some with showers.

The main town of **Estoril** was once a grand resort for titled Europeans. Portugal was neutral during World War II and the resort attracted both spies, including

Graham Greene, and exiled royals, such as Umberto of Italy and Juan Carlos of Spain. The **Casino Estoril** (Avenida Dr Stanley Ho, www.casino-estoril.pt) was the inspiration for Ian Fleming's *Casino Royale*. Now owned by Macao-based tycoon Stanley Ho, it draws legions of slot-machine addicts and has glitzy floor shows and the occasional free concert by Portuguese bands. The local branch of the Cascais **tourist office** (21 466 6230, www.visitcascais.com) is in the nearby Centro de Congressos do Estoril. Over the road is a crafts fair every evening (June-Sept).

For fine dining, the casino's **Estoril Mandarim** (21 466 7270, closed Mon & Tue, €€€) has more than 100 Cantonese dishes to choose from. It's pricey, but you can just drop in for the juicy dim sum at lunchtime. There's a cheaper Italian option, **Al Fresco** (Rua de Lisboa 5, 21 467 6770, €€), opposite the casino's main entrance.

The narrow strand at **Praia do Tamariz**, next to Estoril station, is occupied by tourists and locals. A private seawater pool, **Reverse Pool & Beach Lounge** (www. reversepoolandbeach.com) keeps the mob at bay, staying open until midnight. On the promenade here there's fitness equipment at regular intervals, as well as **Bar Jonas** (Paredão do Estoril, 21 467 6946, www. jonas-bar.com), where you can sip sangria and listen to ambient music. As you near Cascais, **Escotilha Bar** (Piscina Alberto Romano, 21 482 2589) tempts Brits with fish and chips, on a terrace overlooking a seawater pool. Take care – the waves lap over with force.

▶ *The train west from Cais do Sodré, known to locals as a Linha – 'the Line' – is the most scenic, and simplest, way to get anywhere on this coast. There are generally three an hour Mon-Fri (5.30am-1.30am), fewer at weekends. For smaller stations, make sure to load up your rechargeable card (€0.50, one-way tickets from €1.95) with a return, or keep coins handy: counters close early, leaving only a machine.*

Cascais

This ancient fishing port at the end of the rail line from Cais do Sodré is also a busy modern town and resort, with sights that make it worth a trip in its own right.

The first Cascais beach is only a frisbee throw from the train station: **Praia da Conceição**, separated by a strip of sand from Praia da Duquesa. **John David's Café** (Alameda Duquesa de Palmela 175A), at the east end of the beach by the station, panders to Anglo-Saxon palates, while the attached **Cascais Watersport Centre** offers visitors diving, waterskiing, windsurfing or pedal

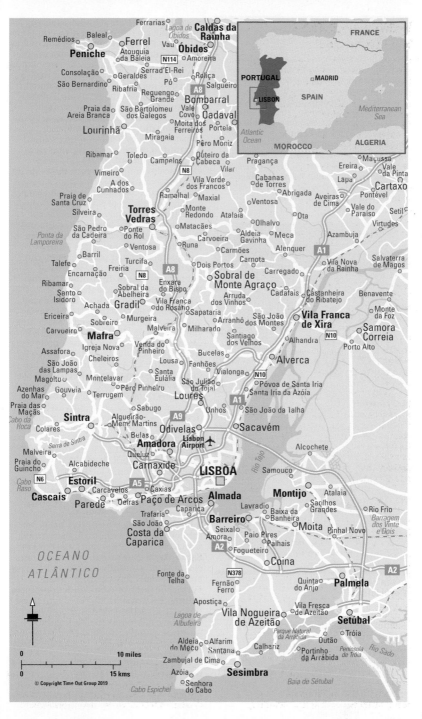

Cascais

boats. Here there are showers, changing rooms and sun loungers for hire. Further on is the tiny **Praia da Rainha**; in front of Praça do 5 de Outubro, **Praia da Ribeira** is bigger but geared to fishing rather than sunbathing.

Around the Baía de Cascais, the town's main bay, are lobster pots, gaily painted boats and old fishermen talking football. (You might also see Portugal's current president, Marcelo Rebelo de Sousa, taking a morning dip – he is often mobbed, trunks and all, by locals wanting selfies.) The **tourist office** is on the square here (Praça 5 de Outubro, 91 203 4214, www.visitcascais.com). In late July, the **Festa do Mar** (Festival of the Sea) includes a parade of boats in the bay, fado singing, fireworks and the procession of Nossa Senhora dos Navegantes (Our Lady of the Seafarers).

There are several fine fish restaurants in the pedestrianised centre, such as **Beira Mar** (Rua das Flores 6, 21 482 7380, www.restaurantebeiramar.pt, €€€). Beer, chips and televised football are available at pubs around **Largo de Camões**. Nearby, **Dom Manolo** (Avenida Marginal 11, 21 483 1126, €€) has good, cheap grilled chicken. Beyond here is the warren-like old town and, beyond that, the **Museu do Mar** (Rua Júlio Pereira de Mello, 21 481 5906, www.cascais.pt/equipamento/museu-do-mar-rei-d-carlos), which pays tribute to fisherfolk and shipwrecks. A little further on is the **Casa das Histórias Paula Rego** (Avenida da República 300, 21 482 6970, www.casadashistoriaspaularego.com; *see also p161* Every Picture Tells a Story), a building designed by Pritzker laureate Eduardo Souto Moura, whose twin peaks echo Sintra's **Palácio Nacional** (*see p163*).

Overlooking the Baía is the **Cidadela** (Avenida 25 de Abril, 21 486 7226, www.hotelcidadela.com), a 16th-century fort that now houses a presidential residence, a fancy hotel and a trendy *taberna* for wine and snacks. Nearby, the modern **Centro Cultural** (Avenida Rei Humberto II de Itália, 21 481 5660, closed Mon) hosts free art exhibits. Past the entrance to the marina, with its bars and restaurants, the **Casa de Santa Maria** (Rua do Farol de Santa Marta, closed Mon) is an early work by Portuguese architect Raúl Lino with a fine interior. Further on is the **Museu Condes de Castro Guimarães** (Avenida Rei Humberto II de Itália, 21 481 5304, closed Mon), a lavish mansion containing Indo-Portuguese furniture, paintings and porcelain that was left to the town by the Count of Guimarães in 1892.

It's a 15-minute walk now to **Boca do Inferno** (Hell's Mouth) where great columns of water shoot up at high tide. It was here, in 1930, that Aleister Crowley faked his own

Every Picture Tells a Story

Paula Rego's brilliance on display

Lisbon-born Paula Rego fled to London during the 1950s to study, and to escape the restrictions imposed on women in ultra-conservative Portugal. But the artist always made regular trips back to her homeland, and particularly the Estoril coast where she grew up. So it's appropriate that Cascais was chosen as the location for the **Casa das Histórias Paula Rego** (see p160), which provides an in-depth introduction to her work, as well as showing works by her late husband, the British artist Victor Willing. The inauguration of the museum in 2009 by Portugal's president confirmed her status as a national treasure, an important moment in a country that hasn't always celebrated the achievements of go-ahead women.

Rego has never shied away from supporting women's causes, such as the campaign against Portugal's strict abortion laws that for years saw tens of thousands risk their health – and lives – in illegal clinics or worse. Her contribution was a viscerating series of works depicting the tribulations of a victim of the prevailing law. In a 2007 referendum – the second on the subject within a decade –voters approved the legalisation of abortion.

In much of Rego's art, women appear in less harrowing circumstances, often emanating energy and determination as much as pathos. As Germaine Greer has written of Rego's works: 'It is not often given to women to recognise themselves in painting, still less to see their private world, their dreams, the insides of their heads, projected on such a scale and so immediately, with such depth and colour.'

The seeds of Rego's mature style can be found in a 1954 nude portrait, which while obeying academic rules, contains raw emotion. After experimenting with collages and abstraction, she returned to figurative work, but with a theatrical element. Clothes are often key: in *The Moth*, a little girl wears a dress that belonged to the artist's mother.

The name Casa das Histórias (House of Stories) was at Rego's suggestion, because nursery rhymes, folk tales and stories in general are central to her work. She harks back to the narrative tradition of Jan Van Eyck, William Hogarth, Zurbarran and others, whose works she often quotes, but reinvents by manipulating the relations between figures and their setting to create new psychological drama. Some critics argue that she's currently the world's leading narrative painter; she's certainly the best-known female artist born in Portugal.

The museum's name was echoed in the title of a 2017 film produced for the BBC, *Paula Rego. Secrets and Stories*. Directed by her son, Nick Willing, it is an intimate and intense portrait of his mother, now in her 80s, in which she spoke frankly about the misogyny and other challenges she had faced – including bankruptcy – and how she drew on her own tribulations as well as more universal inspirations to produce her striking work, so much of which is on display in Cascais.

death. En route is the Grande Villa Real Itália hotel, former home in exile of the last king of Italy, Humberto II; the Duke of Windsor and Mrs Simpson stayed in another villa here after the abdication. At the start of the road to **Guincho** (*see p161*) is the **Casa da Guia**, a 19th-century *palacete* that is now a chic shopping centre flanked by restaurant terraces with sea views.

▶ *All the sights in Cascais are within walking distance from the train station, and the town is served by Scotturb buses (routes and ticket details at www.scotturb.com/turismo). You can hire municipal bikes (€1/30mins, €3.90/ day) at BiCas kiosks: opposite the station, outside the Casa das Histórias, or out at Guia. You'll need a passport or ID card; under-16s must be accompanied by parents.*

Guincho and Cabo da Roca

The sea crashes into the rocks with a new violence beyond Cascais. At **Guincho**, cliffs give way to a great bank of sand, which is ringed by heath and woodland. Further to the north, the Sintra hills end in the cliffs of **Cabo da Roca**. Beyond here the beaches of the Sintra coast are smaller, tucked between

❤ Beaches & watersports

The Algarve may be the country's best-known beach destination, but the Lisbon region offers plenty of opportunities for sunbathing, beachcombing and watersports. West of the city, the Estoril coast has both sheltered beaches and broad strands (*see p158*). Continue round the cape to windswept Guincho (*see p161*) and beyond for spectacular cliffs and coves. South of the Tagus, Caparica (*see p168*) is the gateway to miles of dune-backed sands, served by bars that cater to various tribes. Further south are more isolated beaches.

There are currently 21 Blue Flag beaches in the region, but water quality varies, particularly on the Estoril coast. As for safety, beaches as far as Cascais are fairly sheltered, but take care elsewhere; drownings occur off Portugal's coast every year. Where lifeguards are on duty in the bathing season (June-mid Sept), check the colour of the flag that's flying: if it's red, limit yourself to paddling. Note also that the ocean, particularly north of Cascais, is chilly. Portugal increasingly draws leading surfers and windsurfers, but wetsuits are de rigueur.

For beginners in these sports, including children, there are plenty of opportunities to take individual or cheaper group lessons. You can also learn to bodyboard or kitesurf, or stand up paddle (SUP). For those with experience, the same outfits generally hire out equipment only.

On the Estoril coast, Praia de Carcavelos has several good surfing spots. At the **Windsurf Café** (21 457 8965, www. windsurfcafe.com) you can sign up for kayak, banana-boat or jet-ski outings, or ask the **Carcavelos Surf School** (96 285 0497, www.carcavelossurfschool.com) for group or individual surfing lessons. You can also bodyboard here most of the year with specialists **Pure Emocean** (91 659 9466, www.puremocean.com); between July and September it's based at Praia Grande, near Sintra (*see p163*).

Further west, the beach at São Pedro do Estoril is good for beginners, served by **Surf in São Pedro** (96 114 1667); while at São João do Estoril, **The Blue Room** (92 748 8112, www.theblueroom.pt) team includes Frederico 'Kiko' Morais – the first Portuguese to make the World Surf League Championship Tour roster.

Based in Cascais, and variously working at Carcavelos, Guincho and Praia Grande (depending on weather and waves), the **Cascais Surf School** (21 245 5912, www. surfcascais.com) does group lessons, with equipment and transport included. Also in Cascais, you can learn SUP and surfing with **SurfnPaddle** (93 325 8114, www. surfnpaddle.com) at Praia da Duquesa – or just hire a board, paddle and wetsuit.

Beyond Cascais, at Praia do Guincho, there are veteran instructors at **Guincho Surf School** (91 753 5719, www. guinchosurfschool.com). Or make the most of the strong north wind with **Kitesurf Adventures** (91 312 1606, 96 226 2879, www. kitesurfadventures.com.pt); it also offers SUP and surfing. It has another base at Fonte da Telha at the southern end of the Caparica coast and, in winter, offers kitesurfing on the Lagoa de Albufeira, a lagoon further south. At the lagoon you can also find the more established **Meira Pro Center** (21 268 4527, 96 918 6859, www.meiraprocenter. com) for windsurf, surf and kitesurf lessons or equipment hire.

Also on the Caparica coast, the **Carcavelos Surf School** (*see above*) offers surfing lessons at Praia do Infante. The quieter Praia da Nova Vaga, known for its wind and good waves, is another kitesurfing draw, where the **Boarder Club** school (21 214 1392, www.boarderclubportugal.com) offers lessons – also in SUP.

▶ *For more on surfing in Portugal, see www. portuguesewaves.com.*

dramatic headlands and linked by clifftop trails as far north as Magoito.

Some six kilometres from Cascais, the open sands of **Praia Grande do Guincho** stretch back, forming dunes that reach up the hillside beyond the main road. To the north, the Sintra hills form a craggy horizon, and fresh pine scents mix with the salty ocean tang. Dismissed in the 1940s by *Life* magazine as a beach with no future, Guincho is now a prime destination. But take heed. A breeze in Cascais probably means a gale here. Bathers should be wary of powerful waves and currents; note that there are no lifeguards in the middle of the beach. Guincho is among Europe's top spots for windsurfing, but is no place for beginners. It can also offer good surfing, mainly early and late in the day when the wind dies down.

Fine dining options dot the N247 coast road from Cascais: fish restaurants where you can divide your attention between the sunset and the seafood. **Meste Zé** (Estrada do Guincho, 21 487 0275, www.mesteze. com, €€€), overlooking sheltered **Praia da Cresmina**, offers excellent fare. Overlooking the main **Praia Grande do Guincho** is the Michelin-starred **Fortaleza do Guincho** (Estrada do Guincho, 21 487 0491, www. fortalezadoguincho.com, €€€€). Nearby, the **Estalagem do Muchaxo Hotel** (Praia do Guincho, 21 487 0221, www.muchaxo.com), built around another old fort, also has an excellent restaurant (€€€), as well as its own sheltered seawater pool (mid May-Sept).

At the northern end of the main beach (a 20-minute walk from where the 405 bus turns inland; turn left after the picnic site), **Bar do Guincho** (Estrada do Abano 547, 21 487 1683, www.bardoguincho.pt, closed Mon) draws watersports enthusiasts. The bar's restaurant (€€€) has a decent menu and is cosy in winter. To reach tiny, sheltered **Praia do Abano** follow the track past the capacious car park for another 1.3km (1 mile).

North of Guincho, the N247 turns inland and climbs the Sintra hills; look out for the turn-off for **Cabo da Roca**, continental Europe's westernmost point – Promontorium Magnum to the Romans. Here a wall protects the central area round the raised stone cross but take care elsewhere: there's a flimsy wooden fence or nothing at all stopping you from plunging hundreds of metres on to the rocks below.

Just after the Cabo da Roca turn-off, a dirt track on the left leads to an old windmill, **Moinho Dom Quixoto** (Rua dos Moinhos 5, 21 929 2523), now a cosy bar that also serves food (€€). Its *azulejo*-lined terrace affords breathtaking views of Guincho.

▶ *Guincho is a smooth 20 to 30min bike ride from Cascais, and the 405 and 415 Scotturb buses run about hourly (€3.35), plying a* *circular route in opposite directions and making multiple stopping at sights and restaurants. For sea views on the outward journey, take the 405, on the return leg the 415. Only the keenest cyclists would aim for Cabo da Roca, but the 403 stops on its way between Cascais and Sintra. Cheaper prepaid tickets and day passes with or without rail travel from Lisbon are available.*

Queluz and Sintra

The town of **Sintra** (*see p164*) became a UNESCO World Heritage Site in 1995 thanks to its abundance of mesmerising Romantic architecture. Spreading out from around the town are dense woodlands among which fairytale castles and gardens appear with surprising regularity.

The Sintra train line from Lisbon once ran through bucolic villages but almost all are now concrete suburbs. The only sight along the way well worth a visit, now run in tandem with the palaces of Sintra, is the **Palácio Nacional de Queluz** (Largo Palácio de Queluz, www.parquesdesintra. pt, open winter 9am-5.30pm daily, summer 9am-7pm, €8.50, €7-€8 reductions, free under-6s). The pink edifice was a royal hunting lodge until, in 1747, Prince Dom Pedro decided he fancied it as a home and had it converted into a rococo palace with delightful gardens. In 1760, when he married his niece, the future Queen Maria I, he organised operas and chamber concerts here for her. But in 1788, after the death of their son, Maria went mad, wandering the corridors tearing her hair and shrieking.

When the royal family fled to Brazil to escape the 1807 French invasion, they took most of the furniture with them, but

🖤 Sintra

Lord Byron called Sintra and its setting 'Glorious Eden', and that's only a minor exaggeration. It's a magical (literally, early inhabitants believed) place of lush forests and turreted palaces. Invariably several degrees cooler than Lisbon, it was the royal family's summer retreat. That made it a magnet for Portuguese and foreign aristocrats and also social climbers, who built fantastical residences and laid out fine gardens mixing native and exotic plants.

Today most major sights are run by **Parques de Sintra – Monte da Lua** (www.parquesdesintra.pt, 21 793 7300), called after the ancient name for the Sintra hills, the Mountain of the Moon. It's won prizes for its conservation and restoration work, details of which can be found on the website, which also lists the various combined tickets available.

Hilltop sights

Few visitors are up to exploring all of the surrounding hills on foot, though there are many marked paths, detailed at www.activesintra.com and in leaflets at the **tourist office** (Praça da República 23, 21 923 1157). But the 434 bus links the old town and the hilltop sights (€6.90 hop-on hop-off, €3.90 single). Head first for the **Castelo dos Mouros** (€6.50-€8, free under-6s) or Moorish Castle, whose dragon-tooth walls creep over the crest of one hill. On a clear day there are spectacular views to the sea and, on the next hill, the pink-and-yellow **Palácio Nacional da Pena** (€12.50-€14, free under-6s). Built by German-born Dom Fernando II at the end of the 19th century around a ruined monastery, the Pena Palace is a pastiche of styles. The exterior is covered with gargoyles and has an incredible bay window, held up by a huge stone Triton. You enter through an impressive portcullis. The palace is set in acres of gardens – a wonderful place to walk and picnic, particularly by the swan lake. Motor vehicles can only go up to the main entrance; there's a shuttle (€3) up to the palace. The ticket includes the park, but there's also a park-only ticket (€7.50, reductions €6.50, free under-6s). A free hop-on hop-off minibus tours the grounds, stopping at the **Chalet da Condessa d'Edla**, a chalet that Fernando had built after the queen's death for Elise Hensler, the Swiss-born opera singer who eventually became his second wife. Further uphill, and not on any bus route, is the **Convento dos Capuchos** (€7), an eerie place where Capuchin monks lived in tiny, cork-lined cells.

Palácio Nacional da Pena

The old town

Back down in the old town, the **Palácio Nacional de Sintra** or National Palace dominates, with its two massive white chimneys. It was built in the 14th century by Dom João I – who lived here with his wife, Philippa of Lancaster, daughter of John of Gaunt – but added to over centuries. The tiled Arab Room is striking, as is the Swan Room. The hexagonal Sala dos Brasões ('Coats of Arms Room') is also lined with *azulejos*, while its domed ceilings are painted with the emblems of nobles of the court. One of the oldest parts is the Magpie Room, painted with 136 birds, each bearing a rose and a scroll marked '*Por bem*'. The story goes that Dom João I proffered a rose to a lady-in-waiting when Queen Philippa wasn't looking and a magpie snatched it. The king excused himself by saying '*Por bem*' – 'all to the good'. Beyond the tourist office is **Lawrence's Hotel** (Rua Consiglieri Pedroso 38, 21 910 5500, www. lawrenceshotel.com), said to be the oldest on the Iberian peninsula, where Byron started *Childe Harold's Pilgrimage*. Dotted around town are pricey antique and lace shops, and some famous pastries. At 150-year-old **Casa Piriquita** (Rua das Padarias 1 & 18, 21 923 0626, www.piriquita.pt, closed Tue)

Monserrate

Castelo dos Mouros

❤ Sintra (cont.)

specialities include *queijadas de Sintra* (tartlets filled with sweetened cottage cheese), *travesseiros* (flaky pastry 'pillows' with an egg, almond and gila pumpkin filling) and the simpler egg-and-almond *pastéis de Sintra*. There's a still older tradition of *queijadas* at the **Fábrica das Verdadeiras Queijadas da Sapa** (Volta do Duche 12, 21 923 0493, closed Mon), on the road from the station: the business has been here 125 years but was founded in 1756.

The lower slopes

The privately run **Quinta da Regaleira** (Rua Barbosa du Bocage 5, www.regaleira.pt, 21 910 6650) is a neo-Manueline mansion with a garden full of grottos and a secret passage from a well. You can explore yourself (€4-€6) or take a guided tour (€8-€12, free for under-6s and over-79s).There are more grand houses further on, starting with the **Palácio de Seteais** (Rua Barbosa du Bocage 8, 21 923 3200, www.tivolihotels.com), a hotel with a terrace for tea or cocktails. The **Palácio de Monserrate** (€6.50-€8, free under 6s) was once the Gothic home of English writer and eccentric William Beckford and was later turned into a Moorish fantasy with subtropical gardens. The house and park have been extensively renovated and are now under the Parques de Sintra realm, which recently started a hop-on hop-off minibus in the grounds.

The 435 hop-on hop-off bus (€5) covers these lower slopes, taking in the National Palace, Regaleira, Seteais and Monserrate.

The new town

In the new town beyond the station, **Pastelaria O Moinho** (Avenida Dr Brandão Vasconcelos, 21 929 0267, closed Mon) has revived an old recipe for *nozes douradas* – 'golden walnuts' with egg and caramel. The new town is also home to the Museu das Artes de Sintra or **MU.SA** (Avenida Heliodoro Salgado, 21 923 6106, closed Mon, €1) in a 1920s former casino. It has 19th-century romantic paintings by Columbano Bordalo Pinheiro and Alfredo Keil, works by contemporary artists such as Vitor Pi and Júlio Pomar, and temporary exhibitions, often of photography.

▶ *Sintra is easily reached by train from Lisbon's Rossio or Oriente stations (39 or 51mins, €2.25 on a rechargable €0.50 card), leaving at least half-hourly. From Estoril, you can take bus 418; from Cascais, the 403 (via Cabo da Roca) or 417. You'll need a full day to get the most out of Sintra, though the Train & Bus pass (€15.50) also covers Cascais (see p158).*

Palácio de Monserrate

the palace has been carefully refurbished. One wing accommodates visiting heads of state, and the music room, with its superb acoustics, is used for concerts.

There is a basic café near the palace entrance but **Cozinha Velha** (Largo Palácio de Queluz 11, 21 435 6158, www.pousadas. pt, €€€), in the old kitchens across the road, now part of the Pousadas hotel chain, serves fine food.

▶ *Trains to Sintra leave from Rossio or Oriente. For Queluz, alight at Queluz-Belas (13mins from Rossio; €1.60 on a €0.50 rechargeable card); from there it's a 15-minute walk to the palace. In Sintra (40mins from Rossio, €2.25), the old town is a 10-minute walk from the station.*

NORTH OF LISBON
Mafra and Ericeira

The enormous marble **Palácio Nacional de Mafra** (Terreiro Dom João V, 261 817 550, www.palaciomafra.gov.pt, closed Tue, €3-€6) was begun in 1717 by Dom João V, and financed by gold from Brazil. The project – a combined palace and convent – became ever more elaborate, taking 38 years to finish and employing more than 50,000 builders. The 880 rooms and 300 monks' cells have been fully restored. The dome is one of the world's largest, and the rococo library has a chequered marble floor and more than 38,000 leather-bound books. The monks' pharmacy is quaint, with its old jars and bizarre instruments. Each of the chapel's bell towers has a carillon – at 98 bells in all, this is the world's largest assemblage – whose working is described in detail on the palace website. The chapel's organs are in use; indeed, after lengthy renovation, in 2010 all six were played together for the first time since the 1834 dissolution of Portugal's monasteries, and are now used regularly for concerts. The palace lost its royal status in 1910, after

Portugal's last king, Dom Manuel II, escaped his republican persecutors from here. The local **tourist office** (Avenida Movimento das Forças Armadas 28, 261 817 170, www. cm-mafra.pt) is just beside the palace.

The **Tapada Nacional de Mafra** former hunting grounds (261 817 050, www. tapadademafra.pt), whose main entrance is eight kilometres from Mafra at Codeçal, can be explored on foot (€4) or, at weekends if you book ahead, on a mini-train tour with demonstrations such as falconry and bee-keeping (€9-€12, free under-4s).

For fresh fish, visit **Ericeira**, a laidback fishing village some ten kilometres from Mafra, where the best restaurants are in side streets. It's a magnet for surf freaks: with seven world-class breaks within a few kilometres of coastline, it was named a World Surfing Reserve by the Save the Waves Coalition in 2011. There are several local schools that can teach you a few tricks. The local branch of Mafra's **tourist office** (Rua Dr Eduardo Burnay 46, 261 863 122) can help out with information.

▶ *There are half a dozen direct trains from Lisbon's Sete Rios station to Mafra, but the station is 8km (5 miles) from town. Better to catch a Mafrense bus from Campo Grande bus station (45 minutes, €4.10) that also continues on to Ericeira. From Sintra, there are separate buses from Portela station to Mafra and Ericeira.*

Óbidos

This picture-postcard walled village on a hill was a wedding gift from Dom Dinis to his bride, Isabel of Aragon, in 1282. Its whitewashed houses have terracotta roofs and trademark ochre or blue bands painted around their base, and sport window boxes of geraniums.

Pick up a map at the **tourist office** (Rua da Porta da Vila, 26 295-9231, www.obidos. pt) at the entrance to town. Then pass through the tiled main gate and search out the old pillory with the town's arms – a fishing net with a drowned person inside (Isabel and Dinis's son drowned in the Tagus before being fished out) – and the **Igreja de Santa Maria**, where ten-year-old Dom Afonso V married his eight-year-old wife in 1444. The church has 17th-century tilework, wooden painted ceilings, and panels by Josefa de Óbidos, a Spanish-born artist (1634-84) whose dark still lifes are enjoying a revival. She's buried in the Igreja de São Pedro; there are works by her in the **Museu Municipal** (Rua Direita 97, 26 295 9299, closed Mon). The castle is a *pousada* (luxury hotel) but you can walk the walls and try to spot the sea in the distance.

The annual **Chocolate Festival** in March or April is great fun but a crush at weekends. In July there's a **Mercado Medieval**, complete with a parade in period costume (you can rent outfits and take part), battles, court scenes and hog roasts. Finally, **Óbidos Vila Natal**, starting in mid December, is a Christmas wonderland for children, with puppet shows, ice-skating, Disney characters and Santa Claus (even if the snow is fake).

▶ *From Lisbon, Rodoviário do Tejo runs at least five direct buses (Rápidas) daily from Campo Grande station. There are half a dozen direct trains a day from Sete Rios (1hr 58mins, €8.30); it's then a 15min walk into town from Óbidos station. Phone the tourist office for local taxi phone numbers.*

SOUTH OF LISBON
The Caparica coast

The Caparica coast begins near the mouth of the River Tagus, where a huge maritime grain silo dominates Trafaria village. Although it's one enormous strand, each stretch has its own feel, with the tone set by beach bars.

North from Caparica town, a broad promenade has been laid out with plenty of room to walk, run or cycle. South from the town, dunes rise up a short distance from the sea, and beyond them thickets of green reach inland to the base of a tree-crowned sandstone cliff. In spring, this area is all yellow flowers. The density of the beach population fluctuates with the popularity of the bars spaced along the dunes. The bars are reached by wooden walkways from the mini-train stops and car parks. Many have showers and first-aid posts, some have music and dancing, and most are closed out of season.

Liked by locals but relatively unknown to tourists, the beach of **São João de Caparica**, north of Caparica town, is backed by

Caparica coast

campsites and has a large shaded car park. There are several bars, some serving food, and a crèche. It's highly regarded by surfers and windsurfers, but currents nearer the northern end can be treacherous.

Caparica town is not for those seeking sophistication or seclusion. There are several good seafood restaurants on the promenade, notably the bustling **O Barbas** (Rua Pedro Álvares Cabral, 21 291 3089, €€). Access to the beach is via busy Rua dos Pescadores, near where buses from Lisbon unload. The approach is a jumble of restaurants and stalls.

The **Transpraia** (21 290 0706, June-Sept) is a small open-top train that stops at beaches all the way to Fonte da Telha (*see p169*). Departing at least half-hourly between 9am and 8pm, the train scoots between the dunes: ring the bell to get off; stops are numbered. There are two zones; the most you'll pay is €2.10 single/€4 return, and there are reductions. The last train back leaves Fonte da Telha at 7.30pm.

The first stretches served by the Transpraia mini-train are a rag-bag of wooden beach huts and bars, with families entrenched in the dunes. At **Praia Nova** (train stop 5), **Bar Golfinho** is a popular hangout, with a stoned surfer feel and live bands on summer evenings.

In the know
Monastic lifestyle

Phone ahead for a guided tour of the **Convento da Arrábida** (21 219 7620, www.foriente.pt), a beautifully preserved 16th-century Franciscan monastery in a breathtaking hillside setting overlooking the Atlantic. The convent's owner, Fundação Oriente, uses it as a conference venue: at the annual Arrábida Meetings, bigwigs from around the world discuss security and international affairs.

The true beauty of this coast reveals itself around **Praia da Mata** (train stop 8). This area tends to be busy, as it's the closest point to town where you can enjoy the beauty of the landscape with nothing more than an occasional bar to block the view. **Bar Praia** has a reasonably priced restaurant serving fish and meat dishes.

The next stretch attracts a younger, more middle-class crowd with wheels. At **Praia da Riviera** (stop 9), an eponymous restaurant offers grilled fish in cramped surroundings, but it's fresh and not too expensive. Further along is **Jamming**, a beach club with a surf school (96 602 5252, www.essencia-surf.com) attached. At **Praia do Castelo** (stop 11), where volleyball nets dot the beach in summer, bars serve fish, salads, shots and cocktails. The **Cabana do Pescador** (Praia do Pescador, 21 296 2152, €€), right by stop 12, is a more traditional eaterie which attracts lunch crowds even in winter.

At **Praia do Rei** (stop 13), another eponymous restaurant (€€) offers good fish and seafood. **Hula Hula** bar attracts a younger crowd, serving all the salads, juices and cocktails you'd expect. On **Praia da Morena** (stop 14), **Borda d'Água** (21 297 5213) draws an older middle-class crowd, thanks to discreetly placed sun loungers. At **Praia da Sereia** (stop 15), a Blue Flag beach, **Bar Waikiki** (21 296 2129) is where young poseurs hang out. During the day drinks are served to sun loungers on the beach.

The sands are less crowded from **Praia da Nova Vaga** (stop 16), a kitesurfing favourite. **Tartaruga Bar** is on hand with juices and snacks. After **Praia da Bela Vista** (stop 17), the beach bars disappear. The final three-kilometre stretch to Fonte da Telha is for male nudists and the site of much gay cruising – the dunes are very active, though the beach is fairly quiet. There are peaceful spots on the fringes and things get mixed again soon after stop 19.

The Transpraia train line ends just before the village of **Fonte da Telha**. The beach is busy here, with music bars such as **Cabana** (21 297 7711) pulling in younger customers. Its diving centre functions year round. Restaurant **O Camões** (Avenida 1º de Maio, Lote 94, 21 296 3865, €€) serves fish caught by the owners, while **Inéditu's Bar** (91 724 0460) has good hamburgers for €2. The TST127 bus runs from Fonte da Telha direct to Cacilhas until 11.30pm. A walk up to the wooded hilltop (where buses to and from the Cacilhas ferries stop) yields wonderful views and access to cliff-top paths.

▶ *To reach Caparica from Lisbon by public transport, catch the ferry to Cacilhas from Cais do Sodré boat station (€1.20 on a €0.50 card, every 10-40mins), and from there a 135 TST bus (€3.25, 30mins). The last bus back to Cacilhas is usually at 8pm. There's also bus 153 direct from Lisbon's Praça de Espanha (40mins; €3.25); it drops you in Praça da Liberdade, next to Caparica market, a 5min walk from the open-top train. The last bus to Lisbon (from round the corner) is at midnight. There's also bus 161 from Lisbon's Praça do Areeiro (€4.10). In summer, Lisbon bus company Carris usually lays on at least one beach service too.*

An alternative route is the ferry from Belém to Trafaria (€1.15, about every hr), at the mouth of the Tagus. From there, bus 129 takes you to Caparica town (€2.25, 30mins); or hop off at São João when you see the sign 'Praias'. The last boat back is at 9.30pm on weekdays, 9pm at weekends. It's a 30min walk or 10min cycle ride (bike hire from Lisbon) to the nearest beach.

Sesimbra

Overlooked by a fairy-tale castle, Sesimbra is a busy fishing village-cum-resort with whitewashed streets leading up from the harbour. Not surprisingly for a place that supplies fresh fish to a number of posh Lisbon eateries, it has great seafood. The **tourist office** (93 740 5902) is in a renovated 17th-century fort, the Fortaleza de Santiago.

This beautiful protected area of sandy coves and towering limestone cliffs is covered with pines and thickets of green Mediterranean-style vegetation, which thrive thanks to Arrábida's microclimate. From Sesimbra you can hire a boat to take you to one of the beaches or drive to the sheltered **Praia do Portinho da Arrábida**, whose warm waters attract snorkellers.

▶ *Sesimbra is reached by crossing the Ponte 25 de Abril and then traversing the Serra da Arrábida (Transportes do Sul do Tejo buses leave Praça de Espanha more or less hourly and take an hour; a one-way ticket costs €4.10).*

Experience

Events

Tradition, culture and sport through the year, plus a big party in June

In Portugal, there are *festas* dotted throughout the year – often marking saints' days – and many city dwellers are close enough to their rural roots to keep track of goings-on in their ancestral village. Though religious in origin, *festas* tend to involve drinking, listening and dancing to bad music, setting off firecrackers and eating sugar-covered doughnuts. In the capital, more sophisticated seasonal pleasures are on offer – from jazz festivals to major sporting events.

The city authorities organise or fund free outdoor classical and fado concerts in summer, and indoor ones in winter, and even individual parishes have their own initiatives, ranging from live music or DJ sets in squares and gardens to outdoor screenings of summer blockbusters. With tourism booming, new events are popping up all the time, from hip hop and urban art festivals to ever-more niche cinema showcases.

► *Tickets for most large-scale events are available via www.ticketline.sapo.pt or at the ABEP booth in Praça dos Restauradores. Both music and sports events often have early-bird prices.*

Marchas Populares *p175*

♥ Best events

DocLisboa *p179*
The pick of Lisbon's burgeoning film fests.

Festa do Avante *p177*
A bit of a Cold War hangover but huge fun.

Festa de Santo António *p175*
The high point of the city's month-long party.

Peixe em Lisboa *p174*
Apt alias 'Lisbon Fish & Flavours'.

Super Bock Super Rock *p177*
Top music bash with stars old and new.

Spring

Moda Lisboa
*Various venues (21 321 3000, www.
modalisboa.pt).* **Date** *early Mar, mid Oct.*

Portuguese designers display their wares at
this twice-yearly clothes show.

Meia Maratona de Lisboa
*Ponte 25 de Abril to Mosteiro dos
Jerónimos (21 441 3182, www.
maratonaclubedeportugal.com).* **Admission**
*Half-marathon €20-€26; mini-marathon
€15-€21.* **Date** *late Mar.*

Tens of thousands take part in the 21km (13-
mile)Lisbon Half Marathon, many for the
opportunity to run across the city's Ponte 25
de Abril. There's a parallel elite event that
stays on terra firma (in 2010, the men's world
record for the distance was set here) and a
seven-kilometre mini-marathon, which also
takes in the bridge.

Senhor dos Passos
*Igreja da Graça (21 887 3943, http://
senhorpassosgraca.blogs.sapo.pt).* **Date** *2nd
Sun in Lent.*

This religious procession has been staged
annually since 1587 and in 2013 resumed
its full original route. A figure of a bleeding
Christ is carried on a litter of violets
from the Igreja de São Roque through
the heart of Lisbon and up to the Igreja
da Graça. It's attended by leading public
figures and socialites.

♥ Peixe em Lisboa
*Pavilhão Carlos Lopes, Parque Eduardo VII
(www.peixemlisboa.com). Metro Parque.*
Admission *€15/day; free under-13s.*
Date *mid Apr.*

Also dubbed Lisbon Fish & Flavours for the
benefit of foreign visitors, the city's biggest
gastronomic event focuses on seafood.
As well as the chance to sample a range

of delicious dishes, it features cooking
demonstrations by top local and foreign
chefs, fine Portuguese wines to match with
your food and stalls selling many non-fishy
gourmet ingredients.

Dias da Música
*Centro Cultural de Belém, Praça do Império,
Belém (21 361 2400, www.ccb.pt). Belém rail
from Cais do Sodré, or tram 15, bus 714, 727,
728, 751.* **Tickets** *€4-€14.50.* **Date** *late Apr/
early May.*

Three 'Days of Music' packed with cut-price
classical concerts from morning to night, on a
different musical theme each year. The same
organiser, CCB (*see p207*) also puts on a
one-day Festa da Primavera (Spring Party) in
March, with some free concerts.

Dia da Liberdade
*Information: Associação 25 de Abril, Chiado
(21 324 1420).* **Date** *25 Apr.*

A national holiday for the anniversary of the
1974 coup that ended decades of dictatorship
and ushered in democracy. Official speeches
are made (these days usually outside the
capital), while nostalgic lefties parade down
the capital's Avenida da Liberdade. For a full
list of public holidays, *see p253.*

IndieLisboa
*Various venues (21 315 8399, www.
indielisboa.com).* **Tickets** *€1-€4.* **Date** *late
Apr/early May.*

The Lisbon International Festival of
Independent Cinema has expanded hugely
since its debut in 2004 and now comprises
various competitive sections, as well as
showcases of feature films and shorts from
around the world. There's also a parallel Indie
Júnior festival for kids. Non-English-language
films are screened with English subtitles.

Estoril Open
*Clube de Ténis do Estoril, Avenida
Conde de Barcelona, Estoril (http://
millenniumestorilopen.com). Estoril rail
from Cais do Sodré then 30min walk.* **Tickets**
*Ground admission €10; free under-6s. Centre
court €10-€55.* **Date** *late Apr-early May.*

Portugal's most important tennis tournament
usually attracts a big international
name or two, as well as João Sousa and
other national heroes.

FIMFA Festival Internacional de Marionetas e Formas Animadas
*Various venues (21 242 7621, www.tarumba.
pt).* **Tickets** *free-€15.* **Date** *May.*

Puppeteers from around the world put
on inventive shows, with the language
barrier rarely an issue.

💙 Festa de Santo António

Around town (www.egeac.pt). **Date** *12-13 June.*

Local favourite Santo António, a native of Lisbon who even has his own museum (*see p79*), is the patron saint of lovers, and in the run-up to Dia de Santo António on 13 June, secret admirers hand over pots of *manjerico* (sweet basil) with corny poems attached to a paper carnation of the object of their affection. The afternoon of 12 June sees the wedding of the Noivos de Santo António, in which a dozen or so lucky pairs of *noivos* (fiancés and fiancées) get married with all expenses paid by the city council. That evening – Noite de Santo António – a colourful parade, the Marchas Populares, inches down the Avenida de Liberdade; each *bairro* contributes a group dressed in themed costumes that performs a song written for the competition. There is only limited tiered seating and the pavements are crowded, so to get a proper look at the groups you could instead attend one of the pre-competition showcases held some ten days earlier at the Altice Arena (*see p207*). This will give you a sense not only of how much work goes into the enterprise but of the fierce rivalries involved: the mood in the arena when Alfama, Castelo and Mouraria are in action recalls a football derby – and fists have been known to fly.

After the marches on the night of 12 June, many residents of the older *bairros populares* set up an *arraial* (street party) where grilled sardines and sangria are served to allcomers; in Alfama you may

have to queue to sit down and the area is packed until sunrise. In the early hours, the atmosphere here and in Mouraria can get a little fraught, as the proportion of tipsy teenagers rises. Other traditional *bairros* such as Graça and Madragoa can be just as fun, but with more elbow room.

The following afternoon – St Anthony's Day itself, a municipal holiday – there is a procession from the Igreja de Santo António (*see p79*) to the Sé cathedral (*see p79*). The two are a stone's throw apart, yet it takes a couple of hours for the cortège to snake its way around Alfama. Afterwards, the saint's devotees linger, placing a mountain of candles round his statue.

That, though, is not the end of it. The Festas dos Santos Populares (*see p176*) is a month-long party celebrating 'the people's saints' of António, João and Pedro.

Festival Internacional de Máscara Ibérica

Praça do Império, Belém (21 759 9141, www.fimi.pt). Belém rail from Cais do Sodré or tram 15, bus 714, 727, 728, 751. **Date** *early May*

A riotous open-air showcase for traditional masks (and associated costumes) from rural Portugal and Spain, mostly with pagan origins. The highlight is a parade with hundreds of participants from across Iberia and beyond; there are also dances, traditional food, handicrafts and folk bands.

ARCOlisboa

Cordoaria Nacional, Avenida da Índia, Belém (www.arcolisboa.com). Belém rail from Cais do Sodré or tram 15, bus 714, 727, 728, 751. **Tickets** *€5-€15.* **Date** *mid May.*

Lisbon's International Contemporary Art Fair is a spinoff of Madrid's long-running ARCO event, though not yet with comparable artistic and social cachet. Around 70 commercial galleries, most of them local, tout works from their stable of artists, alongside selected special projects. The four-day programme includes debates and tours of local galleries.

Alkantara Festival

Various venues (21 315 2267, www.alkantarafestival.pt). **Tickets** *free-€17; various reductions; pass €21/3 shows, €42/6 shows; €63/9 shows.* **Date** *late May-early June.*

Cross-cultural fertilisation is the theme of Lisbon's largest performing arts festival, a biennial affair (held on even years) with local and visiting dance and theatre troupes performing around town (*see also 209*).

Feira do Livro

Parque Eduardo VII (21 843 5180, www.feiradolivrodelisboa.pt). Metro Marquês de Pombal. **Date** *late May-early June.*

Book stalls take over Lisbon's central park, with side events such as author talks and concerts.

Summer

Out Jazz

Various venues (21 342 1546, www.ncs.pt/outjazz). **Admission** *free.* **Date** *May-Sept.*

This free outdoor festival of music stretches either side of summer. Concerts take place on weekend afternoons (sometimes on Fridays as well) in a different park or garden each month.

❤ Festas dos Santos Populares/ Festas de Lisboa

Around town (www.egeac.pt). **Date** *June.*

The Festas dos Santos Populares is not one party but a whole month of them during which 'the people's saints' – António, João and Pedro – have their days. Throughout June *arraiais* are held around town on a staggered timetable, and the council invariably puts

---

Music Festivals

Live rock, roots and jazz

As well as the annual **NOS Alive** and **Super Bock Super Rock** and biennial **Rock in Rio Lisboa** (for all, see *p177*) – whose high prices reflect interest from foreign fans – there are other festivals in the region that offer good value.

In June or July, **Lisboa Mistura** (www.sonsdalusofonia.com) brings the sound of the suburbs into the city centre, with free concerts featuring hip hop and Cape Verdean rhythms, plus urban and world music from outside Portugal. **Sumol Summer Fest** (https://sumolsummerfest.com), in early July in surf mecca Ericeira, near Sintra, and **O Sol da Caparica** (www.osoldacaparica-festival.pt), in mid August at Parque Urbano, Costa da Caparica (Almada) south of the River Tagus, are seaside showcases for Portuguese bands. Activities at the latter include windsurfing, bodyboarding, street art and cartoons, with one day set aside for kids. Further down the

coast at Sines, **Festival Músicas do Mundo** (269 630 665, www.fmm.com.pt), in July, has music from around the globe in the castle and on the seafront.

Back in town, **Jameson Urban Routes** (21 343 0107, http://jamesonurbanroutes.com, box office https://musicbox.bol.pt) is hosted by **Musicbox** (see *197*) in late October, its finger firmly on the pulse of modern music at home and abroad, usually with less established acts than **Super Bock em Stock** (see *p179*). In November, **Misty Fest** (www.misty-fest.com) is a showcase above all for singer-songwriters at various downtown venues.

Jazz fans might make a special trip for **Seixal Jazz** (see *179*) or **Jazz em Agosto** (see *177*); Lisbon also has **Festa do Jazz** (21 346 3244, www.sonsdalusofonia.com) with amateurs and professionals performing – often for free – over a weekend in March or April. For classical music, see *p206*.

on lots of free open-air shows as part of the official Festas de Lisboa programme. *See also p175* Festa de Santo António.

Rock in Rio Lisboa
Parque da Belavista, Marvila (http://rockinriolisboa.sapo.pt). Metro Belavista, dedicated buses laid on during festival **Tickets** *€69/day.* **Date** *late June.*

A biennial event (held on even years) spread over two long weekends and several stages, this slick Brazilian import boasts big Portuguese, Brazilian and international names (Katy Perry, Bruno Mars and Muse were on the bill in 2018). DJs keep pumping out the music until the early hours.

Festival Estoril Lisboa
Various venues (www.festorilisbon.com). **Tickets** *free-€24.* **Date** *July.*

Classical concerts by orchestras and soloists in Cascais and Lisbon – at venues that include monuments such as the Jerónimos monastery and Sé (Cathedral) – in a festival that has been going for four decades.

Festival ao Largo
Largo de São Carlos, Chiado (21 325 3000 www.festivalaolargo.pt). Metro Baixa-Chiado or tram 28. **Admission** *free.* **Date** *July.*

Free symphonic, choral, opera and dance performances are laid on in front of the São Carlos opera house on an almost daily basis, in a festival that has become a summer highlight. Come early to secure a seat.

Festival Internacional de Teatro
Various venues (21 273 9360, www.ctalmada.pt). **Tickets** *€8-€17; Festival pass €75.* **Date** *July.*

Also known as the Festival de Almada, after the south-bank town where it is based, Portugal's leading theatre festival encompasses dozens of productions by Portuguese and foreign groups, staged at venues on both sides of the river.

Cool Jazz
Various venues, Cascais (21 133 0783/91 872 7336, www.edpcooljazz.com). **Tickets** *€25-€75.* **Date** *July.*

Even more cool than jazz, this series of concerts features mainly well-known performers, performing in leafy settings; big names in 2018 included David Byrne, Van Morrison and Norah Jones.

NOS Alive
Passeio Marítimo de Algés (21 393 3770, www.nosalive.com). Algés rail from Cais do Sodré, dedicated buses laid on during

festival. **Tickets** *€65/day; €149/3 days.* **Date** *mid July.*

The Lisbon music festival that draws the most fans from abroad: a long weekend by the river with big mainstream, indie and dance names on three stages, and a plethora of sideshows and attractions.

❤ Super Bock Super Rock
Parque das Nações (www.superbock.pt). Metro Oriente. **Tickets** *€55-€60/day; €109-€114/3 days.* **Date** *late July.*

Lisbon's longest-running rock festival, sponsored by national brewer Super Bock, has changed format several times but always keeps its edge. It takes place in various venues at the former site of Expo '98. Big names in 2018 included Stormzy, The The, Benjamin Clementine, Travis Scott and The xx.

Jazz em Agosto
Fundação Calouste Gulbenkian, Avenida de Berna, 45A/Rua Dr Nicolau de Bettencourt (21 782 3483/74, 21 782 3700, www.gulbenkian.pt/jazzemagosto). Metro Praça de Espanh/São Sebastião. **Tickets** *€5-€20; €3-€7 reductions. Pass €40/3 shows, €135/10 shows.* **Date** *early Aug.*

International and local artists – including big names in experimental jazz – perform at the outdoor amphitheatre in the gardens of the Fundação Calouste Gulbenkian or in its main auditorium (*see p146*).

Autumn

❤ Festa do Avante
Quinta da Amora, Seixal (21 222 4000, www.festadoavante.pcp.pt). Dedicated festival transport. **Tickets** *€25-€37.50.* **Date** *1st wknd in Sept.*

They don't get so many votes these days, but Portugal's communists know how to hold a party. Cross the Tagus for this three-day extravaganza featuring rock, roots and even classical music, plus well-priced food and drink from around the country.

TODOS
Various venues, neighbourhood varies (www.festivaltodos.com). **Tickets** *free-€3.* **Date** *Sept.*

The name means 'all' and this festival has since 2009, been celebrating Lisbon's ethnic diversity, encouraging all communities to take part in or at least enjoy its many and varied events – from live music and theatre to guided visits and cookery and graffiti workshops. It changes location every year and is a great way to get off the tourist track and into a local neighbourhood.

Festa do Avante

Festival de Sintra
Various venues in and around Sintra (information 21 910 7110, box office 21 910 7118, www.festivaldesintra.pt). Sintra/Portela de Sintra/Queluz-Belas rail from Rossio/Oriente. Tickets €5-€15. Date mid Sept-mid Oct.

Classical music dominates this highlight of the year for cultured locals, which has been going for more than half a century. Concerts take place at the Centro Cultural Olga de Cadaval in Sintra, and in palaces and country estates around the region.

Open House Lisboa
Various venues (21 346 9366, www.trienaldelisboa.com). Admission free. Date late Sept.

One weekend a year dozens of public and private buildings of architectural interest throw open their doors for free guided visits. It is extremely popular, so book ahead (from mid September).

Festival Iminente
Panorâmico de Monsanto (http://vhils.com). Dedicated festival transport. Tickets €10-€20. Pass €40. Date late Sept.

This three-day festival of urban art and music in Monsanto Forest Park is curated by Portugal's most celebrated urban artist, Vhils (Alexandre Farto).

Queer Lisboa
Various venues (91 376 5343, www.queerlisboa.pt). Tickets free-€4; €16/5 films. Date late Sept.

Portugal's main showcase for gay, lesbian, bisexual, transgender and transsexual cinema

is also Lisbon's longest-established film festival. All non-English-language movies have English subtitles.

Santa Casa Alfama
Various venues in Alfama (21 010 5700/http://santacasaalfama.com). Admission €20-€25. Pass €30-€35. Date Late Sept.

The city's top fado music festival, held over two days, offers scores of shows on a dozen stages scattered around one of the neighbourhoods most closely associated with the genre. The Museu do Fado (see p86), hosts four of the best concerts.

Festa no Chiado
Various venues in Chiado (21 346 6722, www.e-chiado.pt). Date mid Oct.

A week of concerts, exhibitions, open-air bookstalls, free guided tours and talks in one of Lisbon's most fashionable neighbourhoods.

Dia da República
Paços do Concelho, Praça do Município, Baixa. Metro Baixa-Chiado/Terreiro do Paço. Date 5 Oct.

Republic Day (not a public holiday) is a key date for Portugal's leftists – and for Lisbon. The first republic was declared in 1910 from the balcony of City Hall, and it is from that same spot that the mayor and Portugal's president make speeches to mark the date.

Maratona de Lisboa
Cascais to Praçca do Comércio (21 441 3182, www.maratonaclubedeportugal.com). Cascais rail from Cais do Sodré then 15min walk. Admission Marathon €46-€76; half-marathon €20-€26; mini-marathon €15-€21. Date Oct.

The city's marathon avoids hills to attract record-chasing athletes: it starts in Cascais, running along the Atlantic coast and the north bank of the Tagus into the heart of Lisbon. Separate half- and mini-marathon events both start on the Ponte Vascao da Gama pontoon bridge.

Música em São Roque
*Igreja de São Roque, Largo Trindade Coelho, Bairro Alto (21 323 5444, http://mais.scml. pt/tmsr). Metro Baixa-Chiado, tram 24, 28. **Tickets** €3-€3.50. **Date** mid Oct-mid Nov.*

Two or three cut-price concerts a week– mainly *música antiga* (early music) – are staged in the lavish 16th-century Igreja de São Roque and other religious buildings in the neighbourhood.

♥ DocLisboa
*Various venues (information 91 493 7923, box office 21 310 3400, www.doclisboa. org). **Tickets** €3.20-€4.50; €2.15-€3.50 reductions. **Date** late Oct.*

Worth a special trip if you love documentaries, this long-running festival offers a feast of films from around the world in competitive and themed sections, as well as popular debates and director workshops. In 2018 the 236 films screened at the Cinema São Jorge, Culturgest and Cinemateca, with subtitles in English and Portuguese, included 68 world premieres.

Seixal Jazz
*Auditório Municipal do Fórum Cultural do Seixal, Seixal (box office 21 794 1400, www. cm-seixal.pt/seixaljazz). Ferry to Seixal from Cais do Sodré then 20min walk. **Tickets** €12; €7.50 reductions; €70/7 days. **Date** late Oct.*

This south-bank festival is a highlight of the year for jazz fans, attracting international musicians as well as local favourites.

Dia de Todos os Santos
Date 1 Nov.

Florists do a roaring trade on All Saints' Day – also known as *Dia dos Mortos* (Day of the Dead) – selling chrysanthemums at the gates of cemeteries as families leave flowers and candles on graves.

Lisbon & Sintra Film Fest
*Various venues in Lisbon & Sintra (21 099 5662 www.leffest.com) **Admission** Films €4-€7. Pass €60, €50 under-25s. **Date** Nov.*

One of the country's highest-profile film festivals (still also known as LEFFEST despite its move from Estoril), this is the brainchild of veteran Portuguese producer, Paulo Branco, who flies in A-list guests from around the world to take part. For more film festivals, *see p182*.

São Martinho
*Various venues. **Date** 11 Nov.*

Roast chestnut parties are held to celebrate the opening of the first barrels of *água pé* (new wine). Some restaurants and fado houses discreetly observe the tradition, but strict hygiene rules mean that these days *jeropiga* (a sugary fortified wine) is often served instead.

Winter
Super Bock em Stock
*Venues on Avenida da Liberdade (ticket sales 1820, www.superbockemstock.pt). Metro Restauradores/Avenida **Tickets** Pass €45-€50. **Date** late Nov.*

Dozens of contemporary musicians (in 2018 these included Johnny Marr, Jungle and Conan Osiris, but also new talents) are on stage at venues on Lisbon's central axis, with fans rushing between shows to make the most of this two-day musical feast.

Natal
Date 24, 25 Dec.

Christmas announces its arrival early these days, with the Baixa, Chiado and Avenida da Liberdade decked out in fairy lights from late November. Free concerts are often staged in the city's churches (check council website www.egeac.pt for details). Christmas dinner, of *bacalhau*, is on the evening of 24 December; the next day people are out and about, and many cafés are open.

Ano Novo
*Various venues (www.egeac.pt). **Date** 31 Dec, 1 Jan.*

New Year is seen in with fireworks, either downtown at Terreiro do Paço or sometimes out at Parque das Nações (and at several points on the south bank visible from Lisbon), preceded by one or more nights of concerts by leading Portuguese artists.

Carnaval
Date Feb/early Mar (start of Lent).

Children dress up for parties, but otherwise this religious festival is pretty low key in the capital. Carnival is celebrated more enthusiastically in nearby Loures (www. carnaval-loures.pt), with children's processions, masked balls and a final *enterro do entrudo* ('burial' of the festivities) with fireworks; on the south bank, Montijo (http:// carnavaldomontijo.pt) is similarly jolly. Further afield, Sesimbra (*see p169*) has Brazil-style samba parades.

Film

Creativity in adversity, plus plenty of festivals

A small domestic market coupled with chronic underfunding means that the local film industry is tiny compared to that of neighbouring Spain – even if its artiest output has long been prized by foreign critics. Locals, for their part, were mostly indifferent to the meditative fare produced by Manoel de Oliveira – who died in 2015 after a prolific 87-year career – and his followers, and voted with their feet for Hollywood blockbusters. Still, cinephiles in Lisbon can choose from a healthy supply of European arthouse fare, as well as a varied festival selection. And amid the austerity of recent years, plenty of young Portuguese film-makers have defied the odds to turn out prize-winning animations, shorts and, increasingly, features, too.

Portuguese film

Lisbon has always been at the heart of Portugal's film industry. In 1922, businessman Raul de Caldevila bought the Quinta das Conchas estate in Lumiar with plans to build a film city there. After António Oliveira Salazar's Estado Novo regime was installed in 1928, propaganda chief António Ferro oversaw the creation of Cinelândia, housing laboratories and studios. The buildings survive today, dwarfed by high-rise flats.

The first talkie made in Portugal was, fittingly enough, about a fado diva: *A Severa* (1931) by José Leitão de Barros. The next two decades proved to be the golden era of Portuguese cinema, with comedies, musicals and historical dramas aligned with the dictatorship's world view perhaps inevitably dominating.

After the fall of Salazar, the Cinema Novo group was established by the Centro Português de Cinema (with help from the Gulbenkian Foundation), while the government created the Instituto Português de Cinema – now the Instituto do Cinema e Audiovisual (ICA). These twin approaches remain. The 'commercial' school – spearheaded by directors such as João Canijo, Joaquim Leitão, António Pedro Vasconcelos and Leonel Vieira – targets the domestic market, with Vieira often remaking old favourites. Since the 1974 Revolution, though, Portuguese cinema has been dominated by auteurs, usually living a hand-to-mouth existence. The exception for decades was Manoel de Oliveira: a director whose career began in the silent era and reached an early peak with *Aniki-Bóbó* (1942), and whose realist style predated Italy's masters by several years. He was still making movies at the rate of roughly one a year until shortly before his death; he received a lifetime achievement award at Cannes in 2008, at the tender age of 100, and his last feature, *The Old Man of Belem* (2014) was premiered at the Venice festival.

Younger auteurs have looked to follow de Oliveira's lead, exploring themes of colour, space and *saudade* (melancholic nostalgia). This is not, however, the stuff of box-office hits. According to ICA statistics, at present only on one in five weekends does a Portuguese film even make the top ten at the box office.

Festivals and screenings

Lisbon now has several excellent film festivals and, in some of them, movies that are not already in English are subtitled in English as well as Portuguese. So even if you don't understand the local language, it is always worth checking a festival's programme for details.

The last of the city's old picture palaces, **Cinema São Jorge** (Avenida da Liberdade 175, 21 310 3400, www.cinemasaojorge.pt), is now council-owned and has established itself as the city's main venue for festivals. It has one of Lisbon's largest screens, plus two smaller screens, spacious reception areas and a balcony overlooking the avenue. The council's **Fórum Lisboa** (Avenida da Roma 14, 21 817 0400) and **Culturgest** (*see p145*) also host screenings. The various entities behind most of the festivals listed below now share a home in the Bairro Alto, the **Casa do Cinema** (Rua da Rosa 277).

The festival year kicks off in March, with **Monstra** (www.monstrafestival.com), an animation festival for adults and children, with competitive sections. Around the same time there is **FESTin** (http://festin-festival. com), which screens films from Portuguese-speaking countries – with Brazil inevitably supplying the lion's share. In late April, running into May, is **IndieLisboa** (*see p174*), a veritable feast of independent film.

After the summer lull, September sees **MotelX** (www.motelx.org), a horror showcase organised by fans but along increasingly professional lines and now with a competitive section for Portuguese shorts. Later in the same month comes **Queer Lisboa** (*see p178*), a long-running LGBT competitive festival with international pulling power. **DocLisboa** (*see p179*) follows in October, with documentaries from around the world

At November's **Lisbon & Sintra Film Festival** (*see p179*), once known as the Estoril Film Festival, the focus is on European features. In December, Culturgest screens winning films from Cinanima, Portugal's leading festival of animated film, held for the past four decades in the northern town of Espinho.

Lisbon also plays host to film showcases from a number of different nations (whose screenings generally only have subtitles in Portuguese): German films in **Kino** (www.goethe.de/portugal); Italian movies in **Festa do Cinema Italiano**

In the know
Cheap seats

If you want to cut costs, save your movie-going for Monday, when many cinemas offer discounts of up to 30 per cent (Wednesday is the day for cut-price tickets at UCI). Alternatively, head to Medeia Monumental before 8pm on Tuesday or Wednesday, or before 1pm on other days, for reduced-price seats.

(www.festadocinemaitaliano.com) in spring or early summer; and French fare at **Festa do Cinema Francês** (www.festadocinemafrances.com) in October – the last two sometimes with the presence of a leading actor or director.

In August, cinemas **Monumental** and **Nimas** (for both, *see p184*) re-run arthouse films from the past year. But for those who like their summer cinema outdoors, more mainstream fare is screened in late June and July in the Quinta das Conchas park, near the metro station of the same name, as part of the city's free **CineConchas** (www.cineconchas.pt) initiative. There are usually other outdoor screenings around town too. Beware, though: Lisbon summer nights can be cool and windy.

Tickets and information

All the major shopping centres have cinemas run by NÓS; for information and credit card booking for these, *see p184* **Cinemas NÓS Amoreira**s. Similar fare is offered by **UCI** and **Cinema City**, while **Medeia Monumental** and **Nimas** are the best places for European and US indie films. Listings can be found in national newspapers, weekly magazines such as Time Out Lisboa and Visão, and at www.cinecartaz.publico.pt – where the original title of foreign films is always given. NB: On cinemas' own websites the original title of foreign films is not always given and the Portuguese given title may bear little or no relation to the original one.

Weekly programmes change on a Thursday. Films in languages other than Portuguese are subtitled rather than dubbed, except for children's animation – and even for these, there will be some screenings (usually evening ones) in the original version ('VO'). At venues other than the **Cinemateca**, you can reserve over the phone – but tickets need to be collected 30 minutes before the screening.

Foreign cultural institutes, including the **British Council**, have film libraries. Spain's **Instituto Cervantes** (Rua Santa Marta 43, 21 310 5020, www.lisboa.cervantes.es) has occasional screenings. Retailer **Fnac** (*see p101*) also shows the odd topical film in its café, while **Galeria Zé dos Bois** (*see p107*) in the Bairro Alto screens arthouse and experimental film.

Cinemas

Cinema City
Campo Pequeno (21 798 1420, www.cinemacity.pt). Metro Campo Pequeno. **Admission** *€6.50; €5.70 reductions; €5.80 all Mon. 3D films €1.80 extra.* **Map** *p142 Q13.*

It's mainly commercial fare at this small multiplex located in a mall underneath the Lisbon bullring. Rooms are themed, so you may find yourself watching a drama from a chair stamped with cartoon characters. For some films, extra-comfy VIP seats are available; the €18 ticket (€15.50 Mondays) gives you access to a special lounge with free drinks and snacks. Family tickets (from €5.90 per person) are offered for adventure, comedy and animation films. **Other location** Avenida da Roma 100 (21 841 3040/3).

Cinema Ideal
Rua do Loreto 15, Chiado (21 099 8295, www.cinemaideal.pt). Metro Baixa-Chiado. **Open** *Box office 15mins before 1st session.* **Tickets** *€7; €6 reductions; €6 before 8pm; €5 before 1pm and all Thur.* **Map** *p95 P20.*

DocLisboa film festival

Museum 1.30-10pm Mon-Fri. **Tickets** €3.20; €2.15 reductions. Museum free. No cards. **Map** p60 P17.

Lisbon's equivalent of London's BFI Southbank has two screens showing as many as five different films a day, in themed world cinema retrospectives. Tickets are only sold on the day and non-members can't reserve, so there may be queues for rare or popular classics. The Cinemateca has had museum status since cinephile Dr Felix Ribeiro persuaded the government to found it in 1948. The archive in his former home contains historical gadgets, 19,000 books and 1,500 other publications in European languages, plus posters and other Portuguese film memorabilia. To visit the library (biblioteca), bring ID and seek out the helpful English-speaking librarians in the old building. The new building has a restaurant-bar (12.30pm-1am Mon-Sat), a shop selling books, magazines and DVDs (1-10pm Mon-Sat), and space for exhibitions in an atrium with columns made from stacked film reels. Saturday afternoon 'Cinemateca Júnior' screenings for kids take place at Palácio Foz on Praça dos Restauradores; tickets for these are available from the box office from 11am to 3pm or online at http://cinemateca.bol.pt.

Monumental

Avenida Praia Vitória 72 (21 314 2223, www. medeiafilmes.pt). Metro Saldanha. **Tickets** €7; €5 reductions; €5 all Mon, before 8pm Tue, Wed, before 1pm Thur-Sun. 3D films €2 extra. **Map** p142 Q13.

Four screens show leading indie and European arthouse fare. The cinema has excellent acoustics and sightlines, and attracts the highest audiences per screen in town. The café-bar offers a range of Belgian beers and decent food, and there's a quiet mezzanine area with DVDs, books for sale and free Wi-Fi. Round the corner, small sister cinema Nimas (Avenida 5 de Outubro 42B, 21 357 4362) draws local intellectuals with a mix of premieres, classics and film series. **Other location** Medeia Fonte Nova, Estrada de Benfica 503, Benfica (21 714 5088).

UCI El Corte Inglés

Avenida António Augusto Aguiar 31 (box office 707 232 221, www.ucicinemas.pt). Metro São Sebastião. **Tickets** €7; €5.70 reductions; €4.90 Wed. 3D films €2.50 extra. No cards. **Map** p142 O14.

This 14-screen multiplex attached to a Spanish-owned department store offers a mix of artsy films and blockbusters, with the same movie often shown on different screens on the same day, at staggered times. Several of its theatres feature larger, more comfortable VIP seats (€9).

In a space that once housed one of the world's oldest cinemas (but was for many years given over to porn), this new venue, inaugurated in mid 2014, aims to fill the considerable gap left by the closure of all of Lisbon's neighbourhood cinemas. Programming is varied: in part the aim is to serve as a showcase for contemporary Portuguese cinema. The building – restored by prize-winning architect José Neves – also houses a café, which is open during screening hours (as is the box office).

Cinemas NÓS Amoreiras

Avenida Engenheiro Duarte Pacheco, Amoreiras (box office 16996, http:// cinemas.nos.pt). Tram 24, bus 711, 713, 718, 723, 748, 753, 758, 774, 783. **Tickets** €7; €6.30 reductions. 3D films €2 extra. **Map** p132 N16.

You buy your tickets from a single booth at the Amoreiras shopping centre, but the seven screens are scattered around the complex so look for the overhead signs. The booking line (open 11am-11pm daily) is the same for all the company's multiplexes. **Other locations** Centro Colombo (*see* p149); Centro Vasco da Gama (*see* p154); Alváláxia, Estádio José Alvalade, Campo Grande.

Cinemateca Portuguesa/Museu de Cinema

Rua Barata Salgueiro 39 (box office 21 359 6262, recorded information 21 359 6266, museum 21 359 6200, www.cinemateca.pt). Metro Marquês de Pombal. **Open** Box office 2.30-3.30pm, 6-10pm Mon-Sat. Closed Aug.

All Must Have Prizes

Auteurs have carved out a space for Portugal both internationally and on the arthouse circuit

It is what you might call the Portugal paradox. Domestic cinema has among the lowest box office shares in its home market of any European country, yet abroad, the country punches well above its weight at major film festivals.

As a small country with no prospect of sustaining an industry solely on a market basis, Portugal has had laws guaranteeing subsidies for domestic production since 1973. As a result, a more or less unbroken tradition has developed of creatively adventurous cinema.

At times, this results in directors disappearing up their own artistic cul-de-sac. But it also generates surprising, genre-bending works, putting Portugal consistently among countries with the highest proportion of output (in its case, around 20 features a year) winning prizes at major festivals or forming part of official selections.

The 2012 Berlin Film Festival was a milestone, with directors from Portugal winning two top awards – the Alfred Bauer prize for Miguel Gomes' *Tabu* and the Golden Bear for João Salaviza's short *Rafa*. By then, the eurozone crisis had brought a bailout and cuts to state funding. Yet Portugal's artists resisted – Gomes in particular assailing the effects of austerity in his three-part drama *As 1001 Noites* (Arabian Nights) – and then bounced back. At the 2017 Berlinales the official selection included nine films from Portugal (including five co-productions), an all-time record. As filmmaker Teresa Villaverde put it in an interview with *Variety*, she and her compatriots had become 'experts in making omelettes without eggs'.

The consensus in the local industry is that one of its main strengths is a stress on artistic freedom, reflecting the criteria used in selecting projects for public funding, which favour films to showcase at festivals abroad. But funding is notoriously erratic. So the impressive performance is increasingly thanks to producers and directors themselves, not least in finding foreign collaborators.

Documentaries have in recent years accounted for a large proportion of feature-length films, thanks in part to the work of Apordoc, the national association that organises DocLisboa and more grassroots initiatives. At the 2018 First Look showcase in Locarno, four out of six Portuguese productions presented to distributors for release in 2019 were non-fiction. *Viveiro* (Breeding Ground), a study of back-room staff at a suburban football club by award-winning director Pedro Filipe Marques; *Campo*, Thiago Hespanha's 'film essay' set in and around a military base south of Lisbon (which won the showcase's top prize); Rodrigo

Areias's *Halito Azul* (Blue Breath), a portrait of a fishing village in the Azores; and *Terra* (Earth), from Hiroatsu Suzuki and Rossana Torres, with its focus on traditional charcoal making.

The other two films showcased were *A Golpe do Sol* (Sunburn) by Vicente Alves do O, a look at contemporary mores as a group of thirty-somethings gather at a holiday villa to await a long-absent friend; and coming-of-age movie *Gabriel*, the debut feature by Nuno Bernardo, the man behind online fictional vlog *Sofia's Diary*.

Another festival stalwart is Joao Salaviza, whose Amazon-set drama *Chuva é Cantoria na Aldeia dos Mortos* (The Dead and the Others), co-directed with Brazil's Renée Nader Messora, won the jury prize in the Un Certain Regard section at the 2018 Cannes festival.

Meanwhile, the government is stepping up efforts to attract foreign filmmakers, with Terry Gilliam's *The Man Who Killed Don Quixote* (2018) the first film to benefit from a new incentive scheme, with local co-producer Ukbar. Filming in Tomar and elsewhere in Portugal employed hundreds of locals. These incentives have been bolstered further, with up to €4 million (£3.55 million) now on offer per project for film or television production.

Portugal has featured in many films over the decades, including 1969 James Bond movie *On Her Majesty's Secret Service*, but the authorities believe that it has much more to offer – and to gain. In early 2018 the secretary of state for tourism herself flew to Hollywood to tout Portugal in meetings with major studios.

As 1001 Noites

Nightlife

Still a great place to party

Lisbon is an outdoors city and at weekends it can seem as if every partygoer in the country has come to town to let their hair down. Thankfully, even when people are milling around the alleyways of Bairro Alto or sitting in a 3am traffic jam, the atmosphere remains refreshingly relaxed. Still, there are some serious clubbers around, and no shortage of well-versed DJ crews to serve them. There's plenty of variety in the city's music-driven bars and clubs, from style palaces whose snooty doormen enforce strict no-trainers rules to sweaty African dancehalls where you'll hear Cape Verdean and Angolan rhythms – not to mention the parallel universe of fado, the city's archetypal music.

The local scene

A balmy climate and tolerant attitude mean that pop and samba, fado and Cape Verdean *mornas*, northern European techno and local rap all spill on to the streets of Bairro Alto and Cais do Sodré (and the beaches of Caparica). Fado music aside (*see p200*) Lisbon is not really known for its live music; instead, clubs such as **Lux Frágil** and DJ-driven bars provide the main interest. In these venues and at one-off parties you might hear the latest twist on Afro sounds from the suburbs, such as electronic *kuduro* (Buraka Som Sistema have disbanded but its members still DJ around town) or *batida*, *funaná* and Afro house from the likes of DJs Mobuku or Marfox.

Information and tickets

For big shows (see *also p206*), *Público* newspaper has music listings, a showbiz magazine on Fridays, plus online Guia do Lazer (http://lazer.publico.pt). *Time Out Lisboa* is also informative. Tickets can be obtained from **ABEP**, **Fnac** or **Ticketline** (for all, *see p206*). For club nights and parties, browse *Dance Club Mag* on Facebook or the Lisbon section of www. residentadvisor.net, or pick up flyers from **Flur** (*see p91*), near Lux. Most venues let their websitse lapse, but update Facebook regularly. For festivals, *see pp172-179* Events.

Venues

Lisbon is justly famed as a non-stop party town and the scene is best in summer, when things get going later (once people are back from the beach and changed).

Most of the action is west of the Baixa, in Bairro Alto and Cais do Sodre. Elsewhere, the Intendente area is an alternative, especially in summer when the square hosts concerts that delight tourists. Nowadays, it's only in places like Marvila that locals predominate. LGBT venues are clustered in Bairro Alto and Príncipe Real. See also *p193* LGBT Lisbon.

❤ Best DJs

Europa *p197*
'Pink Street' dance devotees.

Jamaica *p197*
Good vibes.

Lux Frágil *p190*
Still ahead of the pack.

Purex *p193*
Small space, great music.

Trumps *p194*
LGBT night's end.

❤ Best rooftop bars

Galeria Zé dos Bois (ZDB) *p192*
Cool place for a warm night.

Park *p192*
Beautiful people, beautiful view.

Silk *p191*
Slick mini-club.

TOPO *p190*
Cocktails and castle view.

❤ Best live music

B.leza *p195*
Danceable African music.

Fábrica Braço de Prata *p199*
Eclectic programming.

Hot Clube de Portugal *p189*
For jazz fiends.

Mesa de Frades *p202*
For fado fiends.

MusicBox *p197*
Quality shows and sets.

Venues are listed below by neighbourhood, except for fado music venues (which are listed together). Admission is free unless otherwise stated; any charge goes towards your drinks bill.

▶ *Night buses (every 30mins-1hr) include the 201, running west via Alcântara to Belém, and 208, which heads through Baixa past Intendente towards the airport. These can get crowded.*

CENTRAL LISBON

While Avenida da Liberdade was, for a time, known for prostitution, the Baixa has never been a nightlife district. Yet there are a few venues worth seeking out.

Baixa
Ministerium
Praça do Comércio, Ala Nascente 72/73 (21 888 8454, www.ministerium.pt). Metro Terreiro do Paço or tram 15, 28. **Open** *times vary (usually midnight-4am Fri, Sat).* **Admission** *free-€15 (incl 1 drink).* **Map** *p60 Q21. Club*

This large central venue in a former government ministry has mostly one-off parties, so check first that there's something on. The attached restaurant and terrace, Ministerium Cantina, is good for a late-night snack in summer.

Avenida da Liberdade
♥ Hot Clube de Portugal
Praça da Alegria 48 (21 346 0305, www. hcp.pt). Metro Avenida. **Open** *10pm-2am Tue-Sat. Jam sessions 10.30pm Tue, Wed. Concerts 10.30pm, midnight Thur-Sat.* **Admission** *Concerts €5-€10. No cards.* **Map** *p60 P18. Live music*

The city's leading dedicated jazz venue, this is one of Europe's most venerable clubs (now next door to its original premises, after a fire a few years ago) and consistently draws the best local and foreign performers. The club has its own jazz school and the best students (and professors) often perform, sometimes as an orchestra, which is worth catching. The suitably laid-back atmosphere is helped by the pouffes scattered about.

Red Frog
Rua do Salitre 5A (21 583 1120). Metro Avenida. **Open** *6pm-2am Mon-Thur; 6pm-3am Fri, Sat.* **Map** *p60 P18. Cocktail bar*

This smart basement 'speakeasy' (ring the bell for admission) is inspired by America's Prohibition era. Some 20 cocktails are available (from €8), with the list changing monthly. Hang around long enough and you might get to see another 'secret' space staff open up only late at night.

EAST OF BAIXA

This side of town has plenty of congenial spots for an *aperitivo* before dinner or an *aguardente* to end the night – such as the *miradouros* on Largo das Portas do Sol and the **Esplanada da Graça** (*see p83*), and is home to DJ-driven outposts **DAMAS** and **Lux**. In Alfama, going out used to mean taking in a fado show (*see pp200-203*) but **Taberna Moderna** (*see p80*) brought gin fever here and there is the odd *ginjinha* bar too (*see p69*). Intendente, by contrast, is something of a summer hub, with the square hosting world music or Portuguese rock concerts.

Castelo
Chapitô
Costa do Castelo 7 (21 885 5550, www. chapito.org/agenda/barto). Tram 12, 28 or bus 737. **Open** *Winter 10pm-2am Tue-Sun. Summer 10pm-2am daily.* **No cards.** **Map** *p80 R20. Bar/Live music*

This bar attached to the Chapitô circus school has a broad terrace from which visitors can enjoy one of the best views in Lisbon. There's also a restaurant upstairs with an international menu. A separately run basement space, Bartô, has exhibitions, poetry recitals and regular live music – from Brazilian sounds to free jazz or electronica (from 10pm Thur-Sat, free-€3); check the Facebook page.

Alfama

Outro Lado

Beco do Arco Escuro 1 (96 006 1470). Metro Terreiro do Paço or tram 15, 28. Open Dec-Feb 3pm-midnight Tue-Thur; 3pm-2am Fri, Sat; 2-11pm Sun. Mar-Nov 3pm-1am Tue-Thur; 3pm-2am Fri, Sat; 2pm-midnight Sun. Map p80 R21. Craft beer bar

This out-of-the-way bar has enough brands of craft beer to make a trip worthwhile: at least 15 on tap (rotated every month or two), plus more bottled – including Portuguese brands Sovina, Letra, Maldita, Passarola and Mean Sardine. It also stocks foreign wines and serves toasties.

Tejo Bar

Beco do Vigário 1A (no phone). Metro Santo Apolónia or tram 28. Open 10pm-2am daily. No cards. Map p80 S20. Bar

An alternative place with a handful of tables with low seats and shelves loaded with books and board games. Anyone may strum the house guitar (don't applaud: patrons instead rub their hands together to show appreciation, thus minimising noise). The bar has many regulars – who help themselves to drinks, noting down what they've taken – and draws students and musicians (even Madonna once).

Sao Vicente & Graça

DAMAS

Rua da Voz do Operário 60, Graça (96 496 4416). Tram 28 or bus 734. Open 1pm-2am Tue-Thur; 1pm-4am Fri, Sat; 5pm-midnight Sun. Map p80 S19. Bar/Live music

DAMAS opened in 2016 and quickly made its mark. During the day and in the early evening it's a restaurant, but it later turns into a bar, then a concert venue with dancefloor. There's music for all tastes in the course of the night (check the Facebook page) and always a good atmosphere.

Mouraria & Intendente

Casa Independente

Largo do Intendente 4 (21 887 2842, http://casaindependente.com). Metro Intendente. Open 2pm-midnight Tue-Thur; 2pm-2am Fri; noon-2am Sat. No cards. Map p80 R18. Bar/Live music

In a decaying mansion that has housed all manner of clubs and associations over the past century or so, this is the latest (and probably the liveliest) incarnation. The large front 'Tiger Room' hosts gigs and DJ sets, there are various small rooms that are good

for a chat or a spot of work on your tablet, and the café and back patio are great places to relax. The bar serves a good range of teas, fresh juices and cocktails, while finger food is served until midnight.

Crew Hassan

Rua Andrade 8 (21 136 1589). Metro Intendente. Open 3pm-midnight daily. Admission Concerts €3-€5. No cards. Map p80 R18. Bar/Live music

This long-established 'cultural cooperative' is a chilled place with friendly service and live music or DJs at weekends (sometimes two sets in a night) or sounds from the vast vinyl collection. Earlier there are cut-price yoga, jiu jitsu and tai chi classes. There's a corner for kids too. Try the house sangria Red Dress cocktail, or the vegetarian pizza, hot from the oven from 6pm.

❤ TOPO

Centro Comercial do Martim Moniz (6th floor), Praça do Martim Moniz (21 588 1322, www.topo-lisboa.pt). Metro Martim Moniz. Open 12.30pm-midnight Mon-Wed; 12.30pm-2am Thur-Sat; 12.30pm-midnight Sun. No cards. Map p80 Q19. Bar

Atop a scruffy shopping centre, this bar boasts the most amazing castle view. There's lots of space on the terrace (which is covered and heated in winter), though it packs out with youngsters at weekends. The attached restaurant has interesting vegetarian options. **Other locations** Terraços do Carmo, Chiado; Centro Cultural de Belém (see p207).

Santa Apolónia

Clube Ferroviário

Rua de Santa Apolónia 59 (92 534 608, 21 815 3196). Metro Santa Apolónia. Open 6pm-2am Tue-Thur; 6pm-4am Fri; 4pm-4am Sat; 4pm-midnight Sun. Map p80 T19. Bar

On warm summer nights the rooftop terrace at the 'Railworker Club' (still functioning downstairs) heaves with a well-heeled crowd, revelling in the amazing river view

❤ Lux Frágil

Avenida Infante Dom Henrique, Armazém A (21 882 0890, www.luxfragil.com). Metro Santa Apolónia. Open 11pm-6am Thur-Sat. Admission €12. Map p80 T20. Club

Lisbon's best club, with two dancefloors (one loungey, one sweaty) and a roof terrace overlooking the river. As the hip furniture indicates, it's a see-and-be-seen place, but the crowd is friendly and the measures Lisbon-large. House and guest DJs offer everything from electro and hip hop to bursts of '80s music. Thursdays are popular with locals keen on leftfield names; on Saturdays the place is mobbed by out-of-towners. Lux's programme – which includes live bands and the odd Sunday afternoon event, as well as big international DJs – and its catch-all social role remain unrivalled. Exude photogenic importance at the door if you arrive after 2am.

WEST OF BAIXA

Chiado has many cafés (*see p99*), although the most popular place to plan a night out in Bairro Alto remains **A Brasileira** (*see p99*). For a civilised start to the night, there are several wine bars in these neighbourhoods and hopefully soon Solar do Vinho do Porto (*see p107*).

Some gay- and lesbian-run places in Bairro Alto are very mixed: **Purex** is among the best. Príncipe Real has fewer bars but more of an LGBT focus. The Bairro Alto scene also extends into Bica and in summer the Santa Catarina *miradouro*, **Esplanada do Adamastor**, with its river view, has a laid-back (sometimes drugged-up) vibe. Nearby, **Noobai** (*see p111*) is more secluded.

Chiado

By the Wine

Rua das Flores 41 (21 342 0319, www. bythewine.pt). Metro Baixa-Chiado, bus 758 or tram 24, 28. **Open** *Sept-June 6pm-midnight Mon, noon-midnight Tue-Sun. July, Aug 6pm-midnight daily.* **Map** *p95 P20.* *Wine bar*

This large, arched space, its ceiling lined with bottles, is a showcase for José Maria da Fonseca, Portugal's first company to sell bottled, labelled table wine. There are some 60 wines to sample, plus nibbles that range from ham and cheese boards to salmon ceviche and braised veal cheek.

🧡 Silk

Rua da Misericórdia 14 (91 300 9193, www. silk-club.com). Metro Baixa-Chiado, bus 758 or tram 24, 28. **Open** *7pm-1am Tue, Wed; 7pm-1.30am Thur; 7pm-4am Fri, Sat (last entry 2.30am).* **Map** *p95 P20. Club*

Located on top of the Espaço Chiado shopping mall, with a 270-degree view of the city and river, Silk aimed to replicate the model of a London club. The difference here being you're all but guaranteed entry if you phone ahead (and, on less busy nights, even if you don't). The effort is worth it for the views and swish decor. In summer, the small terrace is the big draw. Japanese food is served until midnight.

Bairro Alto

Bairru's Bodega

Rua da Barroca 3 (no phone, www. bairrusbodega.com). Metro Baixa-Chiado, bus 758 or tram 24, 28. **Open** *10pm-2am Tue-Thur; 10pm-3am Fri, Sat.* **No cards.** **Map** *p95 P20.* *Wine bar*

This large, sociable corner wine bar welcomes all-comers, but its location round the corner from Purex (*see p193*) makes it something of an LGBT hub. There's a good range of Portuguese wines on offer, as well as hams, cheeses and other snacks.

Silk

A Capela

Rua da Atalaia 45 (21 347 0072). Metro Baixa-Chiado, bus 758 or tram 24, 28. **Open** *8pm-2am Mon-Thur, Sun; 8pm-3am Fri, Sat.* **Map** *p95 P19. DJ bar*

With a bar in front and a few tables at the back, the small, atmospheric 'Chapel' can get overcrowded, especially after 2am at weekends, when other bars close and revellers pile in to continue the party to the sound of dance and electronic music.

▶ *If you need to escape the crush, there's an old-fashioned pool hall across the street.*

❤ Galeria Zé dos Bois (ZDB)

Rua da Barroca 59 (21 343 0205, www. zedosbois.org). Metro Baixa-Chiado, bus 758 or tram 24, 28. **Open** *6pm-2am Mon-Thur, Sun; 6pm-3am Fri, Sat. Live music/DJs from 10pm Wed-Sat.* **Admission** *€3 until 10pm (for exhibitions), then free. DJ sets €2-€3. Concerts €6-€15.* **Map** *p95 P20. DJ bar/ Live music*

ZDB, as this alternative arts space is usually known, has provided a stage for far-out music for 25 years. Its main performance space is a bit of a fish tank, with large floor-to-ceiling windows looking out on to a back street. As well as the large ground-floor bar there's a roof terrace for lounging on warm evenings. Art exhibitions are open until 10pm.

Garrafeira Alfaia

Rua Diário de Notícias 125 (21 343 3079, www.garrafeiraalfaia.com). Metro Baixa-Chiado, bus 758, tram 24, 28 or Ascensor da Glória funicular. **Open** *3pm-1am Mon, Wed-Sat; 4pm-1am Sun.* **Map** *p95 P19. Wine bar*

At this tiny bar-cum-shop opposite the Alfaia restaurant, you can accompany tastings from a large selection of excellent wines with delicious cheeses, hams and sausages. Down the street at no.95, **Artis** (21 342 4795, 91 817 6736, open 5.30pm-2am Tue-Thur, Sun, 5.30pm-3am Fri, Sat) takes a similar approach, to a jazz soundtrack.

Majong

Rua da Atalaia 3-5 (no phone). Metro Baixa-Chiado, bus 758 or tram 24, 28. **Open** *5pm-2am Mon-Thur, Sun; 5pm-3am Fri, Sat.* **No cards.** **Map** *p95 P20. DJ bar*

This busy corner watering hole, run by the same family for almost four decades, is a key Bairro Alto bar, with cool decor and a DJ-driven soundtrack. It now does basic tapas: cheese, salami and the like. After 11pm it can get absurdly crowded. Smoking is allowed here.

Maria Caxuxa

Rua da Barroca 12 (21 346 1311). Metro Baixa-Chiado, bus 758 or tram 24, 28. **Open** *6pm-2am Mon-Thur; 6pm-3am Fri, Sat; 6pm-2am Sun.* **Map** *p95 P20. Bar*

The phrase *'do tempo da Maria Caxuxa'* means old and old-fashioned, but this café-bar in a barely renovated former bakery packs in hip twenty- and thirty-somethings. During the week it's great for winding down to a loungey soundtrack. DJs spin dub and house music on Friday and Saturday, when space is at a premium and drinkers spill out on to the street.

Mezcal

Travessa Água da Flor 20 (96 533 1272). Metro Baixa-Chiado, bus 758, tram 24, 28 or Ascensor da Glória funicular. **Open** *8pm-2am Mon-Thur, Sun; 8pm-3am Fri, Sat.* **No cards.** **Map** *p95 P19. Bar*

Don't be put off by the kids – lured by the cheap takeaway beer and cloying shots such as *pastél da nata* – hanging around outside; this bar is great for tequila fans. The tacos are pretty decent and the music mainly Mexican.

Páginas Tantas

Rua do Diário de Notícias 85-87 (21 133 3697). Metro Baixa-Chiado, bus 758 or tram 24, 28. **Open** *9pm-2am Tue-Thur, Sun; 9pm-3am Fri, Sat. Live music 10pm-1am Tue-Thur, Sun; 10.30pm-2am Fri, Sat.* **No cards.** **Map** *p95 P19. Bar/Live music*

A spacious bar that's a good post-dinner destination if you want to wind down with trad jazz, blues and the occasional bit of bossa nova. It's supposedly a journalists' hangout – hence the name 'so many pages' – but attracts all types (including smokers).

❤ Park

Calçado do Combro 58 (21 591 4011). Metro Baixa-Chiado, bus 758 or tram 24, 28. **Open** *1pm-2am Tue-Sat; 1-8pm Sun.* **Map** *p95 O20. DJ bar*

This sprawling rooftop bar on a multi-storey car park on the edge of the Bairro Alto (the 28 tram stops outside) gets packed on warm evenings. Beautiful young things chat amid giant pot plants, swaying to a soundtrack of jazz, soul and funk. The view over the river and bridge is stunning. Snacks and light meals are available (until 3pm, then 8-11pm).

Portas Largas

Rua da Atalaia 103-105 (no phone). Metro Baixa-Chiado, bus 758, tram 24, 28 or Ascensor da Glória funicular. **Open** *8pm-2am Mon-Thur; 8pm-3am Fri, Sat.* **No cards.** **Map** *p95 P19. Bar/Live music*

LGBT Lisbon

Finally out and proud

Portugal has come a long way since the 1974 Revolution. Traditional family values remain entrenched outside the big cities, but in Lisbon public displays of affection are now common even outside the core LGBT areas of Bairro Alto and Príncipe Real. A milestone was reached in 2010 when parliament voted to allow marriage between same-sex couples – not the halfway house of civil unions that the conservative opposition had proposed at the last minute – although it rejected legislation to allow such couples to adopt. Six years later, a new parliament approved the latter reform.

Well before all that, foreign visitors of every orientation were already getting a warm welcome in a city where mixed bars and clubs often offer the best evening out. In general, different groups socialise happily together – but those who prefer exclusively gay places still have plenty of choice, including nowadays even a few themed or fetish bars.

Pride (www.portugalpride.org) takes place in late June as an official part of the **Festas dos Santos Populares** (see p176), and film festival **Queer Lisboa** (see p178) has also had active support for most of its more than three decades. All in all, from a visitor's point of view, Lisbon's balmy climate, charming locals and rich nightlife make it a great LGBT destination.

Cruising in Lisbon is usually limited to parks, mainly at weekends, and beaches. Be on the alert for muggers and the occasional police patrols. There's plenty of activity on the **Caparica coast** (see p168), where there are nudist and gay beaches at mini-train stops 17, 18 and 19. If you want to cruise on summer days, head for the dunes here; there's nighttime car cruising on access roads and parking areas all year round.

In town, saunas include **Trombeta Bath** (Rua do Trombeta 1C, 21 609 5626, www. trombetabath.com, open noon-6am Mon-Thur, non-stop noon Fri-6am Mon) and **SaunApolo 56** (Rua Luciano Cordeiro 56, 21 828 2854, 92 613 6808, www.saunapolo56. pt, open 3pm-3am daily), which prides itself on being the only sauna that is LGBT and hetero-friendly.

Café A Brasileira (see p99) gets cruisey in the early evening, and the Bairro Alto restaurants **Sinal Vermelho** (see p107) and **Pap' açorda** (see p116), a local staple that's now moved to Mercado da Ribeira, are justly renowned for their welcome. There's also **Stasha** (Rua das Gáveas 33, 21 343 1131, closed Mon), run by the owner of Bar 106, and **Pó-te na Bicha** (Travessa Água da Flôr 34, 21 342 5924, closed Wed), whose punningly suggestive name (*bicha* means queue in Portuguese but is also Brazilian slang for gay) betrays its inclinations. In Príncipe Real, the kitchens at **Frei Contente** (Rua de São Marçal 94, 93 821 2749, closed Sun) and **Gayola** (Rua da Imprensa Nacional 116B, 21 397 4493) bar stay open late, making them pit-stops for those planning a night in the area's clubs (see p194). As for parties, the most popular is the **Conga Club** (monthly, various venues, check Facebook).

To find out what's on, check out www. portugalgay.pt, an informative site in various languages, or chat to staff in bars such as **Portas Largas** (see p192), **Bar 106** (see p194) or **As Primas** (see p193).

Its central location in the Bairro Alto makes this a real hub, and on summer nights the street outside is packed. Gay-owned and -run, it's nevertheless mixed, particularly early on. The decor is unchanged from when it was a scruffy *tasca* before the in-crowd's arrival: same marble tables, peanut-littered floor and music split between fado and dance (unless a Latin band takes over).

Pride Burlesque

Rua da Rosa 159 (21 134 0119). Metro Baixa-Chiado, bus 758, tram 24, 28 or Ascensor da Glória funicular. Open 9pm-2am Mon-Thur; 9pm-3am Fri, Sat. Map p95 P19. Gay bar

A Parisian-themed gay bar that draws plenty of youngsters with its weekday happy hours (10-11.30pm), cocktails and DJ sets. Later on there might be a drag show and plenty of wild dancing.

As Primas

Rua da Atalaia 154-156 (21 342 5925). Metro Baixa-Chiado, bus 758, tram 24, 28 or Ascensor da Glória funicular. Open 10pm-4am Mon-Sat. No cards. Map p95 P19. Lesbian/Mixed bar

You can't get simpler than 'The Cousins', with its two pool tables and a jukebox. The three eponymous owners are all women who know the scene, making the place popular with lesbians. But everyone is welcome.

❤ Purex

Rua das Salgadeiras 28 (no phone). Metro Baixa-Chiado, bus 758 or tram 24, 28. Open 10pm-2am Tue-Thur; 10.30pm-3am Fri, Sat; 10pm-2am. July, Aug also open Mon 10pm-2am. No cards. Map p95 P20. Mixed DJ bar

A trendy, mixed bar that combines arty decor with a cosy, friendly feel. Daily DJs ensure the small dancefloor packs out, making this one of the area's buzziest clubs. The cocktails are worth trying.

Príncipe Real

Bar 106
*Rua de São Marçal 106 (21 342 7373, 96 663 5616, www.bar106.com). Metro Rato or bus 758, 773, 790. **Open** 9pm-2am Mon-Thur, Sun; 9pm-3am Fri, Sat. **No cards**. **Map** p95 O19. Gay bar*

This stylish, modern bar has a fun atmosphere and attracts a wide range of punters with various themed nights. Owner José will fill you in on what's hot (and not) on the Lisbon gay scene.

Bar Cru
*Rua de São Marçal 170 (93 830 6078, www.barcru.eu). Metro Rato or bus 758, 773, 790. **Open** 5pm-2am Mon-Thur, Sun; 5pm-3am Fri, Sat. **Admission** €5. **Map** p95 O18. Gay bar*

As the name hints, this place is an out-and-out cruising bar. Open seven days a week, it organises themed underwear and fetish parties, which progress to nude (including staff) after 10pm.

Cinco Lounge
*Rua Ruben António Leitão 17A (21 342 4033, www.cincolounge.com). Metro Rato or bus 773. **Open** 9pm-2am daily. **No cards**. **Map** p95 O19. Cocktail bar*

This New York-style cocktail bar is a colourful haven in a nightlife no-man's-land. Its British owners have built up a loyal clientele, who lounge on low sofas and savour some of the 100 drinks on offer: from classic martinis through fruity mocktails to sophisticated Madagascar Bourbon and Madeline Hays. Alcoholic cocktails start from €7, mocktails from €5. There's an offshoot in the Time Out Market (*see p116*).

Construction
*Rua Cecílio de Sousa 84 (21 342 8971, http://construction-lisbon.negocio.site). **Open** 11.45pm-6am Fri, Sat; 10pm-6am Sun. **Admission** €10. **Map** p95 O18. Gay club*

This self-declared bear venue welcomes all gays. It has pumping house music, well-built dancers on platforms and a popular dark room. The themed nights, with erotic performances, are fun.

Enoteca-Chafariz do Vinho
Chafariz da Mãe d'Água, below Príncipe Real (21 342 2079, www.chafarizdovinho.

*com). **Open** 6pm-1am Tue-Sat. **Map** p95 P18. Wine bar*

Owned by Portugal's most influential wine writer, this was Lisbon's first proper wine bar and has one of the best ranges from around the world, some sold by the glass. Housed in a former water reservoir that is a national monument, it has a nice terrace and serves interesting snacks.

Finalmente
*Rua da Palmeira 33 (21 347 9923, www.finalmente club.com). Metro Rato or bus 758, 773, 790. **Open** midnight-6am daily. **Admission** €7 (free before 2am). **Map** p95 O19. LGBT club*

The kitsch drag shows here, which start at around 2am, are a Lisbon institution, and the place gets packed at weekends. After the acts, it's dark, clubby and cruisey, with the younger punters on the raised dancefloor almost as entertaining as the show itself. Monday is open-mic night for up-and-coming performers.

Pavilhão Chinês
*Rua Dom Pedro V 89 (21 342 4729). Metro Baixa-Chiado or Rato, or bus 790. **Open** 6pm-2am Mon-Sat; 9pm-2am Sun. **Map** p95 P19. Bar*

Here you will find Lisbon's best bar decor, courtesy of Luís Pinto Coelho. This warren is lined with floor-to-ceiling glass cases stuffed with toy battleships, Eastern European army officers' hats and other grim ornaments. This museum of kitsch is not cheap, but it's definitely worth a look. The back room is an atmospheric setting for a frame of pool. Another Pinto Coelho-designed bar, **Procópio** (Alto de São Francisco 21A, 21 385 2851, www.barprocopio.com), is near Amoreiras.

❤ Trumps
*Rua Imprensa Nacional 104B (91 593 8266, www.trumps.pt). Metro Rato or bus 758, 773, 790. **Open** 11.45pm-6am Thur-Sat. **Admission** €10. **Map** p95 O18. LGBT club*

Two dancefloors and three bars help to make Trumps the place where most LGBT clubbers end their night. There's techno and house in the main space, and pop and Brazilian music elsewhere, plus drag shows and scantily clad go-go boys. It gets busy from 2am, after Bairro Alto bars close.

Bica

A Bicaense
*Rua da Bica de Duarte Belo 42 (21 015 6040). Metro Baixa-Chiado or tram 28. **Open** 8pm-2am Tue-Sat. **No cards**. **Map** p95 P20. DJ bar*

In this large converted *tasca*, fine sounds – dub, electro, funk and reggae from resident DJs, plus indomitable staff and a large range of spirits attract a creative crowd. Smoking is allowed. Opposite, **Baliza** (8pm-2am Fri, Sat) is another local stalwart with wild berry vodkas, great *tostas* and a bubbly gay/straight clientele.

WESTERN WATERFRONT

During the Salazar years, the area by the harbour at Cais do Sodré was the only place where visiting foreigners were able to find late-night drinking or any lowlife action. Until quite recently prostitutes solicited openly in and around Rua Nova de Carvalho, where seedy bars were named after distant port cities. Many retain their tacky 1970s decor, although the street as a whole has been transformed (*see p196* The Pink Street). Nearby **O'Gilins**, with regular live music, is Lisbon's only authentic Irish bar.

In Santos, **Le Chat** (*see p118*) has DJs until the early hours. Further west, Docas is a veritable mall of docklands nightlife, with Cuban-themed bars and the like carrying on until as late as 6am, but there's little for serious clubbers. Alcântara, by contrast, has **LX Factory** (*see p121*) with **Rio Maravilha** and the odd techno party at **Village Underground** (Rua 1º de Maio 103; check the Facebook page).

Cais do Sodré

Bar da Velha Senhora
Rua Nova do Carvalho 40, (21 346 8479). Metro Cais do Sodré. **Open** *6pm-3am Tue-Sat. Shows 10.30pm Tue, Wed; 11pm-midnight Thur-Sat.* **Map** *p114 P20. Bar/Live music*

The name is a sly reference to a nickname for the dictator Salazar, 'the old lady' in power for four decades to 1968. Picking up on the area's louche traditions, this bar hosts burlesque shows towards the end of the week. The stage is small and the space narrow, but there's room to breathe on the terrace. On Tuesdays there's live flamenco, on Wednesdays jazz. This is a good place if you've skipped dinner: it serves elaborate snacks until midnight.

♥ B.Leza
Cais da Ribeira Nova, Rua Cintura do Porto de Lisboa 16, Armazém B (21 010 6837). Metro Cais do Sodré. **Open** *10.30pm-4am Wed-Sun. Live music from 10.30pm or 11pm Wed-Sat.* **Admission** *free-€7.50.* **Map** *p114 O21. Live music*

Lisbon has always been a great place to hear music from Portugal's former African

B.Leza

💜 Rua Cor-de-Rosa

Like any port neighbourhood worth its sea salt, Cais do Sodré long had a red-light neighbourhood, in its case just in from the river on and around Praça de São Paulo and Rua Nova de Carvalho , also known as the 'Pink Street' or Rua Cor-de-Rosa. Here, long-established bars bore the names of old ports of call around Europe and beyond, but both they and most of the ageing prostitutes lolling on street corners had clearly seen better days.

A harbinger of the changes to come was the inauguration in 2010 of **Sol e Pesca** (*see p198*), an old tackle shop that transformed into a modish bar with fishy snacks. But the revolution was under way when **Pensão Amor** (*see p198*) opened a year or so later in a building whose many rooms were once used by prostitutes – here the 'Love' theme recurs in the stairwell's murals, the over-the-top decor in the main bar, and an erotic bookshop. That was when pink paint was first used on the asphalt of Rua Nova de Carvalho for one-off events. But a couple of years later the authorities decided to take things a step further, pedestrianising the street permanently and ensuring that both the paint and the nickname 'Rua Cor-de-Rosa' stuck (with the help of a well-known brand of vodka).

In the meantime, several of the street's other bars have been turned into dance music hubs, such as **Europa** (*see p197*) or live music venues, such as **MusicBox** (*see right*). Others are more unreconstructed, such as **Viking** (no.7), with its daily striptease and karaoke; the newer **Bar da Velha Senhora** (*see p195*) has burlesque shows too, but is more arch about it. Now there's even artisanal ice-cream from local firm **Davvero** (no.81) – including, inevitably, several flavours featuring alcohol.

Ironically, rising rents as a result of growing interest in the area from property developers – several formerly dilapidated buildings have been rehabilitated and turned into luxury apartment blocks, mainly used by tourists – have threatened the survival of several old places that kept the flame burning all these years. The oldest, **Jamaica** (*see right*), seems to be hanging on for now.

Not everyone is happy about these changes. Local residents who had watched the area's transformation with growing alarm finally got organised; campaigns run by the 'Aqui Mora Gente' (Here People Live)

association eventually led to restrictions on opening hours similar to those already in place in the Bairro Alto – at least for venues without soundproofing – plus still stricter limits (1am) on off-licence alcohol sales.

The scene has long since spread to several other streets in the Cais do Sodré, with some interesting developments along Rua de São Paulo such as **A Tabacaria** (*see p198*), and its continuation, Rua da Boavista – such as council-funded **Polo Cultural Gaivotas** (Rua das Gaivotas 8, 21 817 2600), in whose courtyard you can see a work by Vhils, Portugal's best-known urban artist. But if you head for the Pink Street around midnight you won't want for options – or company.

colonies. But B.Leza is the slickest of such venues; it opened in this prime riverfront location in 2012, five years after the club was evicted from a dilapidated palace in São Bento. Now there's lots of space to bump and grind to the *mornas* and *sembas* turned out by the likes of Cape Verdean veteran Tito Paris or Calú Moreira and the house band. On Sundays from 7pm there are dance classes (mainly Angolan *kizomba*, €5) followed by a DJ set. Unattached women will not want for dance partners. *Beleza* means beauty; the club's quirkily spelt name was the stage moniker of a revered Cape Verdean musician celebrated for his Brazilian influenced innovations.

O Bom O Mau e O Vilão

Rua do Alecrim 21 (96 423 1631, https:// thegoodthebadandtheuglybar.com). Metro Cais do Sodré. **Open** *7pm-2am Mon-Thur; 6pm-3am Fri, Sat.* **Map** *p114 P20. DJ bar/ Live music*

The Portuguese title for the Sergio Leone film *The Good, the Bad and the Ugly* provides the name for this multifaceted venture: bar, restaurant, film club and music venue, with concerts or DJ sets daily. Check Facebook for details. In contrast to most Lisbon bars, where electronica rules, here soul, funk, Afrobeat and jazz dominate. Several rooms feature striking murals by local artists.

British Bar

Rua Bernardino Costa 52 (21 342 2367). Metro Cais do Sodré or tram 15, 18, 25. **Open** *10am-2am Mon-Wed; 10am-4am Thur-Sat.* **Map** *p114 P21. Bar*

With a long bar and wooden floor, the British Bar is designed like an English pub, but you'll rarely find a native of the isles here. It has carried on in its own dignified way since 1919, offering a great selection of beers, aperitifs and a digestif of its own. It also has a famous clock that marks the time in reverse.

Copenhagen

Rua de São Paulo 8 (91 711 4670). Metro Cais do Sodré or tram 15, 18, 25. **Open** *10pm-5am Mon-Thur, Sun; 10pm-6am Fri, Sat.* **Map** *p114 P20. Club/Live music*

This legendary Cais do Sodré bar pulls in a young crowd, including many students. The decor has a nautical theme, with lots of timber, and a mural featuring cartoons of recognisable local types. On Thursdays (and some Tuesdays) there's live music; on Wednesdays, Fridays and Saturdays there are DJ sets – mainly hip hop and R&B, filling a gap in the market – from 11pm to closing time.

♥ Europa

Rua Nova do Carvalho 18 (91 848 9595, www.europabar.pt). Metro Cais do Sodré or tram 15, 18, 25. **Open** *11pm-4am Wed-Sun.* **Admission** *free to 1.30am, then €5-€10. No cards.* **Map** *p114 P21. Club*

A bright modern club that buzzes with life most nights, hosting DJs spinning (from midnight) various genres, including cutting-edge electro. It regularly hosts music launches, slam poetry events and exhibitions. Smoking is allowed. Occasional after-hours parties take place at **Europa Sunrise** (Pátio do Pinzaleira 26) off Avenida 24 de Julho (no.68) – check the website for details.

♥ Jamaica

Rua Nova de Carvalho 8 (21 342 1859). Metro Cais do Sodré or tram 15, 18, 25. **Open** *midnight-6am Tue-Sat.* **Admission** *free-€6. No cards.* **Map** *p114 P21. Club*

Still going after 40 years, Jamaica is a world unto itself. The DJs are the nostalgic kind, whether they're spinning rock, soul or reggae, but they know their stuff and unfailingly get the mixed crowd jumping. Bob Marley is always heard at some point in the evening. Smoking is allowed.

Lounge

Rua da Moeda 1 (no phone). Metro Cais do Sodré or tram 15, 18, 25. **Open** *10pm-4am daily.* **No cards.** **Map** *p114 O20. DJ bar*

Lounge has moderate prices, an unkempt crowd, and interesting musical events. On regular nights, decent DJs spin an underground mix of electro and minimal techno, and there's the occasional themed party. It's packed at weekends, when ordering a drink can be a challenge.

♥ MusicBox

Rua Nova do Carvalho 24 (21 347 3188, www. musicboxlisboa.com). Metro Cais do Sodré. **Open** *11pm-4am Mon-Sat. Live music from 10.30pm Wed, Thur; 11pm or midnight Sat.* **Admission** *free-€10. No cards.* **Map** *p114 P21. DJ bar/Live music*

The managers of this key club with an underground feel (it's beneath steep Rua do Alecrim) have music industry connections and exploit them. It's one of Lisbon's most interesting venues, with a regular programme of rock bands, electronic live acts, singer-songwriters and DJ sets (all night on Fridays). Note that some shows start as late as 2am; for details, check the website.

Opened in 2015 by a veteran of the Lisbon nightlife scene, this small bar in a former tobacconist's retains the marvellous wooden panelling. Cocktails and gins (from €8) are made with flavours macerated on site, and there's a tasty range of hot and cold snacks.

Tokyo

Rua Nova do Carvalho 12 (21 347 2429, www.tokyo.com.pt). Metro Cais do Sodré or tram 12, 15, 25. **Open** *10pm-4am Tue-Sat. Live music 11.30pm & 1.45am Tue-Sat.* **Admission** *free-€3.* **Map** *p114 P21. Bar/ Live music*

Formerly one of the area's sleaziest bars, this joint has gained a new lease of life as a rock venue, with local bands pumping out mainstream standards, and the odd night of funk or reggae.

O'Gilins

Rua dos Remolares 8 (21 342 1899). Metro Cais do Sodré or tram 15, 18, 25. **Open** *11am-2am daily. Live music 11pm-2am Mon, Fri, Sat.* **No cards**. **Map** *p114 P21. Pub/ Live music*

This low-key authentic Irish pub attracts a mix of locals and expats with Guinness, televised football and hearty Irish breakfasts (until 6pm Sun). There are jam sessions on Mondays and a band on Fridays and Saturdays; landlord Conor occasionally sings or plays the spoons.

Pensão Amor

Rua Nova do Carvalho 36 (21 314 3399, www. artbuilding.eu). Metro Cais do Sodré. **Open** *noon-2am Mon-Wed; noon-4am Thur, Fri; 6pm-4am Sat.* **Map** *p114 P21. Bar/Club*

The name means 'Love Boarding House' – a nod to the building's past as a place of business for sex workers and their clients. Trendy locals now flock here to see and be seen in the over-the-top lounge bar – a sort of decadent tearoom, open from late afternoon – and attached rooms, which include an old-style disco. There are occasional concerts and the background music is eclectic.

Sol e Pesca

Rua Nova do Carvalho 44 (21 346 7203, www.solepesca.com). Metro Cais do Sodré. **Open** *noon-2am Mon-Wed; noon-3am Thur-Sat; noon-2am Sun.* **Map** *p114 P21. Bar*

This little place metamorphosed from fishing equipment store to trendy snack bar with only the lightest of makeovers. It kept the original name ('Sun and Fishing') and decor, but now sells canned fish and other delicacies to accompany well-priced beer.

A Tabacaria

Rua de São Paulo 75 (21 152 1550). Metro Cais do Sodré. **Open** *6pm-2am Mon-Thur, Sun; 6pm-3am Fri, Sat.* **Map** *p114 O20. Cocktail bar*

Alcântara and Docas

Rio Maravilha

LX Factory, Entrada 3, 4th floor, Rua Rodrigues Faria 103 (www.riomaravilha.pt). Tram 15, 18 or bus 714. **Open** *6pm-2am Wed, Thur; 12.30am-3am Fri, Sat; 12.30-8pm Sun.* **Map** *p114 J20. DJ bar*

In the former workers' recreation room of an old textile factory, Rio Maravilha pays homage to both the River Tagus and Rio de Janeiro. Slurp a cocktail on the terrace at sunset, or drink in the marvellous view any time. There are often DJs on duty, or live Brazilian music. You can eat here, too.

SÃO BENTO & BEYOND

Cerveteca

Praça das Flores 62, São Bento (21 402 3509, www.cervetecalisboa.com). Tram 28. **Open** *3.30pm-1am Mon-Thur, Sun; 3.30pm-2am Sat, Sun.* **Map** *p132 O19. Craft beer*

On a quiet square down the hill from Príncipe Real, this bar has more than 100 craft beers to sample from Lisbon, Portugal and abroad, to drink in or take away. It also serves simple snacks.

Incógnito Bar

Rua dos Poiais de São Bento 37, São Bento (21 390 8755, www.incognitobar.com). Tram 28. **Open** *11pm-4am Wed-Sat.* **Admission** *free-€20.* **Map** *p132 O19. Club*

An established 'alternative dance bar', Incógnito offers a discerning mix of music from across the indie-rock-dance spectrum. A decent small venue, it covers all ages, is low on posers and permits smoking.

FURTHER AFIELD

Northern Lisbon

Templários
Rua Flores de Lima 8A, (21 797 0177, www.templarios.pt). Metro Roma or Entrecampos. **Open** *10.30pm-2am Mon-Thur; 10.30pm-3am Fri, Sat. Live music midnight-2am Mon-Thur; 12.30-2.30am Fri, Sat.* **Admission** *€5-€7.* **Map** *p142 Q11. Live music*

A bar where mainly local punters of all ages sink beer and caipirinhas while listening to Portuguese and international standards, as well as the odd original set. There are smoking and non-smoking areas. Phone reservations (call 2.30-3.30pm or during opening hours to 11.30pm) are guaranteed until 11.45pm.

Eastern Lisbon

Capitão Leitão
Rua Capitão Leitão 5B, Marvila (21 580 9594). Bus 718, 728, 755, 781, 782. **Open** *6pm-midnight Wed, Thur; 6pm-2am Fri, Sat; 6-10pm Sun.* **Map** *p151 W15. Craft beer/DJ bar*

This small space is a hipster magnet, known for its craft beers – this is the area's main outlet for locally brewed Lince – and cocktails. There's also a tiny record shop (the owner is a vinyl freak) and someone is usually spinning disco, house or funk.

Dois Corvos
Rua Capitão Leitão 94, Marvila (21 133 1093, www.doiscorvos.pt). Bus 718, 728, 755, 781, 782. **Open** *2-11pm Mon-Thur, Sun; 2pm-1am Fri, Sat.* **Map** *p151 W15. Craft beer*

In the know
Crafty Marvila

The craft beer revolution came late to Portugal but there are now dozens of brands. Most supermarkets and bars stock one or more, and there are specialist bars such as **Cerveteca** (see left) and **Outro Lado** (see p190). In Marvila, breweries **MUSA** (see above), **Dois Corvos** (see above) and **Lince** (available at **Capitão Leitão**, see above) in 2017 joined with local galleries and restaurants to launch a 'Lisbon Beer District', with an 'Oktober Festa' and other events.

The 'Two Crows' taproom opened in 2015, soon after the couple that founded the company (she's Portuguese, he's American) started brewing in this former wine warehouse. The 12 taps feature their own or guest beers. They do tasting trays with five mini-beers, and bar snacks. You can take away mixed six-packs or cases of 24.

♥ Fábrica Braço de Prata
Rua da Fábrica do Material de Guerra 1, Braço de Prata, Marvila (96 551 8068, www.bracodeprata.com). Bus 718, 728, 755, 781, 782. **Open** *6pm-2am Wed, Thur; 6pm-4am Fri, Sat. Live music from 10pm or 10.30pm Thur-Sat.* **Admission** *free, except €6-€7.50 from 10pm Fri, Sat.* **Map** *p151 W14. Bar/ Live music*

On the city's eastern fringe, the hulking former headquarters of an arms manufacturer now houses this thriving cultural centre. As well as nightly dance classes, it hosts concerts of everything from fado to classical music on Fridays and Saturdays. On Thursdays there are free jam sessions and at other times anyone can play the bar piano. There are also film screenings, talks on philosophy and exhibitions by local artists. The restaurant offers snacks and set menus.

Heterónimo BAAR
Praça David Leandro da Silva 4, Marvila (21 868 8023). Bus 718, 728, 755, 781, 782. **Open** *6pm-2am Tue-Sat.* **Map** *p151 W14. Bar*

This smart place is a homage to modernist poet Fernando Pessoa, said to have frequented the space almost a century ago: its name is made up of the first letters of his best-known heteronyms (Bernardo Soares, Álvaro de Campos, Alberto Caeiro and Ricardo Reis). It serves cocktails (from €5) and food from attached restaurant **Refeitório do Senhor Abel** (*see p152*).

MUSA
Rua do Açúcar 83, Marvila (21 387 7777, www.cervejamusa.com). Bus 718, 728, 755, 781, 782. **Open** *4pm-midnight Tue-Thur; 4pm-2am Fri; 1pm-2am Sat; 1-10 pm Sun.* **Map** *p151 W15. Craft beer/DJ bar/ Live music*

While not the longest-established of Lisbon's craft breweries, MUSA boasts memorable, music-themed beer names (Blondie, Twist and Stout, Red Zeppelin and Mick Lager) and the busiest tap room. Bar food stretches from chicken wings to Mexican tamales. There's a happy hour on Thursdays (6-8pm) and live music or DJ sets Fridays through Sundays.

❤ Fado

There's arguably no cultural expression more unmistakeably Portuguese than fado. But after the 1974 Revolution, Lisbon's traditional music fell out of fashion, tainted as it was by associations with the Salazar dictatorship. The old regime presided over mass poverty and emigration; by contrast, by the mid 1980s, when Portugal joined the then EEC, the future looked bright.

Fado means 'fate' – supposedly an expression of a national trait of fatalism. Whatever the truth of this, many songs, whether performed by men or women, touch on betrayal, jealousy and disappointed love. Fado is also linked with the notion of *saudade*, a longing for something impossible to attain. However, fado can be upbeat. In more informal venues, audiences may interrupt the singer with repartee. In the *desgarrada*, singers challenge each other, often with caustic remarks.

In fado, conveying sentiment is more important than technical perfection (some amateurs are a little harsh on the ear). The *fadista* is accompanied by a *guitarra* (a mandolin-shaped Portuguese guitar) and a *viola* (Spanish guitar). The 12 strings of the *guitarra* are arranged in pairs, producing a resonant sound that at times highlights the singer's melody and at others plays solo, while the *viola* provides rhythm.

In the mid 1800s, fado was performed in the seedy taverns of working-class *bairros*, notably Alfama and Mouraria, where legendary *fadista* Maria Severa Onofriana – known as 'A Severa' – lived and loved until her death at the age of 26. But it was also taken up by some aristocrats – helping fado reach beyond its humble origins – while in the 20th century, poets wrote sophisticated fado lyrics.

Radio, the gramophone and then television made fado a truly national music style – as did the Salazar regime's bid to mythologise it. Perhaps this couldn't have happened without Amália. Born in 1920 to a poor family and possessed of a uniquely expressive voice ('I don't sing fado – it sings

Adega Machado

in me,' she said), she took it from taverns to the stage and then screen in *Capas Negras*, a film that broke national box office records in 1947. The first *fadista* to gain international recognition, she sang at the Paris Olympia, appeared on Broadway, and developed a repertoire beyond Portuguese music.

By the time Amália died in 1999, fado had been fully rehabilitated – a museum dedicated to it had been opened the previous year (*see p134*) – and she was mourned by the nation; her remains were eventually transferred to the Panteão Nacional. Today, her passing can be seen to have marked the end of an era. Since then, fado has been classified as UNESCO Intangible World Heritage (in 2011) and can now be heard not only in *casas de fado* but occasionally even on the street – something the old regime banned, as well as censoring lyrics – and at open-air concerts, often for free. Stars such as Mariza, Camané and Carminho now regularly top the charts and *casas de fado* (*see pp201-203*) are multiplying.

Parque das Nações

Casino Lisboa
Alameda dos Oceanos, Parque das Nações (21 892 9000, www.casinolisboa.pt). Metro Oriente. **Open** *3pm-3am Mon-Thur, Sun; 4pm-4am Fri, Sat.* **Admission** *€12-€35.* **Map** *p154 Z9. Casino/Bar/Live music*

This slick glass complex contains several restaurants and bars, hundreds of slot machines and a 634-seat auditorium with the latest equipment. It often stages concerts by leading Portuguese and foreign artists – jazz in particular. There are also free concerts by local and foreign performers in the Arena Lounge bar (for dates, see www.arenalounge. ws), above which aerial acrobats also perform on weekends.

FADO

Fado needs the right setting to work its magic, and the convention is to stop talking during the performance. At a *casa de fado* – a restaurant where professional musicians perform and customers must dine (relatively expensively) or stump up a *consumo mínimo* ('minimum spend') – the standard of music is good. There are always several singers, so don't worry if you don't like the first performance. On less busy nights, staff may let you come in later and nurse a drink; do check first. In general, kitchens close around midnight, the house when business tails off.

In taverns specialising in *fado vadio* ('vagabond fado', *see p203*), a more laid-back attitude prevails and anyone may get up and sing. Admission is invariably free.

Casas de fado

Adega Machado
Rua do Norte 91, Bairro Alto (21 322 4640). Metro Baixa-Chiado or tram 28. **Open** *5pm-2am daily. Fado 5pm, 9pm.* **Admission** *€17 for 5-6pm session, then minimum spend €27 until 10.30pm, then €17.* **Map** *p95 P19.*

This large, tastefully decorated fado house attracts tour groups, yet retains atmosphere. Performers include Isabel de Noronha, Pedro Viana, Joana Viega and Marco Rodrigues. Accompanying them is a double bass, as well as the traditional Spanish and Portuguese guitars. You'll pay between €40 and €50 a head to eat; for a cheaper taste of fado (tapas included), come at 5pm for a one-hour *apontamento* with two singers.

Café Luso
Travessa da Queimada 10, Bairro Alto (21 342 2281, www.cafeluso.pt). Metro Baixa-

Mesa de Frades

Chiado or bus 758, 790. **Open** *7.30pm-2am daily. Fado 8.30pm, 10.30pm-2am.* **Admission** *minimum spend €25 until 10.30pm, then €17.* **Map** *p95 P19.*

This is the oldest fado joint in Bairro Alto, and where Amália started out. Opened in the 1920s in the former stables of the Palácio de São Roque, it has recently been refurbished. Four or five *fadistas* perform each night, including Catarina Rosa and veteran singer-manager Filipe Acácio. The minimum spend is low and there are set menus.

Clube de Fado

Rua São João da Praça 92-94, Alfama (21 885 2704, 21 888 2694, www.clube-de-fado. com). Tram 28. **Open** *8pm-2am daily. Fado from 9.30pm.* **Admission** *€7.50 plus dinner (average €50) until 11pm, then €10 plus drinks.* **Map** *p80 R20.*

Owned by talented *guitarrista* Mário Pacheco, this club attracts his friends, some of whom may perform, and features sessions by leading *fadistas* such as Cuca Roseta (when she's not off touring), Miguel Capucho, Ana Maria and Cristiana Águas. It has a lovely atmosphere, with stone arches dividing the room into nooks.

O Faia

Rua da Barroca 54-56, Bairro Alto (21 342 6742, www.ofaia.com). Metro Baixa-Chiado or tram 28. **Open** *8pm-2am Mon-Sat. Fado from 9.30pm.* **Admission** *dinner only (average €50); after 11.30pm minimum spend €25.* **Map** *p95 P20.*

An upmarket and slightly antiseptic venue, but offering good-quality *fadistas*. The daily roster includes Anita Guerreiro, who had a career in *revista* (music hall) before focusing on fado; António Rocha, known for his classic style; and Lenita Gentil. You may also catch younger star Ricardo Ribeiro. There's a proper bar area if you just want to look in later for a drink.

Maria da Mouraria

Largo da Severa 2, Mouraria (21 886 0165, 93 445 0130, http://mariadamouraria.pt). Metro Martim Moniz. **Open** *8pm-2am Tue-Sun. Fado from 9pm.* **Admission** *dinner only (set menu €45).* **Map** *p80 R19.*

Housed in the Casa da Severa – the building where 19th-century fado diva Maria da Severa lived out her last years, now redone in contemporary style – this is an offshoot of the Museu do Fado (*see p86*). Well-known *fadista* Hélder Moutinho manages it and performs; other musicians and singers are of high quality.

♥ Mesa de Frades

Rua dos Remédios 139, Alfama (91 702 9436). Metro Santa Apolónia. **Open** *8.30pm-2am Mon-Sat. Fado from 11pm.* **Admission** *dinner only (set menu €45) until 11pm.* **Map** *p80 S20.*

This *azulejo*-lined former chapel of the Quinta da Dona Rosa, a palace built by Dom João V for one of his lovers, is owned by *guitarra*-player Pedro de Castro. It has a reputation as the *fadistas'* canteen: you never know who might roll up in the wee hours for an impromptu performance. The food is Portuguese, prettified, but not up to the fado. Booking is a must, but if you drop in later and can squeeze in there's no minimum spend.

A Parreirinha de Alfama
*Beco do Espírito Santo 1, Alfama (21 886 8209, www.parreirinhadealfama.com). Metro Santa Apolónia. **Open** 8pm-1am Tue-Sun. Fado from 9.15pm. **Admission** dinner only (average €35) until 10.30pm; after 10.30pm minimum spend €15. **Map** p80 S20.*

This low-ceilinged, atmospheric restaurant in an alley off Largo do Chafariz de Dentro is managed by fado legend Argentina Santos – now officially retired – but veteran Maria de Fátima and rising star Joana Amendoeira sing here and are worth catching.

A Severa
*Rua das Gáveas 51, Bairro Alto (21 346 4006, www.asevera.com). Metro Baixa-Chiado or tram 28. **Open** 8pm-2am Mon, Tue, Thur-Sun. Fado from 9pm. **Admission** minimum spend €30. **Map** p95 P20.*

This family-owned fado house has hosted many fine *fadistas* over the years. Current performers are Aina Santos, Natalino de Jésus, Fernando Sousa and Alzira de Sá. The minimum spend always applies and fixed menus cost €55 – it may sound a lot, but you're paying for the show.

Sr Vinho
*Rua do Meio à Lapa 18, Lapa (21 397 2681, www.srvinho.com). Tram 25. **Open** 8pm-2am daily. Fado from 9pm. **Admission** minimum spend €25. Map p132 N19.*

This classic Lisbon venue has helped launch countless *fadistas*, including Mariza and Camané. The best known of the current crop is Aldina Duarte, but Francisco Salvação Barreto and Liliana Silva are also expert singers. 'Mr Wine' is owned by a grande dame of fado, Maria da Fé, though she performs rarely these days. The food is good and booking essential.

Fado vadio
In *fado vadio* venues, don't expect quality food or quality singing – or any singing, for that matter, if you go on an off day. The best bets for enjoyable sessions are **O Jaime** (Rua da Graça 91, Graça, 21 888 1560, fado 4-8pm Sat, Sun & hols) and **Tasca do Chico** (Rua Diário de Notícias 39, Bairro Alto, 96 505 9670, fado 8pm-1am daily), now with an offshoot in Alfama (Rua dos Remédio 83, fado 8pm-1am Thur & Sun). In these places, you can just poke your head in the door; in fact, that's all you can do unless you arrive early to bag a seat and order wine and snacks. **Baiuca** (Rua de São Miguel 20, Alfama, 21 886 7284, fado 8pm-midnight Mon, Thur-Sun) is unusual in that you must dine, but you won't spend much over €25. At nearby **Bela** (Rua dos Remédios 190, Alfama, 92 607 7511, fado from 9pm Thur & Sun) the snacks are tasty and the fado seriously good.

Fado vadio graffiti on Escadinhas de São Cristóvão

Performing Arts

The show must go on

The city's performing arts scene has always been characterised by creativity in the face of adversity – and at times a struggle to identify and attract the audiences to appreciate it. Portuguese composers aren't particularly well known abroad, but the country has strong classical music traditions, underpinned by centuries of royal patronage. Many concerts take place in churches, palaces and monasteries, and summer festivals attract international artists. Funding for opera and ballet – despite or perhaps because of their elite status – can never be entirely cut for reasons of national pride, but theatre and dance in general are chronically short of money. Yet after a lengthy hangover following the post-Revolution party of the 1970s, both have emerged artistically vibrant, despite continuing financial challenges.

Gulbenkian Choir and Orchestra

♥ Best acoustics

Centro Cultural de Belém *p207*
And the seats in the main auditorium are
comfy, too.

Fundação Calouste Gulbenkian *p207*
Sounds even better after its recent refurb.

Teatro Camões *p209*
For ballet lovers.

Teatro Ibérico *p213*
Atmospheric former church.

Teatro Nacional de São Carlos *p208*
Top notes in a baroque setting.

CLASSICAL MUSIC & OPERA

Although Lisbon isn't renowned for
classical excellence, the range and quality
of performances on offer, from home-grown
musicians as much as visiting artists, is
good – and prices are still below what you'd
pay in many other European capitals.

Portugal's early classical repertoire has
been rediscovered of late, and a browse
through the CD racks at **Fnac** (*see p101*)
will throw up excellent recordings of
works penned by Dom Dinis, the medieval
troubadour king; early Renaissance
composers such as Pedro de Escobar; and
later ones such as Manuel Cardoso and João
Rebelo. Modern musicians have also tackled
the 'colossal Baroque' *Te Deum* of António
Teixeira, the virtuoso harpsichord sonatas
of Carlos Seixas and the rococo elegance of
Sousa Carvalho.

From the 18th century, royal initiatives to
send Portuguese composers to study in Italy,
and to bring Domenico Scarlatti to teach
in Lisbon, bore fruit through the likes of
Domingos Bomtempo (1775-1842); Viana da
Mota (1868-1948), a pupil of Liszt; and Luís
de Freitas Branco (1890-1955).

Contemporary Portuguese composers
include Luís Tinoco and the challenging
Eurico Carrapatoso; performers of note
include pianists Maria João Pires, Artur
Pizarro, Pedro Burmester and António
Rosado, as well as Portuguese-born soprano
Jennifer Smith. Elisabete Matos, also
a soprano, is the country's best-known
opera singer.

Information and tickets

Newspapers have daily listings; the
Público culture supplement on Fridays
and *Expresso* on Saturdays are also worth a
look. Municipal monthly *Agenda Cultural*
is available from tourist offices and hotels,
and online at http://agendalx.pt/, while our
sister magazine *Time Out Lisboa* also has
information and reviews (in Portuguese).

You can buy tickets for some shows at
Multibanco (ATM) cash machines, but
people mostly pick them up at the venue,
often after reserving by phone. Most major
venues' websites also allow you to go
through to online ticketing platform **BOL**
(www.bol.pt), where you can also browse
events in English by category as well as by
day. Tickets can also be bought in person
for a fee at the **ABEP** booth on the south-
eastern corner of Praça dos Restauradores
(21 347 0768, 9am-8pm Mon-Sat, 9am-6pm
Sun) at **Fnac** (to reserve in advance call 707
31 34 35 or from abroad +351 211 544 039,
9am-11pm), at **El Corte Inglés** (*see p149*; 707
211 711, 9am-10pm Mon-Sat) or by phone
or online at **Ticketline** (24hr booking line
1820, from abroad +351 21 794 1400, www.
ticketline.sapo.pt).

Orchestras and ensembles

The **Orquestra Gulbenkian**, headquartered
at the private Fundação Calouste
Gulbenkian, (*see p146*) is Portugal's oldest
orchestral group; in it British and other
foreign musicians are well represented. The
state **Orquestra Sinfónica Portuguesa**,
founded just 20 years ago, is based at the
Teatro Nacional de São Carlos (*see p208*)
but also plays at the **Centro Cultural de
Belém** (*see p125*). Its repertoire includes
major symphonies and operas. Since the
beginning of 2014, its resident conductor
has been Joana Carneiro, back from a
successful spell in the US and herself a
product of the Gulbenkian.

Lisbon's third orchestra, the **Orquestra
Metropolitana de Lisboa** (21 361 7320,
www.metropolitana.pt) was founded
in 1992 and, despite a difficult period
financially, takes its role as a municipal
orchestra extremely seriously, putting on
literally hundreds of concerts in Lisbon
and the surrounding region every year,
many of them free. These range from full-
blown orchestral concerts, presided over
by conductor-composer Pedro Amaral,
to solo and chamber performances at the
downtown **Palácio Foz** (*see p207*), **Museu
do Oriente** (*see p119*) and other venues. The
orchestra is also very unusual in having
three music schools attached. Every now
and then it and its student offshoot, the
Orquestra Académica Metropolitana, join
forces to form a full symphony orchestra,
the **Orquestra Sinfónica Metropolitana**,
which has been a resident performer at the
CCB's **Dias da Música** (*see p174*) for the last
three years.

Concert venues

At **Culturgest** (*see p145*), the Grande Auditório (tickets €6-€20) has a capacity of 618 and reasonable acoustics. The **Aula Magna**, the main amphitheatre of the University of Lisbon (21 796 7624, tickets €15-€25) has a wide, steeply banked seating area that affords the whole audience a clear view when hosting orchestral concerts or opera; while this can make rock gigs less than atmospheric, given the right act it can pull off a great show. The **Conservatório Nacional** (Rua Alexandre Sá Pinto 85, Belém, 21 342 5922, www.emcn.edu.pt) hosts interesting performances by its students or teachers.

Lisbon is blessed – or perhaps cursed, given their ruinous maintenance costs – with some lovely 18th-century church organs. The one in the **Igreja de São Vicente** (*see p87*) is used on the second Saturday of the month for free concerts (details at www.althum.com); the **Igreja da Graça** (*see p87*) and **Sé** (*see p79*) also occasionally host similar events.

Altice Arena (Pavilhão Atlântico)
Rossio dos Olivais, Parque das Nações, Eastern Lisbon (21 891 8409, http://arena.meo.pt). Metro Oriente. **Tickets** *€20-€55.* **Map** *p154 AA8.*

Built for Expo '98 to an impressive design by Regino Cruz, this UFO-shaped riverside arena – whose current official name reflects a major sponsorship deal with telecommunications giant Altice – is used for musical spectaculars, as well as being Lisbon's premier indoor rock venue (if not always the most atmospheric). It also hosts tennis and other sports tournaments, ice shows and the like.

♥ Centro Cultural de Belém
Praça do Império (21 361 2627, www.ccb.pt). Belém rail from Cais do Sodré, tram 15, or bus 714, 727, 728, 751. **Box office** *11am-8pm daily (or until 30mins after start of performance).* **Tickets** *€5-€40.* **Map** *p123 D21.*

The CCB's two auditoriums are sometimes used for classical concerts: the Grande Auditório has excellent acoustics for large-scale works and opera, while the Pequeno Auditório is more intimate. The still smaller Sala de Ensaio (Rehearsal Room) is occasionally used for alternative music. The CCB also hosts special musical events throughout the year, such as the Dias da Música festival in May (*see p174*), and has various workshops for children.

Coliseu dos Recreios
Rua das Portas de Santo Antão 96, Baixa (21 324 0585, www.coliseulisboa.com).

Metro Restauradores or Rossio. **Box office** *1-7.30pm Mon-Sat or until 30mins after start of performance.* **Tickets** *€15-€60. No cards.* **Map** *p60 Q19.*

Lisbon's coliseum was completed in 1890 and stages everything from classical operas to rock concerts and circus shows, with seating being added or removed as needed. Acoustics vary; some maintain that the left side is best.

♥ Fundação Calouste Gulbenkian
Avenida de Berna 45A (21 782 3700, www.musica.gulbenkian.pt, www.bilheteira.gulbenkian.pt). Metro Praça de Espanha. **Box office** *10am-7pm Mon-Fri; 10am-6pm Sat (or until start of performance); 1-7pm Sun (concert nights only).* **Tickets** *€4-€70.* **Map** *p142 O13.*

The Gulbenkian's 1,200-seat Grand Auditorium hosts most events in the foundation's rich October-to-May season of orchestral, chamber and solo performances, although the outdoor amphitheatre is also occasionally used. The house Gulbenkian Orchestra, founded as a chamber group in 1962, comprises 66 musicians; despite not being of symphonic dimensions, it has its own distinctive sound. In 2018 Lorenzo Viotti, a 28-year-old Swiss citizen who has won a string of international awards, took over as resident maestro and Giancarlo Guerrero is the principal guest conductor, but others feature during the season. The 100-strong Gulbenkian Choir, founded two years after the orchestra, has been under the baton of Michel Corboz since 1969. The season includes regular broadcasts from the New York Metropolitan Opera House to the Grand Auditorium.

Palácio Foz
Praça dos Restauradores (21 322 1237). Metro Restauradores. **Open** *Irregular performances, check PalacioFozOficial/Events on Facebook.* **Admission** *free.* **Map** *p60 P19.*

At this grand former private residence, free one-hour concerts by members of the Orquestra Metropolitana de Lisboa and visiting international musicians are staged mostly on Mondays and the occasional Saturday in the opulent first-floor Sala de Espelhos (Mirror Room). Enter via the door at the far right of the imposing 18th-century façade; a sheet advertising the month's programme is usually available here. The building now houses government departments, but there are periodic guided tours of the palace, including a basement where the decor is charged with Masonic symbolism.

Teatro Nacional de São Carlos

❤ Teatro Nacional de São Carlos

Rua Serpa Pinto 9, Chiado (21 325 3045/6, http://tnsc.pt, tickets http://tnsc.bol. pt). Metro Baixa-Chiado or tram 28. **Box office** *1-7pm Mon-Fri; 1-7pm Sat, Sun (concert nights only, until 30mins after start of performance).* **Tickets** *Opera €10-€70. Orchestral/choral €10-€20.* **Map** *p95 P20.*

A grand 18th-century opera house inspired by the likes of Milan's La Scala, with a rococo interior, excellent acoustics and good sightlines. Despite chronic under-investment, its artistic profile has been raised over the past decade by a well-connected Italian director, Paolo Pinamonti – now officially with consultant status but still actively involved. As well as the Orquestra Sinfónica Portuguesa, led since 2014 by Joana Carneiro, the theatre is home to the Coro do Teatro Nacional de São Carlos, headed by Giovanni Andreoli, while its well-respected former director João Paulo Santos now oversees musical and dramatic production at the theatre. Note that reservations are accepted only up to 48 hours before a show.

Festivals

The CCB has an annual festival, **Dias da Música** (*see p174*); this is preceded in late March by a one-day **Festa da Primavera** (*see p174*), which includes some free concerts. So does the classy **Festival Estoril Lisboa** (*see p177*), in July, while in the open-air **Festival ao Largo** (*see p177*) all shows are free. The **Festival de Sintra** (*see p178*) is a highlight for classical buffs, with concerts by international artists.

Cantabile Festival (962 335 855, www. cantabilefest.pt), in late September, is coordinated by the local Goethe-Institut (www.goethe.de/lisboa) and features top German and other international soloists and chamber musicians performing inside (and outside) the Teatro São Carlos and churches. The same team works with Almada, a culturally vibrant municipality on the south bank of the River Tagus, on **Os Sons de Almada Velha** (21 272 4008/96 233 5855, www.m-almada.pt – check the 'Agenda' panel) with free concerts – mainly 17th-century music – staged in lovely old churches in early October.

In November in Lisbon, look out for **Música em São Roque** (*see p179*), in the church of that name; and then, in December, the city council's **Concertos de Natal** (www.egeac.pt) .

Those wanting something more experimental might enjoy **Música Viva** (21 457 5068, www.misomusic.com); this festival's dates and venues vary but it invariably includes several world premières and provides an important forum for local musical creativity.

DANCE

A generation of choreographers was nurtured at the Ballet Gulbenkian – for 40 years Portugal's strongest contemporary dance company. It was wound up in 2005, when officials at the **Fundação Calouste Gulbenkian** (*see p146*) decided resources could be better used to fund burgeoning independents, which has produced some promising results. Classical ballet has a short history in Portugal. The **Companhia Nacional de Bailado** (www.cnb.pt), based at the **Teatro Camões** (*see p209*), was set up in 1977.

Away from the big institutions, Lisbon's dance community is good at collaborating with umbrella projects, such as **Forum Dança** (92 510 3596, www.forumdanca.pt), **c.e.m. centro em movimento** (21 887 1763, www.c-e-m.org) and **Alkantara**. Alkantara, as well as organising an ambitious festival (*see p176*), hosts one-off performances, artist residencies, talks and film screenings at its Espaço Alkantara home in Santos. Few companies have their own performance space, but most tour regularly abroad. The **Companhia Portuguesa de Bailado Contemporâneo** (91 978 9675, www.cpbcontemporaneo.pt), founded in 1998 by Gulbenkian veteran Vasco Wellencamp, is among the more accessible.

Olga Roriz and her eponymous company (21 887 2383, www.olgaroriz.com) tackle provocative social, political or religious themes. João Fiadeiro's **RE.AL** company (21 390 9255, www.re-al.org) collaborates with other groups such as Artistas Unidos (*see p213* Teatro da Politécnica), freely mixing in text and drama. Vera Mantero, seen by many as Portugal's most important choreographer, heads **O Rumo do Fumo** (21 343 1646, www.orumodofumo.com). **Clara Andermatt** (21 590 3105) has overseen some interesting work with Cape Verdean artists. Also well known abroad is **Rui Horta**, another Gulbenkian alumnus who has tried his hand in areas from film to circus, but now runs a dance research

centre in the Alentejo (266 899 856, www.oespacodotempo.pt).

If you want to dance yourself, a plethora of courses are advertised in *Agenda Cultural*, including at **Chapitô** (*see p212*). There are also periodic open dances (tango, samba and so on) at the **Teatro Municipal de São Luiz** (*see p210*), while the **CCB** (*see p207*) runs regular workshops. Workshops at **c.e.m.** are also open to amateurs.

Dance venues

The **Coliseu** (*see p207*) hosts visiting ballet companies, as well as circuses and rock concerts. The **CCB** (*see p207*) sometimes offers chances to catch up-and-coming local dancers and choreographers. **Culturgest** (*see p145*) hosts relatively little contemporary dance, but its shows are invariably interesting.

♥ Teatro Camões

Passeio de Neptuno, Parque das Nações (21 892 3477, www.cnb.pt). Metro Oriente. ***Open Box office*** *Nov-Apr 1-5pm Wed-Sun. May-July, Sept, Oct 2-6pm (or until 30mins after start of performance).* ***Tickets*** *€5-€25.* ***Map*** *p154 AA10.*

Built for Expo '98, this big, blue glass-and-metal cube seats 890 amid state-of-the-art acoustics. It's home to the Companhia Nacional de Bailado. Bookings may also be made via the Teatro Nacional de São Carlos (*see p208*), but reservations are not accepted until 48 hours before the performance. The theatre also hosts a variety of other shows and workshops for all ages.

Festivals

The **Alkantara Festival** (*see p176*) was once a small-scale dance event but has blossomed into a major biennial multi-disciplinary festival, with performers from around the globe. Alkantara, the name of a neighbourhood in western Lisbon, means 'bridge' in Arabic, and the festival seeks to foster links between different cultures and disciplines. The **Festival Internacional de Teatro** (*see p177*), held in July, now includes dance too. A couple of months later, the **Quinzena da Dança de Almada** (21 258 3175, www.cdanca-almada.pt) is a 'fortnight' of contemporary dance, staged annually since 1993, which initially showcased Portuguese groups but now casts its net more widely and lasts almost a month. Shows, workshops, exhibitions and meetings (tickets €6-€10) take place mostly in Almada, on the south bank of the Tagus, but some are at more central Lisbon venues.

THEATRE

As with the visual arts scene, Lisbon's relative isolation can spawn both hackneyed pretension and shining originality in theatre. There's now at least plenty of choice: both state and independent companies abound, offering ballet and street theatre, Brecht and Gil Vicente (the 16th-century father of Portuguese drama). There's a growing commercial sector too, embracing comedy and musicals. If you speak little or no Portuguese, then **Estrela Hall** (English-language theatre), newer English-language troupe **Já** (91 194 1163, http://jait.pt), **Chapitô** (mainly physical theatre) and **Teatro Politeama** (with subtitles) will generally be your best bets, although **Teatro Nacional Dona Maria II** and other major theatres – as well as festivals – occasionally host foreign troupes, which may perform in a language you can follow.

Information and tickets

Newspaper listings cover the big theatres and some independents and have reviews, as does our sister publication *Time Out Lisboa*. Poster-spotting, leaflet-gathering and word-of-mouth should do the rest, and even alternative groups such as **Teatro do Vão** (91 897 0961, www.teatrodovao. com) and Palmela-based **O Bando** (21 233 6850, www.obando.pt) now have websites. Shows are usually at 9pm from Wednesday or Thursday to Saturday; there may be a Sunday matinée. Whatever a box office's normal hours, on performance days it will be open at least until showtime, and usually until 30 minutes after the start. Most locals buy tickets at the theatre, after reserving by phone or email, but most theatres' website now have a link that takes you through to an online ticket platform, usually BOL (www. bol.pt), and agencies listed in the Classical Music & Opera section of this chapter also sell tickets for big shows.

Establishment theatres

With Lisbon's largest auditorium, another medium-sized one and a studio theatre, all with machinery, the **Centro Cultural de Belém** (*see p207*) has the best facilities. Its programme encompasses Portuguese and foreign groups. Founded back in 1993, **Culturgest** (*see p145*) usually has more adventurous programming. The **Altice Arena/Pavilhão Atlântico** (*see p207*) hosts musical and ice spectaculars. The **São Luiz Teatro Municipal** (*see below*) has some musicals and drama, though it more often hosts jazz and rock concerts. At the time of writing, details of when two other municipal venues, the **Teatro do Bairro Alto** and **Teatro Maria Matos** – which is now to be privately managed – will reopen, and what fare they will offer, had yet to be released.

LU.CA Teatro Luís de Camões

Calçada da Ajuda, 80, Ajuda (215 939 100, www.lucateatroluisdecamoes.pt). Belém rail from Cais do Sodré then 7min walk, tram 15, bus 714, 727, 728, 751. **Box office** *10am-1pm, 2-6pm Tue-Sun.* **Tickets** *free-€7, €3 children.* **Map** *p123 E20.*

This municipal theatre in Belém, just uphill from the area's famous museums, opened in 2018 as a venue dedicated to entertaining children. As well as hosting drama, dance, puppet shows, circus and film it organises performing arts workshops.

São Luiz Teatro Municipal

Rua António Maria Cardoso 40, Chiado (21 325 7650 box office, www.teatrosaoluiz. pt). Metro Baixa-Chiado. **Box office** *1-8 pm daily. Closed Aug.* **Tickets** *€7-€15. No cards.* **Map** *p95 P20.*

The 1,000-seat main auditorium of this city-run theatre stages everything from children's plays to contemporary dance and jazz concerts. The glass-walled Jardim de Inverno (Winter Garden) hosts talks and concerts. There's a studio theatre downstairs.

Teatro da Trindade

Largo da Trindade 9, Chiado (21 342 0000, http://teatrodatrindade-inatel. bol.pt/). Metro Baixa-Chiado. **Open Box office** *2-8pm Tue-Sat; 2-6pm Sun.* **Tickets** *€5-€18.* **Map** *p95 P20.*

Teatro da Trindade is a 19th-century gilded jewel that specialises in high-profile one-off shows and new plays with a strong political

---

In the know
Cheap seats

Theatre in Lisbon can be very cheap, if you're free on the right night. At Teatro da Trindade, tickets for Wednesday performances bought at the theatre on the day cost just €5, while at Teatro Cinearte that applies on Thursdays; at Teatro Comuna and Teatro da Politécnica, tickets for both these days cost €5. At Teatro Nacional Dona Maria II, tickets to Thursday performances of most shows are 25 per cent off. And if you're too disorganised to manage any of the above, Teatro Municipal de São Luiz and Teatro Cinearte are among venues that offer €5 tickets to under-30s most nights.

theme. The theatre is now striking out in a fresh musical direction too, bringing world music to the masses. There's also a studio theatre and a smoky basement bar that offers music and comedy.

Teatro Nacional Dona Maria II
Praça Dom Pedro IV (Rossio) (800 213 250, www.tndm.pt). Metro Rossio. **Box office** *2-7pm Tue; 11am-10pm Wed-Fri; 2-10pm Sat; 2-7pm Sun.* **Tickets** *€10-€17.* **Map** *p60 Q19.*

Inaugurated in 1846, this is Lisbon's leading national theatre, but it has had no resident company for over a decade. Tiago Rodrigues, the leading actor who has been artistic director since 2014, would like to form one; in the meantime he has won the 2018 European Theatre Award for his work reaching out to and involving the wider community. Its 320-seat Sala Garrett (named after the founder) and 52-seat studio stage in-house productions, some in partnership with independents, and periodically host foreign groups. There are workshops for children, literary readings and talks, Lisbon's only thespian bookshop and a café with great cakes. On Thursdays a limited number of on-the-day tickets are available at a 25% discount. You can also book a guided tour of the theatre (11am Mon, closed Aug; reservations by phone or email bilheteira@tndm.pt).

Teatro da Trindade

Commercial theatres

Teatro Maria Vitória
Parque Mayer, Avenida da Liberdade (21 346 1740, www.teatromariavitoria.com). Metro Avenida. **Box office** *2-9.30pm Tue, 2-7.30pm Wed, 2-9.30pm Thur-Sun.* **Tickets** *€12.50-€30. No cards.* **Map** *p60 P18.*

The only theatre not to have gone dark in Parque Mayer – Lisbon's old theatreland and the home of *revista*, the authentically Portuguese-style music hall that provided an escape valve under Salazar. It stages shows Thursdays through Sundays (plus weekend matinées) with a trademark mix of slapstick, glittery camp and mild satire.

Teatro Politeama
Rua das Portas de Santo Antão 109 (21 340 5700, www.filipelaferia.pt). Metro Restauradores. **Box office** *2-7pm Mon, Tue; 2-9.30pm Wed-Sat; 2-5pm Sun.* **Tickets** *€10-€30. No cards.* **Map** *p60 Q19.*

This 700-seat theatre puts on slick musicals and cabaret-style *revistas* masterminded by impresario Filipe La Feria. One major advantage over just about every other local venue is that shows have English subtitles. The latest long-running production is *Eu Saio na Próxima, e Você?* (meaning 'I get off at the next stop, and you?') – an updated form of classic Portuguese *revista* of the kind found at Teatro Maria Vitória (*see p211*). You can buy tickets for shows via the theatre's website.

Teatro Tivoli BBVA
Avenida da Liberdade 182 (21 357 2025, www.teatrotivolibbva.pt). Metro Avenida. **Box office** *1-2.30pm, 3.30-8pm Tue-Fri, 2-8pm Sat; on performance days 1-2.30pm, 3.30-7.30pm, from 8pm Tue-Fri; from 2pm Sat, Sun.* **Tickets** *€10-€60. No cards.* **Map** *p60 P18.*

This central venue, with more than 1,000 seats, opened in 1924. Now owned by promoter UAU (www.uau.pt), it relies on local and imported (Brazilian) TV stars to pull in the punters, as well as hosting rock concerts.

Teatro Villaret
Avenida Fontes Pereira de Melo 30A (21 353 8586 www.fproducao.pt). Metro Picoas. **Open** *performance days only 6-10pm Tue, 4-10pm Wed-Sat, 1-5pm Sun.* **Tickets** *€10-€20. No cards.*

This 384-seat theatre, named after comic actor João Villaret, has been associated with comedy since its inauguration in 1964 by the late Raúl Solnado, a major influence on today's alternative comedians. Today it hosts mainly commercial comedies, with the occasional classic or contemporary work,

Teatro Nacional Dona Maria II

and shows for children – plus stand-up in the downstairs bar. Note that the website provided is the promoter's, and lists shows at venues around Portugal.

Alternative theatres

Chapitô
Costa do Castelo 1-7, Mouraria (21 885 5550, www.chapito.org). Tram 12, 28 or bus 37. **Box office** *2hrs before performance; phone bookings 10am-8pm daily.* **Tickets** *€5-€12. No cards.* **Map** *p80 R20.*

This venue has a unique atmosphere, with students from the circus school and tourists rubbing shoulders on a restaurant patio that has fabulous views. It's home to the Companhia do Chapitô, a troupe known for inspired comic physical theatre. Chapitô also plays host to an annual female clowns' convention.

Estrela Hall
Rua Saraiva de Carvalho, Estrela (21 396 1946, www.lisbonplayers.com. pt). Tram 28 or bus 9. **Box office** *1hr 30mins before performance; book online or by phone message.* **Tickets** *€8-€10. No cards.* **Map** *p132 M18.*

The Lisbon Players, a long-established amateur group (formed in 1947) that performs regularly in English, was in early 2019 expected to move into a new Estrela Hall some time from late 2020, following the British government's sale of the old venue along with most of the rest of the 'Quarteirão Inglês' (English block) that it has owned for centuries. Until the new theatre is built, shows are to be staged in other venues. The Players' focus is firmly on the classics, but comedy and musicals get a look-in.

Teatro Aberto
Praça de Espanha (21 388 0089, www. teatroaberto.com). Metro São Sebastião or Praça de Espanha. **Box office** *2-7pm Mon-Fri, on performance days from 2pm.* **Tickets** *€7.50-€15. No cards.* **Map** *p142 O14.*

This modern building with two plush auditoriums (one with 400 seats, the other half that) is home to the O Novo Grupo company, successor to the cutting-edge 1970s Grupo 4. Under João Lourenço and his partner, playwright and Germanist Vera San Payo de Lemos, its repertoire – once dominated by heavyweight Germans such as Brecht – now tends to produce more modern fare, including works translated from English.

Teatro Cinearte

Largo dos Santos 2, Santos (21 396 5275/91 334 1683, www.abarraca.com). Tram 15, 25. **Box office** *1hr 30mins before performance; phone bookings 10am-6pm daily.* **Tickets** *€5-€20. No cards.* **Map** *p114 N20.*

Cinearte is the showcase for A Barraca, a troupe founded 30 years ago and led by Maria do Céu Guerra, one of Portugal's handful of established female directors. It stages productions of modern Portuguese and European classics, with hefty discounts on Thursdays. There are two auditoriums, and the upstairs café-bar has an offbeat programme of concerts, poetry and play readings and stand-up comedy, as well as workshops for children.

Teatro da Comuna

Praça de Espanha (21 722 1770/7/9, www.comunateatropesquisa.pt). Metro Praça de Espanha. **Box office** *from 8pm on performance days; phone bookings 10am-7pm Mon-Sat.* **Tickets** *€5-€10. No cards.* **Map** *p142 N13.*

Resident company Comuna Teatro de Pesquisa ('Research Theatre') has a history of experimentation dating from the early 1970s, but today the theatre also plays host to mainstream pieces. Its four show spaces include a café that hosts mainly comedy.

Teatro do Bairro

Rua Luz Soriano 63, Bairro Alto (21 347 3358/91 321 1263, www.teatrodobairro.org). Metro Baixa-Chiado or tram 28. **Box office** *1hr before performance; phone bookings 3-7pm daily.* **Tickets** *€7-€12.* **Map** *p95 P19.*

This neighbourhood theatre, housed in an old newspaper printing works, started out in 2011 professing to offer a distinctive artistic project, but now hosts an eclectic mix of comedy, literary adaptations and dance. Still, it's a stylish venue that's as much bar and social club as theatre, and has regular live music.

❤ Teatro Ibérico

Rua de Xabregas 54, Xabregas (21 868 2531, www.teatroiberico.org). Bus 718, 728. **Box office** *2hrs before performance; phone bookings 10am-6pm daily.* **Tickets** *€5-€10. No cards.* **Map** *p151 V17.*

A former monastery church with magnificent acoustics (it has hosted many classical performances), this theatre in eastern Lisbon in 2016 gained a new lease of life as home to the theatre company formed by João Garcia Miguel (www.joaogarciamiguel.com), one of Portugal's most talented performers and directors, with a strong track record in physical theatre.

Teatro Meridional

Rua do Açúcar 64, Poço do Bispo (91 999 1213, www.teatromeridional.net). Bus 728. **Box office** *1hr before performance; phone bookings 2-10pm Tue-Sun.* **Tickets** *€5-€10. No cards.* **Map** *p151 W15.*

A converted warehouse in eastern Lisbon is the base for Teatro Meridional, a Portuguese-Spanish group that focuses on comic and physical drama. It often stages works by African authors. Shows may start as late as 10pm. On Wednesday tickets are half price.

Teatro da Politécnica

Rua da Escola Politécnica 56, Príncipe Real (21 391 6750, box office 96 196 0281, www.artistasunidos.pt). Metro Rato. **Box office** *5pm-end of performance Tue-Fri; 3pm-end of performance Sat; phone bookings 3-6pm daily.* **Tickets** *€5-€10. No cards.* **Map** *p95 O18.*

The home of Artistas Unidos, one of Lisbon's most vibrant companies, which also stages some shows at larger venues such as the CCB (*see p207*). As well as a core of talented young actors, the group draws on a wider 'family' – including well-known figures from local television and cinema – all overseen by founder-director Jorge Silva Melo, himself a fine actor. On Tuesdays tickets are half-price.

Teatro Taborda

Costa do Castelo 75, Mouraria (21 885 4190, www.teatro dagaragem.com). Tram 12, 28 or bus 37. **Box office** *30mins before performance; phone bookings 3-9pm Tue-Sat.* **Tickets** *€5-€10. No cards.* **Map** *p80 R19.*

This late 19th-century, council-owned theatre is now home to long-established troupe Teatro da Garagem. It has a 150-seat auditorium, a small room for low-budget performances, an exhibition space, and a cosy rear café and terrace with spectacular views (open 5pm-midnight Mon-Fri, 3pm-midnight Sat, 3pm-midnight Sun).

Festivals

The **Festival International de Teatro** (*see p177*), based in the south-bank town of Almada, is firmly established as Portugal's biggest festival of drama, with performances staged both south and north of the River Tagus. Almada also has a smaller **Mostra de Teatro** (www.mostradeteatrodealmada. blogspot.pt) in November. In early summer in Lisbon, there's a veritable orgy of puppet shows in the **FIMFA Festival Internacional de Marionetas e Formas Animadas** (*see p174*).

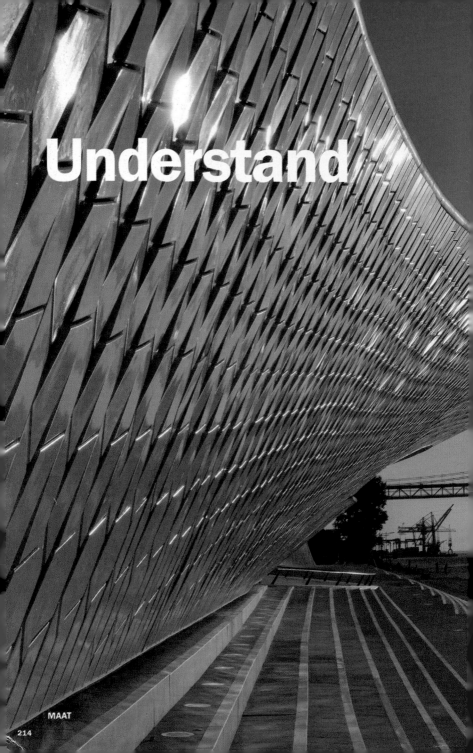

Understand

MAAT

History

From Phoenician outpost to European mainstream

Lisbon's origins may be lost in the mists of the River Tagus but it is one of Europe's oldest cities. Despite its peripheral status under Roman and Moorish rule, after Portugal emerged as an independent kingdom in the 12th century and Lisbon became its capital a century later, the city gained in importance. From the 15th century it was in the vanguard of European exploration and expansion, enjoying a huge inflow of wealth that made it the world's richest trading centre. A period under Spanish rule and a devastating earthquake proved temporary setbacks, but modernity brought political upheavals and uneven economic development. Portugal's joining the European Union seemed to offer a more stable course, but it has not all been plain sailing.

Padrão dos Descobrimentos *p220*

Ancient origins

Before reaching Lisbon, the River Tagus broadens into one of the world's largest natural harbours. It then narrows again and empties into the Atlantic. Its south bank is flat, with inlets famed for millennia for rich oyster beds and fisheries; salt pans still exist around Alcochete and Montijo. On its north bank, freshwater streams flow in from surrounding hills, with Lisbon growing up on the most prominent of these, near where the current runs fastest and deepest. The city owes its eminence largely to the river, the longest in the Iberian peninsula, whose basin stretches beyond Madrid.

One tradition has it that Ulysses founded the city and that its name is a corruption of his. More credible is the story that Phoenician mariners dubbed the place 'Alis Ubbo' – peaceful harbour – which mutated to Olisipo, then Lisbon. In any case, the region has been populated for millennia. Nomadic hunting societies left their mark, while later agricultural populations settled on small tributaries of the Tagus, and the estuary harboured primitive shell-gathering cultures. The area was a crossroads of late Bronze Age trade, and from the eighth to the sixth centuries BC the Phoenicians extended their trade up from Cádiz to the Tagus estuary, where they established an entrepôt for tin coming from Cornwall. Lisbon was a Mediterranean port many centuries before it became the first Atlantic one.

Roman occupation

The Roman presence in Iberia dates to the Second Punic War in the late third century BC, which ended half a century of Carthaginian domination. Putting down restive locals proved more difficult, and it took two centuries to establish the Pax Romana across the peninsula. One local chieftain – Viriatus – gained renown as a resistance leader between 147 BC and 139 BC, harrying Roman legions from the Smerra da Estrela. His Lusitani tribe gave its name to the Roman province of Lusitania, which encompassed most of present-day Portugal.

Lisbon fell in 138 BC and was occupied by the governor Decimus Junius Brutus. He fortified the emergent city, though it's not clear where he built his walls. Lisbon became a district capital under the provincial capital Mérida in what is now Spain. By 30 BC, the city was renamed Felicitas Julia Olisipo after Julius Caesar, then a peninsula commander. The city spread down from today's Castelo de São Jorge to the Tagus and westwards towards what is now Rossio – then a hippodrome. The main exports via its port were the fish paste known as *garum*, salt and local horses; Pliny the Elder described mares from the Tagus as 'fine, docile and impregnated by the west wind, which brought forth offspring of surprising fleetness'.

The principal Roman remains in Lisbon are the Teatro Romano, an amphitheatre built under Emperor Augustus that is only part-excavated. The Forum was probably near an arch that stood by today's Largo da Madalena. In the middle of Rua da Conceição is the entrance to vaulted cellars – probably the foundations of a waterfront temple or similar building, not fish-conserving tanks as once thought. The elongated shape of Rossio, the city's central square, is believed by some historians to follow the perimeter of a Roman hippodrome.

Olisipo prospered for four centuries, ruling a district that extended northwards towards present-day Torres Vedras and Alenquer. Rich farmland was dotted with estates known as *villae*; remains have been found near the airport and around Cascais. Waterfront activity centred on salting fish and maritime commerce.

Christianity was established by the middle of the fourth century, and there's a persistent legend of three Christians – Verissimus, Maximus and Julia – martyred during the persecution by Emperor Diocletian on a river beach later named Santos. (Much later, Portugal's first king was to address his prayers to them before conquering Lisbon.) The city's first bishop was later canonised as St Gens.

Roman rule in Iberia crashed in 409 when hordes of Suevi, Alans and Vandals swept over the Pyrenees. The Suevi swung north, one group of Vandals headed up to Galicia and the other south, and the Alans settled between the Douro and the Tagus. Lisbon fell to this Iranian people, who left few traces. In 418, the Romans called in the Visigoths to kick out the other tribes. The Alans joined with the Vandals in the south (in Vandalusia, later Andalusia), before they all retreated to North Africa. The Visigoths, based in Toledo, soon dominated the peninsula, taking over Olisipo in 469.

Moorish invasion

In 711, Muslim armies landed in southern Spain and within five years conquered most of the peninsula, with Lisbon – now much reduced in size after three centuries of sacking and pillaging – falling in 714. Iberian Christendom regrouped in northern Spain and began the Reconquista. By the mid 800s, northern Portugal was Christian again. The area around Porto was called Portucale, the 'gateway to Cale'. Although forays were made as far as the Tagus, Lisbon remained in Muslim hands for three centuries. Moorish traveller al-Idrisi wrote of the city then called al-Ushbuna: 'This lovely city is defended by a ring of walls and a powerful castle'. That castle was built over the earlier Roman fortification where the Castelo now stands. The Moorish siege walls – Cerca Moura – enclosed about 15 hectares in all, from the Castelo to the present-day Portas do Sol, where one tower houses the Cerca Moura café. From there the line can be traced through Alfama, or over to Largo da Madalena where the Roman arch had become the city gate.

Much of the city stood outside the walls, including most of Alfama. Its name (al-Hama, 'baths' or 'springs') refers to the abundance of water – later medieval fountains on Largo do Chafariz de Dentro and Chafariz d'el Rei are extant.

Moorish Lisbon at its ninth-century peak was a major city of al-Andalus, with 30,000 residents. Immigrants, from Yemenis to newly converted Moroccan Berbers, flooded in and Arabic predominated. Christians (known as *moçárabes*) and Jews could practise their religions, within the strict limits prescribed by their rulers.

Birth of a nation

In 1128, Afonso Henriques wrested control of Portucale from his mother, Teresa, after the death of his father, Henrique. In 1139, he trounced the Moors at Ourique and a year later proclaimed himself king of Portugal. (The pope approved the new nation's foundation in 1179, in exchange for 1,000 gold coins). Aided by northern European crusaders, in 1147 Afonso Henriques attacked Lisbon. On St Crispin's Day, 25 October, a soldier called Martim Moniz led the invading force into the city, where they ran amok.

Later, Afonso Henriques heard of a shrine in the Algarve where relics of St Vincent were guarded by ravens. An expedition of *moçarabes* was sent to retrieve the remains. According to myth, a boat bearing the corpse, circled by ravens, reached Lisbon in September 1173. The image of a boat and ravens duly became the city's symbol.

Capital city

The last Moorish bastions in the Algarve fell in 1249 and Lisbon established itself as the capital, replacing Coimbra. The city huddled within the old walls, with the royal palace in the castle. The Sé Catedral was built soon after. Other houses of worship included the primitive chapels of Santos and St Gens (now Nossa Senhora do Monte). Moors and Jews were permitted to stay on outside the walls – in Mouraria and the Judiarias in the Baixa and Alfama.

For centuries a provincial outpost, Lisbon was now becoming a political and business centre. Portuguese ships plied routes as far as the Baltic and south into the Mediterranean. Medieval Portugal reached its height under poet-king Dom Dinis (1279-1325). He founded the University of Lisbon in 1290 (later moved to Coimbra), planted coastal pine forests to prevent erosion, and built castles to keep out Castilians and Moors. The national borders formalised in the 1297 Treaty of Alcanices with Castile are almost unchanged today.

Portuguese ships plied routes as far north as the Baltic and south into the Mediterranean

By the late 1400s, Lisbon's population was back above 14,000 and the walls expanded to enclose 60 hectares (148 acres). Commerce had moved downhill to the Baixa, with the diagonal Rua Nova (now disappeared) the main street and Rossio a busy open market.

Lisbon suffered several earthquakes during this period. Tremors in 1321 and 1344 damaged the Sé, while another in 1356 set church bells ringing. And the Black Death struck in 1348 and 1349. Despite quakes, plague and persistent grain shortages, Lisbon outgrew its walls once more, creeping up hills north and west of Rossio. When a Castilian raiding party laid waste to much of extramural Lisbon in 1373, Dom Fernando I had new walls built. The Cerca Fernandina was just over five kilometres long with 77 towers and 38 gates and circled Rossio, the Baixa and part of today's Chiado, enclosing 50,000 residents. The Portas de Santa Catarina stood where two churches now face each other in Largo do Chiado. There are remnants of these walls just uphill in the atrium of the Espaço Chiado and downhill on Rua do Alecrim.

When Fernando died in 1383, war broke out between his widow, Leonor Teles, and João, master of the Military Order of Aviz. Leonor sought support in Castile. When the two opposing sides met in 1385 at Aljubarrota, a vastly outnumbered Portuguese force, assisted by English archers, trounced the invaders, cementing Portuguese independence. João I thus

Vasco da Gama

founded Portugal's second ruling house, the Avis dynasty. In gratitude, he ordered the construction of the magnificent monastery of Batalha. He also signed the Treaty of Windsor with England, forging an alliance that stands to this day.

The Discoveries

Portugal's first maritime foray was the 1415 conquest of Ceuta in North Africa. Key to organising and financing this assault was João I's wife, English princess Philippa of Lancaster. Among the participants was João's son, Henriques. Known as Infante Dom Henriques or Prince Henry the Navigator, he soon began training mariners. In 1415 and 1416, expeditions sailed to the Canary Islands; Madeira was discovered around 1419; the Azores in the 1430s. Ships were dispatched to explore the African coast. The psychological barrier of Cape Bojador – people thought they'd fall off the edge of the world – was overcome and charted by Gil Eanes in 1434.

What prompted this sudden burst of activity? Portugal's identity was forged in battle, but it could not expand on land. So it went to sea, driven by greed, adventure and religious fervour – Prince Henry was a master of the Order of Christ, successor to the Knights Templar and a sworn enemy of Islam. After Ceuta, Portugal took Alcacer-Ceguer in 1458, and Arzila and Tangier in 1471.

Madeira and the Azores were by now settled and a brisk trade grew up with these additions to the 'Kingdom of Portugal, the Algarve and the Ocean Seas and Beyond in

Africa'. Henry died in 1460, but by the mid 1470s Portuguese squadrons were active in the Gulf of Guinea and had crossed the equator.

Trade with Asia was at this point in history controlled by Venice, Genoa and Cairo; the only way to reach Asia while avoiding these competitors was to sail all the way south round Africa. Later royals took up this fundamental challenge. Dom João II was nicknamed the Perfect Prince for his Machiavellian talents – he had his rival the Duke of Braganza beheaded in Évora and personally stabbed to death his brother-in-law, the Duke of Viseu. Sailing under the orders of this magnificent schemer, navigator Diogo Cão reached the Zaire river in 1482 and later explored the coast to Angola. Meanwhile, Bartholomew Dias rounded the Cape of Good Hope in 1488 and reported that Africa was circumnavigable. In 1497, Vasco da Gama set out from Restelo (now Belém) with three caravels and a supply ship. Rounding the Cape in November, he sailed up the East African coast and across to India, putting in at Calicut on 20 May 1498. Portugal could now control Indian Ocean trade.

Its only rival at this time was Spain. The 1479 Treaty of Alcaçovas was the two countries' first attempt to carve up the world. The 1494 Treaty of Tordesillas divided the world along a line 370 leagues west of Cape Verde. Portugal could take anything to the east (with the exception of the Canary Islands, already ruled by Spain). This division puts much of present-day Brazil within the Portuguese sphere. There is evidence that, in fact, the Portuguese knew of the South American land mass well before Pedro Álvares Cabral 'discovered' it in 1500.

A fortunate son

Dom Manuel I was dubbed 'the Fortunate' because he came to the throne in 1495, just before Portugal won the India lottery jackpot, which he greedily controlled through royal monopolies. After Vasco da Gama returned with his cargo of spices, the city was overwhelmed by the 'vapours of India', an irresistible force that drew young and old overseas. Many did not return, victims of shipwreck, piracy or disease.

Lisbon's population was now 40,000; it grew west along the river as convents and palaces sprang up. Traders, moneychangers and booksellers jostled along the Rua Nova. The opulence in Europe's richest city was unrivalled – as was its depravity, as caricatured by Gil Vicente in his play *Auto da Índia*, depicting a wife at play while her husband travelled.

The opulence in Europe's richest city was unrivalled – as was its depravity

Dom Manuel spent part of his new-found fortune on two important monuments: the Torre de Belém to guard the harbour entrance, and the Mosteiro dos Jerónimos to thank God for his unexpected wealth. Both are masterpieces of the Portuguese late Gothic style known as Manueline, replete with oriental and maritime motifs.

In 1492, Ferdinand and Isabel of Spain had expelled all non-Christians after conquering Moorish Granada. Portugal at first welcomed fugitive Jews, but in 1496 expelled all Moors and Jews who refused baptism. Those who stayed and officially converted were to form an underclass of 'New Christians'. In 1506, thousands were massacred in a riot that lasted for days. Not surprisingly, after this, most of the Jews fled to North Africa and northern Europe.

Lisbon's population grew fitfully, to 72,000 in 1527 – another plague year. The city had its glories – Renaissance man Damião de Goís described seven of its buildings as wonders of the world, among them the Palácio de Estaus and Hospital de Todos-os-Santos on Rossio, but none survived the 1755 earthquake. Other travellers complained of the stench of slaves' corpses cast into pits such as the Poço dos Negros, and crime was rampant.

Portugal rules the waves

The Indian Ocean, for centuries traversed by Roman, Arab, Indian and Chinese merchants, was lined with prosperous cities and states where standards of living and literacy were often higher than in Europe. The Portuguese sailed in like fundamentalist terrorists armed with bronze cannons – previously unknown in the region – and prepared to use violence on a scale that staggered the locals.

In 1502, Vasco da Gama returned to Calicut in response to the massacre of Portuguese expatriates by local Hindus, a slaughter that had been incited by Muslims. He took terrible revenge, bombarding the city for three days, before he cut off the ears, noses and hands of prisoners he had taken and burned them alive. Elsewhere, he sank a ship of 700 Muslim pilgrims and sent longboats to spear survivors. Other prisoners were rigged up and used for crossbow practice.

In 1510, Viceroy Afonso de Albuquerque conquered Goa, which became the sumptuous seat of the 'pepper empire'. The taking of Malacca in 1511 opened the way to the Far East: caravels soon reached the Spice Islands (Moluccas) and Timor, and by 1513 were trading with China. In 1542, caravels reached Japan, and in 1557 Portugal won the right to administer Macao on the southern coast of China. The poet Luís Vaz de Camões spent time here, as well as in Africa, Goa and the East Indies, during 17 years of travel. At one point he almost lost his epic poem, *The Lusíads,* in a shipwreck, but made it ashore with the poem and later completed it. Published in 1572, it chronicles Vasco da Gama's first voyage to India. Inspired by the origins of empire, Camões saw it come to an end. Young, heirless Dom Sebastião I led a disastrous expedition to Morocco in 1578, where he perished along with much of Portugal's nobility. In 1582, Philip II of Spain snatched the Portuguese crown.

The Spanish move in

The Habsburg Philip backed his claim to the throne by landing an army outside Lisbon and routing the Portuguese in the Alcântara district. As Philip I, he ruled from 1581 to 1598. After modernising the bureaucracy along Spanish lines, he cast his eyes further afield. In 1588, he assembled a fleet of 130 ships and 27,000 men in Lisbon and sent it to attack England. The invincible Armada lost to both the elements and the English, scuttling Spain's ambitions of global domination. Nonetheless, construction of the imposing Igreja de São Vicente de Fora started in 1590, under Juan de Herrera of Escorial fame.

The Inquisition, an agent of state rather than church, had been in Lisbon since 1537, and in 1570 it took over the Estaus Palace on Rossio, where the Teatro Nacional Dona Maria II is now. The inquisitors requested more funds to expand crowded dungeons and organised the notorious autos-da-fé, which began with processions from the Igreja de São Domingos and ended with the condemned being burned.

The Portuguese chafed under Spanish rule – especially when Philip IV (III of Portugal) began appointing Spanish nobles to positions reserved for locals and ignoring the welfare of Portuguese overseas possessions. On 1 December 1640, conspirators overpowered the authorities in Lisbon and proclaimed the Duke of Braganza Dom João IV of Portugal. After a war of secession in 1668, Spain recognised Portugal's independence and possessions, except Ceuta, Ceylon and Malacca. To bolster its position, Portugal matched Catherine of Braganza with England's King Charles II; her dowry included the ports of Bombay and Tangier.

Wealth and reconstruction

Portugal's new-found confidence was soon displayed in the reconstruction of the Igreja do Loreto in Chiado – finished in 1663 – and a start to the building of the Panteão Nacional de Santa Engrácia. Then, in 1699, gold was discovered in Brazil. The flagship of the ensuing construction boom was the massive monastery-palace started by Dom João V in 1717 at Mafra. Elsewhere, artisans created gilded Baroque masterpieces behind the altars of the churches of Madre de Deus (at the Museu Nacional do Azulejo) Santa Catarina and São Roque, and ornate private carriages, some now on display at the Museu Nacional dos Coches. The 1730s also saw construction of the indestructible Aqueduto das Águas Livres. But Lisbon was still mostly a medieval city of narrow lanes. The Bairro Alto became an entertainment centre, as popular theatres staged farces and comedies for plebeians. By 1755, the population had reached 190,000.

On 1 November 1755, Lisbon was struck by a devastating earthquake that lasted six minutes and brought buildings crashing down. It was All Saints' Day, so the churches were packed, while at home candles had been lit in memory of the dead. Panic-stricken citizens racing down to the river were met by a tidal wave that engulfed the Baixa, and a dry north-east wind fanned fires for days.

Dom José I's chief minister, Sebastião José de Carvalho e Melo, threw himself into recovery work. Seen by some as an enlightened despot, by others as high-handed and dictatorial, he is known today as the Marquês de Pombal, a title awarded in 1769. The dust had barely settled when Pombal decreed: 'Bury the dead, feed the living'. Teams searched the rubble for bodies, while taxes on food were dropped and grain was requisitioned: no one starved and no major epidemics followed a disaster that had killed some 15,000.

In the Baixa, hit by the triple scourge of earthquake, tidal wave and fire, Pombal opted to build a new city. The plan, drawn up by Manuel da Maia, Eugénio dos Santos and Hungarian-born Carlos Mardel, was based on the grid scheme of a military encampment, the city's medieval maze overlain by straight roads earmarked for use by distinct trades. Rubble was used as landfill to prevent flooding. Rossio was neatened into a rectangle, and the wide Rua Augusta cut down to the riverside Terreiro do Paço, renamed Praça do Comércio, where Lisbon's rebirth was celebrated 20 years on. The equestrian statue of Dom José I was unveiled in an incomplete square, with wooden façades arranged to fill in the gaps.

In the Baixa, hit by the triple scourge of earthquake, tidal wave and fire, Pombal opted to build a new city

Pombal's authoritarianism brought him results and enemies (see p223 The Making of the Marquês). He cowed the aristocracy by executing nobles accused of plotting to kill the king in 1758. But when José I was succeeded in 1777 by his daughter, Dona Maria I, she dismissed Pombal and cultivated links with France, a policy that had to be reversed after the 1789 revolution there. Her fragile health degenerated into insanity in 1791 and the prince regent, later Dom João VI, took over. She left one important legacy, the Basílica da Estrela, built between 1779 and 1789, while her consort, Pedro, oversaw the building of the Palácio de Queluz, often called the Portuguese Versailles.

In Lisbon, the superintendent of police – or intendente – Diogo Inácio de Pina Manique held sway from 1780. A social reformer, he was instrumental in founding the Casa Pia in 1780, which even now is doing good work for orphans and the poor, despite being buffeted by scandals over

The Making of the Marquês

A visionary but autocratic statesman

A towering figure in Portugal – literally so in Lisbon, where his statue dominates its main traffic intersection, Praça Marquês de Pombal – the man known to posterity as the Marquês de Pombal was graced with that title only towards the end of his long career as a minister. For most of it he was plain Sebastião José Carvalho e Melo.

Born in Lisbon in 1699, in a house that still stands (at Rua do Século 79), Carvalho was the son of a rich provincial squire and cavalry officer. After study at the University of Coimbra and a spell in the army, he eloped with an aristocratic widow; this caused problems initially but was a useful bit of social climbing. From 1738, he served as ambassador in London and then Vienna, before being recalled in 1749. The following year, he was appointed foreign secretary by the newly crowned Dom José I. By the time he was named Secretary of the State of the Kingdom (the top job), he had amassed the unprecedented power that enabled him to govern virtually alone for almost three decades.

Carvalho showed his mettle above all after the 1755 earthquake, and central Lisbon is his most visible legacy. But his deeds were many and varied. A visionary and forceful leader, he made at least as many foes as friends, including a number of prominent aristocrats. After all, Carvalho was not only not one of them, he was also an *estrangeirado*: full of strange foreign ideas.

During his time in power, he abolished slavery in Portugal (though not its colonies), revoked official discrimination against New Christians (descendants of converted Jews) and Freemasons (of which he was assuredly one himself), and ended autos-da-fé. He did not abolish the Inquisition itself, though, not least because he found it to be handy for his own ends. (It was only wound up in 1821.)

The earthquake gave Carvalho the chance to raze the damaged palaces of aristocratic rivals and cut down powerful opponents such as the Society of Jesus (Jesuits). Priests were thrown into prison by the dozen; one, Gabriel Malagrida, was sentenced to death by the Inquisition (headed at the time by Carvalho's brother) for heresy after he attacked a book on public health distributed after the earthquake for explaining it in terms of natural causes rather than as God's wrath.

Carvalho also accused the Jesuits of being involved in the conspiracy to assassinate the king in 1758. A year later, he expelled the order from Portugal and its colonies and instituted reforms at his alma mater, which the Jesuits had dominated for two centuries.

On the economic front, his regime created new industries and fostered existing ones, including the important but abuse-ridden port wine business, with the creation in the Douro of the world's first properly regulated wine region.

For all this and more, a grateful Dom José I ennobled Carvalho in 1759, issuing a royal decree that made him Conde de Oeiras. But it was the title of marquis, conferred a decade later and identifying him with the town where his family's main lands lay, that labelled him for evermore as the Marquês de Pombal.

The backlash against him began the day after the king's death in 1777, with the release of hundreds of political prisoners. Pombal resigned and his carriage was stoned on its way out of Lisbon. Accusations of past misdeeds prompted him to write an apologia that blamed José I for the abuses. Outraged, Dona Maria I issued a decree accusing him of insulting her father. An anonymous 'Letter from Portugal', published in London in response, was ascribed to Pombal. Interrogated for months on end, he eventually implored the queen's pardon. He died, broken and ostracised, in 1782.

With the 1833 triumph of Liberalism, Pombal's posthumous rehabilitation began. The Great Earthquake centenary saw his remains brought to Lisbon amid pomp; today they are in the Igreja da Memória (*see p122*). The centenary of his death was marked by events across Portugal and in the colonies, and work started on the monument that surveys Lisbon today.

Marquês de Pombal

child abuse. He introduced Lisbon's first widespread street lamp-lighting scheme, oversaw the paving of streets, the laying of sewers and the collecting of rubbish, and subjected prostitutes to regular health inspections. He also oversaw the construction of the neoclassical Teatro Nacional de São Carlos in 1793 and planted 40,000 trees in 1799. Meanwhile the population continued to grow: in 1801 it was near 170,000.

Peninsular wars

In 1801, France and Spain joined forces and invaded Portugal. After a brief campaign, the country was forced into submission, ceding to Spain the town of Olivenza (Olivença in Portuguese) near Badajoz; it remains a bone of contention to this day. During Napoleon's rise, Portugal tried quietly to maintain trade with England. But in 1806, he decreed a continental embargo. Portugal faced an unhappy choice: accede and see Britain take over its overseas possessions; or refuse and be invaded. Napoleon gave the Portuguese until September 1807 to declare war on England. Portugal stalled, France invaded and the royal family fled to Brazil, staying for 14 years. Many followed their example: 11,000 passports were issued in short order.

The French invaded three times. In 1808, a British force led by General Arthur Wellesley (better known as the Duke of Wellington) sent them packing after the battles of Roliça and Vimeiro. The French returned under Marshal Soult the following year, but were ejected by Portuguese and British forces. In summer 1810, Marshal Masséna arrived, and after initial setbacks his forces marched on Lisbon. Wellington stopped them with fortifications (the Torres Vedras Lines) stretching north of Lisbon from the Tagus to the sea. The French fled. By 1814, they were back in Toulouse.

The Peninsular Wars left Portugal a wreck. Lisbon's population dipped to 150,000, regaining its turn-of-the-century peak only in 1860. Under the post-war British regency (read, occupation) of Marshal Beresford, unrest was never far from the surface. New ideas took root and words such as 'liberal' and 'constitution' entered the dissident vocabulary. In 1820, Beresford went to Brazil to coax home Dom João VI, who was loath to trade the comforts of Rio for devastated Portugal. In Beresford's absence, the regency was overthrown and liberal rule installed. Elections were held and the Cortes, or parliament, approved a constitution in March 1821.

Now João VI returned and swore allegiance to the new constitution. Crown Prince Pedro, however, stayed in Brazil. In 1822, when the Cortes threatened to strip Brazil of its status as a kingdom, it declared itself independent, and Portugal lost her largest source of overseas income. An ensuing constitutional conflict split the royals. The Absolutists were led by Prince Miguel. The Liberals championed his brother Pedro, whom they proclaimed Dom Pedro IV when João VI died in 1826. Pedro, content as Emperor of Brazil, abdicated the Portuguese throne in favour of his seven-year-old daughter. When she was crowned Dona Maria II in 1828, Miguel declared himself king. So Pedro abdicated the Brazilian throne and returned to head a Liberal counter-revolt.

The war lasted from 1832 – with Lisbon captured by a Liberal army on 24 July 1833 – to 1834, when Miguel was forced into exile. Pedro died months after taking over as regent for the now 13-year-old Maria II, but oversaw the 1834 abolition of religious orders. Monks and nuns were turned out from their cloisters, which were annexed by public and private institutions. Parliament set up in the Mosteiro de São Bento, renamed the Palácio da Assembléia da República, while the monastery in Graça was among religious foundations that became barracks. In 1836, Maria II married Ferdinand of Saxe-Coburg-Gotha, responsible for the fantasy Palácio da Pena on a hilltop at Sintra, which spawned a fashion for Romantic mansions and gardens.

Romanticism, reform and the new republic

In Lisbon, the era saw fado music and military uprisings. Maria Severa Onofriana, the prostitute known as 'A Severa', kept open house in Mouraria, her soprano voice attracting lovers, including the bullfighting Count of Vimioso. She died in 1846, at the age of 26.

Meanwhile there was a series of revolts, the bloodiest occurring on 13 March 1838 when government troops fought rebellious national guardsmen in Rossio. Rossio itself underwent a major facelift in the following years. Black-and-white cobblestones were laid in 1840, and in 1846 the new Teatro Nacional was inaugurated by Dona Maria II. The driving force behind the theatre was Romantic author Almeida Garrett, one of many intellectual former exiles.

By the middle of the 19th century, political stability made possible a major building programme. The grand arch on Praça do Comércio was completed in 1873. Railways had arrived in the 1850s; by the 1860s trains steamed from Santa Apolónia

Swearing-in of Sidónio Pais in Parliament, 1918

station to Porto and Madrid, and by the 1890s from neo-Manueline Rossio station towards Sintra. Prosperity fuelled public entertainment: the Coliseu dos Recreios opened in 1890, followed by the Campo Pequeno bullring in 1892. During Pombaline reconstruction, a green space had been opened north-west of Rossio. The Passeio Público, as it was called, was not a hit at first – the idea of both sexes strolling in a public garden grated with contemporary mores. In the 1830s, it was remodelled as a Romantic garden and became popular with the emergent bourgeoisie. It was extended in the 1880s, becoming the tree-lined Avenida da Liberdade. At its southern end, at Praça dos Restauradores, a monument was raised to the 1640 Restoration. The park laid out to the north was named after Britain's King Edward VII.

Other urban projects of the late monarchy period included the introduction of the first funiculars in 1884, using the water gravity system – a tram filled a tank of water at the top of the hill, and on the downhill run the water provided enough counterweight to pull up another car from the bottom. Electrification began in 1901, and the city soon filled with electric trams.

In the 1870s, a group known as the Cenáculo dominated literary Lisbon. Among its number were storyteller Teófilo Braga, later President of the Republic; historian Oliveira Martins, whose pan-Iberian vision was to shape future generations; and Eça de Queiroz, whose novels *The Maias* and *Cousin Bazilio* offer an unrivalled and at times satirical portrait of Lisbon life. Politically,

intellectuals favoured republicanism, especially after the monarchy gave in to the 1890 British ultimatum that demanded Portugal withdraw from much of south-central Africa.

In 1905, Dom Carlos I appointed João Franco as chief minister. Stepping up censorship and persecution of republicans, Franco only inflamed the situation.

On 1 February 1908, Dom Carlos, his wife Amélia and princes Luís Filipe and Manuel returned from a visit to the Alentejo. Their procession had reached the north-west corner of Praça do Comércio when a black-cloaked figure circled behind the carriage and opened fire. Another conspirator ran out from the arcade. Yet another fired from the central statue. The horseguards rampaged, killing two of the assassins and several bystanders. But the king and crown prince lay dead.

Carlos's second son lasted as Dom Manuel II only until the Republican revolution of 4-5 October 1910. When warships shelled his Palácio das Necessidades, he fled to Ericeira and into exile. From the balcony of the Câmara Municipal (City Hall), the Republic was proclaimed.

Nascent fascism and dictatorship

The optimism accompanying the provisional government set up on 5 October 1910 was soon betrayed by battles over the constitution. A persistent concern was how to hang on to the African colonies, prompting Portugal to enter World War I on the side of the Allies. The Portuguese

Expeditionary Force was virtually wiped out in the April 1918 battle of La Lys.

Back in Lisbon, an army major named Sidónio Pais had led a revolt on 5 December 1917, taking the heights around Parque Eduardo VII and bombarding the Praça do Comércio ministries. Loyalists counter-attacked and hundreds of soldiers died in a brief, bloody fight at Largo do Rato before Sidónio prevailed. What was arguably Europe's first fascist regime saw huge rallies, mass arrests of opposition leaders and heavy censorship. However, Sidónio's chaotic rule lost him allies, and he was assassinated in December 1918.

What was arguably Europe's first fascist regime saw huge rallies, mass arrests of opposition leaders and heavy censorship

Competing local powers threatened to rip Portugal apart. In January 1919, the monarchy was proclaimed in the north; Republican forces took a month to quell the rebellion. In Lisbon, the National Republican Guard (Guarda Nacional Republicana, GNR) was heavily armed and often influenced government. On 19 October 1921 – the Noite Sangrenta or 'bloody night' – members of the GNR and navy revolted; several politicians were massacred, including Prime Minister António Granjo. The next government – the 31st since 1910 – lasted two weeks; 45 Republican administrations would fall before the military definitively took over in 1926.

Meanwhile, despite the political turmoil, intellectual life was thriving. In 1915, the only two issues of the magazine *Orfeu* appeared, introducing painter José de Almeida Negreiros and poets Fernando Pessoa and Mário de Sá Carneiro. In 1924, the Tivoli cinema (now a theatre) opened on Avenida da Liberdade; the Teatro Municipal de São Luíz in Chiado followed in 1928.

This cultural awakening was stifled by the Estado Novo ('New State') regime that prevailed after the May 1926 coup d'état led by Marshal Gomes da Costa. Two years later, a conservative Coimbra professor, António Oliveira Salazar, was named finance minister. In 1932, Salazar became prime minister and was to rule for almost four decades, backed by the infamous

PIDE (Polícia Internacional e de Defesa do Estado) political police. In the early years the regime styled itself as a dictatorship without a dictator, because it eschewed personality cults. But Salazar cracked down on the left and played right-wing rivals off against each other. In 1940, the regime mounted the Exhibition of the Portuguese World in Belém, glorifying national achievements while ignoring World War II and the miserable conditions of rural and industrial workers.

Walking the tightrope

During the war, Portugal was once more forced into a balancing act. When the threat of an Axis invasion evaporated in 1940, Portugal settled into uneasy neutrality, providing tungsten for the Nazi war effort while lending Azores air bases to the Allies. British and German diplomats avoided one another at receptions, and Sintra airport was alone in Europe in offering scheduled flights to both London and Berlin.

Lisbon's cafés were crowded with refugees. Even the king of Romania passed through. *Casablanca* was to have been set here, and Lisbon remained the hoped-for destination in the finished film. French airman-author Antoine de Saint-Exupéry whiled away hours at the Estoril Casino in December 1940, awaiting passage to America; he eventually made it with refugee film director Jean Renoir. Ian Fleming also visited the casino, gleaning ideas for his protagonist by watching Yugoslav spy Darko Popov at the gaming tables.

The Allies' victory in 1945 put Portugal's right-wing dictatorship in a tricky position: celebrating the victory of democracy and communism over its natural allies. The Cold War came to the rescue. After some cosmetic concessions, Portugal aligned with the West in 1949, as a founding member of NATO. Salazar had a scare in 1958 when General Humberto Delgado garnered massive public support and enthused the opposition in show elections for the presidency. But officials rigged the vote, Delgado was forced into exile (and assassinated by PIDE agents in 1965) and internal repression was stepped up. Revolts across the African colonies in 1960 and 1961 became full-blown wars that were only resolved after the 1974 Revolution.

During the 1950s and 1960s, Salazar kept Portugal closed to outside influences. Lisbon was one of the cleanest, quietest cities in Europe: you could chat in the middle of Avenida da Liberdade during rush hour. In the older neighbourhoods, poverty was rampant. Keeping order were the police, who fined citizens for cursing or letting their laundry drip.

at his bedside. Caetano proved unable to unravel the Estado Novo or answer the colonial question. Student demonstrations had been common in the 1960s; now the army joined in. On 25 April 1974, a military coup was masterminded by Otelo Saraiva de Carvalho. Caetano, holed up in the GNR barracks on Largo do Carmo, surrendered after a young captain, Salgueiro Maia, threatened the GNR with tanks, supported by a cheering populace. The only bloodshed came as crowds massed outside the PIDE headquarters on Rua António Cardoso. Shots fired from inside killed three. A plaque marks the spot.

António Oliveira Salazar, 1942

On 25 April 1974, a military coup was masterminded by Otelo Saraiva de Carvalho

Many emigrated. The rest hunkered down and swallowed the regime's three Fs: Fátima, Football, Fado. In 1917, the Virgin Mary supposedly appeared to three shepherd children at Fátima, north of Lisbon. The church had doubts at first, but the regime adopted the cult, building an enormous shrine that became a pilgrimage destination on the 13th of each month from May to October. Football had always been a national passion, but Benfica reached the heights of European club football in the 1960s thanks to the peerless Eusébio, and the national team, inspired by him, finished third in the 1966 World Cup. The 1950s and '60s were also a golden age of fado, dominated by Amália Rodrigues. Down on Praça de Alegria, the Hot Clube turned Lisbon on to jazz.

Major public works were undertaken by the Estado Novo, not least the bridge over the Tagus (Ponte Salazar, later renamed Ponte 25 de Abril after the date of the 1974 Revolution). Linking Lisbon to Almada and its Cristo Rei statue, it was erected in 1958 in thanks for keeping Portugal out of World War II. The Metro was inaugurated in 1959. The city spread outwards. Art nouveau buildings on Avenida da República were demolished and replaced by the first concrete office blocks.

The Revolution

In 1968, Salazar was incapacitated by a stroke after his deckchair collapsed. No one had the heart to tell him President Américo Tomás had appointed the reformist Marcello Caetano in his place; until his death in 1970, ministers held sham meetings

Socialist Party founder (and former PIDE prisoner) Mário Soares and other exiles rushed back to throw themselves into the maelstrom and, soon, take up government posts. General António Spínola headed a Junta de Salvação Nacional, and on 1 May hundreds of thousands demonstrated on Avenida Almirante Reis to back the Revolução dos Cravos – Revolution of the Carnations – as it became known after citizens stuffed soldiers' rifles with the red flowers. Spínola was out by September, and for 14 months right and left, military and civilians, tussled for power. After the 'hot summer' of 1975, when the Communist Party led by Álvaro Cunhal seemed to gain the upper hand but was ultimately outmanoeuvred by Soares, Portugal became a parliamentary democracy.

In the Revolution's aftermath, the colonies won independence, prompting an exodus of hundreds of thousands of Portuguese citizens. These *retornados*, as the white and mixed-race 'returnees' were called (though many had been born in Africa and never seen Portugal), flooded into a post-revolutionary shambles. Later waves of African immigrants came too, for economic or political reasons. Many found low-paid, insecure work in the construction industry, and settled in homes in the shanty towns on the edge of the city.

Catching up (and falling behind again)

In the early 1980s, Lisbon's image was one of genteel decay. Money was scarce, public works were at a standstill, and

Talkin' About the Revolution

More than four decades on, there is finally somewhere to learn about it

For the overwhelming majority of Portuguese who were old enough to understand what was happening – and for many who were not – 25 April 1974 was the happiest day of their lives.

Ask a local to recall the coup that brought down Europe's longest-lived dictatorship and they will lapse into misty-eyed reminiscence about a new dawn that really was bliss.

For such a seismic event, in whose aftermath contemporary Portugal was forged, the Revolution has left surprisingly few visual clues for the visitor. The colourful political murals from the period have either faded or the walls themselves been bulldozed.

The date of the coup remains a national holiday, marked by official and popular celebrations. Over the years, there have been many attempts by politicians to appropriate the Revolution for their own purposes. For example, in the run-up to the 30th anniversary, the right-of-centre government led by José Manuel Barroso launched a poster campaign proclaiming that '*Abril é Evolução*' – 'April is Evolution' (not Revolution) – and listing social and economic statistics to show how much progress Portugal had made.

Barroso's own journey from Maoist firebrand to conservative (some would say neo-liberal) leader represented one kind of evolution (later continued with his moves to head the European Commission and then to Goldman Sachs). But the slogan triggered an outcry from the opposition – and historians – and embarrassment in his own camp. As for the hoardings, leftists daubed a big red 'R' in front of 'Evolução' on most of them.

Ten years later, the 40th anniversary coincided with deep cuts in public spending under a bailout that Portugal sought in the wake of the eurozone crisis. As usual, tens of thousands marched to recall 1974, but many now shouted anti-austerity slogans too.

No one has ownership of the legacy of the Revolution (although not for want of trying in the case of the Communist Party). But the retired officers who toppled the dictatorship have a better claim than most. So, when in 2014 they were not invited to speak at a special session of parliament at which Portugal's conservative president, Aníbal Cavaco Silva, hailed the 1974 coup while calling on the parties to work together to slash the deficit, the grizzled veterans held their own ceremony in Largo do Carmo, the square where the dictatorship had surrendered, complete with (now antique) armoured cars. Thousands of citizens gathered to cheer their speeches accusing politicians of losing sight of the principles of the Revolution: the right to vote, but also universal healthcare, quality education, decent pensions and employment rights.

The charged atmosphere prompted some youngsters to set to with pots of paint and brushes, drawing on the iconography of 1974. The most impressive mural, by the Underdogs collective, is outside Universidade Nova on Avenida da Berna, its centrepiece a portrait of the most widely admired coup leader, the late Salgueiro Maia (see p227).

Still, there was no museum telling the story of the Revolution, or documenting the misdeeds of the dictatorship. The former headquarters of the PIDE, the old secret police, had been converted into luxury flats despite a campaign to turn it into a memorial to the regime's opponents, some of whom were tortured in cells there.

So, when the long-planned **Museu do Aljube** (see p79) finally opened in a former prison in April 2015, it marked an important moment not only for Lisbon – whose mayor, António Costa, was just months later to become prime minister – but for the country.

Former prime minister Mário Soares, seen by many as the father of Portuguese democracy, attended the ceremony, in the very room where he had been married when a political prisoner in the Aljube. He died just two years after the inauguration, his funeral attended by leading political figures from around the world.

The museum's displays contain a wealth of information in Portuguese and English that spans everything from the dictatorship's origins to post-revolutionary turmoil. For a sense of why the Revolution is so important to Portugal and its people, it is the place to visit.

Salgueiro Maia

emigration to northern Europe or the US continued. But, after Portugal joined the European Community in 1986, an inflow of funds provided stability for sustained development. The opening of the Amoreiras shopping centre the previous year had already marked the arrival of mass shopping culture.

The once-quiet streets of Lisbon became clogged with motor vehicles. The Ponte 25 de Abril is notorious for rush-hour jams, barely eased by the newer rail service beneath its carriageway. Another bridge, the Ponte Vasco da Gama, opened in 1998, draining off some weekend traffic. Road-dependent dormitory communities have mushroomed on the outskirts. But in the old city at least, a few more streets are barred to traffic each year.

On 25 August 1988, fire broke out in the Chiado, ripping the heart out of the classy shopping district and ending its long-established outdoor café culture. Renowned Porto architect Álvaro Siza Vieira was called in, and in the face of sloth-like city administration, his sensitive vision of reconstruction was realised.

Further redevelopment took place on the waterfront, where parks, promenades and marinas emerged from Belém to Santa Apolónia station. Upriver, the 1998 Expo was held on former industrial wasteland. Its stated purpose was to mark the 500th anniversary of Vasco da Gama's discovery of the sea route to India, and its hallmark was a giant aquarium, the Oceanário. After Expo ended on 30 September 1998, the site reopened as Parque das Nações, a residential and business district with extensive parkland stretching along the river. Another important legacy was Portugal's new-found confidence in its ability to organise big events, including football's Euro 2004.

Portugal's entry as a founding member to the EU's monetary union on 1 January 1999 underscored its European identity. It handed over its last colony, Macao, to China at the end of that year. Yet a few months earlier, when government-backed militias in Indonesian-ruled East Timor terrorised civilians who had voted for independence, ordinary Portuguese mobilised on behalf of this far-flung former colony with a fervour that recalled revolutionary times.

As the new century dawned Portugal's economy struggled, as EU regional funds and foreign investment switched to Eastern Europe. Politicians lost credibility after three prime ministers departed in quick succession, having failed to tackle deep-rooted problems. The election in 2005 of the first ever majority Socialist administration

was seen as a mandate for reform, and led to transformative investment in renewable energy. But the global financial crisis changed the rules of the game and, though the Socialists were returned to power in 2009 (this time with no absolute majority), public debt ballooned and Portugal was forced to seek a €78 million bailout. After a snap election in 2011, a right-of-centre coalition took over, which professed to want to 'go beyond the troika' – the three international institutions now setting the fiscal rules.

For a while most people seemed ready to swallow the austerity medicine, showing stoicism as public sector wages and pensions were cut and indirect taxes raised. It was only when the government moved to raise workers' social security contributions while trimming those of employers that the average José bridled at this seeming injustice. On 15 September 2012 some half a million people poured onto the streets of Lisbon for the largest protest since the Revolution. The coalition tottered and backed down – though it did go on to implement other painful measures.

The Portuguese are justly proud of social progress made since the Revolution – most dramatically in infant mortality, which is below the EU average, and in education, with about a third of thirty-somethings completing tertiary education (as in Germany).

However, during the economic crisis hundreds of thousands of members of the most highly educated generation in Portugal's history left to seek work abroad. At home, though the minority Socialist government that took office in 2015 (thanks to unprecedented deals with old Communist foes and other leftists) claimed to have 'turned the page on austerity', public services took increasingly threadbare.

The tourism boom of recent years has been an economic boon, with the sector nationally accounting directly or indirectly for perhaps a million jobs. But there has been a downside in Lisbon, where the rapid spread of short-term lets and other tourist-related businesses has sent rents soaring.

Meanwhile, lingering disenchantment with monetary union and the austerity it seems to entail has prompted some to question long-held assumptions about Portugal's place in Europe. Add to that the growing importance of links with former colonies such as Angola and Brazil, and the inflow of people and ideas from outside in the past few years, and many people in Lisbon are again seeing the world through a global prism, just as their rulers did for so many centuries.

Architecture

Whether it's post-quake or postmodernism, Lisbon runs the gamut of architectural glories and horrors.

Though Moorish elements linger, it's the period of the maritime Discoveries that left the first lasting mark on Lisbon's architecture, reflecting the city's prosperity and global links. Later, the devastation of the 1755 earthquake was followed by a pioneering example of Enlightenment town planning that still structures the city's life today. Decorative elements came to loom large, above all *azulejos* – the famous Portuguese ceramic tiles that appear both individually and in ambitious panels.

In more recent times, a great deal of harm was done to the urban fabric. The focus has now shifted to much-needed preservation and rehabilitation work, and away from flagship projects.

Gare do Oriente *p237*

Mosteiro dos Jerónimos

Early origins

Although Lisbon's origins are lost in legend, its days as a Roman provincial city are recalled by the ruins that dot the centre in subterranean (but visitable) pockets. The **Teatro Romano** (*see p79*) is one of these. The centuries after the fall of Rome left little mark and the earliest physical evidence of urban civic life still found in the modern city is of Moorish rule between the eighth and 12th centuries. Surrounded by the Cerca Moura, the Moorish siege walls that skirt the Castelo de São Jorge, Alfama was the city's core. Latticed window shutters to shield women from the glances of passers-by can still be seen on some houses, and the quarter retains the feel of a North African port. Popular style has changed little over the centuries, with the traditional **casa portuguesa** based on simple lines and whitewashed walls with small windows.

Portuguese architecture advanced in the 15th century when Dom Manuel I began putting to use the riches gleaned from the sea route to the Indies. Palaces and churches were built, and royal architects such as Francisco de Arruda devised the new, late Gothic Manueline style. This featured plain walls with extravagant windows and portals decorated with flora and fauna, maritime motifs, the king's seal and the Vera Cruz, or True Cross. Structures still visible today include the **Torre de Belém** and the **Mosteiro dos Jerónimos** (for both, *see p126*), with its spectacular cloister and nave, and the Madre de Deus church, now the **Museu Nacional do Azulejo** (*see p150*). *Lioz*, a local limestone, lent these massive buildings a light, airy look.

Spanish style

Philip II of Spain's ascension to the Portuguese throne in 1582 as Philip I brought a more monumental style, sombre on the outside but gilded within. Still visible are the **Igreja e Mosteiro de São Vicente de Fora** (*see p87*), the **Igreja de São Roque** (*see p105*), the **Mercês church** on Largo do Chiado and the **Convento do Beato** on Alameda do Beato out east in Xabregas. São Vicente, white and imposing on the hill above Alfama, is a prime example. It typifies the mannerist style of the Counter Reformation, rich in ideology and imagery, and its twin bell towers served as models for local architects for two centuries. The interior houses some of Lisbon's most elaborate panels of *azulejos* (tiles). Once imported from Seville, but long since made in Portugal, these tiles remain a consistent presence (*see p234*).

This period also saw the first attempts at town planning. In 1580, the **Bairro Alto** ('Upper Town'; *see p104*) was laid out on a grid of streets that were perceived as wide and regular at the time, even if now they seem cramped and maze-like.

Sobering up and rebuilding

Following the restoration in 1640, a sober style known as the Estilo Chão (Flat or Plain Style) developed, in which massive corner pillars framed horizontally organised façades, with simple balconies topped by stone balustrades or plain railings. Larger country houses and palaces began to mimic the French U-shaped style. Most surviving Lisbon palaces from this period are in Estilo Chão, including the **Palácio Galveias** (Campo Pequeno), now a library, and **Palácio dos Marqueses da Fronteira** (*see p148*).

Artistry and engineering flourished: the **Aqueduto das Águas Livres** (*see p137*) was completed; fancy wood carving and sculpture became de rigueur in royal, church and public interiors; and façades with intricately painted blue-and-white *azulejos* multiplied.

Under Dom João V, the Magnificent, Baroque triumphed in palaces such as the **Paço de Bemposta** (off Campo dos Mártires da Pátria, now a military academy), the **Igreja da Graça** (*see p87*) and the **Palácio das Necessidades** (on Largo das Necessidades, today's Foreign Ministry). Many were inspired by the palace and convent at **Mafra** (*see p167*), north-west of Lisbon, designed by German architect João Frederico Ludovice.

The Great Earthquake of 1 November 1755 left a score of churches, the royal palace, dozens of noble dwellings, and two thirds of the city's medieval housing in rubble. In the aftermath of the ensuing tidal wave and fires, the all-powerful minister of Dom José I, later known as the Marquês de Pombal (*see p223* The Making of the Marquês), sought to impose modernity. He began by forbidding construction outside the city limits and reconstruction inside them until his plans were concluded, and drafted in three bright architects – Manuel da Maia, newly arrived Hungarian Carlos Mardel and Eugénio dos Santos. They plotted out a new Baixa of 200,000 square metres, on a grid of seven streets running north–south, christened after the trades that would operate on them, and eight streets running east–west.

Pombaline style is characterised by scant exterior decoration, although façades were given a glossy finish by pressing the fresh stucco with tin plates – a process known as *estanhado*. The mainly four-storey houses

were built around a *gaiola*, or cage – a flexible structure with wooden joists filled with brick, stone and plaster, intended to withstand earthquakes. Another innovation was to raise the walls separating houses to a level higher than the roof joists, to act as a firewall. Fully equipped with modern sanitation, these blocks were at the very cutting edge of urban planning.

Calcário (limestone) is hewn into tiny blocks to decorate walkways with traditional and modern designs

As soon as Pombal fell from grace, Lisbon resumed its haphazard growth. Dom José's daughter, who became Dona Maria I, was a pious woman responsible for two beautiful churches – the **Igreja da Memória** (*see p122*) and the **Basílica da Estrela** (*see p136*). The latter is an imposing building in white stone, topped by an ornate dome that, when illuminated, dominates the western skyline. Inside is a finely crafted profusion of pink and black marble. The Igreja da Memória is reminiscent of the Basílica – both are mostly the work of Mateus Vicente – but more intimate. Also of note are the 1792 **Teatro Nacional de São Carlos** (*see p208*), perhaps Lisbon's first neoclassical building, and the **Palácio da Ajuda** (*see p128*).

Stagnation and industry

The first half of the 19th century was a turbulent time, and urban planning languished, although the **Teatro Nacional Dona Maria II** (*see p211*) was built between Rossio square and the Passeio Público, a leafy promenade later extended to become the Avenida da Liberdade. The Industrial Revolution brought a new age of engineering (and Romantic nostalgia), epitomised in the neo-Manueline Rossio station and the more French neo-Gothic of the **Elevador de Santa Justa** (*see p64*), designed by Raul Mesnier du Ponsard. The **Campo Pequeno** bullring and the **Casa do Alentejo** in Baixa (Rua das Portas de Santo Antão 58) reflect the neo-Moorish trend that emerged during the 1890s.

Lisbon's distinctive *calçada à portuguesa* (Portuguese paving) came into its own in 1849 with the completion of the dizzy looking wave pattern in Rossio. Even today, *calcário* (limestone) is hewn into tiny

♥ Azulejos

The Portuguese ornamental element that most catches visitors' fancy is the *azulejo*, or tile. They are everywhere: from palaces to the façades of the humblest houses, from butcher's shops to metro stations. There's a **Museu Nacional do Azulejo** (*see p150*) in a former convent, but sometimes the whole city seems like one big tile museum.

The word *azulejo* comes either from *zulej*, 'blue' in Persian, or from *al-zuleycha*, Arabic for polished stone. Tiles from Islamic Asia are on show at the **Museu Calouste Gulbenkian** (*see p147*), but the tradition has deep roots in Iberia. Tiles produced in Seville by Muslim craftsmen were first imported in large numbers during the 14th century; Sintra's **Palácio Nacional** (*see p164*) has some fine examples. But the craze really took off a century later, with the arrival of Italian majolica techniques. After Spain expelled all Mudéjars (local Muslims) in 1610, new factories in Portugal produced flat painted tiles rather than the old relief designs. Made mainly for religious buildings, such as the **Igreja de São Roque** (*see p105*), they depicted biblical landscapes or popular saints.

Larger 'tile tapestries' appeared in the 17th century. Splendid examples survive in the **Igreja de São Vicente** (*see p87*) and the **Palácio dos Marqueses da Fronteira** (*see p148*), whose Sala das Batalhas – full of panels representing battles of the Portuguese Restoration War – has been called 'the Sistine Chapel of tilework'. Mass production began in 1767 when the Marquês de Pombal founded the Real Fábrica do Rato to manufacture tiles for post-Great Earthquake reconstruction. They were used increasingly in façades, in a more restrained, neoclassical style.

The popularity of *azulejos* declined in the early 19th century thanks to the Peninsular War, the court's departure to Brazil and the dissolution of the monasteries; the Real Fábrica closed in 1835. But the industrial age heralded a comeback: examples include the 1865 façade of **Fábrica Viúva Lamego** on Largo do Intendente (which today houses the company's retail outlet, *see p90*, as well as vintage store A Vida Portuguesa, *see p90*), and the façade on Rua da Trindade facing Largo Rafael Bordalo Pinheiro, depicting Progress and Science. Three firms from this period survive today, selling mostly to northern Europe.

The craft moved on. Particularly in Lapa, Campo de Ourique and Saldanha, colourful art nouveau tiles frame doors, windows and balconies. Artists such as Rafael Bordalo Pinheiro and Jorge Colaço created lavish façades and interiors. In later decades, run-of-the-mill tiles were too often slapped on to façades to provide colour or protect against rain. But the latter part of the 20th century saw a revival, with Portuguese and foreign artists designing *azulejos* for sale in specialist shops – and, of course, for Lisbon's metro.

Campo Grande station is graced by Eduardo Néry's 'deconstructions' of traditional blue and white *azulejo* panels; **Campo Pequeno**, two stops away, has fight scenes that recall the nearby bullring. **Parque station** was clad in cobalt blue by Belgium's Françoise Schein and France's Federica Matta, with designs alluding to Portugal's maritime history and noble quotations from poets, philosophers and the Universal Declaration of Human Rights. Out at **Carnide**, José de Guimarães's inimitable style finds expression in neon and stone renditions of wobbly animal forms. At bustling commuter terminal **Cais do Sodré**, António da Costa's giant versions of the White Rabbit from *Alice's Adventures in Wonderland* announce 'I'm late'.

The metro's Linha Vermelha (Red Line), inaugurated to coincide with Expo '98, has been the biggest publicly funded showcase of recent times. At brash **Olaias** station, love-him-or-hate-him architect Tomás Taveira produced a dizzying mosaic of primary colours and restless patterns. For the next station, **Bela Vista**, Querubim Lapa mixed geometric patterns and naïve designs. **Chelas** integrates architecture by Ana Nascimento and decoration by Jorge Martins: tunnels plunge into blue limestone walls with no visible support, slashed by bold rents and asymmetric windows. **Olivais** is one of the network's deepest stations, with fittingly profound artwork by Nuno de Siqueira: panels with images of adversity, war and revolution hint at Portugal's contribution to modernity, while phrases such as 'a thing is not only what we see but also what it signifies' comment obliquely on the artist's own work. At **Cabo Ruivo**, David de Almeida set white Stone Age hunting images on black walls. As your train passes, these flash between pale blue arches, creating a moving-image effect.

The line originally terminated at **Oriente**, designed by Sanchez Jorge. It's a gallery of huge panels on maritime themes by renowned Portuguese and international artists, including Hundertwasser and Erró (more of whose work can also be found in the patio of the nearby **VIP Executive Arts Hotel** on Avenida Dom João II). In 2013, the line was finally extended to the airport – tunnels in the new **Aeroporto** terminus are dotted with mosaic cartoons of Portuguese cultural icons by António Antunes.

Meanwhile, an extension downtown to link up with other lines at **Saldanha** and **São Sebastião** offered fresh opportunities for artistic encounters. At the former, a tribute in tiles to Modernist painter-poet José Almada Negreiros, overseen by his eponymous architect son, incorporates elements from his artworks and aphorisms such as 'Joy is the most serious thing in life'. At São Sebastião, the artist's granddaughters, architects Catarina and Rita Almada Negreiros, worked with Maria Keil, designer of the original 1950s station, to revamp it with panels depicting trees and the odd bird that evoke nearby public gardens, and also to lay out a new twin station with 'kinetic' tiles whose zigzag surfaces suggest movement.

Igreja de São Vicente

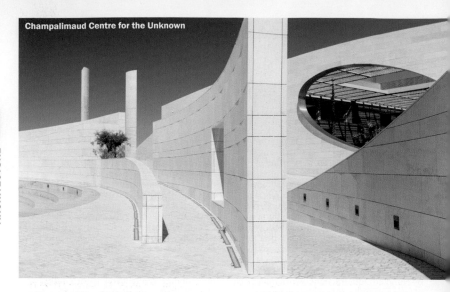

Champalimaud Centre for the Unknown

blocks to decorate walkways with designs traditional and modern, with each stone cut and laid by hand. In 1986, the city set up a vocational school to keep these old skills alive.

Portugal's early 20th-century experiment in democracy produced a precursor of modern social housing in **Arco do Cego** (now dwarfed by Portugal's largest building, the headquarters of state bank **Caixa Geral de Depósitos** and home to Culturgest; *see p145*), as well as the **Parque Mayer** (*see p72*), a cluster of variety theatres off Avenida da Liberdade. The ultra-modern **Teatro Capitólio**, built between 1925 and 1931, was one of these, whose technical innovations included reinforced concrete, a naturally lit auditorium and Portugal's first escalator. Long derelict, in 2009 the theatre was saved from demolition after a vigorous public campaign, and has since been fully restored.

With the rise of Salazar, architecture took on a pseudo-fascist look, with monumental buildings such as the **Palácio da Justiça** at the top of Parque Eduardo VII and the **Biblioteca Nacional** (*see p145*). Modernism struggled in – examples include Cassiano Branco's **Cineteatro Eden** (now a hotel) on Praça dos Restauradores and his **Hotel Victoria** (Avenida da Liberdade 170), as well as the **Instituto Superior Técnico**, an 'acropolis' of learning by Porfírio Pardal Monteiro that was Portugal's first campus. But the regime favoured the Portuguese Modern Traditional style, which featured galleries with round arches and bas-reliefs. The **Igreja da Nossa Senhora da Fátima** on Avenida da Berna and the twin-towered

Igreja São João de Deus on Praça de Londres are outstanding examples.

By 1940, nationalism was in full flow and the Exposição do Mundo Português (Exhibition of the Portuguese World) was held in Belém. It centred on the chauvinistic **Padrão dos Descobrimentos** monument (*see p128*), featuring giant statues of Henry the Navigator and his courtiers, map-makers and sailors advancing along a plinth towards unknown seas. Uptown, the **Fonte Luminosa**, a giant fountain on Alameda Dom Afonso Henriques, with its Tagus nymphs and mythical creatures from Camões's *The Lusíads*, is from the same period.

However, it would be simplistic to write off the Salazar era. It saw the construction of Pardal Monteiro's impressive modernist **Gare Marítima de Alcântara** (1943), with murals by José de Almada Negreiros, while the hyperactive minister of public works, Duarte Pacheco, was a visionary, laying out three large residential neighbourhoods – Alvalade, Restelo and Olivais – and starting the first dual carriageway. By the 1960s, Portugal could no longer avoid international trends: the first metro line opened in 1960, the Ponte Salazar (now **Ponte 25 de Abril**, *see p54*) was built in 1966 and the **Fundação Calouste Gulbenkian** (*see p146*) opened in 1969.

Modern times

Much harm was done to the city's fabric after the 1974 Revolution. In the 1970s and '80s, corrugated-iron shanty towns sprang up and dormitory suburbs were built, largely illegally. Portugal's 1986 entry into the EU generated wealth at a time of minimal public awareness of urban planning, and city officials permitted the rape of several historic zones. On Largo do Martim Moniz, a shopping centre was built on the back of a tiny, ancient chapel. Across town, architect Tomás Taveira tested local humour with his pink and smoked-glass **Amoreiras** office-and-mall complex (*see p139*), which juts out from an old hilltop district, and an office block that echoes the form of a Portuguese guitar (Avenida de Berna 175).

After the 1988 Chiado fire, reconstruction of the historic neighbourhood was assigned to the leading figure of the Porto School of architecture, Álvaro Siza Vieira. He rescued 18 of the 20 damaged façades and rebuilt the gutted insides, restoring the **Armazéns do Chiado** department store as a shopping centre and luxury hotel. The project secured him the 1992 Pritzker Prize, architecture's equivalent of the Nobel Prize.

That same year, Portugal inaugurated the **Centro Cultural de Belém** (*see p207*) to host the EU presidency. Positioned opposite the Mosteiro dos Jerónimos, Vittorio Gregotti and Manuel Salgado's vast *lioz* fortress was controversial at the time but has come to be accepted, if not loved.

The most important urban project of the late 20th century, though, was Expo '98, which rehabilitated a stretch of eastern waterfront polluted by oil refineries, munitions factories and a slaughterhouse. Now called **Parque das Nações** (*see p153*), it boasts such architectural highlights as Peter Chermayev's **Oceanário**, Regino Cruz's UFO-like Pavilhão Atlântico (now renamed the **Altice Arena**, *see p207*), Siza's **Pavilhão de Portugal** with its concave concrete canopy, and Santiago Calatrava's soaring **Gare do Oriente**. Built in conjunction with Expo were the 17-kilometre (10.5-mile) **Ponte Vasco da Gama** and a metro line with some remarkable stations (*see p234* Azulejos).

Since then, several big international names have been bandied about – Jean Nouvel and Norman Foster among them – in plans to provide the city with architectural pizzazz, particularly along the neglected riverfront. The global financial crash and euro crisis sidelined most, but work has now started on a Renzo Piano-designed residential complex at Braço de Prata, in eastern Lisbon.

At the city's western end, in Belém, 2010 saw the inauguration of the **Champalimaud Centre for the Unknown** (*see p125*), a curving hulk designed by Indian architect Charles Correa, and 2016 that of the lower-lying but also impressively swooping

MAAT – Museu de Arte, Arquitetura e Tecnologia (*see p124*), designed by the UK's Amanda Levete. Both were privately funded – the latter by an offshoot of Portugal's biggest company Energias de Portugal (EDP). EDP's own corporate headquarters, by local firm Aires Mateus, has towered over the Cais do Sodré area since 2015.

Expo '98 rehabilitated a stretch of eastern waterfront polluted by oil refineries, munitions factories and a slaughterhouse

As for public buildings, not only is there little or no money for flagship projects, but there has not always been the cash to open those already built. A design by Brazil's Pritztker laureate, Paulo Mendes da Rocha, for a new 16,000 square metre home for Portugal's most visited museum, the **Museu dos Coches** (*see p128*), was approved in 2006; but funds ran out and work halted for several years. The museum's giant raised hangar for exhibits and separate reception block were only inaugurated in 2015 – with many still wondering how the money would be found to run and maintain it. The only major public project to be launched in the last decade is the **Terminal de Cruzeiros** (Cruise Terminal), inaugurated in 2017. Its relatively compact rectangular design, by Lisbon architect José Luís Carrilho da Graça, won out over several foreign rivals.

Nowadays, public and private investment is being ploughed above all into urban rehabilitation – no bad thing when so much of Lisbon's built fabric needs repair. Siza oversaw the overhaul of an old warehouse in the densely packed neighbourhood of São Bento to create the **Atelier-Museu Júlio Pomar** (*see p134*) – a project praised for the elegant simplicity of its 'almost invisible' architecture, as the then mayor (now prime minister), António Costa, put it at the 2013 inauguration.

Another Pritzker Prize-winner from Porto, Eduardo Souto de Moura, has meanwhile been working on a cluster of projects around Praça do Príncipe Real to turn 19th-century mansions into upscale residential and commercial spaces, such as **Embaixada** (*see p110*) and **Palácio Faria**, on the square's eastern side.

Plan

Accommodation

The tourism boom of the past few years has triggered a building bonanza: new hotels, hostels and tourist apartment complexes have been opening on a monthly, if not weekly, basis as the capital extends its lead over the Algarve in terms of visitor numbers. Crumbling mansions in the old central neighbourhoods have emerged as boutique hotels, sometimes with the aid of city funding, while glass towers have multiplied in business hubs such as the Parque das Nacões. Lisbon continues to cater ever more abundantly for the well-heeled, but also welcomes the mid-market tourists and backpackers who were for so long a speciality. Out on the coast, meanwhile, you can find everything from palaces to campsites.

Lisboa Carmo Hotel

New hotels, hostels and tourist apartment complexes have been opening on a monthly, if not weekly, basis

Where to stay

Upmarket hotels are clustered between the Baixa and Parque Eduardo VII, but scattered throughout the city are cheap hotels – often still with *pensão* in their name, although the official classification for non-hotel accommodation now is *alojamento local*. The odd refurbished palace can also be found in Chiado (such as **Verride**, *see p242*) or residential areas away from the centre, such as the **Olissippo Lapa Palace** (*see p242*) in Lapa.

Campsites (*see p244* Get Out of Town) and hostels (*see right* Booking information) – defined as anywhere whose rooms are mostly in dorms – are not always cheaper per head than *pensões*, some of which have triple and quadruple rooms. But hostels do have kitchen and other facilities such as sociable lounges; towels, on the other hand, may not be provided or might cost extra. Almost all budget lodgings tend to have free Wi-Fi throughout, whereas some fancier hotels still make you pay extra in your room. In general,

In the know
Price categories

Our price categories are based on the cost in spring of one night in a double room with en suite shower or bath (not including special offers), breakfast included.

Luxury	€300+
Expensive	€200-€300
Moderate	€100-€200
Budget	up to €100

even budget accommodation is clean, partly because the authorities are strict.

If you want to be sure of LGBT-friendly accommodation, anywhere in the Príncipe Real area, such as **Pensão Londres** (*see p245*) and **Memmo Príncipe Real** (*see p242*), is a good bet.

Prices

It's hard to find rock-bottom prices these days, since even downmarket *pensões* have been forced to upgrade their facilities to compete with hostels and short-let apartments, which has resulted in higher rates to pay for the investment. Still, in some mid-range and lower-priced hotels, rates may be negotiable. Even in fancier establishments, there are bargains to be had if you book ahead or online. In hotels that serve tourists rather than the business trade, prices can double during the summer, particularly along the Estoril coast. Book a fortnight in advance in July and August, especially if you want to be near a beach. For more on out-of-town options, *see p244* Get Out of Town. In Lisbon, rates can depend on the size of the room, the view and whether there's a bathroom. Prices generally include at least a continental breakfast, but not always with online deals.

Booking information

Where booking is concerned, most specialist online sites have a fair range of Lisbon hotels, but sometimes your best bet is to go direct, since even budget places often have online as well as phone/email reservations. Once in town, tourist offices provide only limited help with finding accommodation; there's a comprehensive listing on the **Turismo de Lisboa** website (www.visitlisboa. com) but they have no advance reservation service. Hostellers can use global websites such as **hostelbookers.com** and **hostelworld.com**; Lisbon's downtown YHA can also be booked direct at http://pousadasjuventude.pt.

My Story Hotel Tejo

In the know
Addresses

All of our hotel listings feature a full postal address (including the seven-digit postcode); we have added the neighbourhood only where transport details do not feature a metro station. Note that in Portuguese addresses, where the house number after the street name is followed by a comma and single digit, that digit denotes the floor (most relevant for downtown *pensões*).

Luxury

Four Seasons Hotel Ritz Lisbon

Rua Rodrigues da Fonseca 88, 1099-039 (21 381 1400, www. fourseasons.com/lisbon). Metro Marquês de Pombal. **Rooms** 282. **Map** *p60 O16.*

An art collection worthy of a museum adorns the lounge and lobby of this perennial favourite of visiting statesmen. Guest rooms are understatedly luxurious and all have private terraces with views of Parque Eduardo VII. The Ritz also boasts the most impressive spa in central Lisbon, with an indoor lap pool, solarium, steam room and sauna, while the penthouse fitness centre has a 400m outdoor running track. The fine French- and Portuguese-style food turned out by Pascal Meynard and his team in the Varanda restaurant attracts lots of outside custom – as does the renowned breakfast buffet.

Memmo Príncipe Real

Rua D Pedro V, 56 J, Príncipe Real 1250-094 (21 901 6800, www. memmohotels.com). Metro Rato or tram 24, bus 758. **Rooms** 41. **Map** *p95 P18.*

In the know
Flat out growth

With Lisbon's tourism boom outstripping its hotel-building boom, renting a flat is now popular even for short stays – whether it's a luxury penthouse or a windowless burrow in Alfama. As well as global sites such as **Airbnb** and **Booking.com** there are local platforms such as **www.lisbonapartments.com**, **www.lisbonwindows.com** and **http://feelslikehome.pt**, as well as chains **www.lisbonservicedapartments.com** and **www.hello-lisbon.com**. Just don't expect local flavour or even human contact: decor tends to be bland and keys replaced by access codes.

This self-declared 'hand-made' hotel – the first five-star boutique property in trendy Príncipe Real – opened in 2016, perched on the edge of a hill overlooking the city. Built from scratch, it uses the same local limestone as appears in many of Lisbon's historic buildings and squares, as part of the hotel's tasteful mix of contemporary and classic styles. All guest rooms are spacious; though only the pricier ones have balconies, they all have a great view – as does the small pool on the smart restaurant-bar terrace.

Olissippo Lapa Palace

Rua Pau da Bandeira 4, Lapa, 1249-021 (21 394 9494, www. olissippohotels.com). Tram 25 or 28. **Rooms** 109. **Map** *p132 M20.*

Set in tranquil gardens with wonderful views, this former aristocratic residence in the quiet Lapa neighbourhood is one of Lisbon's classiest hotels. The interior is opulent and there are excellent health and beauty facilities, including sizzling hot stone therapy and sizeable indoor pool. Each room has a terrace or balcony overlooking the lush garden and outdoor pool or the dome of the nearby Basílica de Estrela (*see p136*). There's an amazing breakfast buffet, including champagne, and the main restaurant offers outstanding food and views.

Tivoli Avenida Liberdade Lisboa

Avenida da Liberdade 185, 1269-050 (21 319 8900, www. tivolihotels.com). Metro Avenida. **Rooms** 306. **Map** *p60 P17.*

This landmark hotel combines convenience and creature comforts, attracting a steady stream of business people, honeymooners, families and tour groups to enjoy the spacious public areas and plush rooms. It opened in 1933, but the interior is swish 1950s, with a recent contemporary overhaul. On the rooftop, restaurant SEEN serves contemporary cuisine from 'chefpreneur' Olivier da Costa, while the Sky Bar (Apr-Sept) attracts fashionable locals with a DJ and cocktails. Downstairs,

Cervejaria Liberdade specialises in fine seafood. At the rear is a secluded tropical garden (closed in winter) with a circular pool. The Anantara spa offers therapies from East Asia.

Valverde Hotel

Avenida da Liberdade 164, 1250-146 (21 094 0300, www. valverdehotel.com). Metro Avenida. **Rooms** 25. **Map** *p60 P17.*

There could hardly be a better base for luxury shopping than this drop-dead gorgeous boutique hotel, which aims to serve as a home from home. Its interiors are a well-judged blend of 1950s and contemporary. Service is attentive but discreet. Some rooms only have a shower, but even singles feature spacious bathrooms. All rooms overlook the *avenida*. Breakfast (available up to the civilised hour of 11am) may be taken in the winter garden, which also has a small pool. There's a small restaurant and a tiny private cinema that's ideal for canoodling couples.

Verride – Palácio Santa Catarina

Rua de Santa Catarina 1, 1200-401 (21 157 3055, www.verridesc. pt). Metro Baixa-Chiado or tram 28. **Rooms** 19. **Map** *p95 O20.*

This prize-winning restored hilltop townhouse became a hotel in 2017. Rooms are comfortable and elegant; storage is at a premium but the views make up for it. The King's Suite, with its carved oak panels, is arguably Lisbon's top lodging; the Queen's is all white stucco and tile panels. At breakfast (€30) staff can rustle up anything from a full English to a detox drink. All cakes and biscuits are made in-house. Upstairs, a restaurant serves reinvented Portuguese cuisine while a tiny rooftop terrace bar has a 360-degree view of the old town and River Tagus.

Expensive
EPIC SANA Lisboa Hotel

Avenida Eng Duarte Pacheco 15, 1070- 100 (21 159 7300, www. lisboa.epic.sanahotels.com). Metro Marquês de Pombal or tram 24. **Rooms** 311. **Map** *p132 N16.*

There's no doubt that the rooftop pool and sundeck, plus the huge spa with its view of a lovely botanical garden, are the big draws here. But this hotel's location – halfway between Praça Marquês de Pombal and the Amoreiras mall – also has its attractions, especially if you're planning to drive out to the beaches along the Estoril coast or magical Sintra. Inside, the understated modern decor and furnishings, all cream and brown, are offset by silvery hues in the common areas and turquoise in the 291 rooms and 20 suites. Out at Parque das Nações, sister hotel **Myriad** (21 110 7600, www.myriad.pt) is a riverfront tower with a top-flight (literally) restaurant.

Eurostar das Letras
Rua Castilho 6-12, 1250-069 (21 357 3094, www.eurostarshotels. co.uk). Metro Avenida. **Rooms** *107.* **Map** *p60 P17.*

Spain's Eurostar group caters to better off travellers with modern, arts-themed hotels; this one just up from the Avenida da Liberdade has public areas and guest rooms named for the likes of Stendhal, Shakespeare and Virginia Woolf (with matching bedside reading) and lively literary soirées, and staff can of course point out local literary spots. There's a sauna and gym and a restaurant specialising in Portuguese cuisine with contemporary techniques. In summer you can dine (or eat breakfast) on the terrace.

Hotel do Chiado
Rua Nova do Almada 114, 1200-290 (21 325 6100, www. hoteldochiado.com). Metro Baixa-Chiado. **Rooms** *39.* **Map** *p95 Q20.*

One of Lisbon's best-located hotels, in the middle of the elegant shopping district of the same name. Designed, like much of the area, by Álvaro Siza Vieira, the building's success is most apparent in the morning, when a tall window frames a breakfast backdrop that takes in the Baixa and castle. The interior is clean lines, with hip furniture. Rooms are spacious and light,

Memmo Príncipe Real

with touches of luxury such as fresh flowers, and some have private terraces that look across to the castle. In the seventh-floor Entretanto bar, or on its terrace, snacks or more elaborate dishes are served.

Hotel Miraparque
Avenida Sidónio Pais 12, 1050-214 (21 352 4286, www.miraparque. com). Metro Parque. **Rooms** *96.* **Map** *p60 P16.*

The three-star 1950s 'Parkview' is set in a tranquil location overlooking Parque Eduardo VII, near the El Corte Inglés shopping complex. Rooms are decorated simply and some are on the cramped side – but the proximity of the park, a friendly atmosphere and English-speaking staff go a long way towards making up for that. Aside from breakfast there's no meal service. Local handicrafts are on sale at reception.

My Story Hotel Tejo
Rua dos Condes de Monsanto 2, 1100-059 (21 886 6182, www. lisboatejohotel.com). Metro Rossio or tram 12, 15. **Rooms** *58.* **Map** *p60 Q19.*

Just off Praça da Figueira, these are stylish digs at a reasonable price. Rooms feature brightly coloured walls that contrast with the white-painted furniture, while modern furniture in the common areas is arranged under old stone arches. The lobby bar is a cheerful place for a drink even if you're not staying here. Don't miss the Poço de Borratém in one corner – the water from this ancient well was long used to cure itching and liver ailments, and it's topped with a handsome *azulejo* panel.

PortoBay Liberdade
Rua Rosa Araújo 8, 1250-195 Lisboa (21 001 5700, www. portobay.com). Metro Avenida. **Rooms** *98.* **Map** *p60 P17.*

This newish five-star hotel aims for the feel of an urban resort: located just off the city's main axis, it has an indoor pool, gym with natural light, spa with sauna, Turkish bath and treatment room for couples, plus a rooftop bar with plunge pool. Guest rooms are done out in cream, gold and light brown, and most have balconies. Beds are large, with a pillow menu. The hotel also has a smart modern bistro with patio and a separate cocktail bar. The four-star **PortoBay Marquês** (Rua Duque de Palmela 32, 21 003 2700) is just round the corner.

Pousada de Lisboa
Praça do Comércio 31-34, 1100-148 (21 040 7640, www.pousadas. pt). Metro Terreiro do Paço or tram 12, 15, 28. **Rooms** *90.* **Map** *p60 Q21.*

Standing right on Lisbon's main grand riverside square, this hotel forms part of the now privately run Pousadas de Portugal chain, almost all in historic monuments – in this case, the former home of a government ministry, next to the Triumphal Arch. All guest rooms – including several for families – are classically decorated and have ultra-comfy beds; many have river views. Space is at a premium in this location but there's an inner patio with retractable roof and even a small spa, pool and fitness centre. The trendy RIB Beef & Wine restaurant, in an atmospheric arched space, serves tasty meat and traditional snacks, plus 120 Portuguese wines.

Get Out of Town

Beyond the city limits

Lisbon is the transport hub for the wider region and so a good base for all the places you might want to visit (*see pp156-169* Day Trips). But even if your sightseeing focuses on the city itself, you still might prefer to get away at the end of the day. Unsurprisingly, given the plethora of beaches in the area, there's no shortage of accommodation, especially towards the end of the scenic railway line to Cascais.

Among the latter's top hotels are the boutique **Farol Hotel** (http://farol.com.pt), whose terrace is a rocky shelf looking out onto the open Atlantic, and the **Grande Real Villa Itália Hotel & Spa** (www.granderealvillaitalia.realhotelsgroup.com), housed in the former residence in exile of Italy's last king, Umberto II, with its marble and Venetian mosaics and amazing spa. This includes a thalassotherapy treatment pool, ice fountain and Vichy showers, among other facilities. Out at Guincho (*see p161*), the **Fortaleza do Guincho**, in a sprawling fort dating back to the 17th century, overlooks the beach and has a Michelin-starred restaurant.

Sintra has always been a bit short on hotels, but is known for its charming guesthouses (listed on www.sintrainn.net) as well as **Lawrence's Hotel** (http://lawrenceshotel.com), which claims to be the oldest on the Iberian peninsula.

But if, for you, getting out of the big smoke means camping out amid pine trees, you'll be pleased to learn that there are a some outstanding places to pitch your tent in the region. Just on the edge of Lisbon, **Lisboa Camping** (21 762 8200, www.lisboacamping.com) nestles in Monsanto forest park and boasts a hard-surface football pitch, mini-golf, two tennis courts, a pool with diving area, solarium and terrace, two play pools and children's playgrounds. As well as tent and caravan pitches, there are furnished bungalows sleeping up to six. Buses run into town and to Belém, and if you're here to attend one of the big rock festivals there are usually dedicated shuttles, too.

Beyond Cascais is the **Orbitur-Guincho** campsite (www.orbitur.com), also surrounded by umbrella pines, but just a ten-minute walk from Guincho. Facilities range from a tennis court and games room to a mini-market plus swimming pool with fun slides. It can get busy in high season, but the crowd usually creates a good party atmosphere. An open area is available for motorhomes and there are different-sized bungalows – some with kitchen and bathroom, some without – with prices varying according to the number of guests (two to seven). Bed linen and towels can be supplied if you book ahead online. Orbitur also has a campsite on the Caparica coast (*see p168*).

Sofitel

Avenida da Liberdade 127, 1250-140 (21 322 8300, www.sofitel-lisbon-liberdade.com). Metro Avenida. **Rooms** 163. **Map** p60 P18.

The red, gold and black colour scheme in guest rooms, and sculptures in common areas, recall the voyages to Africa and Asia of Renaissance-era Portuguese mariners. Located on the main drag the hotel has a somewhat business-like atmosphere (and it has a 24-hour business centre and gym), so that while beds are comfortable and the hotel is convenient for sightseeing, it's perhaps not a place to chill out – although it does have a small library and a babysitting service, plus a kids' area in the breakfast room, where

a great buffet is laid out. The ground-floor AdLib restaurant applies French techniques to Portuguese cuisine; its terrace out front is great for people-watching.

Moderate
Altis Avenida Hotel

Rua 1º de Dezembro 120, 1200-360 (21 044 0000, www.altishotels.com). Metro Restauradores. **Rooms** 70. **Map** p60 Q19.

Despite its monolithic exterior (the hotel is housed in a former government building), the Altis Avenida offers plenty of comfort and style, drawing on a 1940s aesthetic. The cheaper Classic rooms overlook the interior patio, while the more expensive Superior and Deluxe rooms have views of Praça dos Restauradores (double glazing blocks out the

traffic noise). There are also two light-filled suites with views up the Avenida; the esplanade of the top-floor Rossio restaurant and bar affords a similar panorama. Guests have free use of the indoor pool, spa and 24-hour gym at the **Altis Grand** (15-minute walk) and discounts at the Altis Belém spa.

BessaHotel Liberdade

Avenida da Liberdade 29, 1250-139 (21 321 0500, www.bessahotel.com). Metro Restauradores. **Rooms** 113. **Map** p60 P18.

This hotel on the Avenida da Liberdade is small but full of cosy corners with big armchairs in keeping with the vintage decor. Some rooms have balconies looking on to the avenue; all have gleaming white bathrooms, and a built-in sound system with

Bluetooth. The covered pool on the roof is a great place to wind down after sightseeing, especially if you can see rain teeming down outside. There's a gym, sauna and Turkish bath too. The ground-floor restaurant has a good reputation for its contemporary take on local cuisine and has a copious wine list.

Hotel Dom Carlos Park
*Avenida Duque de Loulé 121, 1050-089 (21 351 2590, www. domcarloshoteis.com). Metro Marquês de Pombal. **Rooms** 76. **Map** p60 P16.*

Despite the location, right by Praça Marquês de Pombal, this spacious and comfortable three-star hotel is surprisingly secluded, overlooking a leafy square. It is good value too. Bedrooms are comfortable and quiet with roomy en suite marble bathrooms; in most doubles, an extra bed can be added for a small extra charge. The cosy lounge has an honesty bar with drinks and snacks. Round the corner, the slightly smaller **Dom Carlos Liberty** (Rua Alexandre Herculano 13, 21 317 3570) has a rooftop terrace and small gym; there are also rental flats available in the Chiado for long-stay visitors.

Lisboa Carmo Hotel
*Rua da Oliveira ao Carmo 1-3, 1200-307 (21 326 4710, http:// carmo.luxhotels.pt). Metro Baixa-Chiado or Rossio, or tram 24. **Rooms** 45. **Map** p95 P20.*

On the corner of a lovely leafy square just up from the main drag of Chiado, this elegant little hotel is staffed by a friendly, helpful team. Some of the rooms are rather small, but all are prettily decorated in pastel colours and floral motifs, with wood floors and classic or contemporary furniture, and have air-conditioning. Those on the top floors have stunning panoramic views; lower ones overlook the square. There is a stylish restaurant, though you won't want for dining options in this part of town.

Budget
Hotel Duas Nações
*Rua da Vitória 41, 1100-618 (21 346 0710, www.duasnacoes.com). Metro Baixa-Chiado or tram 12, 28. **Rooms** 73. **Map** p60 Q20.*

Now rated as a two-star hotel, this former *pensão* remains one of the best bargains in the Baixa. Rooms are simple and comfortable, and some have been renovated in the past year; the more expensive ones have private bathrooms with showers. Try to avoid those along Rua Augusta, which can be noisy; the rest are fairly quiet. You can even order a basic continental breakfast in bed. The hotel has no bar, but you can buy chilled soft drinks at reception.

Pensão Londres
*Rua Dom Pedro V 53, 1250-092 (21 346 2203, www.pensaolondres. com.pt). Metro Baixa-Chiado or Rato. **Rooms** 36. **Map** p95 P19.*

A decent option, given that prices haven't kept up with those of local rivals (though neither have the facilities). The Londres' location at the Príncipe Real end of Bairro Alto is its trump card: not too noisy, but still close to the city's nightlife. Get a room with a view across Lisbon; the alternative is a distant view of the river or – for those on the lower floor – a busy street. Some of the more expensive rooms have en suites and satellite TV. Staff are friendly and helpful.

Pensão Portuense
*Rua das Portas de Santo Antão 151-153, 1150-167 (21 346 4197, www.pensaoportuense.com) Metro Restauradores. **Rooms** 36. **Map** p60 Q19.*

A first-floor *pensão* run very efficiently by an upbeat, helpful family. The location is fine if you want to be on a street full of restaurants, but it can get noisy at night. Rooms – from single to quadruple – are well furnished and comfortable, and all have clean, modern bathrooms with decent high-pressure showers.

Pensão Praça da Figueira
*Travessa Nova de São Domingos 9, 2D, 1100-372 (21 342 4323, www. pensaopracadafigueira.com). Metro Rossio or tram 12, 15. **Rooms** 32. No cards. **Map** p60 Q19.*

This popular place offers some of the best value in the area. Service is good and the atmosphere friendly. The rooms – each painted a different colour – are large with decent views of the square and the ruins of the Carmo church on the hillside; some have a balcony too. Not all rooms have a shower and barely half have their own toilet.

Residencial Dom Sancho I
*Avenida da Liberdade 202, 1250-147 (21 351 3160, www.domsancho. com). Metro Avenida. **Rooms** 40. **Map** p60 P17.*

Another well-priced, well-run central guesthouse that's now classed as a hotel (with two stars). The decor is nothing special, but the Dom Sancho offers a decent array of services – hairdryers in the rooms, round-the-clock laundry service, theatre and concert bookings, and excursions. All rooms are en suite.

Residencial Estrela dos Santos
*Avenida Almirante Reis 53, 1150-011 (21 317 1030, www. estreladossantos.residencial.com. pt) Metro Anjos or tram 28. **Rooms** 20. **Map** p80 R17.*

This homely, family-run guesthouse has spacious rooms, all with private bathrooms. It's next to Anjos Metro station and you can be in central Lisbon in ten minutes, although traffic can be noisy. Staff at reception (24 hours) will provide hairdryers, robes, ironing kits and more on request, as well as arranging car hire. There's no bar – just a soft-drinks machine in the lobby; a nearby gym has a health club and sauna. The *pensão* shares its entrance with funkier (and slightly pricier) stablemate, **Lisbon Style Guesthouse** (21 317 1035, www.lisbonstyle.pt), which has a cute patio.

Getting Around

ARRIVING & LEAVING

By air

Aeroporto Humberto Delgado (LIS) *21 841 3500, www. aeroportolisboa.pt.*
Lisbon's main international airport is in Portela, in the north-east of the city. There are two **Aerobus** shuttles run by Carris (*see right*), costing €4 (€2 4-10s) or €6 for two (€3 4-10s). Tickets give you 24hrs of travel on both Aerobus routes and there are discounts if you buy online. Line 1, running via the city centre (Entre Campos, Saldanha, Marquês de Pombal, Restauradores and Praça do Comércio) to Cais do Sodré, departs every 20mins 7.30am-7pm, then every 25mins to 11pm, daily. Line 2, running via Entre Campos, Sete Rios and Praça de Espanha to the financial institutions of Avenida José Malhoa, departs every 20mins 7.40am-7pm, then every 25mins to 10.45pm, daily.

A cheaper option is to take the **Metro** (*see right*), which loops out east to Parque das Nações before heading downtown; for most city-centre hotels, you must then change. Alternatively, catch a regular Carris **bus (705 or 722)** to Areeiro, then pick up the Metro, or take **bus 783** all the way to Marquês de Pombal/Amoreiras.

A **taxi** into the centre should be about €12 (plus €1.60 for luggage). There are some dodgy operators, so check the meter is on. You can pay in advance at the Turismo de Lisboa booth in the arrivals hall: staff give you a voucher that you can use in taxis with the relevant sticker. For central Lisbon, this costs €16 during the day (€19.20 9pm-6am). It might work out

slightly more expensive (though the voucher cost includes tip and baggage fee) but you'll know you're not getting ripped off. The airport has a 24hr information line (21 841 3500), and both staffed and automated bureaux de change.

By rail

Trains from Spain, France or north Portugal end at **Santa Apolónia** station (Avenida Infante Dom Henrique, www. cp.pt); it has a tourist information booth, bureau de change, taxi rank and a range of bus services, and is on the Metro. Most trains also call at **Gare do Oriente** station at Parque das Nações, which is about a 20min Metro ride into town. Trains from the Algarve use the rail link under the Ponte 25 de Abril, stop at **Entre Campos** (another Metro station) and terminate at Gare do Oriente.

PUBLIC TRANSPORT

Information

Maps of the bus and tram system are available at Carris booths and maps of the Metro (*see p263 and fold-out map*) at major Metro stations. For **Carris** information, call 21 361 3000 (9.30am-12.30pm, 2.30-5.30pm Mon-Fri) or visit www.carris.pt; there's also a customer service office at Avenida Duque d'Ávila 12 (9am-5pm Mon-Fri). For information on the **Metro**, call 21 350 0115 (8.30am-7pm Mon-Fri) or visit www.metrolisboa.pt.

Fares & tickets

You can buy tickets when boarding a bus (€1.85) or tram (€2.90), but for the Metro you must first get a **7 Colinas** or **Viva Viagem** smart card, chargeable at Metro vending machines or Carris booths, or in post offices or PayShop agents. The card costs €0.50 and is valid for a year; you can either load a €1.45 ticket (for 1hr unlimited Metro and Carris travel) or a 24hr pass (€6.30) on to it, or instead use 'Zapping'. This means charging it up with €2-€15, after which a single Metro or Carris (bus & tram) trip costs €1.25. (Note that if you want to recharge it with a different kind of ticket, you must first use up the original kind.) At Metro gates and on entering buses, hold your card against the electronic pad to validate it.

Lisbon's tourist pass, the **Lisboa Card** (*see p56*), allows the bearer unlimited travel on Metro, buses, trams and trains to Cascais and Sintra, as well as free entry to or reductions at sights and museums.

For all public transport, if you don't have a valid ticket the fine is €120-€350 (plus fare).

Metro

This is the speediest way around Lisbon, though many sights aren't covered by the network. An expansion project is under way, but not expected to be complete before 2023. Trains run about every 5mins 6.30am-1am daily, more frequently during rush hour. The lost property office for the network is at Marquês de Pombal.

Buses

Carris buses provide good services way out into the suburbs. Stops are indicated by a yellow sign.

Tickets can be bought from the driver, but a smart card is better value (*see above*).

Trams

The more traditional *elétricos*, or trams, on the 12, 15, 18, 24, 25 and 28 routes have been joined on the 15 route by modern rapid transport models. All are run by Carris, fares are integrated with the bus system and stops are marked by a yellow sign – often hanging from overhead wires. Don't leave Lisbon without riding the 28, which passes through historic neighbourhoods, from Graça and Alfama through the Baixa, Chiado and Estrela. Beware of pickpockets on this route.

A pricier tourist tram plies much the same route. The circular 12, starting in Praça da Figueira, coincides with the 28 on part of the Alfama stretch; again, a pricier tourist tram covers the same ground. The 25, meanwhile, runs from Cais do Sodré through Lapa and Estrela to Campo de Ourique. The 15, starting downtown at Praça da Figueira, is handy for the sights of Belém, while the 18 coincides with its route for much of the way but starts only at Cais do Sodré and after Alcântara turns uphill to Ajuda. The 24 runs from Praça Luís de Camões via Príncipe Real and Amoreiras to Campolide. *See also p67* Trams & Funiculars.

Funiculars

The city's three funicular trams – officially called *ascensores* but more often known locally as *elevadores* – and the **Elevador de Santa Justa** (*see p64*), which really is a lift, are run by Carris and integrated with its fare system. Note that tickets bought on board these services are much more expensive than those on buses, so you save a lot if you buy a smart card in advance (*see left*). They all run

from 7am or so, an hour or two later on weekends. The **Ascensor da Glória**, which runs from Praça dos Restauradores up to the Bairro Alto, keeps going until 11.50pm (12.25am Fri & Sat), while the **Ascensor da Bica** stops at 9pm and the **Ascensor do Lavra** at 7.55pm.

Local trains

Local train services are mostly run by branches of national rail operator **CP-Caminhos de Ferro Portugueses** (707 210 220, www.cp.pt). Trains run along the Estoril coast from Cais do Sodré station (which is on the Metro) as far as Cascais every 20-30mins (€1.30-€3.45). Here, too, smart cards (*see p246*) are the norm; Zapping works on this route.

Rail services to Queluz and Sintra leave from Rossio, Sete Rios, Entre Campos and Roma-Areeiro – all on the Metro. There are periodic scares about muggings on this line, but it's used by thousands of locals and tourists every day and transport police patrol most trains. A combined train and Scotturb bus pass for the Sintra-Cascais region could be a good option if you're planning several trips out.

Fertagus (707 127 127, www.fertagus.pt) trains serving Almada and Setúbal cross the Tagus using the line beneath the Ponte 25 de Abril.

Ferries

Transtejo ferries (808 203 050, www.ttsl.pt) link the city with the south bank of the Tagus. They are packed with commuters in rush hour, but offer unrivalled views. Boats to Barreiro leave from shabby Terreiro do Paço boat station, near Praça do Comércio; those to Cacilhas, Montijo and Seixal from the ugly new Cais do Sodré boat station, where car ferries also ply the Cacilhas route; and passenger services to Trafaria depart from Belém. Each station has an information office. Fares cost €1.20 to €2.75 – again, loaded on to a Viva Viagem smart card (€0.50). *See also p57* Appreciating the Tagus.

TAXIS

Taxis in Lisbon are common and inexpensive. There's a minimum charge of €3.25 (€3.90 9pm-6am Mon-Fri, all day Sat & Sun). Tipping is optional and even a small amount is appreciated. You are rarely far from a taxi stand: Rossio, Largo do Chiado and Largo de Trindade Coelho/Largo da Misericórdia in the Bairro Alto are reliable. There are several 24hr dial-a-cab services, such as on 21 811 9000 (Retális) and 21 811 1100 (Teletáxis); the booking charge is €0.80. You can also use the **MEOTaxi** and **MyTaxi** mobile apps to connect to licensed taxis. **Uber** is active in Lisbon (it does not work with individual drivers, only companies, hence avoiding labour law issues), as are rival apps **Taxify**, **Cabify** and **Chauffeur Privé**. East of Baixa, **tuk-tuks** proliferate; there's no meter so you have to agree a price.

DRIVING

The Portuguese leave their fabled manners behind when they get behind the wheel. Traffic is chaotic and many streets are narrow, winding and one-way. Police can issue on-the-spot fines for minor driving offences – don't argue. Speed limits are 90km/hr (60km/hr in built-up areas; 120km/hr on *auto-estradas* – motorways), not that many people take notice. Seat belts are obligatory in front and back, and the limit for alcohol is 0.5g/ml (0.2g/ml if you've had your licence for less than three years) – don't drink and drive. You must be 17 to drive a vehicle in Portugal but may encounter problems if you're under 18.

Parking

Cars are often crammed nose to bumper, half on pavements, reflecting a lack of garages. Be sure to tuck the mirror in on your hire car. Underground car parks (signposted with a white P on blue background) have multiplied of late but are not cheap. On-street parking downtown is on a meter system, for which you need coins.

Parking illegally may result in a heavy fine or the vehicle being towed. Even in metered areas, drivers may be met by *arrumadores* – 'fixers' – who will guide you to a place and then, in theory, watch your car. They'll expect an advance tip of about €0.50 for this unsolicited service; refusing to pay will almost certainly trigger no more than unfriendly muttering but you may not want to take the risk.

Car hire

To rent a car in Portugal you must be over 18 (or older for some vehicles) and have had a driving licence for more than one year. All companies listed have a desk at the airport and a booking number; the latter is given first, then details of the main downtown office. In Lisbon car sharing is available via mobile apps **DriveNow** (€10 then from €0.24/min) and electric-car specialist **Emov** (€9 then €0.21/min); parking is included.

Avis *800 201 002 (7am-8pm daily), www.avis.com; Avenida Praia da Vitória 12C (21 351 4560).* **Map** *p142 Q15.*

Budget *808 25 26 27 (8am-8pm daily), www.budget.com.pt; Avenida Praia da Vitória 12C (21 351 4560).* **Map** *p142 Q15.*

Europcar *808 204 050 (8.30am-7.30pm Mon-Fri; 9am-6pm Sat), www.europcar.com; Avenida António Augusto Aguiar 24 C/D (21 353 5115).*

Hertz *808 202 038 (24hr), www.hertz.com; Rua Castilho 72 (21 942 6300).* **Map** *p60 O16.*

CYCLING

Although most of Lisbon's streets are unfriendly to cyclists, with cobbles, tyre-trapping tramlines and bad driving, there is now a total of 60km (37 miles) of cycle routes in the city, including along the river from downtown to Belém. The Estoril and Sintra areas offer the most scenic cycling. As well as private bike hire outfits, there are council schemes in Lisbon (Gira) and Cascais (BiCas). For all, you'll need photo ID.

Belém Bike *Next to MAAT, Avenida de Brasília, Belém (96 378 0233, 93 740 6316, www.belembike.com). Train to Belém from Cais do Sodré or bus 728.* **Open** *Winter 10am-7pm daily. Summer 10am-8pm daily.* **Hire** *from €2.50/30mins. No cards.* **Map** *p123 F21.*
This riverside shack is the cheapest place in town to hire a bicycle for short periods; it does repairs too.

BiCas *Cascais Jovem, Largo da Estação, Cascais (800 203 185). Cascais rail from Cais do Sodré.* **Open** *8am-8pm daily.* **Hire** *from €1/30mins.*
This council-funded outfit has three booths in Cascais: one right by the station, one by the nature tourism booth on Avenida da República, and one on the coast road at Guia. Make use of 16km (9.5 miles) of cycle tracks, including a route along the coast to Guincho beach (20-30mins).

Gira *21 116 3060, www.gira-bicicletasdelisboa.pt* **Open** *24hrs.* **Hire** *from €2/45mins.*
The council's bike-sharing scheme, inaugurated in 2018, already comprises 100 hubs scattered around the city, with both classic and electric bicycles. Download the app and register; your day pass (€10) gives you the first 45mins for free.

Lisbon Hub *Largo Corpo Santo 5, Baixa (21 347 0347, www.lisbonhub.com). Metro Cais do Sodré or tram 15, 18, 25.* **Open** *9.30am-6.30pm daily.* **Hire** *€15/4hrs; €25/day; €75/3 days. Electric bike €30/4hrs. No cards.* **Map** *p114 P21.*
At this well-stocked outlet for tour company Bike Iberia, rental of a sturdy bicycle includes a lock and key, optional helmet and front basket; also available are child seats, trailers, panniers, tool kits and map cases.

▶ *The Parque das Nações is large enough that hiring a Gira bicycle (www.gira-bicicletasdelisboa.pt) at the park could be worth the trouble. There's also the green Parque do Tejo to explore to the north.*

SCOOTERS

In the daytime, central Lisbon is littered with electric scooters from **Lime, Iomo, Hive** and **Voi** (and more firms are on the way). Download an app, register, locate your scooter and unlock it (€1 then €0.15/min). When done, you can in theory leave it anywhere (but don't obstruct pavements), as at night they're returned to hotspots.

WALKING

Our favourite tours are **Inside Tours** (96 841 2612, www.insidelisbon.com), **Lisbon Walker** (96 357 5635, www.lisbonwalker.com) and **Portugal Walks** (96 575 3033, www.portugalwalks.com).
Lisbon's many hills (there are certainly more than the proverbial seven!) make it challenging terrain for even energetic walkers, especially on a hot day. But 20 minutes spent steaming up an incline is often rewarded with a view that takes away what little breath you have left (*see p83* Miradouros).

Resources A-Z

Travel Advice

For up-to-date information on travel to a specific country – including the latest on safety and security, health issues, local laws and customs – contact your home country government's department of foreign affairs. Most have websites with useful advice for would-be travellers.

AUSTRALIA
www.smartraveller.gov.au

CANADA
www.voyage.gc.ca

NEW ZEALAND
www.safetravel.govt.nz

REPUBLIC OF IRELAND
foreignaffairs.gov.ie

UK
www.fco.gov.uk/travel

USA
www.state.gov/travel

ACCIDENT & EMERGENCY

Emergency numbers

Emergency services *112*
Police (*polícia*), fire (*bombeiros*) or ambulance (*ambulância*).

A&E departments

Hospital de Santa Maria *Avenida Professor Egas Moniz, Campo Grande (21 780 5000, information 21 780 5555, www.chln.min-saude.pt). Metro Cidade Universitária or bus 701, 732, 738, 755, 768.* **Open** *A&E 24hrs daily.* **Map** *p142 O11.* This is Lisbon's largest general hospital, with comprehensive emergency services.

ADDRESSES

The name of the road or square comes first, then the number of the building. Numbering starts from the end of the street that is nearest the river. Several major squares have official names and a traditional, more commonly used designation. Prime examples are Praça do Comércio, which is usually known as Terreiro do Paço (also the name of the local Metro station); Praça Dom Pedro IV, which is always known as Rossio (also a Metro station); Largo Trindade Coelho, which is more often known as Largo da Misericórdia; and Campo Mártires da Pátria, invariably

referred to as Campo Santana. In the Baixa, Rua Áurea is also known as Rua do Ouro.

AGE RESTRICTIONS

Drinking alcohol 18.
Buying cigarettes 18.
Driving 18.
Sex (Hetero- and homosexual) 14.

ATTITUDE & ETIQUETTE

The Portuguese are a very courteous people and are sure to say '*com licença*' if they want to edge past you, or '*desculpe*' if they accidentally bump into you; you should do the same. In shops it's normal to greet the assistant with a '*bom dia*' or '*boa tarde*', depending on whether it's morning or afternoon. In addressing people, the Portuguese use different forms for 'you' depending on who's being addressed, and are rather more formal than, say, the Spanish. Young people may launch straight in with '*tu*', but with strangers you're best sticking with '*você*' or even '*o senhor*'/'*a senhora*'.

The Portuguese are also adept at queuing. At bus and tram stops, don't be deceived by the fact that no queue is visible into thinking that one doesn't exist: it almost certainly does, in the heads of the people at the stop. If anyone boards before someone else who's been waiting longer,

it's sure to trigger tutting and resentment.

CLIMATE

Lisbon has long, dry summers and a mild winters, limited to a period of wetter and cooler weather between December and February. Autumn (October and November) and spring (March to May) are mild but sometimes very wet. May is a particularly lovely month. August is generally the hottest month. Excluding July and August, nights can be cool.

CONSUMER

All cafés, restaurants, hotels and other establishments must, by law, have a *livro de reclamações*, where disgruntled customers may write their criticism, and which is periodically inspected by officials. Merely asking for this 'book of complaints' is likely to make your host considerably more emollient. In general, though, consumer rights are not very well protected in Portugal. The most active campaigning organisation is **Deco** (21 841 0800, www.deco.proteste.pt), which can also offer advice.

CUSTOMS

Customs declarations are not usually necessary if you arrive from another EU country and are carrying legal goods for personal use. Guidelines for quantities accepted (for over-16s) as being for personal use include:
• up to 800 cigarettes, 400 small cigars, 200 cigars or 1kg of loose tobacco
• ten litres of spirits (more than 22% alcohol), 20 litres of fortified wine or alcoholic drinks with less than 22% of alcohol, 90 litres of wine (less than 22% alcohol;) or 110 litres of beer.

Coming from a non-EU country (or the Canary Islands) you can bring:

• 200 cigarettes or 100 small cigars or 50 regular cigars or 250g (8.82oz) of tobacco
• one litre of spirits (more than 22% alcohol), two litres of any other alcoholic drink with less than 22% alcohol, four litres of wine (less than 22% alcohol) or 16 litres of beer
• personal items with a total value of up to €430.

Visitors are also allowed to carry up to €10,000 in cash without having to declare it. Non-EU residents can reclaim the VAT (IVA) on certain large purchases when they leave Portugal. For details, *see p253*.

DISABLED ACCESS

With cobbled streets and lots of hills, Lisbon is a challenge for disabled travellers, though rules for new buildings are strict. In museums, hotels and shopping centres, facilities for the disabled are common, as are assigned parking spots.

Public transport company **Carris** has a special minibus service for the disabled (21 361 2141, 6.30am-10pm Mon-Fri, 8am-10pm Sat & Sun) but you need a special card: take a medical certificate proving disability, photograph and passport to the Carris offices in Santo Amaro (Rua 1º de Maio 101). The service must be booked two days in advance and confirmed the next day; the cost is that of an ordinary bus ticket.

Tourism company **Accessible Portugal** (92 691 0989, www.accessibleportugal.com) can hunt down appropriate accommodation for you, as well as offering tours and equipment, from wheelchairs to grab rails.

Cooperativa Nacional de Apoio a Deficientes *Praça Dr Fernando Amado 566-E, Marvila (21 859 5332). Metro Chelas.* **Open** *9am-12.30pm, 2-6pm Mon-Fri.* This association can provide advice and information about tourism services for the disabled.

DRUGS

Consumption or possession of small amounts of any drug are not crimes punishable by imprisonment. Offenders are instead summoned before an administrative tribunal, which can impose a fine or compulsory counselling. Dealing, though, is likely to result in imprisonment.

ELECTRICITY

Electricity in Portugal runs on 220V. Plugs have two round pins. To use UK appliances, purchase a plug adaptor in advance. US appliances run on 110V and require a converter, available at Lisbon's larger specialist electricity stores.

EMBASSIES & CONSULATES

Australian Embassy *Avenida da Liberdade 200, 2º (21 310 1500, www.portugal.embassy.gov.au). Metro Avenida.* **Open** *9.30am-noon, 2-4.30pm Mon-Fri.* **Map** *p60 P17.*

British Consulate *Rua São Bernardo 33, Estrela (21 392 4000, www.gov.uk). Tram 28.* **Open** *9.30am-2pm Mon, Wed, Fri. Phone 9am-5pm.* **Map** *p132 N18.* The community site www.bcclisbon.org also has information.

Embassy of Canada *Edifício Vitória, Avenida da Liberdade 198-200, 3º (21 316 4600, www.canadainternational.gc.ca/portugal). Metro Avenida.* **Open** *9am-noon Mon-Fri.* **Map** *p60 P17.*

Embassy of Ireland *Avenida da Liberdade 200, 4th floor (21 330 8200, www.embassyofireland.pt). Metro Avenida.* **Open** *9.30am-12.30pm Mon-Fri.* **Map** *p60 P17.*

US Embassy *Avenida das Forças Armadas, Sete Rios (21 727 3300, www.pt.usembassy.gov). Metro Jardim Zoológico.* **Open** *Visas 8-10am Mon-Fri. Information 11.30am-4pm Mon-Fri. Commercial section 2-5pm Mon-Fri.* **Map** *p142 N12.*

For all other embassies, see http://embassy.goabroad.com.

HEALTH

There are no special threats to health in Portugal, though strong suncream and sun hats should be kept to hand. EU citizens should get a free **European Health Insurance Card** before leaving home. This does not substitute medical and travel insurance, but entitles you to any state-provided treatment that may become necessary during your trip, whether as a result of illness or accident. Any treatment provided is on the same terms

Local Weather

Average monthly temperatures and rainfall in Lisbon

	High (°C/°F)	Low (°C/°F)	Rainfall (mm/in)
January	15 / 59	8 / 46	100 / 3.94
February	16 / 61	9 / 48	85 / 3.35
March	19 / 66	11 / 52	53 / 2.08
April	20 / 68	12 / 54	68 / 2.67
May	22 / 72	14 / 57	54 / 2.12
June	26 / 79	17 / 63	16 / 0.63
July	28 / 82	18 / 64	4 / 0.15
August	28 / 82	19 / 66	6 / 0.23
September	27 / 81	18 / 64	33 / 1.29
October	23 / 73	15 / 59	101 / 3.97
November	18 / 64	12 / 5	128 / 5.04
December	15 / 59	9 / 48	127 / 5.00

as Portuguese nationals – that is, free except for a symbolic fee. Some hospitals offer both free state and paid-for private healthcare; if you're asked to pay anything more than the symbolic fee up front, then it's being presumed you want private care; make it clear if this is not the case.

Portugal's public health system is poor by western European standards. Once you reach the specialists, standards are reasonable, but GPs are underfunded and burdened with bureaucracy. Those who have insurance should take advantage of a strong private sector. A visit to a private doctor will cost from €60, but the service is good.

▶ UK citizens are urged to seek up-to-date advice on their entitlement to free public healthcare in Portugal from www.gov.uk before they travel.

Complementary medicine

Portugal doesn't have a culture of alternative medicine, apart from the use of traditional herbal remedies. Sweet-smelling ervanárias still thrive, where customers discuss their ailments in hushed tones with the shopkeeper. Herbs come in 100g (3.5oz) bags and are then made into a tea. There's an enormous variety, used to cure everything from alcoholism to haemorrhoids.

Ervanária Rosil Rua da Madalena 210, Baixa (21 887 2097, www.evanararosil.com). Metro Rossio. **Open** 9am-7pm Mon-Fri; 9am-1pm Sat. No cards. **Map** p80 Q20. This long-established herbalist sells local and imported medicinal herbs and potions, many as blends packaged under its own brand name, for everything from eczema to rheumatism and sexual dysfunctions. Rival **Biototal** is at no.150 (21 886 9178, www.biototal.pt). With both companies, you can order online.

Contraception & abortion

Condoms are readily available in supermarkets, from vending machines and in pharmacies, which also sell the 'morning-

after' pill. Abortion is legal. See also right Helplines.

Dentists

Public health dentists charge a nominal fee, but standards are patchy, so go private if you can.

Most younger dentists are likely to speak English. The large dental clinic, **Malo Clinic** (https://maloclinics.com) has its headquarters on Avenida dos Combatentes, Entrecampos (21 722 8100) and also a branch in El Corte Inglés, Praça de Espanha (21 722 8135).

Doctors

Anjos da Noite Rua Dom Luís de Noronha 4, 6º, Praça de Espanha (707 507 707, www.anjosdanoite.pt). Metro Praça de Espanha. **Open** Head office 8am-10pm daily. **Map** p142 O13. Members of 'Night Angels' pay a €2.50 monthly fee for a range of (paid) medical services, with clinics and home visits included. The phone line is manned 24hrs.

Clínica Médica Internacional de Lisboa Avenida Sidónio País 14, Marquês de Pombal (21 351 3310, www.cmil.pt). Metro Parque. **Open** 9am-7pm Mon-Fri. No cards. **Map** p60 P16. A busy practice used to dealing with foreigners.

HELPLINES

Alcoólicos Anónimos 21 716 2969. **Open** 24hrs daily. The local Alcoholics Anonymous.

Centro SOS Voz Amiga 21 354 4545. **Open** 4pm- midnight daily. For those suffering from loneliness and depression.

Intoxicações INEM 808 250 143. **Open** 24hrs daily. Emergency advice on what to do in case of poisoning or overdose.

Linha Verde de Medicamentos 800 202 844. **Open** 9am-6pm daily. Run by the national medicines authority, fielding questions about medicinal drugs.

Narcóticos Anónimos Freephone 800 202 013. **Open** 8.30-10.30pm Mon, Wed, Fri. The local Narcotics Anonymous. If they

don't pick up, leave a message and they'll call back.

Saúde 24 808 24 24 24, www.saude24.pt. **Open** 24hrs daily. Main national health helpline, covering all subjects.

Sexualidade em Linha 800 222 003. **Open** 11am-7pm Mon-Fri; 10am-5pm Sat. State-funded helpline aimed mainly at teenagers.

ID

Legally, you must carry ID at all times; for Britons and non-EU nationals that means a passport. In practice, you'll only need it if you get into trouble.

INSURANCE

For healthcare for EU nationals, see p250 Health. All foreign visitors are advised to take out private travel insurance with a reputable company to cover a wide range of eventualities from injury to theft.

LANGUAGE

Although the language spoken in Portugal can sound indecipherable even to Brazilians, speakers of other Romance languages are in better shape than they might think, as reading Portuguese is a lot easier than understanding it when spoken. Locals are themselves often good linguists. For decades, millions of them have packed their bags to try their luck elsewhere; of those who return, most speak another language. Youngsters, too, invariably speak some English.

LEFT LUGGAGE

Airports

The **Depósito de Bagagem** (21 841 3594) is in the arrivals hall. Cost is according to weight: €3.32 per day for up to 10kg; €4.92 per day for 10kg-30kg; and €9.74 for 30kg-60kg. There's no limit on the number of days that you may leave luggage.

Metro stations

At **Rossio Metro** station **City Lockers** (http://www.citylockers.pt/lisbon-rossio) will store luggage for up to seven days (longer if pre-arranged). Cost is according to size of locker and length of use: a large locker ranges from €2.50 for one hour to €7.50 per day.

LEGAL HELP

If you get into legal difficulties, the **British Consulate** (*see p250*) can provide a list of English-speaking lawyers. Most big local firms of *advogados* (lawyers) have English speakers.

Centro Nacional de Apoio ao Imigrante *Rua Álvaro Coutinho 14-16, Anjos (808 257 257, from abroad +351 21 810 6100, www. acm.gov.pt). Metro Anjos.* **Open** *8.30am-6.30pm Mon-Fri.* **Map** *p142 R17.* Legal and other help and advice specifically for foreign residents, run by ACM, the state agency for migration.

LGBT

Centro LGBT *Rua dos Fanqueiros 40, Baixa (21 887 3918, www. ilga-portugal.pt). Metro Terreiro do Paço or Baixa-Chiado.* **Open** *7-11pm Wed-Sat.* **Map** *p60 Q20.* This friendly council-funded community centre run by the local ILGA (Intervenção, Lésbica, Gay, Bissexual, Trans e Intersexo) affiliate offers advice, information and counselling.

Checkpoint LX *Travessa do Monte do Carmo 2, Príncipe Real (91 069 3158, www.checkpointlx. com). Metro Rato or bus 758.* **Open** *noon-8pm Mon-Fri; 2-6pm Sat.* **Map** *p95 O18.* This free HIV-testing centre in the heart of the Príncipe Real neighbourhood will produce your results in 30 minutes, and also offers advice and health information.

Clube Safo *96 795 7516 (www. clubesafo.com).* National association defending lesbian rights.

LIBRARIES

Specialist libraries are listed in the free council-published *Agenda Cultural* magazine.

Biblioteca Municipal Central *Palácio Galveias, Campo Pequeno (21 817 3090). Metro Campo Pequeno.* **Open**

1-7pm Mon, Sat; 10am-7pm Tue-Fri. **Map** *p142 Q13.* The main municipal lending library. Show ID for access, and proof of residency for borrowing.

Biblioteca Nacional *Campo Grande 83, Entrecampos (21 798 2000). Metro Entrecampos.* **Open** *9.30am-7.30pm Mon-Fri; 9.30am-5.30pm Sat.* **Map** *p142 P10.* Portugal's national library. Use is restricted to over-18s. Show ID for access.

LOST/STOLEN PROPERTY

For lost or stolen property, try the lost and found section of the Lisbon police (*see p253*). Theft should be reported at any police station, in person. For lost or stolen credit cards, contact your bank.

Airport

If your luggage has gone astray, go to the desk in Arrivals set up for this purpose. Items found in the building and handed in go to the PSP police in the airport (21 844 4530).

Public transport

For buses and trams, contact the PSP police station in Olivais (21 853 5403). For the Metro, go to Marquês de Pombal station.

Taxis

If you leave something in a Lisbon taxi, you'll have to phone the company. If you have a receipt with the car's number on it, all the better. If you can't remember the name of the company, and your ride was in central Lisbon, there's a fair chance it will be **Rádio Taxis de Lisboa** (21 811 9000), the largest taxi company.

MEDIA

Newspapers

A Bola *(www.abola.pt)*, **Record** *(www.record.pt)*, **O Jogo** *(www. ojogo.pt)* These three football papers are the country's most popular daily read, respectively biased towards Benfica, Sporting and Porto.

Correio da Manhã *(www. cmjornal.pt)* A diet of crime

and scandal has made this the country's biggest-selling daily.

Diário de Notícias *(www. dn.pt)*, **Jornal de Notícias** *(www. jn.pt)* Oporto-based *Jornal de Notícias* is still a big seller; stable-mate *Diário de Notícias* has good classifieds.

Expresso *(http://expresso.sapo. pt)* Weekly political analysis and an online daily edition.

Jornal i *(http://ionline. sapo.pt)* Self-styled independent daily.

O Jornal Económico *(http:// jornaleconomico.sapo.pt)*, **Jornal de Negócios** *(www.negocios. pt)* Rival business dailies.

Público *(www.publico. pt)* Comprehensive, quality daily coverage; good on global events.

English-language

Delivery of British tabloids is regular, as the *Sun*, the *Daily Mirror*, the *Daily Mail* and the *Daily Express* print in Spain; quality dailies turn up late or even the next day.

The *Portugal News* is a long established, comprehensive English-language newspaper, now only available online at http://theportugalnews.com.

The *Portugal Resident*, an Algarve-based weekly, is available online at http:// portugalresident.com.

Radio

The airwaves are filled with music. Mainstream rock station **Rádio Comercial** (97.4FM) beats the more varied state-run **Antena 3** (100.3FM) at the ratings game, while **Oxigénio** (102.6FM) is wall-to-wall dance music. Church-owned **Rádio Renascença** (103.4FM) has news and talk shows. It and its sister stations have the biggest combined audience. **TSF** (89.5FM) is news radio 24hrs a day. State-run **Antena 1** (95.7 FM) is also a good news and football source. For the **BBC World Service** and other stations you must go online (www.bbc.co.uk/ radio).

Television

Privately owned **TVI** and **SIC** have a diet of *telenovelas* – Brazilian and home-grown soaps, docudramas and absurd game shows. The latter's cable offshoot **SIC Notícias** leads in rolling news. State flagship **RTP1** has upped standards lately after a lengthy period of dumbing down, while **RTP2** caters to a discerning (and tiny) audience.

MONEY

Portugal's currency is the **euro** (€). The notes in public circulation are €5, €10, €20, €50, €100, €200 and €500, while coins come as €1, €2, 1 cent, 2 cents, 5 cents, 10 cents, 20 cents and 50 cents.

ATMs

You're never far from a Multibanco machine in Lisbon, and locals conduct a vast range of day-to-day transactions on them, from paying bills to buying train and even concert tickets. You can withdraw €200 per day – usually in the form of €20 notes (charges may vary). Point-of-sale terminals linked to the Multibanco system are also common in shops, and these and ATMs accept MasterCard, Visa and other major international cards, including Maestro and Cirrus.

Banks

Open 8.30am-3pm, though a few branches stay open later. For travellers' cheques, banks charge hefty commission compared with bureaux de change (*see below*) or the large hotels. All major banks have retail branches throughout the city.

Bureaux de change

There are clusters of these around Rossio. As well as tending to offer a better rate of exchange than banks, they also handle a wider range of currencies.

Credit cards

MasterCard and Visa are the most widely accepted, though use is far from universal. Many shops and restaurants don't take American Express.

Lost/stolen cards

American Express *069 9797 2000.*
Diners Club *21 350 9500.*
Mastercard *800 811 272.*
Visa *800 811 824.*

Tax

Residents of EU member states may not claim back any value-added tax on purchases. Non-EU residents may do so if they buy goods at shops that adhere to the Tax-free scheme; they'll have a sticker displayed in the window. Claims are made by filling in a form available at the Tax-free counter (21 840 8813, 7am-midnight daily) at the airport, near Departures.

NATURAL HAZARDS

There hasn't been a big earthquake in the city since the 1755 disaster. Unlike the Azores, where tremors are relatively common, the very occasional ones that do strike Lisbon are tiny. Otherwise, aside from some fierce Atlantic waves, Portugal is free of natural hazards.

OPENING HOURS

Shops are normally open 9am-1pm and 3-6/7pm, although nowadays many high-street shops stay open during lunch. Most supermarkets stay open until 8pm or later. In shopping centres, hours tend to be 10am-10pm. Post offices (*correios*) are open 9am-6pm, weekdays only (smaller branches may close for lunch). *See also left* Banks.

POLICE

Polícia de Segurança Pública (PSP) officers have a relaxed air, but as is typical in former dictatorships, Portugal's law enforcers are only gradually regaining the trust of the population. Their training and image have improved, and you should find them polite and helpful. But don't try to resist or argue if you get into bother. Quiet politeness is definitely the best approach. There is a police station for tourists in Palácio Foz

on Praça dos Restauradores (21 342 1623).

POSTAL SERVICES

State postal service **CTT** (whose clunky site is at www.ctt.pt) has a monopoly on letter delivery. First-class mail is *correio azul* (blue mail). Costing a minimum €2.80, it should get anywhere in Europe in under four days and to the US in no more than six. Second-class mail, *correio normal*, to Europe (other than Spain) costs €0.86 for a standard-sized letter under 20g (7oz); to the rest of the world it costs €0.91. Within Portugal, sending a 20g letter costs €0.53, or €0.63 for *correio azul*. An alternative is to buy a pre-paid *correio verde* envelope (from €2.40 to send abroad) or box, whose contents may be of any weight; for light packages this works out more expensive, though.

Stamps and envelopes are sold at all post office counters or from nearby machines. Mailing boxes usually have two or more slots to keep *correio azul* apart.

Main post office *Praça dos Restauradores 58, Restauradores (21 326 1370). Metro Restauradores.* **Open** *8am-10pm Mon-Fri; 9am-6pm Sat.* **Map** *p60 Q19.*

Poste restante

Mail can be addressed to someone by name '*Posta restante*' and sent to a particular post office. It costs from €0.98 per item to pick up. If no office is specified then mail ends up at the Cabo Ruivo depot in eastern Lisbon (Avenida Marechal Gomes da Costa 13A, 707 262 626).

PUBLIC HOLIDAYS

Most shops close on public holidays, except for shopping malls and big supermarkets. Restaurants, cafés and cinemas tend not to close either, but museums do.
New Year's Day Ano Novo *1 January*
Good Friday Sexta-Feira Santa *Friday before Easter Sunday*
Freedom Day Dia da Liberdade *25 April*

Worker's Day Dia do Trabalhador *1 May*

Corpus Christi Corpo de Deus *6 June*

Portugal Day Dia de Portugal, de Camões e das Comunidades *10 June*

St Anthony's Day Dia de Santo António *13 June*

Assumption Assunção de Nossa Senhora *15 August*

Republic Day Dia da República *5 October*

Restoration of Independence Day Dia da Restauração da Independência *1 December*

Immaculate Conception Imaculada Conceição *8 December*

Christmas Day Natal *25 December*

RELIGION

Portugal remains a thoroughly Roman Catholic country and you'll never be very far from a church. Check on the doors for mass times.

St George's Church (Anglican) *Rua São Jorge 6, Estrela (21 468 3570, www. lisbonanglicans.org). Tram 25, 28 or bus 709, 720, 738.* **Service** *11.30am Sun.* **Map** *p132 M18.*

Igreja Evangélica Baptista da Graça (Baptist) *Rua Capitão Humberto Ataíde 28, Santa Apolónia (21 813 1563). Metro Santa Apolónia or bus 735.* **Services** *10am, 11.30am, 6pm Sun; 3pm Wed.* **Map** *p80 T18.*

Budismo Tibetano Nyingma (Buddhist) *Rua do Salitre 117, Rato (21 314 2038, 92 548 2986). Metro Avenida/Rato.* **Open** *Reception 10am-3pm, 4.30-7pm Mon-Fri. Practice 7.15am, 9.30pm Mon-Fri; 9am, 9.30pm Sat, Sun.* **Map** *p60 P18.*

Basílica da Estrela (Catholic) *Praça da Estrela, Estrela (21 396 0915). Tram 25, 28.* **Open** *7.30am-1pm, 3-8pm daily.* **Mass** *noon, 7pm Mon-Sat; 10am, noon, 7pm (except July-Sept) Sun.* **Map** *p132 M19.*

Sé Catedral (Catholic) *Largo da Sé, Alfama (21 886 6752). Tram*

12, 28. **Open** *9am-5pm daily. Mass 6.30pm Tue-Sat; 11.30am, 7pm Sun.* **Map** *p80 R20.*

Comunidade Hindú de Portugal (Hindu) *Alameda Mahatma Gandhi, Lumiar (21 757 6524). Metro Campo Grande then bus 778.* **Open** *9am-6pm Mon-Fri.*

Centro Ismaili de Lisboa (Ismaili) *Avendia Lusiada 1, Laranjeiras (21 722 9000). Metro Laranjeiras.* **Open** *9am-7pm daily.* **Map** *p142 N10.*

Mesquita Central de Lisboa (Islamic) *Avenida José Malhôa, Praça de Espanha (21 387 4142/2220). Metro Praça de Espanha.* **Open** *9am-6pm daily.* **Map** *p142 O14.*

Sinagoga Shaaré Tikvá (Jewish) *Rua Alexandre Herculano 59, Rato (21 393 1130). Metro Rato.* **Open** *10am-1pm, 2-5pm Mon-Thur; 9am-1pm Fri.* **Map** *p132 O17.*

St Andrew's Church of Scotland (Presbyterian) *Rua Arriaga 13, Lapa (21 468 0853, www. standrewslisbon.com). Tram 25 or bus 713, 727, 760.* **Worship** *11am Sun.* **Map** *p132 M20.*

SAFETY & SECURITY

Lisbon is a relatively safe town, but be aware of pickpockets in crowds, especially on trams. Violent incidents are rare but basic safety rules apply: carry little cash; avoid dark, deserted places; and look after valuables.

Be particularly alert when visiting the Bairro Alto, Cais do Sodré and the lower Alfama and Mouraria. There's heavier drug-related crime in the peripheral shanty towns. Car crime is common and the usual precautions should be taken.

SMOKING

Smoking isn't permitted on public transport or in museums, and few restaurants opt to install the expensive equipment needed to have licensed smoking sections in closed premises. However, terraces abound.

STUDY

Language classes

Aside from the university's well-regarded summer course (*see right*), several local institutions offer Portuguese language classes, such as the **Cambridge School** (21 312 4600, www. cambridge.pt) which has five schools across Lisbon.

Universities

Universidade de Lisboa *Alameda da Universidade, Cidade Universitária 1649 (21 796 7624, www.ulisboa.pt). Metro Campo Grande.* Portugal's first university, founded around 1288, ended up in Coimbra. It wasn't until the 19th century that higher education regained a foothold in the capital in the form of this institution. Its Faculdade de Letras has run summer courses in Portuguese language since 1934; for information, visit www.iclp. letras.ulisboa.pt.

TELEPHONES

Dialling & codes

The international access code for Portugal is **351**. Lisbon numbers start with 21 (this forms part of the number). To dial another part of Portugal from Lisbon, simply dial the number, which invariably starts with 2; there are no area codes. (If you have an old number together with an area code starting with zero, try replacing the zero with a 2.) To make an international call from Portugal dial 00, followed by the country code (Australia **61**, Canada and the US **1**, New Zealand **64**, United Kingdom **44**) then area code (without the zero if dialling the UK) and number.

Operator services

For directory enquiries (national or international), call **118**, or browse www.118net.pt.

Public phones

MEO still operates some coin- and card-operated booths. Various MEO and other calling cards are available but deals change constantly; look out for leaflets (invariably in English) at kiosks and in shops. Such cards are a boon when phoning from hotels.

Mobile phones

All three main mobile network operators – **MEO**, **NÓS** and **Vodafone** – have good coverage in the city, have counters at the airport, and sell SIM cards with data included and other products online and from agents across the city.

TIME

Portuguese time is always the same as British time, keeping in line with GMT in winter and moving an hour ahead in summer. The 24hr clock is normally used, even in everyday speech.

TIPPING

In restaurants and cafés, a tip of anything between 2% and 10% is normal. Tipping in bars is less common, although meagre wages often warrant it. With taxi drivers, it's less common but we'd encourage tipping if you received good service.

TOILETS

Lisbon isn't overly endowed with public toilets (*sanitários* or *casas de banho*). Café owners aren't fussy about people wandering in off the street, but it's only polite to ask and the facilities may be less than fragrant; museums, restaurants and shopping centres tend to be a better bet. The men's is usually marked with an H for *homens*, the women's with an S for *senhoras*.

TOURIST INFORMATION

As well as the main **Ask Me** tourist office, there are well-stocked booths at several other downtown locations, as well as in front of the Mosteiro dos Jerónimos in Belém and at Parque das Nações and the airport.

Ask Me Lisboa *Praça do Comércio, Baixa (21 031 2810, www.visitlisboa.com or www. askmelisboa.com). Metro Terreiro do Paço or tram 12, 15, 18, 28.* **Open** *9am-8pm daily.* **Map** *p60 Q21.* Helpful staff, leaflets, internet PCs and a shop selling local handicrafts and gourmet products (entry on Rua do Arsenal) are found in the Lisbon tourist board's main complex. Here you can buy a **Lisboa Card** offering up to three days' unlimited public transport – including on trains to Cascais and Sintra – plus a range of discounts (or even free admission) for museums and entertainment (24hr card €19, €12 5-11s; 48hr €32, €18 5-11s; 72hr €40, €22 5-11s). The **Lisboa Eat & Shop card** (€6), offering discounts of up to 20% in 100 restaurants and shops for 72 hours, isn't quite such good value. Staff here will also book you a rental car or pricey sightseeing tour, or help find accommodation. **Other locations** Airport (21 845 0660); Praça do Comércio 78-81 (91 408 1366); Palácio Foz, Praça dos Restauradores (21 346 3314); Rua do Jardim do Regedor 50 (21 347 2134); Rossio train station (91 240 9142); Santa Apolónia train station (91 240 9142); Jardim Vasco da Gama, Belém (21 365 8435); Alameda dos Oceanos, Parque das Nações (91 051 8028).

VISAS & IMMIGRATION

Standard EU immigration law applies: EU citizens planning to stay more than six months will need to apply for a residence permit, but are otherwise free to come and go. Nationals of the US, Australia and New Zealand are entitled to stay up to 90 days with just a passport; Canadians for up to 60 days. If you do have a visa and need to extend it, you should apply at least a week before the previous leave expires.

WOMEN

Lisbon is fairly safe, but it's best not to walk alone late at night in some dingier districts. *See also p254 Safety & security.*

WEIGHTS & MEASURES

Portugal uses the metric system for all weights and measures.

WORK

EU citizens are free to work in Portugal, although if they intend to stay for more than six months they'll need a residence permit. Permits are issued occasionally to other nationals, but aren't easily arranged. For more information, contact the Portuguese embassy or consulate in your home country.

Serviço de Estrangeiros e Fronteiras *Avenida António Augusto de Aguiar 20, Marquês de Pombal (808 202 653, www. sef.pt). Metro Parque.* **Open** *8am-4pm Mon-Fri.* **Map** *p60 P16.* Either you or your *despachante* (agent) must pre-book an appointment at this state immigration office if you intend to get a residence permit.

ERES Relocation Services *Rua João Infante 50, Cascais (21 485 8230, www.eresrelocation.com/ pt). Cais do Sodré rail.* **Open** *9am-6pm Mon-Fri.* Private outfit with decades of experience handling work-related problems.

▶ *UK citizens are urged to seek up-to-date advice on their rights to study and/or work in the EU from www.gov.uk before they travel.*

Vocabulary

Pronunciation

Pronunciation follows some clear rules. The s always takes the sh sound at the end of words. Elsewhere, it becomes sh only when followed by t or c. Watch the latter: Cascais is 'Kashkaish', whereas *piscina* is 'pisheena'. Another feature is the nh and lh consonants, which are similar to the Spanish ñ and ll. Thus Saldanha is 'Saldanya', and *bacalhau* is 'bakalyow'.

The c is soft before e and i, but hard elsewhere. Note also that m takes on a nasal tone at the end of words, as in *sim*, for yes.

Vowels are tricky. Accents denote a stressed syllable, although the tilde (~) and the circumflex (^) also give the vowel a more elongated sound. The ão is unique to Portuguese. A nasal, truncated 'ow' is the best description. Thus *informação* is 'informasow', with a nasal yelp on the last syllable.

The e is silent at the end of the word, unless it has an accent. So *saudade* is 'sowdad', whereas café is 'kaffay'. Also:

- ç – like the **s** in song
- ch and x – both like the sh in ship
- j – like the **s** in treasure
- g – is like **j**, except when it comes before an **a**, **o** or **u** when it is hard
- q – is like **k** in English, even when twinned with u
- ei – like the **ay** in hay
- ou – like the English exclamation **oh**

Basics

- **yes** sim; **no** não; **maybe** talvéz/ se calhar; **with/without** com/sem
- **good** bom (masc), boa (fem); **bad** mau (masc), má (fem)
- **big** grande; **small** pequeno
- **very** muito
- **hot** quente; **cold** frio
- **there is/are...** há...
- **there isn't/aren't...** não há...
- **why** porquê; **when** quando; **who is it?** quem é?
- **I'd like...** queria
- **where is...? (a fixed thing)** onde fica...?
- **where is...? (a movable thing or person)** onde está...?

Useful terms and phrases

- **men's** homens/senhores
- **women's** mulheres/senhoras
- **open** aberto; **closed** fechado
- **entrance** entrada; **exit** saída
- **what is your name?** como se chama? (formal) como te chamas? (informal)
- **my name is...** chamo-me...
- **I am English/American** sou inglês/norte-americano (masc) sou inglesa/norte-americana (fem)
- **I don't speak Portuguese** não falo Português
- **do you speak English?** fala inglês? (formal) falas inglês? (informal)
- **I don't understand** não entendo
- **speak more slowly please** fale mais devagar, por favor
- **where is the toilet?** onde fica a casa de banho?

Polite conversation

- **hello** olá
- **good day/evening/night** bom dia/boa tarde/boa noite
- **goodbye** adeus (formal) ciao (informal); **see you later** até logo
- **how are you?** como está? (formal) como estás? (informal) tudo bem? (more informal)
- **I'm fine** estou bem
- **thank you** obrigado (masc) obrigada (fem)
- **you're welcome** de nada/ não tem de quê
- **please** por favor/se faz favor
- **excuse me** com licença
- **sorry** desculpe (formal) desculpa (informal)
- **that's/it's okay** está bem/ não faz mal

Shops and hotels

- **is it cheap/expensive?** é barato/ caro?
- **how much is it/are they?** quanto é/quanto são?
- **buy** comprar; **rent** alugar
- **I like...** gosto de...; **I don't like...** não gosto de...
- **do you have a single/double room for tonight?** tem um quarto indivíduo/duplo para hoje?
- **bed** cama
- **bathroom** casa de banho; **bath** banheira; **shower** chuveiro/duche

Getting around

- **near** perto; **far** longe
- **left** esquerda; **right** direita
- **straight on** sempre em frente
- **train station** estação de comboios
- **bus station** rodoviário
- **do you know the way to...?** sabe o caminho para...?
- **bus stop** paragem de autocarros
- **petrol** gasolina; **diesel** gasóleo
- **ticket office** bilheteira
- **single** ida; **return** ida e volta
- **I'd like to go to...** queria ir á...
- **one/two/three o'clock** uma/ duas/três horas

Emergencies

- **I feel ill** sinto-me mal
- **doctor** médico
- **pharmacy** farmácia
- **hospital** hospital
- **emergency ward** serviço de urgência
- **ambulance service** ambulância
- **police** polícia
- **fire brigade** bombeiros

Days, times and numbers

- **today** hoje; **tomorrow** amanhã
- **now** agora; **later** mais tarde
- **before** antes
- **Sunday** domingo
- **Monday** segunda-feira
- **Tuesday** terça-feira
- **Wednesday** quarta-feira
- **Thursday** quinta-feira
- **Friday** sexta-feira
- **Saturday** sábado
- **1** um/uma; **2** dois/duas; **3** três; **4** quatro; **5** cinco; **6** seis; **7** sete; **8** oito; **9** nove; **10** dez; **11** onze; **12** doze; **13** treze; **14** quatorze; **15** quinze; **16** dezasseis; **17** dezassete; **18** dezoito; **19** dezanove; **20** vinte; **30** trinta; **40** quarenta; **50** cinquenta; **60** sessenta; **70** setenta; **80** oitenta; **90** noventa; **100** cem; **1,000** mil

Further Reference

BOOKS

Fiction & literature

António Lobo Antunes *The Return of the Caravels* Hallucinatory tale from an author preoccupied with Portugal's tainted historical legacy.

Luís Vaz Camões *The Lusiads* Epic by Portugal's national poet chronicling the adventures of Vasco da Gama. Hard going in English.

José Cardoso Pires *Ballad of Dog's Beach* Detective story set in the Salazar years, based on a real-life murder.

Lídia Jorge *The Murmuring Coast* Draws on the author's experiences in colonial Africa.

Eugénio Lisboa & Helder Macedo (eds) *The Dedalus Book of Portuguese Fantasy* Short stories from leading Portuguese writers.

Eugénio Lisboa (ed.) *The Anarchist Banker and Other Portuguese Stories: Volume I; Professor Pfiglzz and His Strange Companion and Other Portuguese Stories: Volume II* Great primers featuring Fernando Pessoa, Eça de Queirós and others.

Pascal Mercier *Night Train to Lisbon* Mousy Swiss professor obsesses over a dead Portuguese writer. This novel falls short yet captures something of the essence of Lisbon.

Fernando Pessoa *The Book of Disquietude* The savagely solipsistic 'factless autobiography' of Bernardo Soares, now available in Richard Zenith's translation.

Fernando Pessoa *A Centenary Pessoa* Eugénio Lisboa's excellent anthology of Pessoa's poetry and prose with critical commentary, a chronology and two 'posthumous interviews'.

Fernando Pessoa *Selected Poems* Peruse at one of Pessoa's old haunts, such as Café A Brasileira.

Eça de Queirós *Cousin Bazilio* From Lisbon's premier 19th-century novelist; recounts an affair between a bored bourgeois Príncipe Real housewife and her dashing cousin.

Eça de Queirós *The Maias* Sort of a Portuguese version of Mann's *Buddenbrooks*.

Erich Maria Remarque *The Night in Lisbon* The author of *All Quiet on the Western Front* sets an adventure and love story in neutral Lisbon during World War II.

José Saramago *Baltasar and Blimunda* This almost magically realist adventure set in Lisbon and Mafra made the name of the 1998 Nobel Prize-winner for literature.

José Saramago *The History of the Siege of Lisbon* Set both in the present day and the 12th century (during the Christian Reconquest) with a printshop drudge as its anti-hero.

José Saramago *The Year of the Death of Ricardo Reis* One of Pessoa's heteronyms returns from Brazil to Salazar-era Lisbon, and meets the ghost of his creator.

Antonio Tabucchi *Pereira Maintains* A newspaperman questions his life in the face of state censorship during the oppressive Salazar years. Alain Tanner's film of this intriguing classic starred Marcello Mastroianni.

Robert Wilson *A Small Death in Lisbon* Set in 1940s and 1990s Portugal, with an engaging detective as its hero.

Richard Zimler *The Last Cabbalist of Lisbon* This absorbing story is set during the anti-Jewish riots of 1506.

Non-fiction

David Birmingham *A Concise History of Portugal* A short, illustrated classic.

CR Boxer *The Portuguese Seaborne Empire (1415 1825)* Account of Portugal's glory days.

Almeida Garrett *Travels in My Homeland* Witty account from the 19th-century Liberal-Absolutist wars.

Barry Hatton *The Portuguese: A Modern History* Analysis and anecdotes from a foreign correspondent.

Marion Kaplan *The Portuguese: The Land and its People* Updated in 2006, this 1980s classic is a fine single-volume introduction.

Richard Mayson *Portugal's Wine and Wine-Makers: Port, Madeira and Regional Wines* A coffee-table tome, updated in 2013, on local wine history and regions.

AH de Oliveira Marques *History of Portugal* Good, accessible reference work.

Fernando Pessoa *Lisbon: What the Tourist Should See* Guidebook by Lisbon's iconic poet covers the major sights.

Fernão Mendes Pinto *Peregrinations* No-holds-barred account of 20 years of pillaging and adventure during the Discoveries.

José Hermano Saraiva *Portugal: A Companion History* A decent, concise history, with chronology, gazetteer and maps.

Edite Vieira *The Taste of Portugal* Loads of recipes, plus tasty snippets of history and literature.

MUSIC ALBUMS

Zeca Afonso *Cantigas de Maio* A rousing song on this 1971 album by the great folk singer was the signal for the 1974 coup.

Buraka Som Sistema *Black Diamond* Angolan *kuduro*, electronically charged, 'from the Lisbon suburbs to the world'.

Camané *Sempre de Mim* The most impressive of the current crop of male fadistas.

Carlos do Carmo *Um Homem na Cidade* A 1977 landmark, mixing traditional fado with Sinatra-style crooning.

Alfredo Marceneiro *The Fabulous Marceneiro* At the age of 70, the inventor of modern fado was still at his peak.

Mariza *Mariza* The latest from Portugal's most versatile female *fadista*.

Carlos Paredes *Movimento Perpétuo* The art of *guitarra* playing, raised to unprecedented heights.

Amália Rodrigues *Com que Voz* The fado diva is said to embody the soul of Portugal.

Salvador Sobral *Excuse Me ao vivo* Live version of jazz album plus 2017 Eurovision-winning song.

António Zambujo *Do Avesso* Brazil-influenced singer's latest; guests include Luísa Sobral.

WEBSITES

www.transporlis.pt Handy Lisbon route-finder.

www.timeout.pt Your critical guide to arts, culture and going out in Lisbon.

www.visitlisboa.com Official tourist office site.

Picture credits

2 (top), 39 (left), 116 Time Out Market Lisboa; 2 (bottom) Pabkov/Shutterstock; 3 Adam Szuly/Shutterstock; 5 silvia/Shutterstock; 6, 20 Rrrainbow/Shutterstock; 11 (top) Slavko Sereda/Shutterstock; 11 (bottom) Ungvari Attila/Shutterstock; 12 (top) DiegoCityExplorer/Shutterstock; 12 (bottom), 181 Alexandre Rotenberg/Shutterstock; 13 (top) SariMe/Shutterstock; 13 (bottom) Dmitri Ma/Shutterstock; 14 (top) Tupungato/Shutterstock; 14 (bottom) Paulo Alexandrino/MNAA; 15 (top), 26 (bottom), 126 Jose y Estudio/Shutterstock; 15 (bottom), 64, 231; saiko3p/Shutterstock; 16 (top) Andrey Lebedev/Shutterstock; 16 (bottom), 165 (bottom), 167 PSML Luis Duarte; 17 (top) © FG+FS_Courtesy EDP Foundation; 17 (bottom) Olga Moreira/Shutterstock; 18 Beketoff/Shutterstock; 19 (top) Nicholas Courtney/Shutterstock; 19 (bottom) joyfull/Shutterstock; 21 (top), 175 (top) ribeiroantonio/Shutterstock; 21 (bottom), 195 Samuel Sequeira/B.leza; 22 (top), 211 Roman Tiraspolsky/Shutterstock; 22 (middle), 39 (right), 124 Radu Bercan/Shutterstock; 22 (bottom), 202 Mesa de Frades; 23 (top) Jose Alevar/Museu de Lisboa; 23 (middle), 46 Helissa Grundemann/Shutterstock; 23 (bottom) Salvador Aznar/Shutterstock; 24 (top) 4kclips/Shutterstock; 24 (middle) Eugenio Marongiu/Shutterstock; 24 (bottom) positive emotions/Shutterstock; 25 (top) paulzhuk/Shutterstock; 25 (middle top) Ricardo Mateus/Shutterstock; 25 (middle bottom), 57 ELEPHOTOS/Shutterstock; 25 (bottom), 59 Elijah Lovkoff/Shutterstock; 26 (top) Eduardo Jarnac de Freitas/Shutterstock; 26 (middle) Satellite Dani/Shutterstock; 27 (top) S-F/Shutterstock; 27 (middle), 184 Alipio Padilha; 27 (bottom left) Alfredo Garcia Saz; 27 (bottom right), 187 rfranca/Shutterstock; 29, 217 Kyryk Ivan/Shutterstock.com; 30 Yavuz Sariyildiz/Shutterstock.com; 31 Hieronymus Ukkel/Shutterstock.com; 33 Bordalo II; 35 Paulo Barata/LOCO; 36 SEA ME; 37 Restaurante Eleven; 38 Shutterstock/Giorgio Rossi; 40 Tiago Lopes/Dois Corvos; 43 A Arte da Terra; 44 Luis Trancoso/Loja das Conservas; 45 Shutterstock/Phil Darby; 46 klublu/Shutterstock.com; 47 Lidija Kolovrat; 48, 107 Solar Antiques/João Nauman; 49 ingehogenbijl/Shutterstock.com; 51 WBTS/Shutterstock.com; 53 trabantos/Shutterstock.com; 54 Miguel Azevedo e Castro/Shutterstock.com; 56 Nataliya Nazarova/Shutterstock.com; 63 Benny Marty/Shutterstock.com; 66 Tasca Kome; 67 Richie Chan/Shutterstock.com; 70 Balate Dorin/Shutterstock.com; 74 JoaoKrull/Shutterstock.com; 77 anyaivanova/Shutterstock.com; 82 José Frade/Museu do Aljube; 83 Nido Huebi/Shutterstock.com; 85 Neirfy/Shutterstock.com; 88 Christophe Cappelli/Shutterstock.com; 90 Pedro Guimaraes/A Vida Portuguesa; 93 Rob van Esch/Shutterstock.com; 98 Bojan i Jelena/Shutterstock.com; 101 nito/Shutterstock.com; 103 Roman Debree/Shutterstock.com; 104 Pedro Bento/Vista Alegre; 106 Wangkun Jia/Shutterstock.com; 109 Patrick Nouhailler/Wikicommons; 113, 223 byvalet/Shutterstock.com; 117 Zabotnova Inna/Shutterstock.com; 120 Ler Devagar; 121 KajzrPhotography/Shutterstock.com; 127 (top) artem evdokimov/Shutterstock.com; 127 (bottom) Appreciate/Shutterstock.com; 128 Feitoria/Shutterstock.com; 131 vmedia84/Shutterstock.com; 137 Tiago Ladeira/Shutterstock.com; 139 Mikhail Gnatkovskiy/Shutterstock.com; 141 Museu de Lisboa; 144 Anton_Ivanov/Shutterstock.com; 146 Ricardo Oliveira Alves; 148 Jorge Maio; 150 Galeria 111; 153 Bruno Lopes; 155 Taras Chykhman/Shutterstock.com; 157 Cassiohabib/Shutterstock.com; 160 Maria Evseyeva/Shutterstock.com; 161 Carlos Pombo/Museo Berardo; 162 laurah17/Shutterstock.com; 164 PSML Wilson Pereira; 165 (top) Gerald Luckhurst; 166 PSML Emigus; 168 Alexey Ignatiev/Shutterstock.com; 170 Pedro Soares; 173 Peek Creative Collective/Shutterstock.com; 175 (bottom) Olga Moreira/Shutterstock.com; 178 Festa do Avante; 183 Iñigo Sánchez Fuarros; 188 Mathew Gilbert/Shutterstock.com; 191 Silk Restaurant & Club; 196 kavalenkava/Shutterstock.com; 198 Copenhagen; 200 Kat Piwecka/Fado & Food Group; 203 Arsenie Krasnevsky/Shutterstock.com; 205 Gulbenkian Musica; 208 Bruno Simao; 212 Alfredo Garcia Saz/Shutterstock.com; 214 Lethicia Coelho/Shutterstock.com; 220, 225, 227 Wikicommons; 228 stick2target.com; 232 Ary Lopez/Shutterstock.com; 234 Marcel Bakker/Shutterstock.com; 235 Martin Lehmann/Shutterstock.com; 236 Nessa Gnatoush/Shutterstock.com; 238 Yury and Tanya/Shutterstock.com; 240 Lisboa Carmo Hotel; 241 Pedro Sampayo Ribeiro; 243 Memmo Príncipe Real

Index